Fodor's 2000

Maine, Vermont, New Hampshire

The complete guide, thoroughly up-to-date

Packed with details that will make your trip

The must-see sights, off and on the beaten path

What to see, what to skip

City strolls, countryside adventures

Smart lodging and dining options

Essential local do's and taboos

Transportation tips

Key contacts, savvy travel tips

When to go, what to pack

Clear, accurate, easy-to-use maps

Books to read, background essays

Excerpted from *Fodor's New England 2000*

Fodor's Travel Publications, Inc. • New York, Toronto, London, Sydney, Auckland
www.fodors.com

Fodor's Maine, Vermont, New Hampshire

EDITOR: Linda Cabasin

Editorial Contributors: Paula J. Flanders, Hilary M. Nangle, Bill Scheller, Kay Scheller

Editorial Production: Brian Vitunic

Maps: David Lindroth, *cartographer;* Rebecca Baer, Bob Blake, *map editors*

Design: Fabrizio La Rocca, *creative director;* Guido Caroti, *art director;* Jolie Novak, *photo editor*

Cover Design: Pentagram

Production/Manufacturing: Rebecca Zeiler

Cover Photograph: Peter Guttman

Copyright

Important Tip

Although all prices, opening times, and other details in this book are based on information supplied to us at press time, changes occur all the time in the travel world, and Fodor's cannot accept responsibility for facts that become outdated or for inadvertent errors or omissions. So **always confirm information when it matters,** especially if you're making a detour to visit a specific place.

Special Sales

Fodor's Travel Publications are available at special discounts for bulk purchases for sales promotions or premiums. Special editions, including personalized covers, excerpts of existing guides, and corporate imprints, can be created in large quantities for special needs. For more information, contact your local bookseller or write to Special Markets, Fodor's Travel Publications, 201 East 50th Street, New York, NY 10022. Inquiries from Canada should be directed to your local Canadian bookseller or sent to Random House of Canada, Ltd., Marketing Department, 2775 Matheson Boulevard East, Mississauga, Ontario L4W 4P7. Inquiries from the United Kingdom should be sent to Fodor's Travel Publications, 20 Vauxhall Bridge Road, London SW1V 2SA, England.

PRINTED IN THE UNITED STATES OF AMERICA

10 9 8 7 6 5 4 3 2 1

CONTENTS

Maps

ON THE ROAD WITH FODOR'S

EVERY Y2K TRIP is a significant trip. So if there was ever a time you needed excellent travel information, it's now. Acutely aware of that fact, we've pulled out all stops in preparing *Fodor's Maine, Vermont, New Hampshire 2000*. To guide you in putting together your Maine, Vermont, and New Hampshire experience, we've created multiday itineraries and neighborhood walks. And to direct you to the places that are truly worth your time and money in this important year, we've rallied the team of endearingly picky know-it-alls we're pleased to call our writers. Having seen all corners of Maine, Vermont, and New Hampshire, they're real experts. If you knew them, you'd poll them for tips yourself.

Originally from Maine but now an 18-year-resident of New Hampshire, **Paula J. Flanders** writes travel features for newspapers and magazines around the country. New Hampshire, her Fodor's territory, remains one of her favorite subjects.

Hilary M. Nangle, formerly travel editor for a daily newspaper in Maine, is now a freelancer based in the state's scenic mid-coast. She writes regularly about travel, food, and skiing for publications in the United States and Canada.

Kay and Bill Scheller, who revised the Vermont chapter, have a total of more than 30 years' experience as contributors to Fodor's guides. They are the authors of several books on travel in New England and the Northeast. The Schellers live in northern Vermont.

Don't Forget to Write

Keeping a travel guide fresh and up-to-date is a big job. So we love your feedback—positive and negative—and follow up on all suggestions. Contact the Maine, Vermont, and New Hampshire editor at editors@fodors.com or c/o Fodor's, 201 East 50th Street, New York, New York 10022. And have a wonderful trip!

Karen Cure

Karen Cure
Editorial Director

Maine, Vermont, and New Hampshire

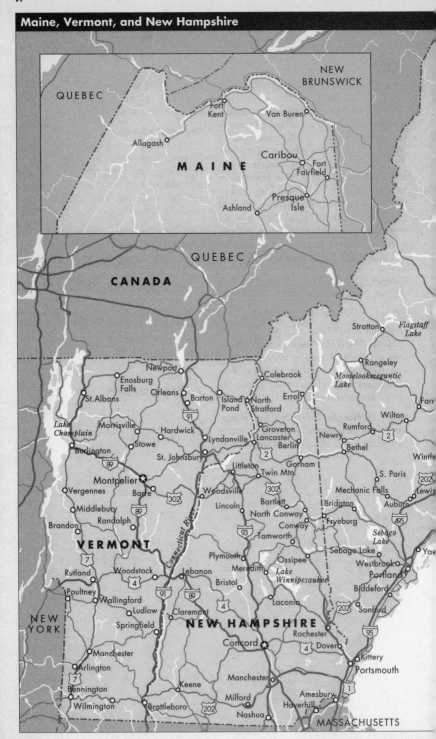

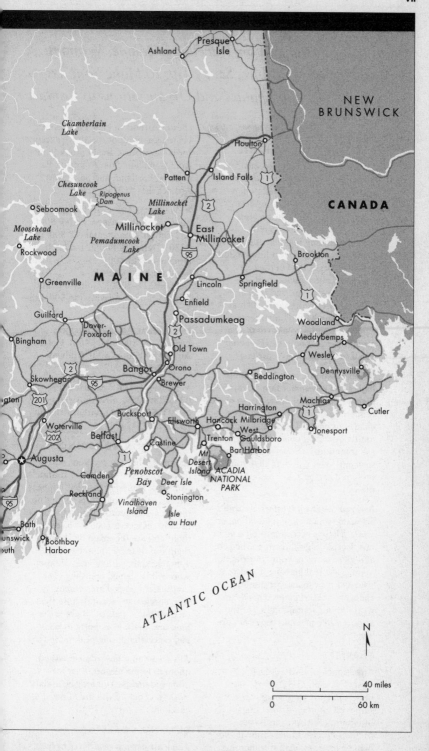

SMART TRAVEL TIPS A TO Z

Basic Information on Traveling in Maine, Vermont, and New Hampshire, Savvy Tips to Make Your Trip a Breeze, and Companies and Organizations to Contact

AIR TRAVEL

BOOKING YOUR FLIGHT

Price is just one factor to consider when booking a flight: Frequency of service and even a carrier's safety record are often just as important. Major airlines offer the greatest number of departures. Smaller airlines—including regional and no-frills airlines—usually have a limited number of flights daily. On the other hand, so-called low-cost airlines usually are cheaper, and their fares impose fewer restrictions, such as advance-purchase requirements. Safety-wise, low-cost carriers as a group have a good history—about equal to that of major carriers.

When you book, **look for nonstop flights** and **remember that "direct" flights stop at least once.** Try to **avoid connecting flights,** which require a change of plane. Two airlines may jointly operate a connecting flight, so ask if your airline operates every segment—you may find that your preferred carrier flies you only part of the way.

Ask your airline if it offers electronic ticketing, which eliminates all paperwork. There's no ticket to pick up or misplace. You go directly to the gate and give the agent your confirmation number—a real blessing if you've lost your ticket or made last-minute changes in travel plans. There's no worry about waiting in line at the airport while precious minutes tick by.

CARRIERS

American, Continental, Delta, Northwest, TWA, and US Airways serve (independently or through partnership with another airline) Logan International Airport in Boston, Maine's Portland International and Bangor International, Burlington International in Vermont, and Man-chester Airport in New Hampshire. United serves all of the above except for Bangor; Air Canada offers flights from Canadian cities to Logan, Bangor, and Portland; and Southwest Airlines flies to Manchester.

➤ MAJOR AIRLINES: **Air Canada** (☎ 800/776–3000). **American** (☎ 800/433–7300). **Continental** (☎ 800/525–0280). **Delta** (☎ 800/221–1212). **Northwest** (☎ 800/225–2525). **Southwest** (☎ 800/435–9792). **TWA** (☎ 800/221–2000). **United** (☎ 800/241–6522). **US Airways** (☎ 800/428–4322).

➤ REGIONAL AIRLINES: **Business Express** (☎ 800/345–3400). **Colgan Air** (☎ 800/206–1800). **Midway** (☎ 800/446–4392).

➤ FROM THE U.K.: **American** (☎ 0345/789–789). **British Airways** (☎ 0345/222–111). **Virgin Atlantic** (☎ 01293/747–747).

CHECK-IN & BOARDING

Assuming that not everyone with a ticket will show up, airlines routinely overbook planes. When that happens, airlines ask for volunteers to give up their seats. In return these volunteers usually get a certificate for a free flight and are rebooked on the next flight out. If there are not enough volunteers, the airline must choose who will be denied boarding. The first to get bumped are passengers who checked in late and those flying on discounted tickets, so **get to the gate and check in as early as possible,** especially during peak periods.

Always **bring a government-issued photo ID to the airport,** even for domestic flights. You may be asked to show it before you are allowed to check in.

CUTTING COSTS

The least-expensive airfares to New England must usually be purchased in advance and are non-refundable. It's smart to **call a number of airlines, and when you are quoted a good price, book it on the spot**—the same fare may not be available the next day. Always **check different routings** and look into using different airports. Travel agents, especially low-fare specialists (☞ Discounts & Deals, *below*), are helpful.

Consolidators are another good source. They buy tickets for scheduled international flights at reduced rates from the airlines, then sell them at prices that beat the best fare available directly from the airlines, usually without restrictions. Sometimes you can even get your money back if you need to return the ticket. Carefully read the fine print detailing penalties for changes and cancellations, and **confirm your consolidator reservation with the airline.**

When you **fly as a courier** you trade your checked-luggage space for a ticket deeply subsidized by a courier service. There are restrictions on when you can book and how long you can stay.

➤ CONSOLIDATORS: **Cheap Tickets** (☎ 800/377–1000). **Up & Away Travel** (☎ 212/889–2345). **Discount Airline Ticket Service** (☎ 800/576–1600). **Unitravel** (☎ 800/325–2222). **World Travel Network** (☎ 800/409–6753).

ENJOYING THE FLIGHT

For more legroom **request an emergency-aisle seat.** Don't sit in the row in front of the emergency aisle or in front of a bulkhead, where seats may not recline. If you have dietary concerns, **ask for special meals when booking.** These can be vegetarian, low-cholesterol, or kosher, for example. On long flights, try to maintain a normal routine, to help fight jetlag. At night **get some sleep.** By day **eat lightly, drink water** (not alcohol), and **move around the cabin** to stretch your legs.

FLYING TIME

Flying time is about 1 hour from New York, 2 hours and 15 minutes from Chicago, 6 hours from Los Angeles, 4 hours from Dallas, and 8 hours from London.

HOW TO COMPLAIN

If your baggage goes astray or your flight goes awry, complain right away. Most carriers require that you **file a claim immediately.**

➤ AIRLINE COMPLAINTS: U.S. Department of Transportation **Aviation Consumer Protection Division** (✉ C-75, Room 4107, Washington, DC 20590, ☎ 202/366–2220). Federal Aviation Administration Consumer Hotline (☎ 800/322–7873).

AIRPORTS

A major gateway to New England is Boston's Logan International Airport, the largest airport in New England. Additional New England airports served by major carriers include those in Manchester, New Hampshire (growing rapidly and a lower-cost alternative to Boston); Portland and Bangor, Maine; and Burlington, Vermont (☞ regional and state A to Z sections *in* corresponding chapters for information).

➤ AIRPORT INFORMATION: **Logan International Airport** (✉ Exit 24 off I–93 N, East Boston, MA, ☎ 800/235–6426). **Portland International Airport** (✉ Exit 7 off I–95, Portland, ME, ☎ 207/775–5809). **Bangor International Airport** (✉ Godfrey Blvd., off Union St., Bangor, ME, ☎ 207/947–0381). **Burlington International Airport** (✉ Exit 14E off I–89, Burlington, VT, ☎ 802/863–2874). **Manchester International Airport** (✉ Exit 2 off I–93, Manchester, VT, ☎ 603/624–6539).

BIKE TRAVEL

BIKES IN FLIGHT

Most airlines accommodate bikes as luggage, provided they are dismantled and boxed. For bike boxes, often free at bike shops, you'll pay about $5 (at least $100 for bike bags) from airlines. International travelers can sometimes substitute a bike for a piece of checked luggage at no charge; otherwise, the cost is about $100. Domestic and Canadian airlines charge $25–$50.

BOAT & FERRY TRAVEL

See the A to Z sections at the end of Chapters 2 through 4.

THE GOLD GUIDE / SMART TRAVEL TIPS

BUS TRAVEL

All New England states have bus service; fares are cheap and buses normally run on schedule, although service can be infrequent and travel time can be long due to traffic and frequent stops.

FARES & SCHEDULES

➤ BUS INFORMATION: **Bonanza** (☎ 800/556–3815). **Concord Trailways** (☎ 800/639–3317). **Greyhound Lines** (☎ 800/231–2222). **Peter Pan Trailways** (☎ 800/343–9999). **Vermont Transit** (☎ 802/864–6811 or 800/451–3292).

BUSINESS HOURS

Banks in Maine, Vermont, and New Hampshire are generally open weekdays from 9 AM until 3 PM, post offices weekdays between 8 AM and 5 PM; many branches operate Saturday morning hours. Business hours tend to be weekdays from 9 to 5. Many stores may not open until 10 or 11, but they remain open until 6 or 7; most carry on brisk business on Saturday as well. Stores in tourist areas may be open on Sundays, too. Suburban shopping malls are generally open seven days a week, with evening hours every day except Sunday. All across these states, so-called convenience stores sell food and sundries until about 11 PM. Along the highways and in major cities you can usually find all-night diners, supermarkets, drugstores, and convenience stores.

CAMERAS & PHOTOGRAPHY

➤ PHOTO HELP: **Kodak Information Center** (☎ 800/242–2424). *Kodak Guide to Shooting Great Travel Pictures,* available in bookstores or from Fodor's Travel Publications (☎ 800/533–6478; $16.50 plus $4 shipping).

EQUIPMENT PRECAUTIONS

Always **keep your film and tape out of the sun.** Carry an extra supply of batteries, and **be prepared to turn on your camera or camcorder** to prove to security personnel that the device is real. Always **ask for hand inspection of film,** which becomes clouded after successive exposures to airport X-ray machines, and **keep videotapes away from metal detectors.**

CAR RENTAL

Rates begin at $41 a day and $200 a week for an economy car with air-conditioning, an automatic transmission, and unlimited mileage. This does not include tax on car rentals, which is 5%.

➤ MAJOR AGENCIES: **Alamo** (☎ 800/327–9633; 020/8759–6200 in the U.K.). **Avis** (☎ 800/331–1212; 800/879–2847 in Canada; 02/9353–9000 in Australia; 09/525–1982 in New Zealand). **Budget** (☎ 800/527–0700; 0144/227–6266 in the U.K.). **Dollar** (☎ 800/800–4000; 020/8897–0811 in the U.K., where it is known as Eurodollar; 02/9223–1444 in Australia). **Hertz** (☎ 800/654–3131; 800/263–0600 in Canada; 020/8897–2072 in the U.K.; 02/9669–2444 in Australia; 03/358–6777 in New Zealand). **National InterRent** (☎ 800/227–7368; 0345/222525 in the U.K., where it is known as Europcar InterRent).

CUTTING COSTS

To get the best deal **book through a travel agent who will shop around.** Also **price local car-rental companies,** although the service and maintenance may not be as good as those of a major player. Remember to ask about required deposits, cancellation penalties, and drop-off charges if you're planning to pick up the car in one city and leave it in another. If you're traveling during a holiday period, also make sure that a confirmed reservation guarantees you a car.

INSURANCE

When driving a rented car you are generally responsible for any damage to or loss of the vehicle as well as for any property damage or personal injury that you may cause. Before you rent, see what coverage your personal auto-insurance policy and credit cards already provide.

For about $15 to $20 per day, rental companies sell protection, known as a collision- or loss-damage waiver (CDW or LDW), that eliminates your liability for damage to the car.

In Massachusetts the car-rental company must pay for damage to third parties up to a preset legal limit, beyond which your own liability insurance kicks in. However, **make sure you have enough coverage to pay for the car.** If you do not have auto insurance or an umbrella policy that covers damage to third parties, purchasing liability insurance and a CDW or LDW is highly recommended.

REQUIREMENTS & RESTRICTIONS

You must be 21 to rent a car, and rates may be higher if you're under 25. You'll pay extra for child seats (about $3 per day), which are compulsory for children under five, and for additional drivers (about $2 per day). Non-U.S. residents will need a reservation voucher, a passport, a driver's license, and a travel policy that covers each driver, in order to pick up a car.

SURCHARGES

Before you pick up a car in one city and leave it in another **ask about drop-off charges or one-way service fees,** which can be substantial. Note, too, that some rental agencies charge extra if you return the car before the time specified in your contract. To avoid a hefty refueling fee **fill the tank just before you turn in the car,** but be aware that gas stations near the rental outlet may overcharge.

CAR TRAVEL

Because public transportation is spotty or completely lacking in the outer reaches of these states, a car is the most convenient means of transportation.

AUTO CLUBS

➤ IN AUSTRALIA: **Australian Automobile Association** (☎ 02/6247–7311).

➤ IN CANADA: **Canadian Automobile Association** (CAA, ☎ 613/247–0117).

➤ IN NEW ZEALAND: **New Zealand Automobile Association** (☎ 09/377–4660).

➤ IN THE U.K.: **Automobile Association** (AA, ☎ 0990/500–600). **Royal Automobile Club** (RAC, ☎ 0990/722–722 for membership; 0345/121–345 for insurance).

➤ IN THE U.S.: **American Automobile Association** (☎ 800/564–6222).

GASOLINE

Self-service gas stations are the norm in Maine, Vermont, and New Hampshire, though in some of the less populated regions you'll find stations with one or two pumps and a friendly attendant who provides full service (pumping your gas, checking your tires and oil, washing your windows). At press time, rates for unleaded regular gas at self-service stations in New England were about $1.09 per gallon (somewhat higher in Connecticut); rates at full-service stations ranged from 10¢ to 30¢ more.

ROAD MAPS

Each of the states in New England makes available a map that has directories, mileage, and other useful information—contact the state offices of tourism (☞ Visitor Information, *below*). Delorme publishes topographical atlases of Connecticut/Rhode Island, Maine, New Hampshire, and Vermont that include most back roads and many outdoor recreation sites. The maps are widely available in the state.

RULES OF THE ROAD

The speed limit in much of New England is 65 mph on interstate and some limited-access highways (55 mph in densely populated areas), and 50 mph on most other roads (25–30 mph in towns and cities). In Maine, Vermont, and New Hampshire, drivers can turn right at a red light (unless signs indicate otherwise) providing they come to a full stop and check to see that the intersection is clear first.

CHILDREN IN MAINE, VERMONT, AND NEW HAMPSHIRE

In these states, there's no shortage of things to do with children. Major museums have children's sections, and there are children's museums in cities large and small. Children love the roadside attractions found in many tourist areas, and miniature golf courses are easy to come by. Attractions such as beaches and boat rides, parks and planetariums, lighthouses and llama treks are fun for youngsters as are special events, such as crafts fairs and food festivals.

Be sure to plan ahead and **involve your youngsters** as you outline your trip. When packing, include things to keep them busy en route. On sightseeing days try to schedule activities of special interest to your children. If you are renting a car don't forget to **arrange for a car seat** when you reserve.

➤ LOCAL INFORMATION: Consult Fodor's lively by-parents, for-parents *Where Should We Take the Kids? Northeast* (available in bookstores, or ☎ 800/533–6478; $16).

FLYING

If your children are two or older **ask about children's airfares.** As a general rule, infants under two not occupying a seat fly at greatly reduced fares or even for free. Experts agree that it's a good idea to use safety seats aloft for children weighing less than 40 pounds. Airlines set their own policies: U.S. carriers usually require that the child be ticketed, even if he or she is young enough to ride free, since the seats must be strapped into regular seats. Do **check your airline's policy about using safety seats during takeoff and landing.** And since safety seats are not allowed just everywhere in the plane, get your seat assignments early.

When reserving, **request children's meals or a freestanding bassinet,** if you need them. But note that bulkhead seats, where you must sit to use the bassinet may lack an overhead bin or storage space on the floor.

LODGING

Chain hotels and motels welcome children, and Maine, Vermont, and New Hampshire have many family-oriented resorts with lively children's programs. You'll also find farms that accept guests and that are lots of fun for children; the Vermont Chamber of Commerce (☞ Visitor Information, *below*) publishes a directory. Rental houses and apartments abound, particularly around ski areas; off-season, these can be economical as well as comfortable touring bases. Some country inns, especially those with a quiet, romantic atmosphere and those furnished with antiques, are less enthusiastic about little ones, so **be up front about your traveling companions** when you reserve.

Most hotels allow children under a certain age to stay in their parents' room at no extra charge; others charge them as extra adults; be sure to **find out the cutoff age for children's discounts.**

SIGHTS & ATTRACTIONS

Places that are especially good for children are indicated by a rubber duckie icon in the margin.

COMPUTERS ON THE ROAD

Checking your e-mail or surfing the Web can sometimes be done in the business centers of major hotels, which usually charge an hourly rate. Web access is also available at many fax and copy centers, many open 24 hours and on weekends. In major cities look for cyber cafés, where tabletop computers allow you to log on while sipping coffee or listening to live jazz. Whether you have e-mail at home or not, you can **arrange to have a free temporary e-mail address** from several services, including one available at www.hotmail.com (the site explains how to apply for an address).

CONSUMER PROTECTION

Whenever shopping or buying travel services in Maine, Vermont, or New Hampshire, **pay with a major credit card** so you can cancel payment or get reimbursed if there's a problem. If you're doing business with a particular company for the first time, **contact your local Better Business Bureau and the attorney general's offices** in your state and the company's home state, as well. Have any complaints been filed? Finally, if you're buying a package or tour, always **consider travel insurance** that includes default coverage (☞ Insurance, *below*).

➤ LOCAL BBBs: Council of Better Business Bureaus (✉ 4200 Wilson Blvd., Suite 800, Arlington, VA 22203, ☎ 703/276–0100, FAX 703/525–8277).

CUSTOMS & DUTIES

When shopping, **keep receipts** for all purchases. Upon reentering the country, **be ready to show customs officials what you've bought.** If you feel a duty is incorrect or object to the way your clearance was handled, note the inspector's badge number and ask to see a supervisor. If the problem isn't resolved, write to the appropriate authorities, beginning with the port director at your point of entry.

IN AUSTRALIA

Australia residents who are 18 or older may bring home $A400 worth of souvenirs and gifts (including jewelry), 250 cigarettes or 250 grams of tobacco, and 1,125 ml of alcohol (including wine, beer, and spirits). Residents under 18 may bring back $A200 worth of goods. Prohibited items include meat products. Seeds, plants, and fruits need to be declared upon arrival.

➤ INFORMATION: **Australian Customs Service** (Regional Director, ✉ Box 8, Sydney, NSW 2001, ☎ 02/9213–2000, ꜰᴀx 02/9213–4000).

IN CANADA

Canadian residents who have been out of Canada for at least 7 days may bring home C$500 worth of goods duty-free. If you've been away less than 7 days but more than 48 hours, the duty-free allowance drops to C$200; if your trip lasts 24–48 hours, the allowance is C$50. You may not pool allowances with family members. Goods claimed under the C$500 exemption may follow you by mail; those claimed under the lesser exemptions must accompany you. Alcohol and tobacco products may be included in the 7-day and 48-hour exemptions but not in the 24-hour exemption. If you meet the age requirements of the province or territory through which you reenter Canada, you may bring in, duty-free, 1.14 liters (40 imperial ounces) of wine or liquor *or* 24 12-ounce cans or bottles of beer or ale. If you are 16 or older you may bring in, duty-free, 200 cigarettes and 50 cigars. Check ahead of time with Revenue Canada or the Department of Agriculture for policies regarding meat products, seeds, plants, and fruits.

You may send an unlimited number of gifts worth up to C$60 each duty-free to Canada. Label the package UNSOLICITED GIFT—VALUE UNDER $60. Alcohol and tobacco are excluded.

➤ INFORMATION: **Revenue Canada** (✉ 2265 St. Laurent Blvd. S, Ottawa, Ontario K1G 4K3, ☎ 613/993–0534; 800/461–9999 in Canada).

IN NEW ZEALAND

Homeward-bound residents 17 or older may bring back $700 worth of souvenirs and gifts. Your duty-free allowance also includes 4.5 liters of wine or beer; one 1,125-ml bottle of spirits; and either 200 cigarettes, 250 grams of tobacco, 50 cigars, or a combination of the three up to 250 grams. Prohibited items include meat products, seeds, plants, and fruits.

➤ INFORMATION: **New Zealand Customs** (Custom House, ✉ 50 Anzac Ave., Box 29, Auckland, New Zealand, ☎ 09/359–6655, ꜰᴀx 09/359–6732).

IN THE U.K.

From countries outside the EU, including the United States, you may bring home, duty-free, 200 cigarettes or 50 cigars; 1 liter of spirits or 2 liters of fortified or sparkling wine or liqueurs; 2 liters of still table wine; 60 milliliters of perfume; 250 milliliters of toilet water; plus £136 worth of other goods, including gifts and souvenirs. If returning from outside the EU, prohibited items include meat products, seeds, plants, and fruits.

➤ INFORMATION: **HM Customs and Excise** (✉ Dorset House, Stamford St., Bromley Kent BR1 1XX, ☎ 020/7202–4227).

IN THE U.S.

Non-U.S. residents ages 21 and older may import into the United States 200 cigarettes or 50 cigars or 2 kilograms of tobacco, 1 liter of alcohol, and gifts worth $100. Meat products, seeds, plants, and fruits are prohibited.

➤ INFORMATION: **U.S. Customs Service** (inquiries, ✉ 1300 Pennsylvania Ave. NW, Washington, DC 20229, ☎ 202/927–6724; complaints, ✉ Office of Regulations and Rulings, 1300 Pennsylvania Ave. NW, Washington, DC 20229; registration of equipment, ✉ Resource Management, 1300 Pennsylvania Ave. NW, Washington, DC 20229, ☎ 202/927–0540).

DINING

Seafood is king throughout Maine, Vermont, and New Hampshire.

THE GOLD GUIDE / SMART TRAVEL TIPS

Clams, quahogs, lobster, and scrod are prepared here in an infinite number of ways, some fancy and expensive, others simple and moderately priced. One of the best ways to enjoy seafood is in the rough—off paper plates on a picnic table at a clam boil or clambake—or at one of the many shacklike eating places along the coast, where you can smell the salt air.

Among the quintessentially New England dishes served at inland resorts and inns are Indian pudding, clam chowder, fried clams, and cranberry anything. You can also find multicultural variations on themes, such as Portuguese *chouriço* (a spicy red sausage that transforms a clam boil into something heavenly) and the mincemeat pie made with pork in the tradition of the French Canadians who populate the northern regions.

The restaurants we list are the cream of the crop in each price category. Properties indicated by an ✕⛱ are lodging establishments whose restaurant warrants a special trip. Following is the price chart used in this book; note that prices do not include tax, which is 7% in Maine, 8% in New Hampshire, and 9% in Vermont.

CATEGORY	COST*
$$$$	over $40
$$$	$25–$40
$$	$15–$25
$	under $15

cost of a three-course dinner, per person, excluding drinks, taxes, and tip

RESERVATIONS & DRESS

Reservations are always a good idea: we mention them only when they're essential or are not accepted. Book as far ahead as you can, and reconfirm as soon as you arrive. We mention dress only when men are required to wear a jacket or a jacket and tie.

DISABILITIES & ACCESSIBILITY

In Kennebunkport, as in many of Maine's coastal towns south of Portland, travelers with mobility impairments will have to cope with crowds as well as with narrow, uneven steps and sporadic curb cuts. L.L. Bean's outlet in Freeport is fully accessible, and Acadia National Park has some 50 accessible mi of carriage roads that are closed to motor vehicles. In New Hampshire, many of Franconia Notch's natural attractions are accessible.

➤ LOCAL RESOURCES: The **New Hampshire Office of Vacation Travel** (☎ 603/271–2343) puts out "New Hampshire Guide Book," which includes accessibility ratings for lodgings and restaurants.

LODGING

When discussing accessibility with an operator or reservations agent **ask hard questions.** Are there any stairs, inside *or* out? Are there grab bars next to the toilet *and* in the shower/tub? How wide is the doorway to the room? To the bathroom? For the most extensive facilities meeting the latest legal specifications **opt for newer accommodations.**

➤ COMPLAINTS: **Disability Rights Section** (✉ U.S. Department of Justice, Civil Rights Division, Box 66738, Washington, DC 20035-6738, ☎ 202/514–0301; 800/514–0301; 202/514–0301 TTY; 800/514–0301 TTY, FAX 202/307–1198) for general complaints. **Aviation Consumer Protection Division** (☞ Air Travel, *above*) for airline-related problems. **Civil Rights Office** (✉ U.S. Department of Transportation, Departmental Office of Civil Rights, S-30, 400 7th St. SW, Room 10215, Washington, DC 20590, ☎ 202/366–4648, FAX 202/366–9371) for problems with surface transportation.

TRAVEL AGENCIES

In the United States, although the Americans with Disabilities Act requires that travel firms serve the needs of all travelers, some agencies specialize in working with people with disabilities.

➤ TRAVELERS WITH MOBILITY PROBLEMS: **Access Adventures** (✉ 206 Chestnut Ridge Rd., Rochester, NY 14624, ☎ 716/889–9096), run by a former physical-rehabilitation counselor. **CareVacations** (✉ 5-5110 50th Ave., Leduc, Alberta, Canada T9E 6V4, ☎ 780/986–6404 or 780/986–8332) has group tours and is especially helpful with cruise vacations. **Flying Wheels Travel** (✉ 143 W. Bridge St., Box 382, Owatonna, MN

55060, ☎ 507/451–5005 or 800/
535–6790, FAX 507/451–1685). **Hinsdale Travel Service** (✉ 201 E. Ogden
Ave., Suite 100, Hinsdale, IL 60521,
☎ 630/325–1335).

➤ TRAVELERS WITH DEVELOPMENTAL
DISABILITIES: **Sprout** (✉ 893 Amster-
dam Ave., New York, NY 10025,
☎ 212/222–9575 or 888/222–9575,
FAX 212/222–9768).

DISCOUNTS & DEALS

Be a smart shopper and **compare all
your options** before making decisions.
A plane ticket bought with a promotional coupon from travel clubs,
coupon books, and direct-mail offers
may not be cheaper than the least
expensive fare from a discount ticket
agency. And always keep in mind that
what you get is just as important as
what you save.

DISCOUNT RESERVATIONS

To save money **look into discount-
reservations services** with toll-free
numbers, which use their buying
power to get a better price on hotels,
airline tickets, even car rentals. When
booking a room, always **call the
hotel's local toll-free number** (if one
is available) rather than the central
reservations number—you'll often
get a better price. Always ask about
special packages or corporate rates.

➤ AIRLINE TICKETS: ☎ **800/FLY–4–
LESS.**

➤ HOTEL ROOMS: **RMC Travel**
(☎ 800/245–5738).

PACKAGE DEALS

Don't confuse packages and guided
tours. When you buy a package, you
travel on your own, just as though
you had planned the trip yourself.
Fly/drive packages, which combine
airfare and car rental, are often a
good deal.

ELECTRICITY

Overseas visitors will need to bring
adapters to convert their personal
appliances to the U.S. standard: AC,
110 volts/60 cycles, with a plug of two
flat pins set parallel to one another.

GAY & LESBIAN TRAVEL

➤ RESOURCE: *Fodor's Gay Guide to
the USA, 2nd edition,* provides infor-

mation on travel in Ogunquit, Maine
(available in bookstores, or from
Fodor's at ☎ 800/533–6478; $20
plus shipping).

➤ GAY- AND LESBIAN-FRIENDLY TRAVEL
AGENCIES: **Different Roads Travel** (✉
8383 Wilshire Blvd., Suite 902, Bev-
erly Hills, CA 90211, ☎ 323/651–
5557 or 800/429–8747, FAX 323/651–
3678). **Kennedy Travel** (✉ 314 Jeri-
cho Turnpike, Floral Park, NY
11001, ☎ 516/352–4888 or 800/
237–7433, FAX 516/354–8849). **Now
Voyager** (✉ 4406 18th St., San Fran-
cisco, CA 94114, ☎ 415/626–1169
or 800/255–6951, FAX 415/626–8626).
Yellowbrick Road (✉ 1500 W. Bal-
moral Ave., Chicago, IL 60640,
☎ 773/561–1800 or 800/642–2488,
FAX 773/561–4497). **Skylink Travel
and Tour** (✉ 1006 Mendocino Ave.,
Santa Rosa, CA 95401, ☎ 707/546–
9888 or 800/225–5759, FAX 707/546–
9891), serving lesbian travelers.

HEALTH

MEDICAL PLANS

No one plans to get sick while traveling, but it happens, so **consider signing up with a medical-assistance
company.** Members get doctor referrals, emergency evacuation or repatri-
ation, 24-hour telephone hot lines for
medical consultation, cash for emergencies, and other personal assistance.
Coverage varies by plan, so **review
the benefits of each carefully.**

➤ MEDICAL-ASSISTANCE COMPANIES:
International SOS Assistance (✉ 8
Neshaminy Interplex, Suite 207,
Trevose, PA 19053, ☎ 215/245–4707
or 800/523–6586, FAX 215/244–9617;
✉ 12 Chemin Riantbosson, 1217
Meyrin 1, Geneva, Switzerland, ☎
4122/785–6464, FAX 4122/785–6424;
✉ 10 Anson Rd., 14-07/08 International Plaza, Singapore, 079903,
☎ 65/226–3936, FAX 65/226–3937).

LYME DISEASE

Lyme disease, so named for its having
been first reported in the town of
Lyme, Connecticut, is a potentially
debilitating disease carried by deer
ticks, which thrive in dry, brush-
covered areas. **Use insect repellent;**
outbreaks of Lyme disease all over
the East Coast make it imperative
(even in urban areas) that you protect

yourself from ticks from early spring through summer. To prevent bites, **wear light-colored clothing and tuck pant legs into socks.** Look for black ticks about the size of a pin head around hairlines and the warmest parts of the body. If you have been bitten, **consult a physician, especially if you see the telltale bull's-eye bite pattern.** Influenza-like symptoms often accompany a Lyme infection. Early treatment is imperative. Also **ask your physician about Lymerix, the new Lyme disease vaccine;** it takes three shots and 12 months to be 80% effective but is worth considering.

HOLIDAYS

Major national holidays include New Year's Day (Jan. 1); Martin Luther King, Jr., Day (3rd Mon. in Jan.); President's Day (3rd Mon. in Feb.); Memorial Day (last Mon. in May); Independence Day (July 4); Labor Day (1st Mon. in Sept.); Thanksgiving Day (4th Thurs. in Nov.); Christmas Eve and Christmas Day (Dec. 24 and 25); and New Year's Eve (Dec. 31). Patriot's Day (3rd Mon. in Apr.) is a Massachusetts state holiday.

INSURANCE

The most useful travel insurance plan is a comprehensive policy that includes coverage for trip cancellation and interruption, default, trip delay, and medical expenses (with a waiver for preexisting conditions).

Without insurance you will lose all or most of your money if you cancel your trip, regardless of the reason. Default insurance covers you if your tour operator, airline, or cruise line goes out of business. Trip-delay covers expenses that arise because of bad weather or mechanical delays. Study the fine print when comparing policies.

British and Australian citizens need extra medical coverage when traveling overseas.

Always **buy travel policies directly from the insurance company**; if you buy it from a cruise line, airline, or tour operator that goes out of business you probably will not be covered for the agency or operator's default, a major risk. Before you make any

purchase **review your existing health and home-owner's policies** to find what they cover away from home.

➤ TRAVEL INSURERS: In the U.S. Access America (✉ 6600 W. Broad St., Richmond, VA 23230, ☎ 804/285–3300 or 800/284–8300), **Travel Guard International** (✉ 1145 Clark St., Stevens Point, WI 54481, ☎ 715/345–0505 or 800/826–1300). In Canada **Voyager Insurance** (✉ 44 Peel Center Dr., Brampton, Ontario, Canada L6T 4M8, ☎ 905/791–8700; 800/668–4342 in Canada).

➤ INSURANCE INFORMATION: In the U.K. the **Association of British Insurers** (✉ 51–55 Gresham St., London EC2V 7HQ, ☎ 020/7600–3333, ℻ 020/7696–8999). In Australia the **Insurance Council of Australia** (☎ 03/9614–1077, ℻ 03/9614–7924).

LODGING

Hotel and motel chains provide standard rooms and amenities in major cities and at or near traditional vacation destinations. At small inns, where each room is different and amenities vary in number and quality, price isn't always a reliable indicator; fortunately, when you call to make reservations, most hosts will be happy to give all manner of details about their properties, down to the color scheme of the handmade quilts—so **ask all your questions before you book.** Also **ask if the property has a Web site**; sites can have helpful information and pictures, although it's always wise to confirm how up-to-date the information is. At small inns, **don't expect a telephone, TV, or honor bar in your room**; you may even have to share a bathroom. The rooms in the lodgings reviewed here have private baths unless otherwise indicated.

The lodgings we list are the cream of the crop in each price category. We always list the facilities that are available—but we don't specify whether they cost extra: When pricing accommodations, always ask what's included and what costs extra. Properties indicated by an ✕☷ are lodging establishments whose restaurant warrants a special trip. Following is the price chart used in this book; note that prices do not include tax, which is 7% in Maine, 8% in New Hampshire, and 9% in Vermont.

CATEGORY	COST*
$$$$	over $180
$$$	$130–$180
$$	$80–$130
$	under $80

All prices are for a standard double room during peak season and do not include tax or gratuities. Some inns add a 15% service charge.

Assume that hotels operate on the European Plan (EP, with no meals) unless we specify that they use the Continental Plan (CP, with a Continental breakfast daily) or serve a full breakfast daily (indicated in the italicized service information at the end of the review). If more than breakfast is served, we specify whether the lodging operates on the Modified American Plan (MAP, with breakfast and dinner daily), or the American Plan (AP, with all meals).

B&BS

The bed-and-breakfasts and small inns of Maine, Vermont, and New Hampshire offer some of the region's most distinctive lodging experiences. Some are homey and casual, others provide a stay in a historic property in a city or out in the country, and still others are modern and luxurious. Most inns offer breakfast—hence the name bed-and-breakfast—yet this formula varies, too; at one B&B you may be served muffins and coffee, at another a multicourse feast with fresh flowers on the table. Many inns prohibit smoking, which is a fire hazard in older buildings, and some of the inns with antiques or other expensive furnishings do not allow children. Almost all say no to pets. Always be sure to **ask about any restrictions** when you're making a reservation.

➤ RESERVATION SERVICES: *See* Contacts and Resources *in* the A to Z sections at the end of Chapters 2 through 4.

CAMPING

The state offices of tourism (☞ Visitor Information, *below*) supply information about privately operated campgrounds and ones in parks run by state agencies and the federal government.

HOME EXCHANGES

If you would like to exchange your home for someone else's **join a home-exchange organization,** which will send you its updated listings of available exchanges for a year and will include your own listing in at least one of them. It's up to you to make specific arrangements.

➤ EXCHANGE CLUBS: **HomeLink International** (✉ Box 650, Key West, FL 33041, ☎ 305/294–7766 or 800/638–3841, FAX 305/294–1448; $88 per year). **Intervac U.S.** (✉ Box 590504, San Francisco, CA 94159, ☎ 800/756–4663, FAX 415/435–7440; $83 per year).

HOSTELS

No matter what your age you can **save on lodging costs by staying at hostels.** In some 5,000 locations in more than 70 countries around the world, Hostelling International (HI), the umbrella group for a number of national youth-hostel associations, offers single-sex, dorm-style beds and, at many hostels, couples rooms and family accommodations. Membership in any HI national hostel association, open to travelers of all ages, allows you to stay in HI-affiliated hostels at member rates (one-year membership is about $25 for adults; hostels run about $10–$25 per night). Members also have priority if the hostel is full; they're eligible for discounts around the world, even on rail and bus travel in some countries.

➤ ORGANIZATIONS: **Hostelling International—American Youth Hostels** (✉ 733 15th St. NW, Suite 840, Washington, DC 20005, ☎ 202/783–6161, FAX 202/783–6171). **Hostelling International—Canada** (✉ 400–205 Catherine St., Ottawa, Ontario K2P 1C3, ☎ 613/237–7884, FAX 613/237–7868). **Youth Hostel Association of England and Wales** (✉ Trevelyan House, 8 St. Stephen's Hill, St. Albans, Hertfordshire AL1 2DY, ☎ 01727/855215 or 01727/845047, FAX 01727/844126). **Australian Youth Hostel Association** (✉ 10 Mallett St., Camperdown, NSW 2050, ☎ 02/9565–1699, FAX 02/9565–1325). **Youth Hostels Association of New Zealand** (✉ Box 436, Christchurch, New Zealand, ☎ 03/379–9970,

FAX 03/365–4476). Membership in the U.S. $25, in Canada C$26.75, in the U.K. £9.30, in Australia $44, in New Zealand $24.

HOTELS

Hotel chains are amply represented in Maine, Vermont, and New Hampshire. Some of the large chains, such as Holiday Inn, Hilton, Hyatt, Marriott, and Ramada, operate all-suites, budget, business-oriented, or luxury resorts, often variations on the parent corporation's name (Courtyard by Marriott, for example). Though some chain hotels may have a standardized look to them, this "cookie-cutter" approach also means that you can rely on the same level of comfort and efficiency at all properties in a well-managed chain, and at a chain's premier properties—its so-called flagship hotels—the decor and services may be outstanding.

Most hotels will hold your reservation until 6 PM; **call ahead if you plan to arrive late.** Some will hold a late reservation for you if you reserve with a credit-card number.

When you call to make a reservation, **ask all the necessary questions up front.** If you are arriving with a car, ask if the hotel has a parking lot or covered garage and whether there is an extra fee for parking. If you like to eat your meals in, ask if the hotel has a restaurant or whether it has room service (most do, but not necessarily 24 hours a day—and be forewarned that it can be expensive). Most hotels and motels have in-room TVs, often with cable movies, but verify this if you like to watch TV. If you want an in-room crib for your child, there will probably be an additional charge.

All hotels listed have private bath unless otherwise noted.

➤ TOLL-FREE NUMBERS: **Adam's Mark** (☎ 800/444–2326). **Baymont Inns** (☎ 800/428–3438). **Best Western** (☎ 800/528–1234). **Choice** (☎ 800/221–2222). **Clarion** (☎ 800/252–7466). **Colony** (☎ 800/777–1700). **Comfort** (☎ 800/228–5150). **Days Inn** (☎ 800/325–2525). **Doubletree and Red Lion Hotels** (☎ 800/222–8733). **Embassy Suites** (☎ 800/362–2779). **Fairfield Inn** (☎ 800/228–2800).

Forte (☎ 800/225–5843). **Four Seasons** (☎ 800/332–3442). **Hilton** (☎ 800/445–8667). **Holiday Inn** (☎ 800/465–4329). **Howard Johnson** (☎ 800/654–4656). **Hyatt Hotels & Resorts** (☎ 800/233–1234). **Inter-Continental** (☎ 800/327–0200). **La Quinta** (☎ 800/531–5900). **Marriott** (☎ 800/228–9290). **Le Meridien** (☎ 800/543–4300). **Nikko Hotels International** (☎ 800/645–5687). **Omni** (☎ 800/843–6664). **Quality Inn** (☎ 800/228–5151). **Radisson** (☎ 800/333–3333). **Ramada** (☎ 800/228–2828). **Renaissance Hotels & Resorts** (☎ 800/468–3571). **Ritz-Carlton** (☎ 800/341–3333). **ITT Sheraton** (☎ 800/325–3535). **Sleep Inn** (☎ 800/221–2222). **Westin Hotels & Resorts** (☎ 800/228–3000). **Wyndham Hotels & Resorts** (☎ 800/822–4200).

MONEY MATTERS

Prices throughout this guide are given for adults. Substantially reduced fees are almost always available for children, students, and senior citizens. For information on taxes, *see* Taxes, *below.*

ATMS

Automatic teller machines (ATMs) are a useful way to obtain cash. A debit card, also known as a check card, deducts funds directly from your checking account and helps you stay within your budget. When you want to rent a car, though, you may still need an old-fashioned credit card. Although you can always *pay* for your car with a debit card, some agencies will not allow you to *reserve* a car with a debit card.

➤ ATM LOCATIONS: **Cirrus** (☎ 800/424–7787). **Plus** (☎ 800/843–7587) for locations in the U.S. and Canada, or visit your local bank.

BANKS

In general, U.S. banks will not cash a personal check for you unless you have an account at that bank (it doesn't have to be at that branch). Only in major cities are large bank branches equipped to exchange foreign currencies. Therefore, it's best to rely on credit cards, cash machines, and traveler's checks to handle expenses while you're traveling.

CREDIT CARDS

Using a credit card on the road allows you to delay payment and gives you certain rights as a consumer (☞ Consumer Protection, *above*).

Throughout this guide, the following abbreviations are used: **AE**, American Express; **D**, Discover; **DC**, Diners Club; **MC**, MasterCard; and **V**, Visa.

➤ REPORTING LOST CARDS: To report lost or stolen credit cards, call the following toll-free numbers: **American Express** (☎ 800/327–2177); **Discover Card** (☎ 800/347–2683); **Diners Club** (☎ 800/234–6377); **MasterCard** (☎ 800/307–7309); and **Visa** (☎ 800/847–2911).

TRAVELER'S CHECKS

Do you need traveler's checks? It depends on where you're headed. If you're going to rural areas and small towns, go with cash; traveler's checks are best used in cities. Lost or stolen checks can usually be replaced within 24 hours. To ensure a speedy refund, buy your own traveler's checks—don't let someone else pay for them: irregularities like this can cause delays. The person who bought the checks should make the call to request a refund.

NATIONAL AND STATE PARKS AND FORESTS

NATIONAL PARK PASSES

Look into discount passes to save money on national park entrance fees. The Golden Eagle Pass ($50) gets you and your companions free admission to all parks for one year. (Camping and parking are extra.) Both the Golden Age Passport ($10), for those 62 and older, and the Golden Access Passport (free), for travelers with disabilities, entitle holders to free entry to all national parks, plus 50% off fees for the use of many park facilities and services. You must show proof of age and of U.S. citizenship or permanent residency (such as a U.S. passport, driver's license, or birth certificate) and, if requesting Golden Access, proof of disability. All three passes are available at all national park entrances where entrance fees are charged. Golden Eagle and Golden Access passes are also available by mail.

➤ PASSES BY MAIL: **National Park Service** (✉ National Capitol Area Office, 1100 Ohio Dr. SW, Washington, DC 20242, ☎ 202/208–4747).

PACKING

The principal rule on weather in Maine, Vermont, and New Hampshire is that there are no rules. A cold, foggy morning in spring can and often does become a bright, 60-degree afternoon. A summer breeze can suddenly turn chilly, and rain often appears with little warning. Thus, the best advice on how to dress is to **layer your clothing** so that you can peel off or add garments as needed for comfort. Showers are frequent, so **pack a raincoat and umbrella.** Even in summer you should bring long pants, a sweater or two, and a waterproof windbreaker, for evenings are often chilly and sea spray can make things cool.

Casual sportswear—walking shoes and jeans—will take you almost everywhere, but swimsuits and bare feet will not: Shirts and shoes are required attire at even the most casual venues. Dress in restaurants is generally casual.

In summer, **bring a hat and sunscreen.** Remember also to **pack insect repellent**; to prevent Lyme disease you'll need to guard against ticks from early spring through the summer (☞ Health, *above*).

In your carry-on luggage **bring an extra pair of eyeglasses or contact lenses** and **enough of any medication you take** to last the entire trip. You may also want your doctor to write a spare prescription using the drug's generic name, since brand names may vary from country to country. In luggage to be checked, **never pack prescription drugs or valuables.** To avoid customs delays, carry medications in their original packaging. And don't forget to copy down and carry addresses of offices that handle refunds of lost traveler's checks.

CHECKING LUGGAGE

How many carry-on bags you can bring with you is up to the airline. Most allow two, but not always, so **make sure that everything you carry aboard will fit under your seat, and**

get to the gate early. Note that if you have a seat at the back of the plane, you'll probably board first, while the overhead bins are still empty.

If you are flying internationally, note that baggage allowances may be determined not by piece but by weight—generally 88 pounds (40 kilograms) in first class, 66 pounds (30 kilograms) in business class, and 44 pounds (20 kilograms) in economy.

Airline liability for baggage is limited to $1,250 per person on flights within the United States. On international flights it amounts to $9.07 per pound or $20 per kilogram for checked baggage (roughly $640 per 70-pound bag) and $400 per passenger for unchecked baggage. You can buy additional coverage at check-in for about $10 per $1,000 of coverage, but it excludes a rather extensive list of items, shown on your airline ticket.

Before departure **itemize your bags' contents** and their worth, and label the bags with your name, address, and phone number. (If you use your home address, cover it so that potential thieves can't see it readily.) Inside each bag **pack a copy of your itinerary.** At check-in **make sure that each bag is correctly tagged** with the destination airport's three-letter code. If your bags arrive damaged or fail to arrive at all, file a written report with the airline before leaving the airport.

PASSPORTS & VISAS

When traveling internationally **carry a passport even if you don't need one** (it's always the best form of ID), and **make two photocopies of the data page** (one for someone at home and another for you, carried separately from your passport). If you lose your passport promptly call the nearest embassy or consulate and the local police.

➤ U.K. CITIZENS: **U.S. Embassy Visa Information Line** (☎ 01891/200–290; calls cost 49p per minute, 39p per minute cheap rate) for U.S. visa information. **U.S. Embassy Visa Branch** (✉ 5 Upper Grosvenor Sq., London W1A 1AE) for U.S. visa information; send a self-addressed, stamped envelope. Write the U.S. **Consulate General** (✉ Queen's

House, Queen St., Belfast BTI 6EO) if you live in Northern Ireland. Write the **Office of Australia Affairs** (✉ 59th fl., MLC Centre, 19-29 Martin Pl., Sydney NSW 2000) if you live in Australia. Write the **Office of New Zealand Affairs** (✉ 29 Fitzherbert Terr., Thorndon, Wellington) if you live in New Zealand.

PASSPORT OFFICES

The best time to apply for a passport or to renew is during the fall and winter. Before any trip, check your passport's expiration date, and, if necessary, renew it as soon as possible.

➤ AUSTRALIAN CITIZENS: **Australian Passport Office** (☎ 131–232).

➤ CANADIAN CITIZENS: **Canadian Passport Office** (☎ 819/994–3500 or 800/567–6868).

➤ NEW ZEALAND CITIZENS: **New Zealand Passport Office** (☎ 04/494–0700 for information on how to apply; 04/474–8000 or 0800/225–050 in New Zealand for information on applications already submitted).

➤ U.K. CITIZENS: **London Passport Office** (☎ 0990/210–410) for fees and documentation requirements and to request an emergency passport.

SENIOR-CITIZEN TRAVEL

To qualify for age-related discounts **mention your senior-citizen status up front** when booking hotel reservations (not when checking out) and before you're seated in restaurants (not when paying the bill). When renting a car ask about promotional car-rental discounts, which can be cheaper than senior-citizen rates.

➤ EDUCATIONAL PROGRAMS: **Elderhostel** (✉ 75 Federal St., 3rd fl., Boston, MA 02110, ☎ 877/426–8056, ℻ 877/426–2166).

STUDENTS IN MAINE, VERMONT, AND NEW HAMPSHIRE

➤ STUDENT I.D.s & SERVICES: **Council on International Educational Exchange** (CIEE, ✉ 205 E. 42nd St., 14th fl., New York, NY 10017, ☎ 212/822–2600 or 888/268–6245, ℻ 212/822–2699) for mail orders only, in the U.S. **Travel Cuts** (✉ 187 Col-

lege St., Toronto, Ontario M5T 1P7,
☎ 416/979–2406 or 800/667–2887)
in Canada.

TAXES

SALES TAX

Sales taxes in New England are as
follows: Maine 6% and Vermont 5%.
No sales tax is charged in New Hampshire. Some states and municipalities
levy an additional tax (from 1% to
10%) on lodging or restaurant meals.

TELEPHONES

COUNTRY CODES

The country code for the United
States is 1.

DIRECTORY & OPERATOR INFORMATION

To reach an operator in Maine,
Vermont, and New Hampshire, dial
0. To reach directory assistance
information, dial 1, then the area
code and 555–1212. Within immedi-
ate local calling areas, dial 411.

INTERNATIONAL CALLS

From the United States, dial 011,
followed by the country code, the city
code, and the phone number. To have
an operator assist you, dial 0 and ask
for the overseas operator. The country
code for Australia is 61; New
Zealand, 64; and the United Kingdom, 44. To reach Canada, dial 1+
area code + number.

LONG-DISTANCE CALLS

Competitive long-distance carriers
make calling within the United States
relatively convenient and let you
avoid hotel surcharges. By dialing an
800 number, you can get connected to
the long-distance company of your
choice.

➤ LONG-DISTANCE CARRIERS: **AT&T**
(☎ 800/225–5288). **MCI** (☎ 800/
888–8000). **Sprint** (☎ 800/366–2255).

PUBLIC TELEPHONES

Instructions for pay telephones should
be posted on the phone, but generally
you insert your coins—anywhere from
25¢ to 35¢ for a local call in Maine,
Vermont, or New Hampshire—in a
slot and wait for the steady hum of a
dial tone before dialing the number
you wish to reach. If you dial a long-
distance number, the operator will
come on the line and tell you how
much more money you must insert for
your call to go through.

TIME

Maine, Vermont, and New Hampshire are in the Eastern time zone.

TIPPING

At restaurants, a 15% tip is standard
for waiters; up to 20% is expected at
more expensive establishments. The
same goes for taxi drivers, bartenders,
and hairdressers. Coat-check operators usually expect $1; bellhops and
porters should get 50¢ to $1 per bag;
hotel maids in hotels should get about
$1.50 per day of your stay. On pack-
age tours, conductors and drivers
usually get $10 per day from the
group as a whole; check whether this
has already been figured into your
cost. For local sightseeing tours, you
may individually tip the driver-guide
$1–$5, depending on the length of the
tour and the number of people in
your party, if he or she has been
helpful or informative. Ushers in
theaters do not expect tips.

TOURS & PACKAGES

On a prepackaged tour or independent vacation everything is prear-
ranged so you'll spend less time
planning—and often get it all at a
good price.

BOOKING WITH AN AGENT

Travel agents are excellent resources.
But it's a good idea to collect
brochures from several agencies
because some agents' suggestions may
be influenced by relationships with
tour and package firms that reward
them for volume sales. If you have a
special interest **find an agent with
expertise in that area;** ASTA (☞
Travel Agencies, *below*) has a data-
base of specialists worldwide.

Make sure your travel agent knows
the accommodations and other services of the place they're recommend-
ing. Ask about the hotel's location,
room size, beds, and whether it has a
pool, room service, or programs for
children, if you care about these. Has
your agent been there in person or
sent others whom you can contact?

Do some homework on your own, too: Local tourism boards can provide information about lesser-known and small-niche operators, some of which may sell only direct.

BUYER BEWARE

Each year consumers are stranded or lose their money when tour operators—even large ones with excellent reputations—go out of business. So **check out the operator.** Ask several travel agents about its reputation, and try to **book with a company that has a consumer-protection program.** (Look for information in the company's brochure.) In the United States, members of the National Tour Association and United States Tour Operators Association are required to set aside funds to cover your payments and travel arrangements in case the company defaults. It's also a good idea to choose a company that participates in the American Society of Travel Agent's Tour Operator Program (TOP); ASTA will act as mediator in any disputes between you and your tour operator.

Remember that the more your package or tour includes the better you can predict the ultimate cost of your vacation. Make sure you know exactly what is covered, and **beware of hidden costs.** Are taxes, tips, and transfers included? Entertainment and excursions? These can add up.

➤ TOUR-OPERATOR RECOMMENDATIONS: **American Society of Travel Agents** (☞ Travel Agencies, *below*). **National Tour Association** (NTA, ✉ 546 E. Main St., Lexington, KY 40508, ☎ 606/226–4444 or 800/682–8886). **United States Tour Operators Association** (USTOA, ✉ 342 Madison Ave., Suite 1522, New York, NY 10173, ☎ 212/599–6599 or 800/468–7862, FAX 212/599–6744).

TRAIN TRAVEL

State-run, national, and international train service are options in New England: Amtrak offers frequent daily service along its Northeast Corridor route from Washington and New York to Boston and Vermont. Amtrak plans to introduce high-speed service along the Boston–Washington corridor by 2000.

➤ TRAIN INFORMATION: **Amtrak** (☎ 800/872–7245).

TRAVEL AGENCIES

A good travel agent puts your needs first. Look for an agency that has been in business at least five years, emphasizes customer service, and has someone on staff who specializes in your destination. In addition, **make sure the agency belongs to a professional trade organization.** The American Society of Travel Agents (ASTA), with 27,000 agents in some 170 countries, is the largest and most influential in the field. Operating under the motto ìIntegrity in Travel,î it maintains and enforces a strict code of ethics and will step in to help mediate any agent-client disputes if necessary. ASTA also maintains a website that includes a directory of agents. (Note that if a travel agency is also acting as your tour operator, *see* Buyer Beware *in* Tours & Packages, *above*.)

➤ LOCAL AGENT REFERRALS: **American Society of Travel Agents** (ASTA, ☎ 800/965–2782 24-hr hot line, FAX 703/684–8319, www.astanet.com). **Association of Canadian Travel Agents** (✉ 1729 Bank St., Suite 201, Ottawa, Ontario K1V 7Z5, ☎ 613/521–0474, FAX 613/521–0805). **Association of British Travel Agents** (✉ 55–57 Newman St., London W1P 4AH, ☎ 020/7637–2444, FAX 020/7637–0713). **Australian Federation of Travel Agents** (✉ Level 3, 309 Pitt St., Sydney 2000, ☎ 02/9264–3299, FAX 02/9264–1085). **Travel Agents' Association of New Zealand** (✉ Box 1888, Wellington 10033, ☎ 04/499–0104, FAX 04/499–0786).

VISITOR INFORMATION

➤ TOURIST INFORMATION: **Maine Tourism Association** (✉ 325-B Water St., Box 2300, Hallowell, ME 04347, ☎ 207/623–0363 or 800/533–9595 for brochures). **New Hampshire Office of Travel and Tourism Development** (✉ Box 1856, Concord, NH 03302, ☎ 603/271–2343, 800/258–3608 for seasonal events, 800/386–4664 for brochures). **Vermont Department of Tourism and Marketing** (✉ 134 State St., Montpelier, VT 05602, ☎ 802/828–3237 or 800/837–6668 for brochures). **Vermont Chamber of Commerce, Department of Travel and**

Tourism (✉ Box 37, Montpelier, VT 05601, ☎ 802/223–3443).

➤ IN THE U.K.: **Discover New England** (✉ Admail 4 International, Greatness La., Sevenoaks TN14 5BQ, ☎ 01732/742777).

WEB SITES

Do **check out the World Wide Web** when you're planning. You'll find everything from up-to-date weather forecasts to virtual tours of famous cities. Fodor's Web site, www.fodors.com, is a great place to start your travels. For more information specifically on Maine, Vermont, and New Hampshire, take a look at the sites listed below. Besides material on sights and lodgings, most have a calendar of events and other special features, some of which are noted.

MAINE

The comprehensive Maine State Government site (www.state.me.us) has two notable links: "Tourism Office" brings you to www.visitmaine.com, which has an events calendar, links to local and regional chambers of commerce, and sightseeing, lodging, and dining information; "Maine's State Parks" provides details about park fees, facilities, and regulations.

NEW HAMPSHIRE

The resources on the New Hampshire Office of Travel and Tourism Development site (www.visitnh.gov) can be explored by region or activity. Regional sections have links to local chamber of commerce web sites.

VERMONT

The newly redesigned Vermont Department of Travel and Tourism (www.1-800-vermont.com) site can help you find just about any kind of information with links from the home page.

GENERAL INTEREST

A must-visit for anyone interested in the greener side of travel, the Great Outdoor Recreation Page (www.gorp.com) is arranged into three easily navigated categories: attractions, activities, and locations; within most of the "locations" are links to the state parks office. Another helpful resource is the National Park Service site (www.nps.gov), which lists all the national parks and has extensive historical, cultural, and environmental information.

➤ MAINE

www.state.me.us

➤ NEW HAMPSHIRE

www.visitnh.gov

➤ VERMONT

www.1-800-vermont.com

➤ GENERAL INTEREST

www.gorp.com; www.nps.gov

WHEN TO GO

All three states are largely year-round destinations. But you might want to **stay away from rural areas during mud season in April and black-fly season in the last two weeks of May.** Many smaller museums and attractions are open only from Memorial Day to mid-October, at other times by appointment only.

Memorial Day is the start of the migration to the beaches and the mountains, and summer begins in earnest on July 4.

Fall is the most colorful season in New England, a time when many inns and hotels are booked months in advance by foliage-viewing visitors. New England's dense hardwood forests explode in color as the diminishing hours of autumn daylight signal trees to stop producing chlorophyll. As green is stripped away from the leaves of maples, oaks, birches, beeches, and other deciduous species, a rainbow of reds, oranges, yellows, purples, and other vivid hues is revealed. The first scarlet and gold colors emerge in mid-September in northern areas; "peak" color occurs at different times from year to year. Generally, it's best to **visit the northern reaches in late September and early October and move southward as the month progresses.**

All leaves are off the trees by Halloween, and hotel rates fall as the leaves do, dropping significantly until ski season begins. November and early December are hunting season in much of New England; those who venture into the woods then should wear bright orange clothing.

Winter is the time for downhill and cross-country skiing. Maine, Vermont, and New Hampshire's major ski resorts, having seen dark days in years when snowfall was meager, now have snowmaking equipment.

In spring, despite mud season, maple sugaring goes on in Maine, Vermont, and New Hampshire, and the fragrant scent of lilacs is never far behind.

CLIMATE

BURLINGTON, VT

Jan.	29F	– 2C	May	67F	19C	Sept.	74F	23C
	11	–12		45	7		50	10
Feb.	31F	– 1C	June	77F	25C	Oct.	59F	15C
	11	–12		56	13		40	4
Mar.	40F	4C	July	83F	28C	Nov.	45F	7C
	22	– 6		59	15		31	– 1
Apr.	54F	12C	Aug.	79F	26C	Dec.	31F	– 1C
	34	1		58	14		16	– 9

PORTLAND, ME

Jan.	31F	– 1C	May	61F	16C	Sept.	68F	20C
	16	– 9		47	8		52	11
Feb.	32F	0C	June	72F	22C	Oct.	58F	14C
	16	– 9		54	15		43	6
Mar.	40F	4C	July	76F	24C	Nov.	45F	7C
	27	– 3		61	16		32	0
Apr.	50F	10C	Aug.	74F	23C	Dec.	34F	1C
	36	2		59	15		22	– 6

➤ FORECASTS: **Weather Channel Connection** (☎ 900/932–8437), 95¢ per minute from a Touch-Tone phone.

1 DESTINATION: MAINE, VERMONT, AND NEW HAMPSHIRE

DEEP ROOTS IN STONY SOIL

BACK IN THE 1940S photographer Paul Strand took two pictures that capture the essence of northern New England. One photograph, "Susan Thompson, Cape Split Maine," shows a late-middle-aged woman standing perfectly still at the entrance to her barn. She stands, as if pausing in her work, with her worn hands resting at her sides and her wistful, rather tired eyes just averted from the camera. Susan Thompson has the composure of a person who has lived long and hard in a single place.

The second picture, "Side Porch, New England," is a stark, almost abstract composition. Broad, rough-sawn, white painted boards frame the porch. A ladder-back chair with a cane seat (unoccupied) stands on the cracked, weathered boards of the porch floor. A broom and a wire rugbeater hang from nails on the wall. The scene is one of poverty, but not of neglect. The broom has obviously swept the porch clean that very morning, and, though the house has not been painted in years, one imagines that the rugs inside receive regular and thorough beatings.

Susan Thompson is gone, and so, most likely, is the old farmhouse with the clean-swept side porch. But even today, you don't have to travel far off the interstates that knife through Maine, Vermont, and New Hampshire before you run across people and houses and landscapes that are hauntingly similar to those Paul Strand photographed 50 years ago. The serenity, the austere beauty, the reverence for humble objects, the unassuming pride in place, the deep connection between man and landscape—all of these remain very much alive in northern New England.

In northern New England, the people and the land (and in Maine, the sea) seem bound by a marriage that has withstood many hardships. The relationship derives its character in part from the harsh climate. Spring withholds its flowers until mid-May, winter blows through in November, and a summer sunny spell is interrupted by rainstorms before it's had time to settle in properly. (There's a saying that there are two seasons in the north country—winter and July.)

There is a heritage here of self-reliance: the hardship of scratching out a living in small farms; the loneliness of sailing onto the cold northern waters to fish. In some places, isolation and hardship breed suspicion and meanness of spirit; in northern New England, they have engendered patience, endurance, a shrewd sardonic humor, and bottomless loyalty.

People sink deep roots in the thin, stony soil. They forgive the climate its cruelty. The north has a way of taking hold of the body and the spirit, as if weaving a kind of spell. It's not just the residents who are susceptible; summer visitors who have endured years of humid, overcast Julys and fog-shrouded Augusts keep coming back.

Distinct as they are in landscape, geology, and feeling, Maine, Vermont, and New Hampshire are linked by their northerness. There is something pure and fine and mystical about the North, just as there is something lush and soft and voluptuous about the South. You can feel the spirit of the North in the very light. The sun seems to burn more sharply and cleanly in the north country: It scours the rocks on the Maine coast, fills Vermont valleys with powdered gold in September, and turns the new snow of January into sapphires and diamonds.

Even more evocative than the light are the sounds of the North: the mournful, five-note whistle of the white-throated sparrow piercing the stillness of a June morning; the slap of lake water against a sandy shore; or the more insistent murmur of the sea reaching into a cove.

The explosions of warfare have not sounded in northern New England since the War of 1812, but throughout the 19th century the explosions of the industrial revolution ripped through the rural quiet in parts of these three states, particularly in southern New Hampshire. But eventually the noise of this revolution subsided. For the first half of the 20th century, the history of northern New England was primarily a history of decline. Mills and quarries were closed.

Farms were abandoned. Fishing villages dwindled to a handful of old folks. Fields were overgrown by maple and spruce.

It was only when Americans began to have the time, money, and inclination to travel that the region had a resurgence. Motor courts popped up along Maine's coastal Route 1 during the 1950s. Ski chalets peeked above the pines in Vermont and New Hampshire. Artists, teachers, and urban professionals snatched up the old farmhouses, and hippies set up communes in southern Vermont.

In the 1970s and '80s gentrification began to alter the towns and villages of the North. Second homes and condominiums went up in record numbers on the shores of Lake Winnepesaukee, alongside Maine's Casco and Linekin bays, and throughout the green countryside of southern Vermont.

Gentrification looks lovely compared with some of the other changes that have overtaken northern New England in the past couple of decades. Strip development has swallowed long stretches of Vermont's Route 4, especially around Rutland; and a good deal of southern New Hampshire has a distinctly suburban cast. Factory-outlet fever has reached epidemic proportions in Maine and New Hampshire. It used to be that tourists came to northern New England to buy a jug of maple syrup or a little pillow stuffed with balsam needles—now it's a pair of Bass shoes or Calvin Klein jeans.

Equally distressing are the crowds that have brought urban headaches into the heart of the northern wilderness. An endless caravan of leaf peepers crawls along the Kancamagus Highway in late September. The lift lines at Mt. Snow or Killington can be long enough to make you want to trade skiing for shopping at Manchester's boutiques and outlets. I have found few vacation experiences more depressing than slogging up the long, increasingly steep trail of Vermont's Camel's Hump mountain only to find the summit mobbed with fellow hikers. "Do we seat ourselves, or should we wait for the maitre d'?" one hiker remarked as he surveyed the scores of picnickers who had beat him to the top.

BUT EVEN IN THE MIDST of the changes and crowding of the present, the eternal images,

tastes, and experiences of the North endure. The steam of boiling maple sap still rises from sugarhouses all over the Green and White mountains every March. In May, lilacs bloom in fragrant, extravagant mounds beside seemingly every old farmhouse in the North. Loons flapping through the dawn mist rising off a lake, a scarlet-maple branch blazing beside a white church, cows grazing on a lush, green hillside—these images have become cliches, but they are nonetheless stirring and satisfying.

Whenever I feel the first chill of autumn in the air, whenever I see a flock of geese winging north, whenever I come upon a stand of spruce and white pine rising at the end of a freshly mown hay field, I feel the tug of northern New England. The drive north from my home outside New York City is long and dull, and, on the way up, there always comes a moment of doubt: Will it be worth the time and money? Will it have changed? Will it rain or fog the entire time?

Then I see the first ramshackle house with a side porch, the first rough pasture strewn with stones and humps of grass, the first kind wistful face, and I know it will be all right.

– David Laskin

David Laskin has written for The New York Times *and* Travel and Leisure.

WHAT'S WHERE

Maine

Maine is by far the largest state in New England. At its extremes it measures 300 mi by 200 mi; all other New England states could fit within its perimeters. Because of overdevelopment, Maine's southernmost coastal towns won't give you the rugged, "down-east" experience, but the Kennebunks will: classic townscapes, rocky shorelines punctuated by sandy beaches, quaint downtown districts. Purists hold that the Maine coast begins at Penobscot Bay, where the vistas over the water are wider and bluer, the shore a jumble of granite boulders. Beautiful Acadia National Park is Maine's principal tourist attraction; and in Freeport, numerous outlet stores and specialty shops have sprung up around the famous outfitter L. L. Bean. The vast north woods is a destination for outdoors enthusiasts. Tourism has supplanted fishing, logging, and potato farming as Maine's number one industry: The visitor seeking an untouched fishing village with locals gathered around a potbellied stove in the general store may be sadly disappointed; that innocent age has passed in all but the most remote of villages.

Vermont

Southern Vermont has farms, freshly starched New England towns, quiet back roads, bustling ski resorts, and even some strip-mall sprawl. Central Vermont's trademarks include famed marble quarries, just north of Rutland, and large dairy herds and pastures that create the quilted patchwork of the Champlain Valley. The heart of the area is the Green Mountains and the surrounding wilderness of the Green Mountain National Forest. Both the state's largest city (Burlington) and the nation's smallest state capital (Montpelier) are in northern Vermont, as are some of the most rural and remote areas of New England. Much of the state's logging, dairy farming, and skiing take place in the north. With Montréal only an hour from the border, the Canadian influence is strong, and Canadian accents and currency common.

New Hampshire

Portsmouth, the star of New Hampshire's 18-mi coastline, has great shopping, restaurants, music, theater, and one of the best historic districts in the nation. Exeter is New Hampshire's enclave of Revolutionary War history. The Lakes Region, rich with historic landmarks, also has good restaurants, several golf courses, hiking trails, and antiquing. People come to the White Mountains to hike and climb, to photograph the dramatic vistas and the vibrant sea of foliage, and to ski. More than a mile high, Mt. Washington's peak claims the harshest winds and lowest temperatures ever recorded. Western and central New Hampshire is the unspoiled heart of the state: This region has managed to keep the water slides and the outlet malls at bay. Beyond the museums and picture-perfect greens, this area offers Lake Sunapee and Mt. Monadnock, the second-most-climbed mountain in the world. It is also an informal artists' colony where people come to write, paint, and weave in solitude.

PLEASURES AND PASTIMES

Beaches

Long, wide beaches edge the New England coast from southern Maine to southern Connecticut; the most popular are on Maine's York County coast and the coastal region of New Hampshire. Many are maintained by state and local governments and have lifeguards on duty; they may have picnic facilities, rest rooms, changing facilities, and concession stands. Depending on the locale, you may need a parking sticker to use the lot. The waters are at their warmest in August, though they're cold even at the height of summer along much of the Maine coast. Inland, there are small lake beaches, most notably in New Hampshire and Vermont.

Biking

Biking is popular in the New Hampshire lakes region and Vermont's Northeast Kingdom. Biking in Maine is especially scenic in and around Kennebunkport, Camden, and Deer Isle; the carriage paths in Acadia National Park are ideal.

Boating

In most lakeside and coastal resorts, sailboats and powerboats can be rented at a local marina. Maine's Penobscot Bay is a famous sailing area. Lakes in New Hampshire and Vermont are splendid for all kinds of boating.

Dining

Seafood is king throughout New England. Clams, quahogs, lobster, and scrod are prepared here in an infinite number of ways, some fancy and expensive, others simple and moderately priced. One of the best ways to enjoy seafood is in the rough—off paper plates on a picnic table at a clamboil or clambake—or at one of the many shacklike eating places along the coast, where you can smell the salt air.

At inland resorts and inns, traditional fare dominates many menus, although an increasing number of innovative chefs are bringing contemporary regional fare to the table. Among the quintessentially New England dishes are Indian pudding, clam chowder, fried clams, and cranberry anything. You can also find multicultural variations on themes, such as Portuguese *chouriço* (a spicy red sausage that transforms a clamboil into something heavenly) and the mincemeat pie made with pork in the tradition of the French Canadians who populate the northern regions.

Fishing

Anglers will find sport aplenty throughout the region—surf-casting along the shore, deep-sea fishing in the Atlantic on party and charter boats, fishing for trout in rivers, and angling for bass, landlocked salmon, and other fish in freshwater lakes. Maine's Moosehead Lake is a draw for serious anglers. Sporting goods stores and bait-and-tackle shops are reliable sources for licenses—necessary in fresh waters—and for leads to the nearest hot spots.

Hiking

Probably the most famous trails are the 255-mi Long Trail, which runs north–south through the center of Vermont, and the Maine-to-Georgia Appalachian Trail, which runs through New England on both private and public land. You'll find good hiking in many state parks throughout the region.

National and State Parks and Forests

National and state parks offer a broad range of visitor facilities, including campgrounds, picnic grounds, hiking trails, boating, and ranger programs. State forests are usually somewhat less developed. For more information on any of these, contact the state tourism offices or parks departments (☞ Visitor Information *in* Smart Travel Tips A to Z).

MAINE➤ Acadia National Park, which preserves fine stretches of shoreline and high mountains, covers much of Mount Desert Island and more than half of Isle au Haut and Schoodic Point on the mainland.

Baxter State Park comprises more than 200,000 acres of wilderness surrounding Katahdin, Maine's highest mountain. Hiking and moose-watching are major activities. The Allagash Wilderness Waterway is a 92-mi corridor of lakes and rivers surrounded by vast commercial forest property.

VERMONT➤ The 275,000-acre Green Mountain National Forest extends south from the center of the state to the Massachusetts border. Hikers treasure the miles of trails; canoeists work its white waters; and campers and anglers find plenty to keep them happy. Among the most popular spots are the Falls of Lana and Silver Lake near Middlebury; Hapgood Pond between Manchester and Peru; and Chittenden Brook near Rochester.

NEW HAMPSHIRE➤ The White Mountain National Forest covers 770,000 acres of northern New Hampshire. New Hampshire parklands vary widely, even within a region. Major recreation parks are at Franconia Notch, Crawford Notch, and Mt. Sunapee. Rhododendron State Park (near Fitzwilliam in the Monadnock region) has a singular collection of wild rhododendrons; Mt. Washington Park (White Mountains) is on top of the highest mountain in the Northeast.

Shopping

Antiques, crafts, maple syrup and sugar, fresh produce, and the greatly varied offerings of the factory outlets lure shoppers to New England's outlet stores, flea markets, shopping malls, bazaars, yard sales, country stores, and farmers' markets. Maine sales tax is 5½%; Vermont, 5%. New Hampshire has no sales tax.

ANTIQUES➤ In Maine, antiques shops are clustered in Searsport and along U.S. 1 between Kittery and Scarborough. People sometimes joke that New Hampshire's two cash crops are fudge and antiques. Particularly in the Monadnock region, dealers abound in barns and home stores that are strung along back roads. Best antiquing concentrations are in North Conway; along Route 119, from Fitzwilliam to Hinsdale; Route 101, from Marlborough to Wilton; and the towns of Hopkinton, Hollis, and Amherst. The stretch of U.S. 4 between Barrington and Concord is another mecca.

CRAFTS➤ On Maine's Deer Isle, Haystack Mountain School of Crafts attracts internationally renowned craftspeople to its summer institute. In Vermont, Burlington and Putney are crafts centers.

OUTLET STORES➤ In Maine shop along the coast, in Kittery, Freeport, Kennebunkport, Wells, and Ellsworth; in New Hampshire, North Conway; and in Vermont, Manchester.

PRODUCE➤ Opportunities abound for obtaining fresh farm produce from the source; some farms allow you to pick your own strawberries, raspberries, blueberries, and apples. October in Maine is prime time for pumpkins and potatoes. There are maple-syrup producers who demonstrate the process to visitors, most noticeably in Vermont. Maple syrup is available in different grades; light amber is the most refined; many Vermonters prefer grade C, the richest in flavor and the one most often used in cooking. A sugarhouse can be the most or the least expensive place to shop, depending on how tourist-oriented it is. Small grocery stores are often a good source of less-expensive syrup.

Skiing

The softly rounded peaks of New England have been attracting skiers for a full century.

LIFT TICKETS➤ A good bet is that the bigger and more famous the resort, the higher the price of a lift ticket. A single-day, weekend-holiday adult lift ticket always has the highest price; astute skiers look for off-site purchase locations, senior discounts and junior pricing, and package rates, multiple days, stretch weekends (a weekend that usually includes a Monday or Friday), frequent-skier programs, and season-ticket plans to save their skiing dollars. Some independently owned areas are bona fide bargains for skiers who don't require the glamour and glitz of the high-profile resorts.

LODGING➤ Lodging is among the most important considerations for skiers who plan more than a day trip. Although some of the ski areas described in this book are small and draw only day trippers, most offer a variety of accommodations—lodges, condominiums, hotels, motels, inns, bed-and-breakfasts—close to or at a short distance from the action.

For a longer vacation, you should request and study the resort area's accommodations brochure. For stays of three days or more, a package rate may offer the best deal. Packages vary in composition, price, and availability throughout the season; their components may include a room, meals, lift tickets, ski lessons, rental equipment, transfers to the mountain, parties, races, and use of a sports center, tips, and taxes.

EQUIPMENT RENTAL➤ Rental equipment is available at all ski areas, at ski shops around resorts, and even in cities far from ski areas. Shop personnel will advise customers on the appropriate equipment for an individual's size and ability and on how to operate the equipment. Good skiers should ask to "demo," or test, premium equipment.

TRAIL RATING➤ Ski areas have devised standards for rating and marking trails and slopes that offer fairly accurate guides. Trails are rated Easier (green circle), More Difficult (blue square), Most Difficult (black diamond), and Expert (double diamond). Keep in mind that trail difficulty is measured relative to that of other trails *at the same ski area*, not to those of an area down the road, in another state, or in another part of the country; a black-diamond trail at one area may rate only a blue square at a neighboring area. In spite of this, the trail-marking system throughout New England is remarkably consistent and reliable.

LESSONS➤ Within the United States, the Professional Ski Instructors of America (PSIA) have devised a progressive teaching system that is used with relatively little variation at many ski schools, though not the ones at the New England resorts run by the American Skiing Company. This allows skiers to take lessons at ski schools in different ski areas and still improve. Class lessons usually last 1½–2 hours and are limited in size to 10 participants.

Some ski schools have adopted the PSIA teaching system for children, and many also use SKIwee, which awards progress cards and applies other standardized teaching approaches. Many ski schools offer sessions in which the children ski together with an instructor and eat together.

CHILDCARE➤ Nurseries can be found at virtually all ski areas and often accept children aged 6 weeks to 6 years. Parents must usually supply formula and diapers for infants; reservations are strongly advised.

GREAT ITINERARIES

Kancamagus Trail

This circuit takes in some of the most spectacular parts of the White and Green mountains, along with the upper Connecticut River valley. In this area the antiques hunting is exemplary and the traffic is often almost nonexistent. The scenery evokes the spirit of Currier & Ives.

DURATION➤ 3–6 days

1–3 DAYS➤ From the New Hampshire coast, head northwest to Wolfeboro, perhaps detouring to explore around Lake Winnipesaukee. Take Route 16 north to Conway, then follow Route 112 west along the scenic Kancamagus Pass through the White Mountains to the Vermont border.

1–2 DAYS➤ Head south on Route 10 along the Connecticut River, past scenic Hanover, New Hampshire, home of Dartmouth College. At White River Junction, cross into Vermont. You may want to follow Route 4 through the lovely town of Woodstock to Killington, then travel along Route 100 and I–89 to complete the loop back to White River Junction. Otherwise, simply proceed south along I–91, with stops at such pleasant Vermont towns as Putney and Brattleboro.

1–2 DAYS➤ Take Route 119 east to Rhododendron State Park in Fitzwilliam, New Hampshire. Nearby is Mt. Monadnock, the most-climbed mountain in the United States; in Jaffrey take the trail to the top. Dawdle along back roads to visit the preserved villages of Harrisville, Dublin, and Hancock, then continue east along Route 101 to return to the coast.

FODOR'S CHOICE

Even with so many special places in New England, Fodor's writers and editors have their favorites. Here are a few that stand out.

Flavors

★ **White Barn Inn, Kennebunkport, ME.** One of Maine's best restaurants, the White Barn combines superb dining with unblemished service in a rustic setting. $$$$

★ **Fore Street, Portland, ME.** From the open kitchen here, two of Maine's best chefs create culinary magic in dishes such as roasted lobster and applewood-grilled swordfish. $$–$$$

★ **Round Pond Lobstermen's Co-op, Round Pond, ME.** For lobster-in-the-rough, you can't beat this dockside takeout with views over Round Pond Harbor. $

★ **The Balsams Grand Resort Hotel, Dixville Notch, NH.** The summer buffet lunch is heaped upon a 100-ft-long table; dinners might include chilled strawberry soup spiked with Grand Marnier and poached salmon with caviar sauce. $$–$$$

★ **Porto Bello Ristorante Italiano, Portsmouth, NH.** Pure Italian food from grilled calamari to spinach gnocchi is served up at a family-run establishment downtown. $$–$$$

★ **Hemingway's, Killington, VT.** Superb seasonal cuisine that focuses on local game and fresh seafood has won this restaurant a reputation as one of the state's best. $$$$

★ **Prince and the Pauper, Woodstock, VT.** A Colonial dining room is the setting for creative French and American dishes that come with Vermont accents. $$$–$$$$

★ **Villa Tragara, Stowe, VT.** Italian tapas and dishes such as roasted quail have won this romantic northern Italian eatery a devoted following. $$–$$$

Comforts

★ **Lodge at Moosehead Lake, Greenville, ME.** This lumber baron's mansion overlooking Moosehead Lake is as luxurious as it gets in the North Woods. All rooms have whirlpool baths, fireplaces, and four-poster beds; most have lake views. $$$$

★ **Ullikana, Bar Harbor, ME.** Hidden within this staid Tudor mansion is a riot of color and art. Fireplaces, private decks, water views, and gourmet breakfasts make it a real treat. $$–$$$$

★ **Manor on Golden Pond, Holderness, NH.** The rooms in this English-style manor on exclusive Squam Lake are filled with luxurious touches. $$$$

★ **Snowvillage Inn, Snowville, NH.** Rooms in this book-filled inn near North Con-

8

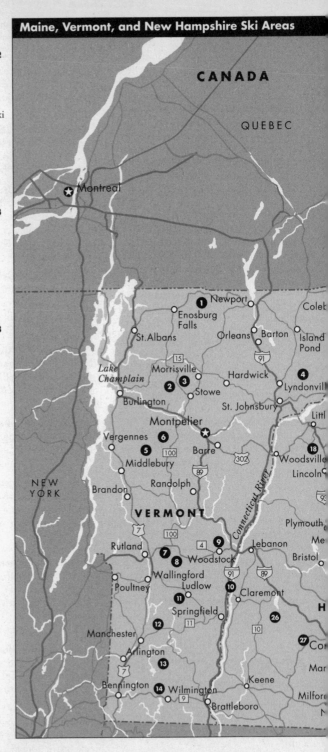

Maine, Vermont, and New Hampshire Ski Areas

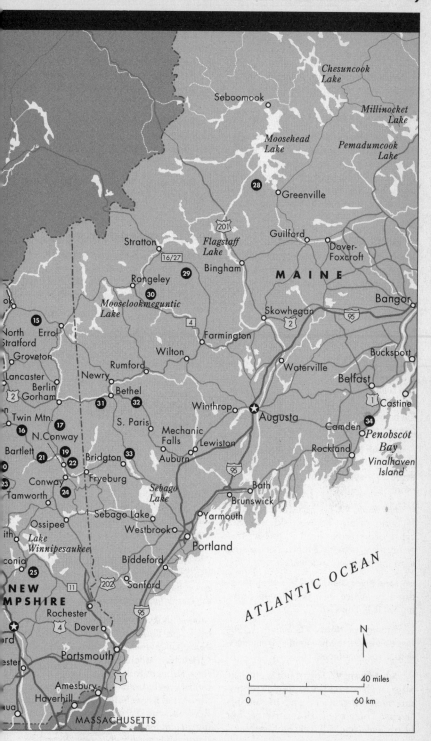

way are named after authors; the nicest, with 12 windows that look out over the Presidential Range, is a tribute to Robert Frost. $$–$$$$

★ **West Mountain Inn, Arlington, VT.** A former farmhouse from the 1840s has a llama ranch on the property and sits on 150 acres with glorious views. $$$$

★ **Inn at Shelburne Farms, Shelburne, VT.** This is storybook land: A Tudor-style inn built for William Seward and Lila Vanderbilt Webb sits on the edge of Lake Champlain and has views of the Adirondack Mountains. $$–$$$$

Ski Resorts

★ **Big Squaw Mountain, ME.** A down-home, laid-back atmosphere prevails at Squaw, which overlooks Moosehead Lake. This is no frills, big mountain skiing at bargain basement prices.

★ **Sugarloaf/USA, ME.** At 2,820 ft, Sugarloaf/USA's vertical drop is greater than that of any other New England ski peak except Killington.

★ **Sunday River, ME.** Good snowmaking and reliable grooming ensure great snow from November to May at this resort, the flagship of the American Skiing Company empire.

★ **Attitash Bear Peak, NH.** There's always something innovative happening here—demo days, special events, race camps, and more.

★ **Jay Peak, VT.** Jay gets the most natural snow of any Vermont ski area. Because of its proximity to Québec, this resort attracts many Montréalers, giving it an international ambience.

★ **Mad River Glen, VT.** The apt motto at this area owned by a skiers cooperative is "Ski It If You Can."

★ **Smugglers' Notch, VT.** With its 1,150-ft vertical, Morse Mountain at Smugglers' is tops for beginners.

★ **Sugarbush, VT.** Sugarbush is an overall great place to ski; it has beginner runs, intermediate cruisers, and formidable steeps. There's a with-it attitude, but nearly everyone will feel comfortable.

Memorable Sights

★ **Sunrise from Cadillac Mountain, Mount Desert Island, ME.** From the summit you have a 360° view of the ocean, islands, jagged coastline, woods, and lakes.

★ **Yacht-filled Camden Harbor, ME, from the summit of Mt. Battie.** Mt. Battie may not be very tall, but it has a memorable vista over Camden Harbor, which shelters a large fleet of windjammers.

★ **Early October views, Kancamagus Highway, NH.** The classic White Mountain vistas on this popular 34-mi drive burst into fiery color each fall.

★ **The trip up Mt. Washington, NH.** Whether you hike, drive the toll road, or take the Mt. Washington Cog Railway, the journey up the Northeast's tallest mountain yields spectacular panoramas.

★ **The Appalachian Gap, Route 17, VT.** Views from the top and on the way down this mountain pass near Bristol are a just reward for the challenging drive.

★ **Village green, Woodstock, VT.** The spirit of New England's past is preserved in the lovely Federal homes that surround the green in this handsome town.

BOOKS AND VIDEOS

New England has been home to some of America's classic authors, among them Herman Melville, Edith Wharton, Mark Twain, Robert Frost, Ralph Waldo Emerson, Henry Wadsworth Longfellow, and Emily Dickinson. Henry David Thoreau wrote about New England in *Cape Cod, The Maine Woods,* and his masterpiece, *Walden.* Modern New England literary voices have included that of Stephen King, the horrormeister of Bangor, Maine.

Among books written about the Maine islands are Philip Conkling's *Islands in Time,* Bill Caldwell's *Islands of Maine,* and Charlotte Fardelmann's *Islands Down East.* Kenneth Roberts set a series of historical novels, beginning with *Arundel,* in the coastal Kennebunk region during the Revolutionary War and also wrote *Trending into Maine,* a book of essays on traditional but rapidly changing Down East ways of life. Sarah Orne Jewett's 1896 novel, *The Country of the Pointed Firs,* describes the heart of small-town life with sympathy. Ruth Moore's *Candalmas Bay, Speak to the Winds,* and *The Weir* and Elisabeth Ogilvie's "Tide Trilogy" books capture both the romanticism and hardships of coastal life. Carolyn Chute's 1985 bestseller, *The Beans of Egypt, Maine,* offers a fictional glimpse of the hardships of contemporary rural life. The 1994 movie version of the book, starring Martha Plimpton, is in video stores with the title *Forbidden Choices.*

Charles Morrissey's *Vermont: A History* delivers just what the title promises; it's part of a series of bicentennial histories, all published by Norton, in which the other five New England states are also represented. *Without a Farmhouse Near,* by Deborah Rawson, describes the impact of change on small Vermont communities, as does Joe Sherman's *Fast Lane on a Dirt Road. Real Vermonters Don't Milk Goats,* by Frank Bryan and Bill Mares, looks at the lighter side of life in the Green Mountain state. Howard Frank Mosher, long a resident of Vermont's sparsely populated, bleakly beautiful Northeast Kingdom, has written works of fiction including *A Stranger in the Kingdom, Northern Borders,* and *Where the Rivers Flow North,* all dealing with the hard lives and bristly independence of the region's natives. *Where the Rivers Flow North* was made into an acclaimed independent film in 1993, with stars Rip Torn and Michael J. Fox. Another video with a Vermont locale—although in a vastly different, comic vein—is John O'Brien's 1996 *Man with a Plan,* about a retired dairy farmer who decides to run for Congress.

Visitors to New Hampshire may enjoy the classic 19th-century history-cum-travel guide *The White Mountains: Their Legends, Landscape, and Poetry,* by Thomas Starr King, and *The Great Stone Face and Other Tales of the White Mountains,* by Nathaniel Hawthorne. New Hampshire was also blessed with the poet Robert Frost, whose first books, *A Boy's Way* and *North of Boston,* are set here, as is his long poem *New Hampshire.* It's commonly accepted that the Grover's Corners of Thornton Wilder's play *Our Town* is the real-life Peterborough. The 1981 movie *On Golden Pond* was partially filmed on Squam Lake.

Also published by Fodor's, *New England's Best Bed & Breakfasts* has more than 300 reviews of places to stay and things to do in the region; *National Parks and Seashores of the East* covers many New England destinations; and *Where Should We Take the Kids? The Northeast* provides ideas on what to do with the little ones while in New England. Fodor's Compass American Guides, handsomely illustrated with color photographs, provide topical and cultural essays and historical background. Look for *Vermont,* by Don Mitchell, and *Maine,* by Charles Calhoun.

FESTIVALS AND SEASONAL EVENTS

WINTER

DECEMBER:➤ Historic **Strawberry Banke** (NH) has a Christmas Stroll, with carolers, through nine historic homes decorated for the season. **Christmas Prelude** in Kennebunkport (ME) celebrates winter with concerts, caroling, and special events. The final day of the year is observed with festivals, entertainment, and food in many locations during **First Night Celebrations.** Some of the major cities hosting First Nights are Portland (ME) and Burlington, Montpelier, and St. Johnsbury (all in VT).

JANUARY:➤ The Bethel (ME) **Winter Festival** has snowshoe and cross-country races, sleigh rides, fireworks, ice-skating, and a snowman contest. Stowe's (VT) **Winter Carnival** heats up around mid-month; it's among the country's oldest such celebrations. Brookfield (VT) holds its **Ice Harvest Festival,** one of New England's largest. The weeklong **Winter Carnival** in Jackson (NH) includes ski races, ice sculptures, and parades. The University of Vermont **Lane Series,** in Burlington, showcases internationally known performers in music, dance, and theater this month and throughout the winter.

FEBRUARY:➤ The Camden Snow Bowl in Camden (ME) is the site of the **U.S. National Toboggan Championships.** On tap at the

Brattleboro Winter Carnival, held during the last week of the month in Vermont, are jazz concerts and an ice fishing derby. The **Mad River Valley Winter Carnival** (VT) is a week of winter festivities, including dogsled races and ski races and fireworks; Burlington's **Vermont Mozart Festival** showcases the Winter Chamber Music Series.

SPRING

MARCH:➤ This is the season for **maple-sugaring festivals and events:** Throughout the month and into April, the sugarhouses of Maine, New Hampshire, and Vermont demonstrate procedures from maple-tree tapping to sap boiling. During **Maine Maple Sunday** Maine sugarhouses open for tours and tastings. Maine's Moosehead Lake has a renowned **Ice-Fishing Derby,** and Rangeley's **New England Sled Dog Races** attract more than 100 teams from throughout the Northeast and Canada. Devotees of chocolate head to Portland (ME) in late March for the **Chocolate Lovers' Fling.** Stratton Mountain (VT) hosts the **U.S. Open Snowboarding Championships.**

APRIL:➤ During **Reggae Weekend** at Sugarloaf/USA (ME), Caribbean reggae bands play outdoors and inside throughout the weekend. During Sunday River's (ME) annual **Bust 'n' Burn**

Mogul Competition, professional and amateur bump skiers test their mettle on the notorious White Heat trail's man-eating moguls. You can gorge on sea grub at Boothbay Harbor's (ME) **Fisherman's Festival,** held on the third weekend in April. At the **Maple Festival,** held early each April in St. Albans (VT), the state's sweetest specialty takes the spotlight; you can try Sugar on Snow, a taffylike treat.

MAY:➤ The Shelburne Museum in Shelburne (VT) is awash in purple glory in mid-May, when the **Lilac Festival** blossoms. If you want to see a moose, visit Greenville (ME) during **Moose-Mainea,** which runs from mid-May to mid-June. Events include moose safaris, mountain bike and canoe races, a parade, and a family fun day.

SUMMER

JUNE:➤ In Vermont, you can listen to jazz at Burlington's **Discover Jazz Festival** or folk at Warren's **Ben & Jerry's One World One Heart Festival,** which is held at Sugarbush. The spring thaw calls for a number of boating celebrations, including the **Vermont Canoe and Kayak Festival** in Stowe and the **Boothbay Harbor Windjammer Days,** which starts the high season for Maine's boating set. Young ones are the stars of Somerworth's (NH) **International Children's Festival,** where games, activities, and crafts keep everybody busy. Nothing is sweeter than a fresh Maine strawberry, and during the **Strawberry Festival** in Wiscasset you can get your fill of strawberry shortcake and other goodies.

JULY:➤ **Fourth of July** parties and parades occur throughout New England; concerts, family entertainment, an art show, a parade, and fireworks are held in Bath (ME). Later in the month, Exeter (NH) holds a **Revolutionary War Festival** at the American Independence Museum with battle reenactments, period crafts and antiques, and a visit from George Washington himself.

Some of the better music festivals include the **Marlboro Music Festival** of classical music, held at Marlboro College (VT); the **Bar Harbor Festival** (ME), which hosts classical, jazz, and popular music concerts into August; and the **Bowdoin Summer Music Festival** (ME), a six-week series of chamber music concerts. Glorious outdoor concert sites and sumptuous picnics are sidelights to fine music at the **Vermont Music Festival,** held throughout northern Vermont in July and August.

Shoppers can rummage through major **antiques fairs** in Wolfeboro (NH) and Dorset (VT), or simply admire the homes during **Open House Tours** in Camden (ME). The **Yarmouth Clam Festival** (ME) is more than a seafood celebration—

expect fireworks, a parade, continuous entertainment, and a crafts show throughout the three-day event. One of the region's most popular **country fairs** is held in Bangor (ME).

AUGUST:➤ Stowe (VT) hosts a popular **Antique and Classic Car Rally.** Popular arts, crafts, and antiques festivals include the **Southern Vermont Crafts Fair** in Manchester (VT), the **Maine Antiques Festival** in Union, and at the **Fair of the League of New Hampshire Craftsmen** at Mt. Sunapee State Park in Newbury. There's a **Lobster Festival** in Rockland (ME) and a **Blueberry Festival** in Rangeley Lake (ME). Most summers find a **major air show** with precision teams, acrobats and stunt pilots, and military planes both flying and on display at the Brunswick (ME) Naval Air Station. Brunswick's **Maine Festival** is a four-day celebration of Maine arts.

AUTUMN

SEPTEMBER:➤ New England's dozens of Labor Day fairs include the **Vermont State Fair** in Rutland, with agricultural exhibits and entertainment; the **International Seaplane Fly-In Weekend,** which sets Moosehead Lake (ME) buzzing; and the **Champlain Valley Exposition,** a Burlington (VT) event with all the features of a large county fair. Foot stomping and guitar strumming are the activities of choice at

several musical events: the **National Traditional Old-Time Fiddler's Contest** in Barre (VT), the **Bluegrass Festival** in Brunswick (ME), and the **Rockport Folk Festival** in Rockport (ME). In Stratton (VT), artists and performers gather for the **Stratton Arts Festival.**

Agricultural fairs not to be missed are the **Common Ground Country Fair** in Unity (ME), an organic farmer's delight, and the **Deerfield Fair** (NH), one of New England's oldest. The six small Vermont towns of Walden, Cabot, Plainfield, Peacham, Barnet, and Groton host the weeklong **Northeast Kingdom Fall Foliage Festival** (VT). The weekend-long **Eastport Salmon Festival** (ME) hosts entertainers and crafts artists. At the **Annual Seafood Festival** in Hampton Beach (NH), you can sample the seafood specialties of more than 50 local restaurants, dance to live bands, and watch fireworks explode over the ocean.

OCTOBER:➤ The **Fryeburg Fair** (ME) presents agricultural exhibits, harness racing, an iron-skillet-throwing contest, and a pig scramble.

NOVEMBER:➤ In Vermont there are two major events in this otherwise quiet month: The **International Film Festival** presents films dealing with environmental, human rights, and political issues for a week in Burlington, and the **Bradford Wild Game Supper** draws thousands to taste large and small game animals and birds.

2 MAINE

At its extremes Maine measures 300 miles by 200 miles; all the other states in New England could fit within its perimeters. The Kennebunks hold classic townscapes, rocky shorelines, sandy beaches, and quaint downtown districts. Portland has the state's best selection of restaurants, shops, and cultural offerings, and Freeport is a mecca for outlet shoppers. North of Portland, sandy beaches give way to rocky coast. Acadia National Park is one of Maine's treasures. Outdoors enthusiasts head to inland Maine's lakes and mountains and the vast North Woods.

Revised and
updated by
Hilary M.
Nangle

ON THE MAINE–NEW HAMPSHIRE BORDER is a sign that plainly announces the philosophy of the region: WELCOME TO MAINE: THE WAY LIFE SHOULD BE. Local folk say too many cars are on the road when you can't make it through the traffic signal on the first try. Romantics luxuriate upon the feeling of a down comforter on an old, yellowed pine bed or in the sensation of the wind and salt spray on their faces while cruising in a historic windjammer. Families love the unspoiled beaches and safe inlets dotting the shoreline and the clear inland lakes. Hikers and campers are revived by the exalting and exhausting climb to the top of Mt. Katahdin, and adventure seekers get their thrills rafting the Kennebec or Penobscot river.

There is an expansiveness to Maine, a sense of distance between places that hardly exists elsewhere in New England, and along with the sheer size and spread of the place there is a tremendous variety of terrain. People speak of "coastal" Maine and "inland" Maine, as though the state could be summed up under the twin emblems of lobsters and pine trees. Yet the topography and character in this state are a good deal more complicated.

Even the coast is several places in one. Portland may be Maine's largest city, but its attitude is decidedly more big town than small city. South of this rapidly gentrifying city, Ogunquit, Kennebunkport, Old Orchard Beach (sometimes called the Québec Riviera because of its popularity with French Canadians), and other resort towns predominate along a reasonably smooth shoreline. North of Portland and Casco Bay, secondary roads turn south off U.S. 1 onto so many oddly chiseled peninsulas that it's possible to drive for days without retracing your route. Slow down to explore the museums, galleries, and shops in the larger towns and the antiques and curio shops and harborside lobster shacks in the smaller fishing villages on the peninsulas. Freeport is an entity unto itself, a place where numerous name-brand outlets and a variety of specialty stores have sprung up around the retail outpost of famous outfitter L. L. Bean.

Inland Maine likewise defies characterization. For one thing, a lot of it is virtually uninhabited. This is the land Henry David Thoreau wrote about in *The Maine Woods* more than 150 years ago; aside from having been logged over several times, much of it hasn't changed since Thoreau and his Native American guides passed through. Ownership of vast portions of northern Maine by forest-products corporations has kept out subdivision and development; many of the roads here are private, open to travel only by permit.

Wealthy summer visitors, or "sports," came to Maine beginning in the late 1800s to hunt, fish, and play in the clean air and clean water. The state's more than 6,000 lakes and more than 3,000 mi of rivers and streams still attract such people, and more and more families, for the same reasons. Sporting camps still thrive around Greenville, Rangeley, and in the Great North Woods.

Logging in the north created the culture of the mill towns, the Rumfords, Skowhegans, Millinockets, and Bangors that lie at the end of the old river drives. The logs arrive by truck today, but Maine's harvested wilderness still feeds the mills and the nation's hunger for paper.

Our hunger for potatoes has given rise to an entirely different Maine culture, in one of the most isolated agricultural regions of the country. Northeastern Aroostook County is where the Maine potatoes come from. This place is also changing. In what was once called the

Potato Empire, farmers are as pressed between high costs and low prices as any of their counterparts in the Midwest, and a growing national preference for Idaho baking potatoes to small, round Maine boiling potatoes has only compounded Aroostook's troubles.

If you come to Maine seeking an untouched fishing village with locals gathered around a potbellied stove in the general store, you'll likely come away sadly disappointed; that innocent age has passed in all but the most remote villages. Tourism has supplanted fishing, logging, and potato farming as Maine's number one industry; most areas are well equipped to receive the annual onslaught of visitors. But whether you are stepping outside a motel room for an evening walk or watching a boat rock at its anchor, you can sense the infinity of the natural world. Wilderness is always nearby, growing to the edges of the most urbanized spots.

Pleasures and Pastimes

Boating
Maine's long coastline is justifiably famous: All visitors should get on the water, whether on a mail boat headed for Monhegan Island for the day or on a windjammer for a relaxing weeklong vacation. Windjammers, traditional two- or three-masted tall ships, sail past long, craggy fingers of land that jut into a sea dotted with more than 2,000 islands. Sail among these islands and you'll see hidden coves, lighthouses, boat-filled harbors, and quiet fishing villages. Most windjammers depart from Rockland, Rockport, or Camden, all ports on Penobscot Bay. Boating trips, including whale-watching, run in season, mid- to late May through September or mid-October.

Dining
Lobster and Maine are synonymous. As a general rule, the closer you are to a working harbor, the fresher your lobster will be. Aficionados eschew ordering lobster in restaurants, preferring to eat them "in the rough" at classic lobster pounds, where you select your dinner out of a pool and enjoy it at a waterside picnic table. Shrimp, scallops, clams, mussels, and crab are also caught in the cold waters off Maine. Restaurants in Portland and in resort towns prepare shellfish in creative combinations with lobster, haddock, salmon, and swordfish. Blueberries are grown commercially in Maine, and Maine cooks use them generously in pancakes, muffins, jams, pies, and cobblers. Full country breakfasts of fruit, eggs, breakfast meats, pancakes, and muffins are commonly served at inns and bed-and-breakfasts.

Hiking
From seaside rambles to backwoods hikes, Maine has a walk for everyone. This state's beaches are mostly hard packed and good for walking. Many coastal communities, such as York, Ogunquit, and Bar Harbor, have shoreside paths for people who want to keep sand out of their shoes yet enjoy the sound of the crashing surf and the cliff-top views of inlets and coves. Those who like to walk in the woods will not be disappointed: Ninety percent of the state is forested land. Acadia National Park has more than 150 mi of hiking trails, and within Baxter State Park are the northern end of the Appalachian Trail and Mt. Katahdin. At nearly 1 mi high, Katahdin is the tallest mountain in the state.

Lodging
The beach communities in the south beckon visitors with their weathered look. Stately digs can be found in the classic inns of Kennebunkport. Bed-and-breakfasts and Victorian inns furnished with lace, chintz, and mahogany have joined the family-oriented motels of Ogunquit, Booth-

bay Harbor, Bar Harbor, and the Camden–Rockport region. Although accommodations tend to be less luxurious away from the coast, Bethel, Carrabassett Valley, and Rangeley have sophisticated hotels and inns. Greenville and Rockwood have the largest selection of restaurants and accommodations in the North Woods region. Lakeside sporting camps, which range from the primitive to the upscale, are popular around Rangeley and the North Woods. Many have cozy cabins heated with woodstoves and serve three hearty meals a day (American Plan, or AP). At some of Maine's larger hotels and inns with restaurants, the Modified American Plan (MAP; rates include breakfast and dinner) is either an option or a requirement during the peak summer season. B&Bs generally prepare full breakfasts, though some serve only a Continental breakfast of pastries and coffee.

Skiing

Weather patterns that create snow cover for Maine ski areas may come from the Atlantic or from Canada, and Maine may have snow when other New England states do not—and vice versa. Thanks to Sunday River's owner, Les Otten, Maine is moving to the forefront of the regional skiing scene. Otten developed Sunday River from a small operation into one of New England's largest and best-managed ski resorts. Since acquiring Sugarloaf/USA in 1996, he's focused much-needed attention here, upgrading lifts and snowmaking. It's worth the effort to get to Sugarloaf, which provides the only above-tree-line skiing in New England and also has a lively base village. Mt. Abram, which sits in Sunday River's shadow, has also blossomed under new ownership, becoming a true family area with reliable skiing day and night as well as snow tubing.

Saddleback, in Rangeley, has big-mountain skiing at little-mountain prices. Its lift system is sorely out of date, but many would have it no other way, preferring its down-home, wilderness atmosphere. New ownership at Squaw Mountain in Greenville is making improvements. Its remote location ensures few crowds, and its low prices make it an attractive alternative to other big mountains. Shawnee Peak remains popular with families and for night skiing; by day the resort has awesome views of Mt. Washington in New Hampshire.

Exploring Maine

Maine is a large state that offers many different experiences. The York County Coast, in the southern portion of the state, has easy access, long sand beaches, historic homes, and good restaurants. The coastal geography changes in Portland, the economic and cultural center of southern Maine. From there north, long fingers of land jut into the sea, sheltering fishing villages. Penobscot Bay is famed for its sailing, rockbound coast, and numerous islands. Mount Desert Island lures crowds of people to Acadia National Park, which is filled with jaw-dropping natural beauty. Way down east, beyond Acadia, the tempo changes; fast food joints and trinket shops all but disappear, replaced by family-style restaurants and artisans' shops. Inland, the western lakes and mountains provide an entirely different experience. Summer camps, ski areas, and small villages populate this region. People head to Maine's North Woods to escape the crowds and to enjoy the great outdoors by hiking, rafting, camping, or canoeing.

Numbers in the text and in the margin correspond to numbers on the maps: Southern Maine Coast, Portland, Penobscot Bay, Mount Desert Island, Way Down East, Western Maine, and the North Woods.

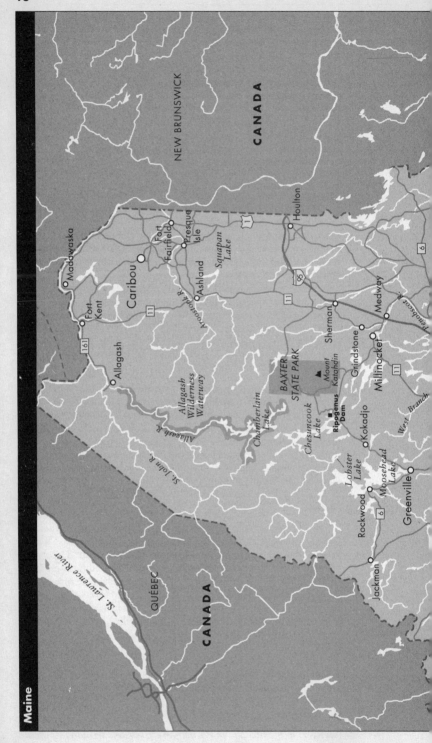

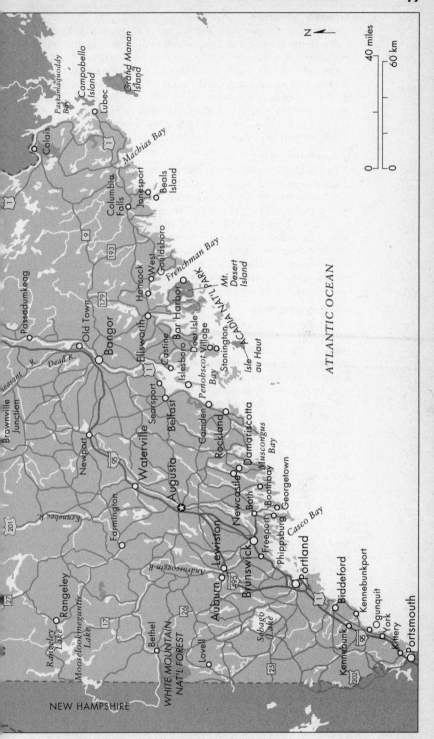

Great Itineraries

You can spend days exploring just the coast of Maine, as these itineraries indicate, so plan ahead and decide whether you want to ski and dogsled in the western mountains, raft or canoe in the North Woods, or simply meander up the coast, stopping at museums and historic sites, shopping for local arts and crafts, and exploring coastal villages and lobster shacks. Trying to see everything in one visit is complicated by the lack of east–west roads in the state and heavy traffic on popular routes, such as U.S. 1 and U.S. 302. Build extra time into your schedule and relax. You'll get there eventually, and in the meantime, enjoy the view.

IF YOU HAVE 2 DAYS

A two-day exploration of the southern coast provides a good introduction to different aspects of the Maine coast. Begin in **Ogunquit** ③ with a morning walk along the Marginal Way. Then head north to **Kennebunkport** ⑥, allowing at least two hours to wander through the shops and historic homes around Dock Square. Relax on the beach for an hour or so before heading to ⊡ **Portland** ⑧–⑬. If you thrive on arts and entertainment, spend the night here. Otherwise, continue north to ⊡ **Freeport** ⑯, where you can shop all night at L. L. Bean. On day two, head north, stopping in **Bath** ⑱ to tour the Maine Maritime Museum, and finish up with a lobster dinner on **Pemaquid Point** ㉑.

IF YOU HAVE 4 DAYS

A four-day tour of midcoast Maine up to Acadia National Park is one of New England's classic trips. From New Harbor on **Pemaquid Point** ㉑, take the boat to ⊡ **Monhegan Island** ㉓ for a day of walking the trails and exploring the artists' studios and galleries. The next day, continue northeast to **Rockland** ㉔ and ⊡ **Camden** ㉕. On day three, visit the Farnsworth Museum in Rockland, hike or drive to the top of Mt. Battie in Camden, and meander around Camden's boat-filled harbor. Or, bypass midcoast Maine in favor of ⊡ **Mount Desert Island** ㉝–㊶ and Acadia National Park. To avoid sluggish traffic on U.S. 1, from Freeport, stay on I–95 to Augusta and the Maine Turnpike; then take Route 3 to Belfast and pick up U.S. 1 north there.

IF YOU HAVE 8 DAYS

An eight-day trip allows time to see a good portion of the coast. Spend two days wandering through gentrified towns and weather-beaten fishing villages from ⊡ **Kittery** ① to ⊡ **Portland** ⑧–⑬. On your third day explore Portland and environs, including a boat ride to **Eagle Island** ⑮ or one of the other Casco Bay islands and a visit to Portland Head Light and Two Lights in Cape Elizabeth. Continue working your way up the coast, letting your interests dictate your stops: outlet stores in **Freeport** ⑯, Maine Maritime Museum in ⊡ **Bath** ⑱, antiques shops in **Wiscasset** ⑲, fishing villages and a much-photographed lighthouse on **Pemaquid Point** ㉑. Allow at least one day in the **Rockland** ㉔ and ⊡ **Camden** ㉕ region before taking the leisurely route to **Bar Harbor** ㉝ via the **Blue Hill** ㉙ peninsula and ⊡ **Deer Isle Village** ㉚. Finish up with two days on ⊡ **Mt. Desert Island** ㉝–㊶.

When to Tour Maine

From July to September is the choice time for a vacation in Maine. The weather is warmest in July and August, though September is less crowded. In warm weather, the arteries along the coast and lakeside communities inland are clogged with out-of-state license plates, campgrounds are filled to capacity, and hotel rates are high. Midweek is less busy, and lodging rates are often lower then than on weekends.

Fall foliage can be brilliant in Maine and is made even more so by its reflection in inland lakes or streams or off the ocean. Late September is peak season in the north country, while in southern Maine the prime viewing dates are usually from October 5 to 10. In September and October the days are sunny and the nights crisp.

In winter, the coastal towns almost completely close down. If the sidewalks could be rolled up, they probably would be. Maine's largest ski areas usually open in mid-November and, thanks to excellent snow-making facilities, provide good skiing often into April.

Springtime is mud season here, as in most other rural areas of New England. Mud season is followed by spring flowers and the start of wildflowers in meadows along the roadsides.

YORK COUNTY COAST

Maine's southernmost coastal towns, most of them in York County, won't give you the rugged, wind-bitten "down-east" experience, but they are easily reached from the south, and most have the sand beaches that all but vanish beyond Portland.

These towns are highly popular in summer, an all-too-brief period. Crowds converge and gobble up rooms and dinner reservations at prime restaurants. You'll have to work a little harder to find solitude and vestiges of the "real" Maine here. Still, even day-trippers who come for a few fleeting hours to southern Maine will appreciate the magical warmth of the sand along this coast.

North of Kittery, the Maine coast has long stretches of hard-packed white-sand beach, closely crowded by nearly unbroken ranks of beach cottages, motels, and oceanfront restaurants. The summer colonies of York Beach and Wells Beach have the crowds and ticky-tacky shorefront overdevelopment. Ogunquit is more upscale and offers much to do, from shopping to taking a cliff-side walk. Farther inland, York's historic district is on the National Register of Historic Places.

More than any other region south of Portland, the Kennebunks—and especially Kennebunkport—provide the complete Maine-coast experience: classic townscapes where white clapboard houses rise from manicured lawns and gardens; rocky shorelines punctuated by sandy beaches; quaint downtown districts packed with gift shops, ice cream stands, and tourists; harbors where lobster boats bob alongside yachts; lobster pounds and well-appointed dining rooms.

These towns are best explored on a leisurely holiday of two days—more if you require a fix of solid beach time. U.S. 1 travels along the coast. Inland, the Maine Turnpike (I–95) is the fastest route if you want to skip some towns.

Kittery

❶ *55 mi north of Boston, 5 mi north of Portsmouth, New Hampshire.*

Kittery, which lacks a large sand beach of its own, hosts a complex of factory outlets that makes it more popular, or at least better known with visitors, than the summer beach communities.

As an alternative to shopping, drive north of the outlets and go east on Route 103 for a peek at the hidden Kittery most people miss. Along this winding stretch are two forts, both open in summer. **Ft. Foster** (1872), off Route 103, was an active military installation until 1949. **Ft. McClary** (1690) was staffed during five wars. There are also hiking and biking trails and, best of all, great views of the water.

Southern Maine Coast

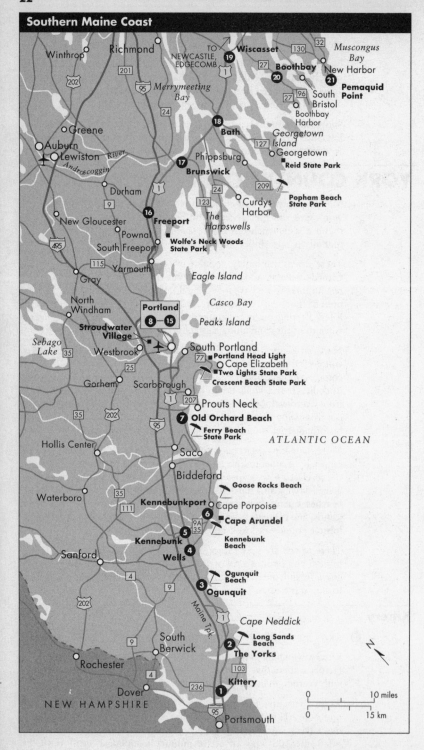

Dining and Lodging

$–$$$ ✕ **Warren's Lobster House.** A local institution, this waterfront restaurant specializes in lobster and seafood but also serves steak and chicken and has a huge salad bar. In season, you can dine outdoors overlooking the water. ⊠ *U.S. 1 and Water St.,* ☎ *207/439–1630. AE, MC, V.*

$$$ ▣ **The Inn at Portsmouth Harbor.** This brick Victorian built in 1889 on the old Kittery town green overlooks the Piscataqua River and Portsmouth Harbor. The convenient location is an easy walk over the bridge into Portsmouth or a quick drive up U.S. 1 to the Kittery outlets. English antiques and Victorian watercolors decorate the inn, and all rooms have cable TV as well as phones with voice mail. ⊠ *6 Water St., 03904,* ☎ *207/439–4040,* FAX *207/438–9286. 6 rooms. Full breakfast. AE, MC, V.*

Nightlife and the Arts

Hamilton House (⊠ Vaughan's La., South Berwick, ☎ 603/436–3205), the Georgian home featured in Sarah Orne Jewett's historical romance novel, *The Tory Lover,* presents "Sundays in the Garden" in July and August, a series of six summer concerts ranging from classical to folk music. Concerts ($5) begin at 4; the grounds are open from noon until 5 for picnicking.

Shopping

Kittery has more than 120 outlet stores. Along a several-mile stretch of U.S. 1 you can find just about anything, from hardware to underwear. Among the stores you'll encounter are Crate & Barrel, Eddie Bauer, Jones New York, Esprit, Waterford/Wedgwood, Lenox, Ralph Lauren, Tommy Hilfiger, DKNY, and J. Crew.

The Yorks

❷ *4 mi north of Kittery.*

The Yorks—York Village, York Harbor, York Beach, and Cape Neddick—are typical of small-town coastal communities in New England and are smaller than most. Many of their nooks and crannies can be explored in a few hours. The beaches are the big attraction here.

Most of the 18th- and 19th-century buildings within the **York Village Historic District** are clustered along York Street and Lindsay Road in York Village; some charge admission. You can buy an admission ticket for all the buildings at the **Jefferds Tavern** (⊠ U.S. 1A at Lindsay Rd.), a restored late-18th-century inn. The **Old York Gaol** (1720) was once the King's Prison for the Province of Maine; inside are dungeons, cells, and the jailer's quarters. The 1731 **Elizabeth Perkins House** reflects the Victorian style of its last occupants, the prominent Perkins family. Members of the Old York Historical Society lead tours. ☎ 207/363–4974. ⊡ $6 for all buildings. ☉ Mid-June–mid-Oct., Tues.–Sat. 10–5, Sun. 1–5.

The waterfront **Sayward-Wheeler House** (1718) mirrors the fortunes of a coastal village in the transition from trade to tourism. Jonathan Sayward prospered in the West Indies trade in the 18th century; by 1860 his descendants had opened the house to share the story of their Colonial ancestors. The house reflects both these eras. You must take a guided tour to see the house. ⊠ *79 Barrell La. extension, York Harbor,* ☎ *603/436–3205.* ⊡ *$4.* ☉ *June–mid-Oct., weekends noon–5; tours on the hr, 11–4.*

If you drive down Nubble Road from U.S. 1A and go to the end of Cape Neddick, you can park and gaze out at the **Nubble Light** (1879), which sits on a tiny island just offshore. The keeper's house is a tidy Victorian cottage with gingerbread woodwork and a red roof.

U.S. 1A runs right behind **Long Sands Beach,** a 1½-mi stretch of sand in York Beach that has roadside parking and a bathhouse. **Short Sands Beach** in York Beach has a bathhouse and is convenient to restaurants and shops.

Dining and Lodging

$$$ ✕ **Cape Neddick Inn.** The American bistro-style menu at this restaurant and art gallery changes with the seasons. Past offerings have included entrées such as sage-roasted quail and poached Atlantic salmon on lobster succotash. ✉ *U.S. 1, Cape Neddick,* ☎ *207/363–2899. D, MC, V. Closed Mon. and mid-Oct.–May. No lunch.*

$–$$$ ✕ **Cafe Shelton.** This perky restaurant decorated in blue and white sits across from Short Sands Beach. Lunch fare includes soups, sandwiches, and salads. Dinner is more elaborate, with entrées such as Grand Marnier salmon and lobster ravioli sharing the menu with linguine and meatballs. A children's menu is available. ✉ *1 Ocean Ave., York Beach,* ☎ *207/363–0708. MC, V.*

$$–$$$ ✕▥ **York Harbor Inn.** A mid-17th-century fishing cabin with dark
  ★   timbers and a fieldstone fireplace forms the heart of this inn, to which various wings and outbuildings have been added over the years. The rooms are furnished with antiques and country pieces; many have decks overlooking the water, and a few have whirlpool tubs or fireplaces. Room in the Harbor Cliffs next door, acquired in 1998, have the intimate appeal of a classic Maine cottage. The dining room (no lunch off-season) has great ocean views. For dinner, start with Maine crab cakes, a classic Caesar salad, or a creamy seafood chowder, and then try the lobster-stuffed chicken breast or the angel-hair pasta with shrimp and scallops. The Cellar Pub ($) offers soups, salads, burgers, and sandwiches. ✉ *Box 573, U.S. 1A, York Harbor 03911,* ☎ *207/ 363–5119 or 800/343–3869,* ▥ *207/363–7151. 25 rooms, 15 suites. Restaurant, pub. Continental breakfast. AE, DC, MC, V.*

$$–$$$ ▥ **Cutty Sark Motel.** The rooms are standard motel fare, but you can't beat the oceanfront location, right on the edge of Long Sands Beach. Every room has an ocean view. ✉ *58 Long Beach Ave., York Beach 03910,* ☎ *207/363–5131 or 800/543–5131,* ▥ *207/351–1335. 42 rooms. Refrigerators. Continental breakfast. D, MC, V.*

$$–$$$ ▥ **Union Bluff.** This fortresslike modern white structure, with balconies across the front and turrets on the ends, sits right across from Short Sands Beach with views to forever. The best rooms are in the front of the inn, but many on the north side, which cost less, also have ocean views. The front rooms in the adjacent motel have ocean views, but the motel has fewer services. ✉ *Box 1860, 8 Beach St., York Beach 03910,* ☎ *207/363–1333 or 800/833–0721,* ▥ *207/363–1381. 36 rooms, 4 suites in inn; 21 rooms in motel. Restaurant, pub. AE, D, MC, V.*

$–$$ ▥ **Edward's Harborside.** This turn-of-the-century B&B sits on the harbor's edge and is just a two-minute walk from the beach. Rooms are spacious, with big windows to take in the water views. One room has a whirlpool tub. ✉ *Box 866, Stage Neck Rd., York Harbor 03911,* ☎ *207/363–3037. 4 rooms share 2 baths, 3 suites. Dock. Continental breakfast. MC, V.*

Outdoor Activities and Sports

Capt. Tom Farnon (✉ Rte. 103, Town Dock #2, York Harbor, ☎ 207/ 363–3234) takes passengers on lobstering trips, weekdays 10–2.

Ogunquit

❸ *10 mi north of the Yorks, 39 mi southwest of Portland.*

Probably more than any other south-coast community, Ogunquit combines coastal ambience, style, and good eating. The village became a resort in the 1880s and gained fame as an artists' colony. A mini Provincetown, Ogunquit has a gay population that swells in summer; many inns and small clubs cater to a primarily gay and lesbian clientele. Families love the protected beach area and friendly environment. Shore Road, which takes you into downtown, passes the 100-ft **Bald Head Cliff,** with views up and down the coast. On a stormy day the surf can be quite wild here.

Perkins Cove, a neck of land connected to the mainland by Oarweed Road and a pedestrian drawbridge, has a jumble of sea-beaten fish houses. These have largely been transformed by the tide of tourism to shops and restaurants. When you've had your fill of browsing and jostling

★ the crowds at Perkins Cove, stroll out along the **Marginal Way,** a mile-long footpath that hugs the shore of a rocky promontory known as Israel's Head. Benches along the route give walkers an opportunity to stop and appreciate the open sea vistas, flowering bushes, and million-dollar homes.

The **Ogunquit Museum of American Art,** in a low-lying concrete building overlooking the ocean, is set amid a 3-acre sculpture garden. Inside are works by Henry Strater, Marsden Hartley, Winslow Homer, Edward Hopper, Gaston Lachaise, Marguerite Zorach, and Louise Nevelson. The huge windows of the sculpture court command a view of cliffs and ocean. ⊠ *183 Shore Rd.,* ☎ *207/646-4909.* ⊡ *$4.* ☉ *July–Sept., Mon.–Sat. 10:30–5, Sun. 2–5.*

Ogunquit Beach, a 3-mi-wide stretch of sand at the mouth of the Ogunquit River, has snack bars, a boardwalk, rest rooms, and, at the Beach Street entrance, changing areas. Families gravitate to the ends; gay visitors camp at the beach's middle. The less-crowded section to the north is accessible by footbridge and has portable rest rooms, all-day paid parking, and trolley service.

Dining and Lodging

$$$$ ✕ **Arrows.** Elegant simplicity is the hallmark of this 18th-century farmhouse, 2 mi up a back road. Grilled salmon and radicchio with marinated fennel and baked polenta and Chinese-style duck glazed with molasses are typical entrées on the daily-changing menu. The Maine crabmeat mousse and lobster risotto appetizers and desserts like strawberry shortcake with Chantilly cream and steamed chocolate pudding are also beautifully executed. ⊠ *Berwick Rd.,* ☎ *207/361–1100. Reservations essential. MC, V. Closed Mon. and Dec.–late Apr. No lunch.*

$$$–$$$$ ✕ **Hurricane.** Don't let the weather-beaten exterior deter you—this small
★ seafood bar and grill with spectacular views of the crashing surf turns out first-rate dishes. Start with lobster chowder, a chilled fresh-shrimp spring roll, or the house salad (assorted greens with pistachio nuts and roasted shallots). Entrées may include lobster cioppino, rack of lamb, and fire-roasted veal chop. Save room for the classic crème brûlée. ⊠ *Oarweed La., Perkins Cove,* ☎ *207/646–6348. AE, D, DC, MC, V. Closed late Dec.–mid-Jan.*

$–$$ ✕ **The Impastable Dream.** If it's good pasta you crave, you'll find it in abundance at this cozy restaurant. Dining rooms are bright and decorated with stenciling and floral linens. Favorites include Greek pasta (with feta cheese, spinach, and black olives) and lobster ravioli. The food is reasonably priced and plentiful; a children's menu is offered from 5 to 6:30. ⊠ *105 Shore Rd.,* ☎ *207/646–3011. Reservations not accepted. AE, D, MC, V. Closed Jan. and midweek off-season. No lunch.*

$$$$ ⌼ **Cliff House.** Elsie Jane Weare opened the Cliff House in 1872. Her granddaughter Kathryn now presides over this sprawling oceanfront resort comprising three buildings atop Bald Head Cliff. Every room has a view of the water, which makes up for the unremarkable decor. This place has a loyal following, so reserve well in advance. ⊠ *Box 2274, Shore Rd., 03907,* ☎ *207/361–1000,* FAX *207/361–2122. 162 rooms. Restaurant, 1 indoor and 1 outdoor pool, hot tub, sauna, 2 tennis courts, exercise room. AE, D. Closed mid-Dec.–late Mar.*

$$–$$$ ⌼ **The Rockmere.** Midway along Ogunquit's Marginal Way, this shingle-style Victorian cottage is an ideal retreat from the hustle and bustle of Perkins Cove. All the rooms have corner locations and are large and airy, and all but one have ocean views. You'll find it easy to laze the day away on the wraparound porch or in the gardens. ⊠ *Box 278, 40 Stearns Rd., 03907,* ☎ *207/646–2985. 8 rooms. Continental breakfast. AE, D, MC, V.*

Nightlife and the Arts

Much of the nightlife in Ogunquit revolves around the precincts of Ogunquit Square and Perkins Cove, where people stroll, often enjoying an after-dinner ice cream cone or espresso. Ogunquit is popular with gay and lesbian visitors, and its club scene reflects this.

The **Club** (⊠ 13 Main St., ☎ 207/646–6655) is Ogunquit's main gay disco. **Jonathan's Restaurant** (⊠ 7 Bourne La., ☎ 207/646–4777) has live entertainment, usually blues, in season. The **Ogunquit Playhouse** (⊠ U.S. 1, ☎ 207/646–5511), one of America's oldest summer theaters, mounts plays and musicals with name entertainment from late June to Labor Day.

Outdoor Activities and Sports

Finestkind (⊠ Perkins Cove, ☎ 207/646–5227) operates cocktail cruises, lobstering trips, and cruises to Nubble Light.

Wells

❹ *5 mi north of Ogunquit, 35 mi southwest of Portland.*

This family-oriented beach community consists of several densely populated miles of shoreline interspersed with trailers and summer and year-round homes.

The **Wells Reserve** sprawls over 1,600 acres of meadows, orchards, fields, and salt marshes, as well as two estuaries and 9 mi of seashore. This nature preserve has extensive trails through its diverse habitats. The visitor center screens an introductory slide show and holds five rooms of exhibits. In winter, cross-country skiing is permitted. ⊠ *342 Laudholm Farm Rd.,* ☎ *207/646–1555.* ⌑ *$2 July–Aug. and weekends Sept.–mid-Oct.* ☉ *Grounds daily 8–5. Visitor center May–Dec., Mon.–Sat. 10–4, Sun. noon–4; weekends only in winter.*

Rachel Carson National Wildlife Refuge (⊠ Rte. 9, ☎ 207/646–9226) has a mile-long loop nature trail through a salt marsh. The trail borders the Little River and a white-pine forest where migrating birds and waterfowl of many varieties are regularly spotted.

☾ A must for motor fanatics and youngsters, the **Wells Auto Museum** has 70 vintage cars, antique coin games, and a restored Model T you can ride in. ⊠ *U.S. 1,* ☎ *207/646–9064.* ⌑ *$3.50.* ☉ *Mid-June–Labor Day, daily 10–5; Labor Day–Columbus Day, weekends 10–5.*

Dining and Lodging

$–$$ ✕ **Billy's Chowder House.** Visitors and locals head to this simple restaurant in a salt marsh for the generous lobster rolls, haddock sandwiches, and chowders. ⊠ *216 Mile Rd.,* ☎ *207/646–7558. AE, D, MC, V. Closed mid-Dec.–mid-Jan.*

$–$$ ✕▥ **Grey Gull.** A century-old Victorian inn, the Grey Gull has views of the open sea and rocks on which seals like to sun themselves. The unpretentious rooms, most with ocean views, have shared or private baths. The restaurant ($$–$$$) serves excellent seafood dishes like soft-shell crabs almandine and regional fare such as Yankee pot roast or chicken breast rolled in walnuts and baked with maple syrup. Breakfast is popular here in summer: Blueberry pancakes or eggs McGull served on crab cakes with hollandaise sauce are good choices. ⊠ *475 Webhannet Dr., at Moody Point,* ☎ *207/646–7501,* 𝖥𝖠𝖷 *207/646–0938. 8 rooms, 6 with bath. Restaurant. Continental breakfast; MAP available. AE, D, MC, V.*

Shopping

Kenneth & Ida Manko (⊠ Seabreeze Dr., ☎ 207/646–2595) sells folk art, rustic furniture, paintings, and 19th-century weather vanes. From U.S. 1 head east on Eldridge Road for a half mile, and then turn left on Seabreeze Drive. **Douglas N. Harding Rare Books** (⊠ 2152 Post Rd./U.S. 1, ☎ 207/646–8785) has many old books, maps, and prints. **R. Jorgensen** (⊠ 502 Post Rd./U.S. 1, ☎ 207/646–9444) stocks 18th- and 19th-century formal and country antiques from the British Isles, Europe, and the United States.

The **Lighthouse Depot** (⊠ U.S. 1, ☎ 207/646–0608) calls itself the world's largest lighthouse gift store.

Kennebunk

❺ *5 mi north of Wells, 30 mi southwest of Portland.*

Handsome white clapboard homes with shutters lend Kennebunk, a shipbuilding center in the first half of the 19th century, a look that's quintessential New England. The historic town is a fine place for a stroll. The cornerstone of the **Brick Store Museum,** a block-long preservation of early 19th-century commercial buildings, is **William Lord's Brick Store.** Built as a dry-goods store in 1825 in the Federal style, the building has an open-work balustrade across the roof line, granite lintels over the windows, and paired chimneys. Walking tours of Kennebunk's National Historic Register District depart from the museum on Friday at 1 and Wednesday at 10 from June to October. ⊠ *117 Main St.,* ☎ *207/985–4802.* ▧ *$5.* ☉ *Tues.–Sat. 10–4:30.*

The **Taylor-Barry House** house, owned by the Brick Store Museum (☞ above), is an early 19th-century sea captain's home that's open for tours. ⊠ *24 Summer St.,* ☎ *207/985–4802.* ▧ *$4.* ☉ *July–Oct., Tues.–Fri. 1–4:30.*

Kennebunk Beach has three parts: **Gooch's Beach, Mother's Beach,** and **Kennebunk Beach.** Beach Road, with its cottages and old Victorian boardinghouses, runs right behind them. Gooch's and Kennebunk attract teenagers; Mother's Beach, which has a small playground and tidal puddles for splashing, is popular with families. For parking permits (a fee is charged in summer), go to the **Kennebunk Town Office** (⊠ 1 Summer St., ☎ 207/985–2102).

The **Wedding Cake House** (⊠ 104 Summer St./Rte. 35) has long been a local landmark. The legend behind this confection in fancy wood fretwork is that its builder, a sea captain, was forced to set sail in the middle of his wedding, and the house was his bride's consolation for the lack of wedding cake. The home, built in 1826, is not open to the public, but the attached carriage house holds a gallery and studio.

Lodging

$ ⊞ **St. Anthony's Franciscan Monastery Guest House.** Individuals and families in search of a quiet, contemplative retreat may want to choose one of the simple, unadorned, motel-style rooms in a former dormitory on the grounds of a riverside monastery. The guest house is private yet within walking distance of Dock Square and the beach. The landscaped grounds, open to the public, have trails and shrines. The monks live in a Tudor mansion on the property, where Mass is said daily in an attached chapel. This place is not recommended for those uncomfortable with Christian symbolism, although no religious participation is required. ⊠ *28 Beach Ave., Kennebunk 04043,* ☎ *207/ 967–2011. 60 rooms. No credit cards. Closed Oct.–May.*

Shopping

J. J. Keating (⊠ 70 Portland Rd./U.S. 1, ☎ 207/985–2097) deals in antiques, reproductions, and estate furnishings. **Marlow's Artisans Gallery** (⊠ 39 Main St., ☎ 207/985–2931) carries a large and eclectic collection of crafts.

Kennebunkport

❻ *10 mi northeast of Ogunquit.*

When George Bush was president, Kennebunkport was his summer White House. But long before Bush came into the public eye, visitors were coming to Kennebunkport to soak up the salt air, seafood, and sunshine. This is a picture-perfect town with manicured lawns, elaborate flower beds, freshly painted homes, and a small-town wholesomeness. People flock to Kennebunkport mostly in summer; some come in early December when the **Christmas Prelude** is celebrated on two weekends. Santa arrives by fishing boat and the Christmas trees are lighted as carolers stroll the sidewalks.

Route 35 merges with Route 9 in Kennebunk and takes you right into Kennebunkport's **Dock Square,** the busy town center. Boutiques, T-shirt shops, a Christmas store, a decoy shop, and restaurants encircle the square. Although many businesses close in winter, the best bargains often are had in December. Walk onto the drawbridge to admire the tidal Kennebunk River.

The very grand **Nott House,** known also as White Columns, is an imposing Greek Revival mansion with Doric columns that rise the height of the house. It is a gathering place for village walking tours; call for schedule. ⊠ *8 Maine St.,* ☎ *207/967–2751.* ⊠ *$3.* ☉ *Mid-June–mid-Oct., Tues.–Fri. 1–4.*

Ocean Avenue follows the Kennebunk River from Dock Square to the sea and winds around the peninsula of **Cape Arundel.** Parson's Way, a small and tranquil stretch of rocky shoreline, is open to all. As you round Cape Arundel, look to the right for the entrance to George Bush's summer home at Walker's Point.

★ ♺ The **Seashore Trolley Museum** displays streetcars built from 1872 to 1972 and includes trolleys from major metropolitan areas and world capitals—Boston to Budapest, New York to Nagasaki, and San Francisco to Sydney, Australia—all beautifully restored. Best of all, you can take a trolley ride for nearly 4 mi over the tracks of the former Atlantic Shoreline trolley line, with a stop along the way at the museum restoration shop, where trolleys are transformed from junk into gems. Both guided and self-guided tours are available. ⊠ *Log Cabin Rd.,* ☎ *207/967–2800.* ☞ *$7.* ⊙ *Late May–mid-Oct., daily 10–5; reduced hrs in spring and fall.*

Goose Rocks, a few minutes' drive north of town, is the largest beach in the Kennebunk area and the favorite of families with small children. You can pick up a parking permit ($5 a day, $15 a week), at the **Kennebunkport Town Office** (⊠ 6 Elm St., ☎ 207/967–4244) or the **police department** (⊠ 1 Main St./Rte. 9, ☎ 207/967–2454).

Dining and Lodging

$$$–$$$$ ✕ **Seascapes.** The emphasis is on seafood at this pretty harborfront restaurant where the view takes center stage. You can begin with pan-fried oysters or lobster spring rolls, then move on to roasted lobster or try the Mediterranean-inspired saddle of lamb. ⊠ *Pier Rd., Cape Porpoise Harbor, Cape Porpoise,* ☎ *207/967–8500. AE, D, MC, V. Closed mid-Oct.–mid-May.*

$$$–$$$$ ✕ **Windows on the Water.** This restaurant overlooks Dock Square and the working harbor of Kennebunkport. Lobster ravioli and rack of lamb are two noteworthy entrées. The special five-course dinner for two, including wine, tax, and gratuity (total: $87), is a good value if you have a healthy appetite. ⊠ *12 Chase Hill Rd.,* ☎ *207/967–3313. Reservations essential. AE, D, DC, MC, V.*

$–$$$ ✕ **Alisson's.** A year-round favorite, this restaurant in the heart of Dock Square serves reliable salads, burgers, sandwiches, and dinner fare. ⊠ *5 Dock Square,* ☎ *207/967–4841,* ℻ *207/967–2532. AE, D, MC, V.*

$–$$ ✕ **Cape Porpoise Lobster Co., Inc.** You can watch the surf crash over distant ledges near the Goat Island lighthouse and see lobster boats returning with their day's catch at this oceanfront lobster shack. Seating is on the deck or inside. The fare includes lobster, clams, and fried foods. ⊠ *15 Pier Rd., Cape Porpoise,* ☎ *207/967–4268 or 800/967–4268. MC, V. Closed early Nov.–late Mar.*

$$$–$$$$ ✕▥ **White Barn Inn.** For a romantic overnight stay or a superb meal,
★ you need look no further than the exclusive White Barn Inn, known for its attentive service. The meticulously appointed rooms have luxurious baths and are decorated with a blend of hand-painted pieces and period furniture; some rooms have fireplaces and whirlpool baths. Regional New England fare is served at the rustic but elegant dining room ($$$$; jacket required), one of the region's best. The fixed-price menu, which changes weekly, might include steamed Maine lobster nestled on fresh fettuccine with carrots, ginger, and snow peas. ⊠ *Box 560C, 37 Beach St., 04046,* ☎ *207/967–2321,* ℻ *207/967–1100. 16 rooms, 9 suites. Restaurant, pool, bicycles. Continental breakfast. AE, MC, V.*

$$$ ✕▥ **Cape Arundel Inn.** This shingle-style inn commands a magnificent ocean view that takes in the Bush estate at Walker Point. The spacious rooms are furnished with country-style furniture and antiques, and most have sitting areas with ocean views. You can relax on the front porch, furnished with antique white wicker, or in front of the living-room fireplace. In the candlelighted dining room ($$$–$$$$), open to the public for dinner, every table has a view of the surf. The entrées include seafood, lamb, duckling, and steak. ⊠ *Ocean Ave., 04046,* ☎ *207/967–2125,* ℻ *207/967–1199. 13 rooms, 1 apartment. Restaurant. AE, D, MC, V. Closed early Dec.–early May.*

$$$$ ▥ **Captain Lord Mansion.** Of all the mansions in Kennebunkport's historic district that have been converted to inns, the 1812 Captain Lord Mansion is the most stately and sumptuously appointed. The three-story Federal inn is topped with a widow's walk, from which you can peer out over the town and harbor, just three blocks away. Distinctive architecture, including a suspended elliptical staircase and gas fireplaces in 15 rooms, and decorating of near museum quality make for a for-

mal but not stuffy atmosphere. Five rooms have whirlpool tubs. The most extravagant suite has fireplaces in the bathroom and the sleeping area, a double whirlpool, a hydro-massage body spa, a TV/VCR and stereo system, exercise equipment, and a king-size canopy bed. ⊠ *Box 800, Pleasant and Green Sts., 04046,* ☎ *207/967–3141,* 𝖥𝖠𝖷 *207/ 967–3172. 16 rooms, 1 suite. Full breakfast. D, MC, V.*

$$$–$$$$ 🖭 **Maine Stay Inn and Cottages.** On a quiet residential street a short walk from Dock Square is the circa 1860 Maine Stay Inn. Three of the accommodations in the Italianate main house have fireplaces. Families often stay in the cottages behind the inn; some have fireplaces, whirlpools, and kitchens. ⊠ *Box 500A, 34 Maine St., 04046,* ☎ *207/ 967–2117 or 800/950–2117,* 𝖥𝖠𝖷 *207/967–8757. 4 rooms, 2 suites, 11 rooms in cottages. Full breakfast. AE, MC, V.*

$$$–$$$$ 🖭 **The Seaside.** This handsome seaside property has been in the hands of the Severance family for 12 generations. The modern motel units, all with cable TVs and sliding-glass doors that open onto private decks or patios (half with ocean views), are appropriate for families; so are the cottages, which have from one to four bedrooms. The four bedrooms in the 1756 inn, furnished with antiques, are more suitable for adults. ⊠ *80 Beach Ave., 04046,* ☎ *207/967–4461,* 𝖥𝖠𝖷 *207/967– 1135. 26 rooms, 10 cottages. Beach, playground, laundry service. Continental breakfast. AE, MC, V. Inn rooms closed Labor Day– June; cottages closed Nov.–Apr.*

$$$ 🖭 **Bufflehead Cove.** On the Kennebunk River at the end of a winding dirt road, this gray-shingle B&B amid quiet country fields and apple trees is only five minutes from Dock Square. Rooms in the main house have white wicker and flowers handpainted on the walls. The Hideaway Suite, with a two-sided gas fireplace, king-size bed, and large whirlpool tub, overlooks the river. The Garden Studio has a fireplace and the most privacy. ⊠ *Box 499, 18 Bufflehead Cove Rd., 04046,* ☎ 𝖥𝖠𝖷 *207/967–3879. 2 rooms, 3 suites, 1 cottage. Dock. D, MC, V.*

Outdoor Activities and Sports

Cape-Able Bike Shop (⊠ Townhouse Corners, ☎ 207/967–4382) rents bicycles. **Chick's Marina** (⊠ 75 Ocean Ave., ☎ 207/967–2782) conducts sightseeing and fishing cruises for up to six people. **First Chance** (⊠ Arundel Wharf, Lower Village, ☎ 207/967–5912) guarantees whale sightings in season. **Venture Inn Charters** (⊠ Performance Marine, near the Rte. 9 bridge, ☎ 207/967–0005 or 800/853–5002) operates full- and half-day deep-sea fishing trips.

Old Orchard Beach

❼ *15 mi north of Kennebunkport, 18 mi south of Portland.*

Old Orchard Beach, a few miles north of Biddeford on Route 9, is a 7-mi strip of sand beach with an amusement park that's like a small Coney Island. Despite the summertime crowds and fried-food odors, the atmosphere can be captivating. During the 1940s and '50s, in the heyday of the Big Band era, the pier had a dance hall where stars of the era performed. Fire claimed the end of the pier, but booths with games and candy concessions still line both sides. In summer the town sponsors fireworks (usually on Thursday night). The many places to stay run the gamut from cheap motels to cottage colonies to full-service seasonal hotels. The area is popular from July 4 to Labor Day with people from Québec. You won't find free parking anywhere in town, but there are ample lots.

A world away in atmosphere from the beach scene is **Ocean Park** (☎ 207/934–9068), on the southwestern edge of town. This vacation community was founded in 1881 as a summer assembly, following the example of Chautauqua, New York. Today the community still has a wide range of cultural offerings, including movies, concerts, workshops, and religious services. Most are presented in the Temple, which is on the National Register of Historic Places.

☾ **Palace Playland** (⊠ 1 Old Orchard St., ☎ 207/934–2001), open from Memorial Day to Labor Day, has rides, booths, and a roller coaster
☾ that drops almost 50 ft. **Funtown/Splashtown** (⊠ U.S. 1, Saco, ☎ 207/284–5139 or 800/878–2900) has more than 30 rides and amusements, including miniature golf, waterslides, a wave pool, and Excalibur, a new wooden roller coaster.

Lodging

$$$$ ⚷ **Black Point Inn.** Toward the top of the peninsula that juts into the ocean at Prouts Neck, 12 mi south of Portland and about 10 mi north of Old Orchard Beach by road, stands a stylish shingled, tastefully updated, old-time resort with views up and down the Maine coast. Mahogany or maple bedsteads, Martha Washington bedspreads, and white-ruffle priscilla or print curtains decorate the rooms, which are in the main house or four cottages. The extensive grounds contain beaches, trails, a bird sanctuary, and sports facilities. You can access the Cliff Walk and walk along the dramatic Atlantic headlands that Winslow Homer (his studio is nearby) often painted. New this year are three dining rooms: one formal, one casual, and one for family dining. ⊠ *510 Black Point Rd., Scarborough 04074,* ☎ *207/883–4126 or 800/258–0003,* FAX *207/883–9976. 68 rooms, 12 suites. Restaurant, bar, 1 indoor and 1 outdoor pool, hot tub, golf, 14 tennis courts, croquet, volleyball, boating, bicycles. MAP. AE, D, MC, V. Closed mid-Nov.–Apr.*

Outdoor Activities and Sports

Bird-watchers can check out the shorebirds that congregate at the **Biddeford Pool East Sanctuary** (⊠ Rte. 9, Biddeford). The **Maine Audubon Society** (⊠ Rte. 9, Scarborough, ☎ 207/781–2330; 207/883–5100 from mid-June to Labor Day) operates guided canoe trips and rents canoes in Scarborough Marsh, the largest salt marsh in Maine. Programs at Maine Audubon's Falmouth headquarters (north of Portland) include nature walks and a discovery room for children.

York County Coast A to Z

Arriving and Departing

BY CAR

U.S. 1 from Kittery is the shopper's route north; other roads hug the coastline. Interstate 95 is usually faster for travelers headed to towns north of Ogunquit. The exit numbers can be confusing: As you go north from Portsmouth, Exits 1–3 lead to Kittery and Exit 4 leads to the Yorks. After the tollbooth in York, the Maine Turnpike begins, and the numbers start over again, with Exit 2 for Wells and Ogunquit and Exit 3 (and Route 35) for Kennebunk and Kennebunkport. Route 9 goes from Kennebunkport to Cape Porpoise and Goose Rocks.

BY PLANE

The closest airport is the Portland International Jetport (☞ Arriving and Departing *in* Maine A to Z, *below*), 35 mi northeast of Kennebunk.

Getting Around

BY CAR

Parking is tight in Kennebunkport in peak season. Possibilities include the municipal lot next to the Congregational Church ($2 an hour from May to October), the Consolidated School on School Street (free from late June to Labor Day), and, except on Sunday morning, St. Martha's Church (free year-round) on North Street.

Trolleys ($1–$3) serve several areas. A trolley circulates among the Yorks from June to Labor Day. Eight trolleys serve the major tourist areas and beaches of Ogunquit, including four that connect with Wells from mid-May to mid-October. The trolley from Dock Square in Kennebunkport to Kennebunk Beach runs from late June to Labor Day.

Contacts and Resources

EMERGENCIES

Maine State Police (✉ Gray, ☎ 207/793–4500 or 800/482–0730). **Kennebunk Walk-in Clinic** (✉ U.S. 1 N, ☎ 207/985–6027). **York Hospital** (✉ 15 Hospital Dr., ☎ 207/351–2157) also operates Tel-A-Nurse (☎ 800/283–7234). **Southern Maine Medical Center** (✉ Rte. 111, Biddeford, ☎ 207/283–7000; 207/283–7100 for emergency room).

VISITOR INFORMATION

Maine Tourism Association Visitor Information Center (✉ U.S. 1 and I–95, Kittery 03904, ☎ 207/439–1319). **Kennebunk-Kennebunkport Chamber of Commerce** (✉ 17 Western Ave., Kennebunk 04043, ☎ 207/967–0857). **Kittery-Eliot Chamber of Commerce** (✉ 191 State Rd., Kittery 03904, ☎ 207/384–3338). **Ogunquit Chamber of Commerce** (✉ Box 2289, U.S. 1, Ogunquit 03907, ☎ 207/646–2939). **Old Orchard Beach Chamber of Commerce** (✉ Box 600, 1st St., Old Orchard Beach 04064, ☎ 207/934–2500 or 800/365–9386). **Wells Chamber of Commerce** (✉ Box 356, Wells 04090, ☎ 207/646–2451). The **Yorks Chamber of Commerce** (✉ 571 U.S. 1, York 03903, ☎ 207/363–4422).

PORTLAND TO PEMAQUID POINT

Maine's largest city, Portland, is small enough to be explored in a day or two. It holds some pleasant surprises, including the Old Port, among the finest urban renovation projects on the East Coast. Freeport, north of Portland, was made famous by its L. L. Bean store, whose success led to the opening of scores of other clothing stores and outlets. Brunswick is best known for Bowdoin College. Bath has been a shipbuilding center since 1607; the Maine Maritime Museum preserves its history. Wiscasset contains many antiques shops and galleries.

The Boothbays—the coastal areas of Boothbay Harbor, East Boothbay, Linekin Neck, Southport Island, and the inland town of Boothbay—attract hordes of vacationing families and flotillas of pleasure craft. The Pemaquid peninsula juts into the Atlantic south of Damariscotta and just east of the Boothbays. Near Pemaquid Beach you can view the objects unearthed at the Colonial Pemaquid Restoration.

This south–mid-coast area provides an overview of Maine: a little bit of city, a little more coastline, and a nice dollop of history and architecture.

Portland

105 mi northeast of Boston, 320 mi northeast of New York City, 215 mi southwest of St. Stephen, New Brunswick.

Portland's role as a cultural and economic center for the region has given the gentrifying city of 65,000 a variety of attractions. Its restored Old Port balances modern commercial enterprise and salty waterfront character in an area bustling with restaurants, shops, and galleries. Water tours of the harbor and excursions to the Calendar Islands depart from the piers of Commercial Street. Downtown Portland, in a funk for years, is now a burgeoning arts district connected to the Old Port by a revitalized Congress Street, where L. L. Bean operates a factory store.

Portland's first home was built on the peninsula now known as Munjoy Hill in 1632. The British burned the city in 1775, when residents refused to surrender arms, but it was rebuilt and became a major trading center. Much of Portland was destroyed on July 4 in the Great Fire of 1866, when a boy threw a celebration firecracker into a pile of wood shavings; 1,500 buildings burned to the ground. Poet Henry Wadsworth Longfellow said at the time that his city reminded him of the ruins of Pompeii. The Great Fire started not far from where people now wander the streets of the Old Port.

Congress Street runs the length of the peninsular city from alongside the Western Promenade in the southwest to the Eastern Promenade on Munjoy Hill in the northeast, passing through the small downtown area. A few blocks southeast of downtown, the bustling Old Port Exchange sprawls along the waterfront. Below Munjoy Hill is India Street, where the Great Fire of 1866 started.

8 One of the notable homes on Congress Street is the **Neal Dow Memorial,** a brick mansion built in 1829 in the late Federal style by General Neal Dow, an abolitionist and prohibitionist. The library has fine ornamental ironwork, and the furnishings include the family china, silver, and portraits. Don't miss the grandfather clocks. ⊠ *714 Congress St.,* ☎ *207/773–7773.* ⊡ *Free.* ☉ *Tours weekdays 11–4.*

★ **9** The Italianate-style Morse-Libby Mansion, known as **Victoria Mansion,** was built between 1858 and 1860 and is widely regarded as the most sumptuously ornamented dwelling of its period remaining in the country. Architect Henry Austin designed the house for hotelier Ruggles Morse and his wife, Olive; the interior design—everything from the plasterwork to the furniture (much of it original)—is the only surviving commission of noted New York designer Gustave Herter. The elegant brownstone exterior of this National Historic Landmark is understated compared to the interior, which has colorful frescoed walls and ceilings, ornate marble mantelpieces, gilded gas chandeliers, stained-glass windows, and a freestanding mahogany staircase; guided tours cover all the details. ⊠ *109 Danforth St.,* ☎ *207/772–4841.* ⊡ *$6.* ☉ *May–Oct., Tues.–Sat. 10–4, Sun. 1–5.*

☙ **10** Touching is okay at the relatively small but fun **Children's Museum of Maine,** where kids can pretend they are fishing for lobster or are shopkeepers or computer experts. The majority of the museum's exhibits, many of which have a Maine theme, are best for children 10 and younger. Camera Obscura, an exhibit about optics that provides fascinating panoramic views of the city, charges a separate admission fee ($3); call for times. ⊠ *142 Free St.,* ☎ *207/828–1234.* ⊡ *$5, $6 for combination ticket with Camera Obscura.* ☉ *Summer and school vacations, Mon.–Sat. 10–5, Sun. noon–5; during school yr, Wed.–Sat. 10–5, Sun. noon–5.*

★ **11** The **Portland Museum of Art,** Maine's largest public art institution, has a number of strong collections, including fine seascapes and landscapes by Winslow Homer, John Marin, Andrew Wyeth, Edward Hopper, Marsden Hartley, and other painters. Homer's *Pulling the Dory* and *Weatherbeaten,* two quintessential Maine-coast images, are here; the museum owns 17 paintings by Homer. The Joan Whitney Payson Collection of Impressionist and Postimpressionist art includes works by Monet, Picasso, and Renoir. Harry N. Cobb, an associate of I. M. Pei, designed the strikingly modern Charles Shipman Payson building. ⊠ *7 Congress Sq.,* ☎ *207/775–6148, 800/639–4067 for recorded information.* ⊡ *$6; free Fri. evenings 5–9.* ☉ *Columbus Day–Memorial Day, Tues.–Wed. and weekends 10–5, Thurs.–Fri. 10–9; Memorial Day–Columbus Day, Mon.–Wed. and weekends 10–5, Thurs.–Fri. 10–9.*

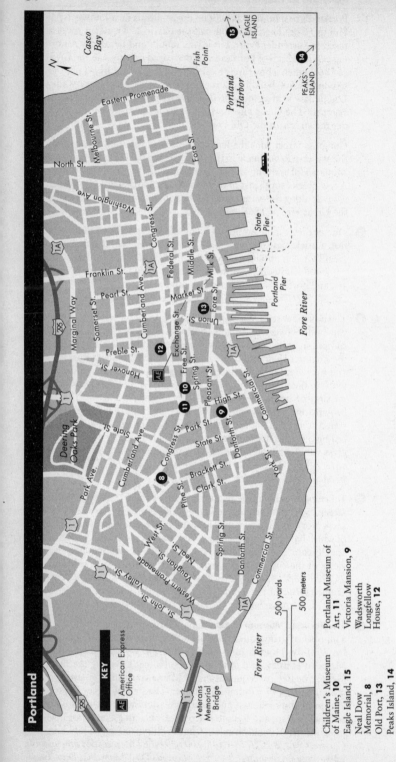

Portland

Casco Bay

Eastern Promenade

Fish Point

Portland Harbor

15 EAGLE ISLAND

14 PEAKS' ISLAND

Melbourne St.

North St.

Fore St.

Washington Ave.

Congress St.

State Pier

Federal St.

Middle St.

Milk St.

Franklin St.

Marginal Way

Pearl St.

Cumberland Ave.

Market St.

Fore St.

13

Portland Pier

Somerset St.

Union St.

Preble St.

Exchange St.

12

Hanover St.

Free St.

AE

Spring St.

Fore River

Pleasant St.

10

11

High St.

9

State St.

Congress St.

Park St.

Danforth St.

Commercial St.

Deering Oaks Park

Park Ave.

Cumberland Ave.

8

Brackett St.

Clark St.

York St.

Pine St.

Spring St.

West St.

Vaughan St.

Neal St.

Danforth St.

Western Promenade

St. John St.

Valley St.

Commercial St.

Fore River

Veterans Memorial Bridge

KEY

AE American Express Office

0   500 yards

0   500 meters

Children's Museum of Maine, **10**
Eagle Island, **15**
Neal Dow Memorial, **8**
Old Port, **13**
Peaks Island, **14**

Portland Museum of Art, **11**
Victoria Mansion, **9**
Wadsworth Longfellow House, **12**

⑫ The **Wadsworth Longfellow House,** the boyhood home of the poet and the first brick house in Portland, is particularly interesting because most of the furnishings are original to the house. The late-Colonial-style structure, built in 1785, sits back from the street and has a small portico over its entrance and four chimneys surmounting the hip roof. Special December tours of the house highlight a particular period in the life of the poet. The house is part of the Center for Maine History, which includes the adjacent Maine History Gallery and a research library; the gift shop has a good selection of books about Maine. ⊠ *489 Congress St.,* ☎ *207/879–0427.* ⊡ *$5.* ⊙ *June–Oct., daily 10–4.*

★ ⑬ The **Old Port** bridges the gap between the city's 19th-century commercial activities and those of today. Like the Customs House, the brick buildings and warehouses of the Old Port were built following the Great Fire of 1866 and were intended to last for ages. When the city's economy slumped in the mid-20th century, however, the Old Port declined and seemed slated for demolition. Then artists and craftspeople began opening shops in the late 1960s, and restaurants, boutiques, bookstores, and gift shops followed. Allow a couple of hours to wander at leisure on Market, Exchange, Middle, and Fore streets. You can park your car at the city garage on Fore Street (between Exchange and Union streets) or opposite the U.S. Customs House at the corner of Fore and Pearl streets.

Crescent Beach State Park (⊠ Rte. 77, Cape Elizabeth, ☎ 207/767–3625), about 8 mi south of Portland, has a sand beach, picnic tables, a seasonal snack bar, and a bathhouse. Popular with families with young children, it charges a nominal fee for admittance. **Scarborough Beach Park** (⊠ Rte. 207, Scarborough, ☎ 207/283–0067) is a long, sandy ocean beach with primitive facilities; admission is charged in season.

OFF THE BEATEN PATH

CAPE ELIZABETH – This upscale Portland suburb juts out into the Atlantic. Take Route 77 south and east from Portland and follow signs to Two Lights State Park, home to Two Lights, one of the Cape's three lighthouses. You can wander through old World War II bunkers and picnic on the rocky coast. Stay on Two Lights Road to the end, where you'll find another lighthouse, privately owned, and the Lobster Shack, a seafood-in-the-rough restaurant where you can dine inside or out. Return to the center of Cape Elizabeth and turn right on Shore Road, which winds along the coast to Portland.

Historic **Portland Head Light,** about 2 mi from town center in Fort Williams Park, was commissioned by George Washington in 1791. Besides a harbor view, the park has walking paths and picnic facilities. The keeper's house is now the Museum at Portland Head Light. *Museum:* ⊠ *1000 Shore Rd.,* ☎ *207/799–2661.* ⊡ *$2.* ⊙ *June–Oct., daily 10–4.*

Dining and Lodging

$$–$$$ ✕ **Café at Wharf Street & the Wine Bar.** Tucked away on cobblestoned Wharf Street, an alley that runs parallel to Fore Street between Moulton and Union, this place is really two finds in one. The small, informal restaurant has a partially exposed kitchen, brick walls, and a painted floor. The menu changes seasonally, but the house specialty, lobster and brie ravioli with roasted grapes and caramelized onion sauce, is a mainstay. After dinner, head upstairs to the Wine Bar for dessert, wine, espresso, and drinks. ⊠ *38 Wharf St.,* ☎ *207/773–6667 for restaurant, 207/772–6976 for wine bar. Reservations essential. AE, MC, V. No lunch.*

$$–$$$ ✕ **Fore Street.** Two of Maine's best chefs, Sam Hayward and Dana Street,
★ opened this restaurant in a renovated old warehouse on the edge of

the Old Port. Every table in the two-level main dining room has a view of the enormous brick oven and hearth and the open kitchen, where entrées such as roasted Maine lobster, applewood-grilled Atlantic swordfish loin, and wood-oven-braised cassoulet are prepared. ⊠ *288 Fore St.,* ☎ *207/775–2717. AE, MC, V. No lunch.*

$$–$$$ ✕ **Street and Co.** You enter through the kitchen, with all its wonder-
★ ful aromas, and dine, amid dried herbs and shelves of staples, on one of a dozen copper-topped tables (so your waiter can place a skillet of steaming seafood directly in front of you). In one dining room is a beer and wine bar. Fish and seafood are the specialties here, and you won't find any better or fresher. The entrées include lobster diavolo for two, scallops in Pernod and cream, and sole Française. A vegetarian dish is the only alternative to seafood. ⊠ *33 Wharf St.,* ☎ *207/775–0887. AE, MC, V. No lunch.*

$$ ✕ **Aubergine.** This bistro and wine bar has staked out a prime down-town location, across the street from L. L. Bean and down the street from the Portland Museum of Art. The atmosphere is casual and the food is very good. The menu changes daily but might include appe-tizers such as Swiss onion soup with fresh tarragon or fried Pemaquid oysters, and entrées like spiced duck breast with fennel sauce or crispy salmon with spinach and Pernod. Wines by the glass are chosen to com-plement the dishes. ⊠ *555 Congress St.,* ☎ *207/874–0680. Closed Sun. night and Mon. No lunch. MC, V.*

$$ ✕ **Katahdin.** Painted tables, flea-market decor, mismatched dinnerware, and a log-pile bar provide a fun and unpretentious setting for dining on large portions of home-cooked New England fare. Try the chicken potpie, fried trout, crab cakes, or the nightly blue-plate special, and save room for the fruit cobbler. ⊠ *106 High St.,* ☎ *207/774–1740. D, MC, V. Closed Sun. No lunch.*

$–$$ ✕ **Portland Public Market.** The more than 20 locally owned businesses inside this handsome, airy new market specialize in fresh foods, or-ganic produce, and imported specialty foods, including fresh-baked goods, soups and chowders, smoked seafood, rotisserie chicken, aged cheeses, and German meats. It's a fun place to grab lunch or an early dinner. At Hanson Bros. Seafood Café, you can choose a fresh Maine lobster roll or a blackened swordfish wrap; Salumeria Rex has great grilled vegetable sandwiches and Italian salads. A skywalk con-nects the market to the third floor of a parking garage on Elm Street; parking is free if a vendor stamps your ticket. Most merchants ac-cept a number of credit cards. The market is open Monday–Satur-day 9–7, Sunday 10–5; some vendors open at 7. ⊠ *25 Preble St.,* ☎ *207/228–2000.*

$$$$ ✕🖬 **Inn by the Sea.** On greater Portland's most prime real estate, this all-suites inn is set back from the shoreline and has views of the ocean—Crescent Beach and Kettle Cove in particular. The dining room ($$–$$$$), open to nonguests, serves fine seafood and regional dishes. The cottage-style architecture throughout is typical New England. ⊠ *40 Bowery Beach Rd., Cape Elizabeth 04107 (7 mi south of Portland),* ☎ *207/799–3134 or 800/888–4287,* 🖷 *207/799–4779. 25 suites, 18 cottage condominiums. Restaurant, pool, tennis court, croquet, bicy-cles. AE, D, MC, V.*

$$$$ 🖬 **Portland Regency Hotel.** The only major hotel in the center of the Old Port, the Regency building was Portland's armory in the late 19th century. Rooms have four-poster beds, tall standing mirrors, floral cur-tains, and love seats. ⊠ *20 Milk St., 04101,* ☎ *207/774–4200 or 800/ 727–3436,* 🖷 *207/775–2150. 87 rooms, 8 suites. Restaurant, massage, sauna, steam room, health club, nightclub, meeting rooms. AE, D, DC, MC, V.*

$$$ ⊡ **Inn on Carleton.** After a day of exploring Portland's museums and shops, you'll find a quiet retreat at this elegant brick town house on the city's Western Promenade. Built in 1869, it is furnished throughout with period antiques as well as artwork by contemporary Maine artists. The entryway features a restored trompe l'oeil painting by Charles Schumacher, and more of his work has been uncovered in the back dining room. ⊠ *46 Carleton St., 04102,* ☎ *207/775–1910 or 800/ 639–1779,* ℻ *207/761–0956. 6 rooms. Full breakfast. D, MC, V.*

Nightlife and the Arts

NIGHTLIFE

Asylum (⊠ 121 Center St., ☎ 207/772–8274) has live entertainment and dancing. **Brian Boru** (⊠ 57 Center St., ☎ 207/780–1506) is an Irish pub with occasional entertainment and an outside deck. **Comedy Connection** (⊠ 6 Custom House Wharf, ☎ 207/774–5554) hosts stand-up comedians from Wednesday to Sunday.

Gritty McDuff's—Portland's Original Brew Pub (⊠ 396 Fore St., ☎ 207/ 772–2739) brews fine ales and serves British pub fare and seafood dishes. **Stone Coast Brewery** (⊠ 14 York St., ☎ 207/773–2337) is a brew pub with entertainment. The **Wine Bar** (⊠ 38 Wharf St., ☎ 207/772– 6976) has comfortable chairs, couches, and a fireplace. A dozen of the 250 wines by the bottle can be ordered by the glass. Espresso, light meals, and desserts are served.

THE ARTS

Portland Performing Arts Center (⊠ 25A Forest Ave., ☎ 207/761–0591) presents music, dance, and theater performances. **Cumberland County Civic Center** (⊠ 1 Civic Center Sq., ☎ 207/775–3458) hosts concerts, sporting events, and family shows.

Portland City Hall's Merrill Auditorium (⊠ 20 Myrtle St., ☎ 207/874– 8200) is home to the Portland Symphony Orchestra and Portland Concert Association and the site of numerous theatrical and musical events. **Portland Symphony Orchestra** (⊠ 30 Myrtle St., ☎ 207/773– 8191) concerts take place from October to August. **Mad Horse Theatre Company** (⊠ 92 Oak St., ☎ 207/797–3338) performs classic, contemporary, and original works. **Portland Stage Company** (⊠ 25A Forest Ave., ☎ 207/774–0465) mounts productions year-round at the Portland Performing Arts Center.

Outdoor Activities and Sports

BALLOON RIDES

Balloon Rides (⊠ 17 Freeman St., ☎ 207/772–4730) operates scenic flights over southern Maine.

BASEBALL

The Class AA **Portland Sea Dogs** (☎ 207/879–9500), a farm team of the Florida Marlins, play at Hadlock Field (⊠ 271 Park Ave.). Tickets cost from $4 to $6.

BOAT TRIPS

For tours of the harbor, Casco Bay, and the nearby islands, try **Bay View Cruises** (⊠ Fisherman's Wharf, ☎ 207/761–0496), **Casco Bay Lines** (⊠ Maine State Pier, ☎ 207/774–7871), **Eagle Tours** (⊠ Long Wharf, ☎ 207/774–6498), **Old Port Mariner Fleet** (⊠ Long Wharf, ☎ 207/ 775–0727, 207/642–3270, or 800/437–3270), or **Palawan Sailing** (⊠ Old Port, ☎ 207/774–2163).

HOCKEY

The **Portland Pirates,** the farm team of the Washington Capitals, play home games at the Cumberland County Civic Center (⊠ 85 Free St., ☎ 207/828–4665). Tickets cost from $8 to $13.

Shopping

For a city its size, Portland has a satisfying variety of locally owned stores, particularly those in or near the Old Port; trendy Exchange Street is great for browsing.

ART, CRAFTS, AND ANTIQUES

Abacus (✉ 44 Exchange St., ☎ 207/772–4880), an appealing crafts gallery, has unusual gift items in glass, wood, and textiles, plus fine modern jewelry. **F. O. Bailey Antiquarians** (✉ 141 Middle St., ☎ 207/774–1479), Portland's largest retail showroom, carries antique and reproduction furniture and jewelry, paintings, rugs, and china.

Greenhut Galleries (✉ 146 Middle St., ☎ 207/772–2693) carries contemporary Maine art. The **Pine Tree Shop & Bayview Gallery** (✉ 75 Market St., ☎ 207/773–3007 or 800/244–3007) has original art and prints by prominent Maine painters.

Representing 100 American artists, the spacious **Stein Gallery** (✉ 195 Middle St., ☎ 207/772–9072) showcases functional, decorative, and sculptural contemporary glass—everything from perfume bottles and vases to larger display pieces.

BOOKS AND PRINTS

Carlson and Turner (✉ 241 Congress St., ☎ 207/773–4200) is an antiquarian book dealer with an estimated 50,000 titles. Besides new and used books, many of regional interest, **Emerson Books, Maps, and Prints** (✉ 18 Exchange St., ☎ 207/874–2665) stocks antique maps of Maine and elsewhere, botanical and bird prints, and old posters and magazine covers.

FURNITURE

Designed and made locally, the handsome cherrywood pieces at **Green Design Furniture** (✉ 267 Commercial St., ☎ 207/775–4234; 800/853–4234 for orders) have a classic feel—somewhat Asian, somewhat Mission; a unique system of joinery allows the pieces to be assembled easily after shipping.

MALL

Maine Mall (✉ 364 Maine Mall Rd., South Portland, ☎ 207/774–0303), 5 mi south of Portland, has 145 stores, including Sears, Filene's, JCPenney, and Macy's.

Casco Bay Islands

The islands of Casco Bay are also known as the Calendar Islands because an early explorer mistakenly thought there was one for each day of the year (in reality there are only 140). The brightly painted ferries of Casco Bay Lines (☞ Getting Around *in* Portland to Pemaquid Point A to Z, *below*) are the islands' lifeline. There is frequent service to the most populated ones, including Peaks, Long, Little Diamond, and Great Diamond. A ride on the bay is a great way to appreciate the Maine coast.

⓮ **Peaks Island,** nearest to Portland, is the most developed of the Calendar Islands, but you can still commune with the wind and the sea, explore an old fort, and ramble along the alternately rocky and sandy shore. The trip to the island by boat is particularly enjoyable at or near sunset. Order a lobster sandwich or cold beer on the outdoor deck of **Jones' Landing** restaurant, steps from the dock. A circle trip without stops takes about 90 minutes. On the far side of the island you can stop on the rugged shoreline and have lunch. A small museum with Civil War artifacts, open in summer, is maintained in the **Fifth Maine Regiment** building. When the Civil War broke out in 1861,

day) in the heart of Freeport's shopping district. You can still find the original hunting boots, along with cotton, wool, and silk sweaters; camping and ski equipment; comforters; and hundreds of other items for the home, car, boat, or campsite. The **L. L. Bean Factory Store** (⊠ Depot St., ☎ 800/341–4341) has seconds and discontinued merchandise at discount prices. **L. L. Bean Kids** (⊠ 8 Nathan Nye St., ☎ 800/341–4341) specializes in children's merchandise and has a climbing wall and other kid-appealing activities.

Harrington House Museum Store (⊠ 45 Main St., ☎ 207/865–0477) is a restored 19th-century merchant's home owned by the Freeport Historical Society; all the period reproductions that furnish the rooms are for sale, as well as books, rugs, jewelry, crafts, Shaker items, and kitchen utensils. You can obtain a brochure with a good walking tour of Freeport here, too. **Green Design Furniture** (⊠ 45 Main St., ☎ 207/865–0342), in an 1830 carriage house near Harrington House, sells Maine-designed solid cherrywood furniture that can be shipped.

Brunswick

17 *10 mi north of Freeport.*

Lovely brick and clapboard homes and structures are the highlights of the town's **Federal Street Historic District**, which includes Federal Street and Park Row and the stately campus of Bowdoin College. Pleasant Street, in the center of town, is the business district. Harriet Beecher Stowe wrote *Uncle Tom's Cabin* while living in Brunswick.

The 110-acre campus of **Bowdoin College** (⊠ Maine, Bath, and College Sts., off east end of Pleasant St.) holds an enclave of distinguished architecture, gardens, and grassy quadrangles, along with several museums (☞ *below*). Campus tours (☎ 207/725–3000) depart daily except Sunday from the admissions office in Chamberlain Hall. Among the historic buildings are Massachusetts Hall, a stout, sober, hip-roofed brick structure dating from 1802 that once housed the entire college. Nathaniel Hawthorne and the poet Henry Wadsworth Longfellow attended the college.

Bowdoin's Hubbard Hall, an imposing 1902 neo-Gothic building, is home to Maine's only gargoyle and the **Peary–MacMillan Arctic Museum.** The museum contains photographs, navigational instruments, and artifacts from the first successful expedition to the North Pole, in 1909, by two of Bowdoin's most famous alumni, Admiral Robert E. Peary and Donald B. MacMillan. (In summer you can vist Peary's nearby home on Eagle Island; ☞ Casco Bay Islands, *above*.) ☎ 207/725–3416. ◪ *Free.* ⊗ *Tues.–Sat. 10–5, Sun. 2–5.*

The **Bowdoin College Museum of Art,** in a splendid Renaissance Revival–style building designed by Charles F. McKim in 1894, has small but good collections that encompass Assyrian and classical art and works by Dutch, Italian, French, and Flemish old masters; a superb gathering of Colonial and Federal paintings, notably Gilbert Stuart portraits of Madison and Jefferson; and a Winslow Homer Gallery with engravings, etchings, and memorabilia (open in summer only). The museum's collection also includes 19th- and 20th-century American painting and sculpture, with works by Mary Cassatt, Andrew Wyeth, and Robert Rauschenberg. ⊠ *Walker Art Bldg.,* ☎ *207/725–3275.* ◪ *Free.* ⊗ *Tues.–Sat. 10–5, Sun. 2–5.*

The **General Joshua L. Chamberlain Museum** displays memorabilia and documents the life of Maine's most celebrated Civil War hero. The general, who played an instrumental role in the Union army's victory at

Gettysburg, was elected governor in 1867. From 1871 to 1883 he served as president of Bowdoin College. ⊠ *226 Main St.,* ☎ *207/729–6606.* ☞ *$3.* ☉ *Tues.–Sat. 10–4.*

OFF THE BEATEN PATH	**THE HARPSWELLS –** A side trip from Bath or Brunswick on Route 123 or Route 24 takes you to the peninsulas and islands known collectively as the Harpswells. Small coves along Harpswell Neck shelter the boats of lobstermen, and summer cottages are tucked away amid the birch and spruce trees. Along Route 123, signs with blue herons mark the studios and galleries of the Harpswell Craft Guild. For lunch, follow the signs off Route 123 to **Dolphin Marina** (⊠ End of Basin Point Rd., off Ash Point Rd.) and try the delicious fish stew and a blueberry muffin.

Dining and Lodging

$$ ✕ **The Great Impasta.** You can match your favorite pasta and sauce to create your own dish at this storefront restaurant, which is a good choice for lunch, tea, or dinner. The seafood lasagna is tasty, too. ⊠ *42 Maine St.,* ☎ *207/729–5858. Reservations not accepted. D, DC, MC, V.*

$ ✕ **Fat Boy Drive-In.** Put your lights on for service at this old-fashioned drive-in restaurant renowned for its BLTs made with Canadian bacon, frappes (try the blueberry), and onion rings. ⊠ *Bath Rd.,* ☎ *207/729–9431. No credit cards. Closed mid-Oct.–mid-Mar.*

$$$ ▥ **Captain Daniel Stone Inn.** This Federal inn overlooks the Androscoggin River. No two rooms are furnished identically, but all contain executive-style comforts and many have whirlpool baths, queen-size beds, and pullout sofas. A guest parlor, a breakfast room, and excellent service in the Narcissa Stone Restaurant (no lunch on Saturday) make this an upscale escape from college-town funkiness. ⊠ *10 Water St., 04011,* ☎ FAX *207/725–9898. 30 rooms, 4 suites. Restaurant. Continental breakfast. AE, DC, MC, V.*

$$–$$$ ▥ **Captain's Watch Bed and Breakfast and Sail Charter.** Built in 1862 and originally known as the Union Hotel, the Captain's Watch is the oldest surviving hotel on the Maine coast. Although much smaller than originally built, this National Historic Register property retains its distinctive octagonal cupola and a homey, old-fashioned feel. Two guest rooms share access to the cupola. Others have less inspired but still pleasant water views. Guests can arrange to go on a day sail aboard the inn's 37-foot sloop, *Symbion.* ⊠ *2476 Cundy's Harbor Rd., Cundy's Harbor 04011,* ☎ *207/725–0979. 4 rooms, 1 suite. Full breakfast. MC, V.*

$–$$$ ▥ **Harpswell Inn.** Spacious lawns and neatly pruned shrubs surround the stately white clapboard Harpswell Inn, built in 1761. The three-story inn was the center of a shipbuilding operation on Lookout Point, and the living room faces Middle Bay and Birch Island. Half the rooms have water views, as do the three carriage-house suites, one with a whirlpool. The inn is no-smoking. ⊠ *141 Lookout Point Rd., South Harpswell 04079,* ☎ *207/833–5509 or 800/843–5509. 9 rooms, 7 with bath, 1 with half bath; 3 suites. Full breakfast. MC, V.*

Nightlife and the Arts

Bowdoin Summer Music Festival (☎ 207/725–3322 for information; 207/725–3895 for tickets) is a six-week concert series featuring performances by students, faculty, and prestigious guest artists. **Maine State Music Theater** (⊠ Pickard Theater, Bowdoin College, ☎ 207/725–8769) stages musicals from mid-June to August. **Theater Project of Brunswick** (⊠ 14 School St., ☎ 207/729–8584) performs semiprofessional, children's, and community theater.

Outdoor Activities and Sports

H2Outfitters (☎ 207/833–5257) provides sea-kayaking instruction and rentals and conducts day or overnight trips. **Logan's Marina** (✉ Off Rte. 24, Bailey Island, ☎ 207/833–2810) rents small power boats.

Shopping

ICON Contemporary Art (✉ 19 Mason St., ☎ 207/725–8157) specializes in modern art. **O'Farrell Gallery** (✉ 58 Maine St., ☎ 207/729–8228) represents artists such as Neil Welliver, Marguerite Robichaux, and Sheila Geoffrion. **Wyler Craft Gallery** (✉ 150 Maine St., ☎ 207/729–1321) carries an intriguing selection of crafts, jewelry, and clothing.

Tontine Fine Candies (✉ Tontine Mall, 149 Maine St., ☎ 207/729–4462) has chocolates and other goodies. A **farmers' market** takes place on Tuesday and Friday from May to October, on the town mall between Maine Street and Park Row.

Bath

18 *11 mi northeast of Brunswick, 38 mi northeast of Portland.*

Bath has been a shipbuilding center since 1607, so it's appropriate that a museum here explores the state's rich maritime heritage. These days the Bath Iron Works turns out guided-missile frigates for the U.S. Navy and merchant container ships. It's a good idea to avoid Bath and U.S. 1 on weekdays between 3:15 and 4:30 PM, when BIW's major shift change occurs. The massive exodus can tie up traffic for miles.

★ At the **Maine Maritime Museum,** displays in the Maritime History Building and in the buildings of the former Percy & Small shipyard examine the world of shipbuilding and the relationship between Mainers and the sea. The history building contains themed exhibits with maritime paintings, ship models, journals, photographs, artifacts, and videos. From May to November, one-hour tours (call for times) of the shipyard explain how wooden ships were built; at other times you can visit the buildings on your own. You can also watch boatbuilders wield their tools on classic Maine boats in the boatshop and learn about lobstering in a special exhibit building. In summer the *Chippewa* sails the scenic Kennebec River (extra charge); a number of boats, including the 142-ft Grand Banks fishing schooner *Sherman Zwicker,* are on display when in port. The museum has a fine gift shop and bookstore, and you can picnic on the grounds. ✉ *243 Washington St.,* ☎ *207/443–1316.* ▭ *$8.50; tickets valid for 2 consecutive days.* ☉ *Daily 9:30–5.*

The **Chocolate Church Arts Center** (☞ Nightlife and the Arts, *below*) offers guided walking tours of private homes and historic buildings from mid-June to mid-September. Call for schedule and fees.

Reid State Park (☎ 207/371–2303), on Georgetown Island, off Route 127, has 1½ mi of sand on three beaches. Facilities include bathhouses, picnic tables, fireplaces, and snack bar. Parking lots fill by 11 AM on summer Sundays and holidays; admission is charged.

OFF THE
BEATEN PATH

POPHAM – Follow Route 209 south from Bath to Popham, the site of the short-lived 1607 Popham Colony, where the *Virginia,* the first European ship built in the New World, was launched. Benedict Arnold set off from Popham on his ill-fated march against the British in Québec. Granite-walled **Ft. Popham** (✉ Phippsburg, ☎ 207/389–1335) was built in 1607. **Popham State Park,** at the end of Route 209, has a good sand beach, a marsh area, bathhouses, and picnic tables; admission is charged.

Dining and Lodging

$$$–$$$$ ✕ **Robinhood Free Meetinghouse.** Chef Michael Gagne, one of Maine's
★ best, finally has a restaurant that complements his classic and creative
multi-ethnic cuisine. The 1855 Greek Revival–style meetinghouse has
large-pane windows and is decorated simply: cream-color walls, pine
floorboards, cherry Shaker-style chairs, white table linens. You might
begin with the artichoke strudel; veal saltimbocca and confit of duck
are two entrées. Finish up with Gagne's signature Obsession in Three
Chocolates. Jazz and theme nights take place in the off-season. ⊠ *Robin-
hood Rd., Georgetown,* ☎ *207/371–2188. AE, D, MC, V. Closed some
weeknights mid-Oct.–mid-May. No lunch.*

$$–$$$ ✕ **Kristina's Restaurant & Bakery.** This restaurant in a frame house
with a front deck prepares some of the finest pies, pastries, and cakes
on the coast. The satisfying new American cuisine served for dinner
usually includes fresh seafood and grilled meats. All meals can be
packed to go. ⊠ *160 Centre St.,* ☎ *207/442–8577. D, MC, V. Closed
Jan. No dinner Sun. Call ahead in winter.*

$$–$$$ ▥ **The Inn at Bath.** Filled with antiques, this handsome 1810 Greek
Revival inn in the town's historic district makes a convenient and
comfortable base for exploring Bath on foot. Five rooms have wood-
burning fireplaces, and two of these also have two-person whirlpool
tubs. ⊠ *969 Washington St., 04530,* ☎ *207/443–4294,* ⅎ *207/443–
4295. 9 rooms. Full breakfast. AE, D, MC, V.*

$$–$$$ ▥ **The 1774 Inn.** On the National Register of Historic Places, the
1774 Inn is a pre-Revolutionary mansion. Architecture buffs will savor
the interior detailing and antiques lovers will appreciate the magnifi-
cent pieces in the house. The inn, on a bend in the Kennebec River, has
large corner guest rooms, two with fireplaces, two with river views.
⊠ *44 Parker Head Rd., Phippsburg Center 04562,* ☎ *207/389–1774.
4 rooms. Full breakfast. No credit cards.*

Nightlife and the Arts

Chocolate Church Arts Center (⊠ 804 Washington St., ☎ 207/442–8455)
hosts folk, jazz, and classical concerts, theater productions, and per-
formances for children. The gallery presents exhibits of works in var-
ious media by Maine artists.

Shopping

The **Montsweag Flea Market** (⊠ U.S. 1 between Bath and Wiscasset,
☎ 207/443–2809) is a roadside attraction with trash and treasures. It
takes place on weekends from May to October and also on Wednes-
day (for antiques) and Friday during the summer. **West Island Gallery**
(⊠ 27 Centre St., ☎ 207/443–9625) carries contemporary Maine art,
quality crafts, and clothing.

Wiscasset

⑲ *10 mi northeast of Bath, 46 mi northeast of Portland.*

Settled in 1663 on the banks of the Sheepscot River, Wiscasset fittingly
bills itself as Maine's Prettiest Village. Stroll through town and you'll
pass by elegant sea captains' homes (many now antiques shops or gal-
leries), old cemeteries, churches, and public buildings.

The **Nickels-Sortwell House,** maintained by the Society for the Preser-
vation of New England Antiquities, is an outstanding example of Fed-
eral architecture. ⊠ *Main St.,* ☎ *207/882–6218.* ▦ *$4.* ☉ *June–Sept.,
Wed.–Sun. 11–5; tours on the hr, 11–4.*

The 1807 **Castle Tucker,** one of the properties maintained by the Soci-
ety for the Preservation of New England Antiquities, is known for its
extravagant architecture, Victorian decor, and freestanding elliptical

staircase. ⊠ *Lee and High Sts.,* ☎ *207/882–7364.* 🖾 *$4.* ⊙ *July–Aug., Thurs.–Sat. noon–5; tours on the hr, noon–4.*

The **Musical Wonder House** contains a vast collection of antique music boxes from around the world. ⊠ *18 High St.,* ☎ *207/882–7163.* 🖾 *1/2-hr presentation on main floor $6.50; 1-hr presentation $12; 3-hr tour of entire house $30 or $50 for 2 people.* ⊙ *Memorial Day–late Oct., daily 10–6; last tour usually at 4; call ahead for 3-hr tours.*

Ⓒ The restored 1930s coaches of the **Maine Coast Railroad** travel from Wiscasset to Bath and Newcastle. ⊠ *Water St.,* ☎ *207/882–8000 or 800/795–5404.* 🖾 *$10.* ⊙ *Late June–early Sept., daily; late May–late June and early Sept.–mid-Oct., weekends only; call for schedule.*

Dining and Lodging

$–$$ ✕ **Sarah's.** Locals and visitors alike rely on this popular family restaurant for breakfast (weekends only), lunch, and dinner. The dining room and the deck have views over the Sheepscot River. Soups, pizzas, Mexican-style foods, hearty sandwiches, and fresh-baked goodies are on the menu. ⊠ *U.S. 1 and Water St.,* ☎ *207/882–7504. AE, D, MC, V.*

$$–$$$$ ✕🏠 **Squire Tarbox.** The Federal-style Squire Tarbox is equal parts inn, restaurant, and working goat farm. Its country setting toward the end of Westport Island, midway between Bath and Wiscasset, is far removed from the rushing traffic of U.S. 1, yet area attractions are easily accessible. Rooms are simply furnished with antiques and country pieces; four have fireplaces. The menu at the dining room ($$$; reservations essential) changes nightly but always includes a vegetarian entrée and a sampling of the inn's own goat cheese. ⊠ *Box 1181, Rte. 144, Westport 04578,* ☎ *207/882–7693,* 𝔽𝔸𝕏 *207/882–7107. 11 rooms. Restaurant. Full breakfast; MAP available. AE, D, MC, V. Closed late Oct.–mid-May.*

Shopping

The Wiscasset area rivals Searsport (☞ Penobscot Bay, *below*) as a destination for antiquing. Shops line Wiscasset's main and side streets and extend over the bridge into Edgecomb.

The **Butterstamp Workshop** (⊠ Middle St., ☎ 207/882–7825) carries handcrafted folk-art designs from antique molds. The **Maine Art Gallery** (⊠ Warren St., ☎ 207/882–7511) carries the works of local artists. **Treats** (⊠ Main St., ☎ 207/882–6192) is a good place to pick up fancy foods for a picnic at Waterfront Park. The **Wiscasset Bay Gallery** (⊠ Main St., ☎ 207/882–7682) specializes in the works of 19th- and 20th-century American and European artists.

Boothbay

⑳ *10 mi southeast of Wiscasset, 60 mi northeast of Portland, 50 mi southwest of Camden.*

When Portlanders want a break from what they know as city life, many come north to the Boothbay region, which comprises Boothbay proper, East Boothbay, and Boothbay Harbor. This part of the shoreline is a craggy stretch of inlets where pleasure craft anchor alongside trawlers and lobster boats. Commercial Street, Wharf Street, the By-Way, and Townsend Avenue are filled with shops, galleries, and ice cream parlors. Excursion boats (☞ Outdoor Activities and Sports, *below*) leave from the piers off Commercial Street. From the harbor, you can catch a boat to Monhegan Island.

Ⓒ At the **Boothbay Railway Village,** about a mile north of Boothbay, you can ride 1½ mi on a narrow-gauge steam train through a re-creation of a century-old New England village. Among the 24 buildings is a museum with more than 50 antique automobiles and trucks. ✉ *Rte. 27,* ☎ *207/633–4727.* ✆ *$7.* ⊙ *Early June–Columbus Day, daily 9:30–5; special Halloween schedule.*

The **Department of Marine Resources Aquarium** has a shark you can pet, touch tanks, and rare blue and multiclawed lobsters. ✉ *McKown Point Rd., West Boothbay Harbor,* ☎ *207/633–9559.* ✆ *$2.50.* ⊙ *Memorial Day–Columbus Day, daily 10–5.*

Dining and Lodging

$$–$$$ ✕ **Christopher's Boathouse.** You can't beat the harbor view or the food at this restaurant in a renovated boathouse where you can watch the chefs at work. The lobster and mango bisque with hot and spicy lobster wontons is noteworthy. Some main-course options are lobster succotash and Asian-spiced tuna steak with Caribbean salsa; finish off with the raspberry almond flan. ✉ *25 Union St., Boothbay Harbor,* ☎ *207/633–6565. MC, V. Mid-Oct.–mid-May; call in advance.*

$ ✕ **Lobstermen's Coop.** Crustacean lovers and landlubbers will find something to like at this dockside working lobster pound. Lobster, steamers, hot dogs, hamburgers, sandwiches, and desserts are on the menu. Eat indoors or outside and watch the lobstermen at work. ✉ *Atlantic Ave., Boothbay Harbor,* ☎ *207/633–4900. Closed mid-Oct.–mid-May.*

$$$$ ✕⌂ **Spruce Point Inn.** Escape the hubbub of Boothbay Harbor at this sprawling resort, which is a short shuttle ride to town yet a world away. Guest rooms are in the main inn, family cottages, and condominiums. Most rooms are comfortable but not fancy and have ocean views. Lobster cioppino made with local shellfish and served over cappellini is the signature dish at the dining room ($$$–$$$$), which has an unparalleled view of the outer harbor and open ocean. ✉ *Box 237, Atlantic Ave., Boothbay Harbor 04538,* ☎ *207/633–4152 or 800/553–0289,* ℻ *207/633–7138. 37 rooms, 26 suites, 7 family cottages, 4 condominiums. Lounge, freshwater pool, saltwater pool, 2 tennis courts, health club, spa, dock. MAP. MC, V. Closed mid-Oct.–mid-May.*

$$–$$$ ⌂ **Admiral's Quarters Inn.** This renovated 1830 sea captain's house is ideally situated for those wanting to explore Boothbay Harbor by foot, a good thing since in-town parking is limited and expensive. The rooms have private decks, many overlooking the harbor, and on rainy days you can relax by the woodstove in the solarium. ✉ *71 Commercial St., Boothbay Harbor 04538,* ☎ *207/633–2474,* ℻ *207/633–5904. 2 rooms, 4 suites. Full breakfast. D, MC, V. Closed mid-Dec.–mid-Feb.*

Outdoor Activities and Sports

Balmy Day Cruises (☎ 207/633–2284 or 800/298–2284) operates day boat trips to Monhegan Island and tours of the harbor and nearby lighthouses. **Cap'n Fish's Boat Trips** (✉ Pier 1 for departures, ☎ 207/633–3244 or 800/636–3244) operates sightseeing cruises throughout the region, including puffin-watching cruises, lobster-hauling and whale-watching rides, and trips to Damariscove Harbor, Pemaquid Point, and up the Kennebec River to Bath.

Shopping

BOOTHBAY HARBOR

Gleason Fine Art (✉ 15 Oak St., ☎ 207/633–6849) carries fine art—regional and national, early 19th century and contemporary. **House of Logan** (✉ 32 Townsend Ave., ☎ 207/633–2293) stocks upscale casual and fancy attire for men and women. Beautiful housewares and attractive children's clothes can be found at the **Village Store & Children's Shop** (✉ 34 Townsend Ave., ☎ 207/633–2293).

EDGECOMB

Edgecomb Potters (✉ Rte. 27, ☎ 207/882–6802) sells high-end glazed porcelain pottery and other crafts at rather high prices; some discontinued items or seconds are discounted. These potters have an excellent reputation. There's a store in Freeport if you miss this one. **Sheepscot River Pottery** (✉ U.S. 1, ☎ 207/882–9410) has original hand-painted pottery as well as a large collection of American-made crafts, including jewelry, kitchenware, furniture, and home accessories.

Pemaquid Point

㉑ *8 mi southeast of Wiscasset.*

A detour off U.S. 1 via Routes 130 and 32 leads to the Pemaquid Peninsula and a satisfying microcosm of coastal Maine. Art galleries, country stores, antiques and crafts shops, and lobster shacks dot the country roads that meander to the tip of the point, where you'll find a much-photographed lighthouse perched on an unforgiving rock ledge, as well as a pleasant beach. Exploring here reaps many rewards, including views of salt ponds, the ocean, and boat-clogged harbors. The twin towns of Damariscotta and Newcastle anchor the region, but small fishing villages such as Pemaquid, New Harbor, and Round Pond give the peninsula its purely Maine flavor.

At what is now the **Colonial Pemaquid Restoration,** on a small peninsula jutting into the Pemaquid River, English mariners established a fishing and trading settlement in the early 17th century. The excavations at Ft. **William Henry,** begun in the mid-1960s, have turned up thousands of artifacts from the Colonial settlement, including the remains of an old customs house, a tavern, a jail, a forge, and homes. Some items are from even earlier Native American settlements. The state operates a museum displaying many of the artifacts. ✉ *Off Rte. 130, New Harbor,* ☎ *207/677–2423.* ▣ *$2.* ☉ *Memorial Day–Labor Day, daily 9:30–5.*

★ Route 130 terminates at the **Pemaquid Point Light,** which looks as though it sprouted from the ragged, tilted chunk of granite that it commands. The former lighthouse-keeper's cottage is now the **Fishermen's Museum,** with photographs, models, and artifacts that explore commercial fishing in Maine. Here, too, is the **Pemaquid Art Gallery,** which mounts exhibitions from July to Labor Day. ✉ *Museum: Rte. 130,* ☎ *207/677–2494.* ▣ *Donation requested.* ☉ *Memorial Day–Columbus Day, Mon.–Sat. 10–5, Sun. 11–5.*

Pemaquid Beach Park (✉ Off Rte. 130, New Harbor, ☎ 207/677–2754) has a good sand beach, a snack bar, changing facilities, and picnic tables overlooking John's Bay; admission is charged.

Dining and Lodging

$ ★ **× Round Pond Lobstermen's Co-op.** Lobster doesn't get much rougher, any fresher, or any cheaper than that served at this no-frills dockside takeout. The best deal is the dinner special: a 1-pound lobster, steamers, and corn-on-the-cob, with a bag of chips. Regulars often bring beer, wine, bread, and/or salads. Settle in at a picnic table and breathe in the fresh salt air while you drink in the view over dreamy Round Pond Harbor. ✉ *Round Pond Harbor, off Rte. 32, Round Pond,* ☎ *207/ 529–5725. MC, V.*

$$–$$$$ **×🏠 Newcastle Inn.** This classic country inn with a riverside location and an excellent dining room attracts guests year-round. All the rooms are filled with country pieces and antiques; some rooms have fireplaces and whirlpool baths. Guests spread out in the cozy pub, comfortable living room, and sunporch overlooking the river. Breakfast is served

on the back deck in fine weather. The four-course dinners ($$$$) at the inn, which is open to the public by reservation, emphasize Pemaquid oysters, lobster, Atlantic salmon, and other Maine seafood. ✉ *60 River Rd., Newcastle 04553,* ☎ *207/563–5685 or 800/832–8669,* FAX *207/563–6877. 14 rooms, 2 suites. 2 dining rooms, pub, TV room. Full breakfast. AE, MC, V.*

$$ 🏨 **Briar Rose.** Round Pond is a sleepy harborside village with an old-fashioned country store, two lobster co-ops, a nice restaurant, and a handful of antiques and crafts shops. The mansard-roof Briar Rose commands a ship captain's view over it all. Antiques and whimsies decorate the airy rooms. ✉ *Box 27, Rte. 32, Round Pond 04556,* ☎ *207/ 529–5478. 2 rooms, 1 suite. Full breakfast. No credit cards.*

$$ 🏨 **Mill Pond Inn.** A quiet residential street holds this circa-1780 inn, which is on a mill pond across the street from Damariscotta Lake. Loons, otters, and bald eagles reside on the lake, and you can arrange a trip with the owner, a Registered Maine Guide, on the inn's 17-ft antique lapstrake boat. The rooms are warm and inviting and there's a pub for guests, though you may find it hard to tear yourself away from the hammocks-for-two overlooking the pond. ✉ *50 Main St., off Rte. 215 N, Nobleboro 04555,* ☎ *207/563–8014. 5 rooms, 1 suite. Horseshoes, boating, bicycles. Full breakfast. No credit cards.*

Nightlife and the Arts

Round Top Center for the Arts (✉ Business Rte. 1, Damariscotta, ☎ 207/563–1507) has a gallery with rotating exhibits and a performance hall where classical, folk, operatic, and jazz concerts are regularly held.

Shopping

Of the villages on and near the Pemaquid Peninsula, downtown Damariscotta offers boutiques, a book shop, clothing stores, and galleries. New Harbor and Round Pond have crafts and antiques shops as well as artisans' studios.

You never know what you'll find at **Reny's** (✉ Rte. 1A, Damariscotta, ☎ 207/563–5757)—perhaps merchandise from L. L. Bean or a designer coat. This bargain chain has outlets in many Maine towns, but this is its hometown, and there are outlets on both sides of the street: one for clothes, the other for everything else. **Granite Hill Store** (✉ Backshore Rd., Round Pond, ☎ 207/529–5864) has penny candy, kitchen goodies, baskets, and cards on the first floor, antiques and books on the second, and an ice cream window on the side. The **Roserie at Bayfields** (✉ Rte. 32, Waldoboro, ☎ 207/832–6330) specializes in practical roses for tough places in your yard. The gardens here have sweeping views over the Medomak River.

Portland to Pemaquid Point A to Z

Arriving and Departing

See Arriving and Departing *in* Maine A to Z, *below.*

Getting Around

BY BUS

Greater Portland's **Metro** (☎ 207/774–0351) runs seven bus routes in Portland, South Portland, and Westbrook. The fare is $1; exact change ($1 bills accepted) is required. Buses run from 5:30 AM to 11:45 PM.

BY CAR

Congress Street leads from I–295 into the heart of Portland; the Gateway Garage on High Street, off Congress, is a convenient place to leave your car while exploring downtown. North of Portland, I–95 takes you to Exit 20 and U.S. 1, Freeport's Main Street, which continues on to Brunswick and Bath. East of Wiscasset you can take Route 27 south to the Boothbays, where Route 96 is a good choice for further exploration.

Casco Bay Lines (☎ 207/774–7871) provides ferry service from Portland to the islands of Casco Bay.

Contacts and Resources

CAR RENTAL

See Contacts and Resources *in* Maine A to Z, *below.*

EMERGENCIES

Maine Medical Center (✉ 22 Bramhall St., Portland, ☎ 207/871–0111). **Mid Coast Hospital** (✉ 1356 Washington St., Bath, ☎ 207/443–5524; ✉ 58 Baribeau Dr., Brunswick, ☎ 207/729–0181). **Miles Memorial Hospital** (✉ Bristol Rd., Damariscotta, ☎ 207/563–1234). **St. Andrews Hospital** (✉ 3 St. Andrews La., Boothbay Harbor, ☎ 207/633–2121).

GUIDED TOURS

Greater Portland Landmarks (✉ 165 State St., ☎ 207/774–5561) offers 1½-hour walking tours of the city from July through September; tours begin at the Convention and Visitors Bureau (✉ 305 Commercial St., ☎ 207/772–5800) and cost $8.

In Portland, the informative van tours of **Mainely Tours** (✉ 5½ Moulton St., ☎ 207/774–0808) cover the city's historical and architectural highlights (with a stop at Portland Head Light, too) from Memorial Day through October. Other tours combine a city tour with a bay cruise, take shoppers to Freeport, or visit Wiscasset or Kennebunkport.

VISITOR INFORMATION

Boothbay Harbor Region Chamber of Commerce (✉ Box 356, Boothbay Harbor 04538, ☎ 207/633–2353). **Chamber of Commerce of the Bath/Brunswick Region** (✉ 45 Front St., Bath 04530, ☎ 207/443–9751; ✉ 59 Pleasant St., Brunswick 04011, ☎ 207/725–8797). **Convention and Visitors Bureau of Greater Portland** (✉ 305 Commercial St. 04101, ☎ 207/772–5800 or 877/833–1374). **Damariscotta Region Chamber of Commerce** (✉ Box 13, Damariscotta 04543, ☎ 207/563–8340). **Freeport Merchants Association** (✉ Box 452, Freeport 04032, ☎ 207/865–1212 or 877/865–1212). **Greater Portland Chamber of Commerce** (✉ 145 Middle St., Portland 04101, ☎ 207/772–2811). **Maine Tourism Association** (✉ U.S. 1, Exit 17 off I–95, Yarmouth 04347, ☎ 207/846–0833).

PENOBSCOT BAY

Purists hold that the Maine coast begins at Penobscot Bay, where the vistas over the water are wider and bluer; the shore a jumble of broken granite boulders, cobblestones, and gravel punctuated by small sand beaches; and the water numbingly cold. Port Clyde in the southwest and Stonington in the southeast are the outer limits of Maine's largest bay, 35 mi apart across the bay waters but separated by a drive of almost 100 mi on scenic but slow two-lane highways. From Pemaquid Point at the western extremity of Muscongus Bay to Port Clyde at its eastern extent, it's less than 15 mi across the water, but it's 50 mi for the motorist, who must return north to U.S. 1 to reach the far shore.

Rockland, the largest town on the bay, is Maine's major lobster distribution center and the port of departure for trips to Vinalhaven, North Haven, and Matinicus islands. The Camden Hills, looming green over Camden's fashionable waterfront, turn bluer and fainter as you head toward Castine, the small town across the bay. In between Camden and Castine are Belfast and the antiques and flea-market mecca of Searsport. Deer Isle is connected to the mainland by a slender, high-arching bridge, but Isle au Haut, accessible from Deer Isle's fishing town of Stonington, can be reached by passenger ferry only: More than half of this steep, wooded island is wilderness, the most remote section of Acadia National Park.

The most promising shopping areas are Main Street in Rockland, Main and Bay View streets in Camden, Main Street in Blue Hill, and Main Street in Stonington. Antiques shops are clustered in Searsport and scattered around the outskirts of villages, in farmhouses and barns. Yard sales abound in summer.

Tenants Harbor

㉒ *13 mi south of Thomaston.*

Tenants Harbor is a quintessential Maine fishing town, its harbor dominated by lobster boats, its shores rocky and slippery, its center a scattering of clapboard houses, a church, a general store. The fictional Dunnet Landing of Sarah Orne Jewett's classic book *The Country of the Pointed Firs* is based on this region.

The keeper's house at the **Marshall Point Lighthouse** has been turned into a museum containing memorabilia from the town of St. George (a few miles north of Tenants Harbor). The setting has inspired Jamie Wyeth and other artists. You can stroll the grounds and watch the boats go in and out of Port Clyde. ⊠ *Marshall Point Rd., Port Clyde,* ☎ *207/372–6450.* ⊡ *Free.* ☉ *June–Sept., weekdays 1–5 and Sat. 10–5.*

Dining and Lodging

$$–$$$ ✕⊡ **East Wind Inn & Meeting House.** Overlooking the harbor and the islands, the East Wind has unadorned but comfortable rooms, suites, and apartments in three buildings; some accommodations have fireplaces. The inn is open to the public for dinner, breakfast, and Sunday brunch. Dinner options include prime rib, boiled lobster, and baked stuffed haddock. ⊠ *Mechanic St., 04860,* ☎ *207/372–6366 or 800/241–8439,* ⅢX *207/372–6320. 23 rooms, 9 with bath; 3 suites; 4 apartments. Restaurant. AE, D, MC, V. Closed Dec.–Apr. No lunch.*

Shopping

Gallery-by-the-Sea (⊠ Port Clyde Village, Port Clyde, ☎ 207/372–8631) carries works by a dozen local artists including Leo Brooks, Lawrence Goldsmith, and Emily Muir.

Monhegan Island

★ **㉓** *East of Pemaquid Point, 10 mi south of Port Clyde.*

Remote Monhegan Island, with its high cliffs fronting the open sea, was known to Basque, Portuguese, and Breton fishermen well before Columbus "discovered" America. About a century ago Monhegan was discovered again by some of America's finest painters, including Rockwell Kent, Robert Henri, A. J. Hammond, and Edward Hopper, who sailed out to paint its meadows, savage cliffs, wild ocean views, and fishermen's shacks. Tourists followed, and today three excursion boats dock here. The village bustles with activity in summer, but you can escape the crowds on the island's 17 miles of hiking trails, which lead from the village to the lighthouse, through the woods and to the cliffs. Those who choose to overnight here have a quieter experience, since lodging is limited. Day visitors should bring a picnic lunch, as restaurants can have long waits at lunchtime.

Penobscot Bay

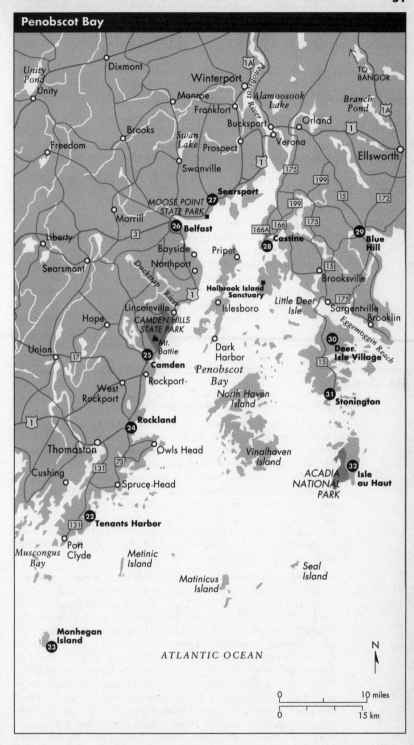

TO BANGOR

Unity Pond
Unity
Dixmont
1A
Winterport
Penobscot River
Branch Pond
1A
Monroe
Alamoosook Lake
Frankfort
Brooks
Bucksport
Orland
1
Freedom
Swan Lake
Prospect
Verona
Ellsworth
175
Swanville
1
199
Morrill
Searsport 27
MOOSE POINT STATE PARK
15
172
Liberty
Belfast 26
3
199
175
Blue Hill 29
Searsmont
Bayside
Pripet
166A 166
175
Castine 28
Northport
Duckham River
15
Brooksville
Hope
Holbrook Island Sanctuary
Little Deer Isle
Sargentville
175
Lincolnville
Islesboro
Brooklin
CAMDEN HILLS STATE PARK
Eggemoggin Reach
Mt. Battie
Dark Harbor
Deer Isle Village 30
Union
17
Camden 25
Penobscot Bay
15
Rockport
West Rockport
North Haven Island
Stonington 31
1
Rockland 24
Thomaston
Owls Head
Vinalhaven Island
ACADIA NATIONAL PARK
Cushing
131
73
Isle au Haut 32
Spruce Head
131
Tenants Harbor 22
Muscongus Bay
Port Clyde
Metinic Island
Seal Island
Matinicus Island
Monhegan Island 23

ATLANTIC OCEAN

N

| 0 | | 10 miles |
| 0 | | 15 km |

Port Clyde, a fishing village at the end of Route 131, is the point of departure for the *Laura B.* (☎ 207/372–8848 for schedules), the mail boat that serves Monhegan Island. The *Balmy Days* (☎ 207/633–2284 or 800/298–2284) sails from Boothbay Harbor to Monhegan on daily trips in summer. **Hardy Boat Cruises** (☎ 207/677–2026 or 800/278–3346) leaves daily from Shaw's Wharf in New Harbor.

The **Monhegan Museum,** in an 1824 lighthouse and an adjacent, newly built assistant-keeper's house, has wonderful views of Manana Island and the Camden Hills in the distance. Inside, artworks and displays depict island life and local flora and birds. ⊠ *White Head Rd.,* ☎ *no phone.* 🖾 *Donations accepted.* ☉ *July–mid-Sept., daily 11:30–3:30.*

Swim Beach, a five-minute walk from the ferry, is rocky but rarely has more than a few sun worshipers.

Lodging

$$$–$$$$ 🖼 **Island Inn.** This three-story inn, which dates from 1807, has a commanding presence on Monhegan's harbor. The waterside rooms, though mostly small, are the nicest, with sunset views over the harbor and stark Manana Island. Some of the meadow-view rooms have the distinct disadvantage of being over kitchen vents. New owners are updating and redecorating the property, which includes the main inn, the adjacent Pierce Cottage, a small bakery-café, and a good dining room that serves breakfast, lunch, and dinner. ⊠ *Box 128, Monhegan Island 04852,* ☎ *207/596–0371,* 𝔽𝔸𝕏 *207/594–5517. 29 rooms, 12 with bath; 4 suites in 2 buildings. Restaurant, café. Full breakfast. MC, V. Closed Columbus Day–Memorial Day.*

Rockland

㉔ *27 mi south of Belfast, 53 mi northeast of Brunswick.*

A large fishing port and the commercial hub of the coast, with working boats moored alongside a flotilla of cruise schooners, Rockland retains a working-class flavor. The expansion of the Farnsworth Museum and the opening of more boutiques, restaurants, and bed-and-breakfasts have increased its appeal to coastal travelers. Day trips to Vinalhaven and North Haven islands and distant Matinicus depart from the harbor, the outer portion of which is bisected by a nearly mile-long granite breakwater. At the end of the breakwater is a late-19th-century lighthouse, one of the best places in the area to watch the many windjammers sail in and out of Rockland Harbor. Owl's Head Lighthouse, off Route 73, is also a good vantage point.

★ The **Farnsworth Art Museum** is an excellent small museum of American art. Artists represented in the permanent collection include Andrew, N. C., and Jamie Wyeth; Fitz Hugh Lane; George Bellows; Frank W. Benson; Edward Hopper; Louise Nevelson; and Fairfield Porter. The **Wyeth Center,** which opened in summer 1998, is devoted to Maine-related works of Andrew Wyeth and other members of the Wyeth family. Works from the personal collection of Andrew and Betsy Wyeth include *The Patriot, Adrift, Maiden Hair, Dr. Syn, The Clearing, Geraniums, Watch Cap,* and other paintings. Between the museum and the new gallery is the **Farnsworth Homestead,** a handsome circa-1852 Greek Revival dwelling that retains its original lavish Victorian furnishings. The museum also operates the **Olson House** (⊠ Hathorn Point Rd., Cushing), which was depicted in Andrew Wyeth's famous painting *Christina's World.* ⊠ *356 Main St.,* ☎ *207/596–6457.* 🖾 *$9.* ☉ *Museum Memorial Day–Columbus Day, daily 9–5; Columbus Day–Memorial Day, Tues.–Sat. 10–5, Sun. 1–5. Homestead Memorial Day–Columbus Day, daily 9–5. Olson House Memorial Day–Columbus Day, daily 11–4.*

○ The **Shore Village Museum** displays many lighthouse and Coast Guard artifacts and has exhibits of maritime and Civil War memorabilia. ⊠ *104 Limerock St.,* ☎ *207/594–0311.* ☞ *Donation suggested.* ☉ *June– mid-Oct., daily 10–4; rest of yr "by chance and appointment."*

○ **Owls Head Transportation Museum** displays antique aircraft, cars, and engines and stages weekend air shows. ⊠ *Rte. 73, Owls Head (2 mi south of Rockland),* ☎ *207/594–4418.* ☞ *$6.* ☉ *Apr.–Oct., daily 10– 5; Nov.–Mar., daily 10–4.*

Montpelier: General Henry Knox Museum was built in 1930 as a replica of the late-18th-century mansion of Major General Henry Knox, a general in the Revolutionary War and secretary of war in Washington's Cabinet. Antiques and Knox family possessions fill the interior. Architectural features of note include an oval room and a double staircase. ⊠ *U.S. 1 and Rte. 131, Thomaston,* ☎ *207/354–8062.* ☞ *$5.* ☉ *Early June–early Oct., Tues.–Sat. 10–4, Sun. 1–4.*

The **Maine Watercraft Museum** displays more than 125 antique and classic small craft both in and out of the water. ⊠ *4 Knox St. Landing, Thomaston,* ☎ *207/354–0444.* ☞ *$4.* ☉ *Memorial Day–Sept., Wed.–Sun. 10–5.*

OFF THE BEATEN PATH	**VINALHAVEN –** You can take the ferry from Rockland to this island for a pleasant day of bicycling or walking. A number of parks are within walking distance of the ferry dock, including Armbrust Hill, the site of an abandoned quarry, and Lane's Island Preserve, a 40-acre site of moors, granite shoreline, tide pools, and beach. You can learn about the island's quarrying history at the Historical Society Museum on High Street and even take a dip in the cool, clear waters of two quarries. Lawson's is 1 mi out on the North Haven Road; Booth Quarry is 1½ mi out East Main Street. Neither has changing facilities, so go prepared. For ferry information, call Maine State Ferry Service (☎ 207/596–2202).

Dining and Lodging

$$ ✕ **Café Miranda.** Expect to wait for a table at this cozy bistro, where the daily-changing menu reflects fresh, seasonal ingredients and the chef's creative renditions of both new American and traditional home-style foods. You can make a meal from the 20 or so appetizers, many roasted in the brick oven. The two dozen entrées may include crispy pan-fried soft-shell crabs with red bean ragout and yellow jasmine rice. If you sit at the small counter, you can watch the chef prepare your meal. ⊠ *15 Oak St.,* ☎ *207/594–2304. MC, V. Closed Sun.–Mon. No lunch.*

$$ ✕ **Jessica's Bistro.** Jessica's occupies four cozy rooms in a Victorian
★ home on a hill at the southern end of Rockland. Billed as a European bistro, the restaurant lives up to its Continental label with creative entrées that include veal Zurich, paella, and pork Portofino; other specialties of the Swiss chef are risottos, pastas, and focaccia. ⊠ *2 S. Main St. (Rte. 73),* ☎ *207/596–0770. D, MC, V. Closed Tues. in winter.*

$–$$ ✕ **Waterworks.** This restaurant in a brick building off Main Street serves light pub fare, including soups and home-style suppers like turkey and meat loaf. Maine microbrewery beers are on tap, and the selection of single-malt Scotches is excellent. A wall of water decorates the small dining room, and a stone fireplace dominates the pub. A children's menu is available. ⊠ *Lindsey St.,* ☎ *207/596–2753. AE, D, MC, V.*

$$$$ ☲ **Samoset Resort.** On the Rockland-Rockport town line next to the breakwater, this sprawling oceanside resort has excellent golf and fitness facilities. Most of the spacious rooms, decorated in soothing blue and rose tones, have views of Penobscot Bay over the fairways; all have patios or decks. ⊠ *220 Warrenton St., Rockport,* ☎ *207/594–2511;*

800/341–1650 outside ME; FAX *207/594–0722. 132 rooms, 18 suites. Restaurant, 1 indoor and 1 outdoor pool, 18-hole golf course, 2 tennis courts, exercise room, racquetball, children's programs. AE, D, DC, MC, V.*

$$–$$$ 🏨 **Limerock Inn.** You can walk to the Farnsworth and the Shore Vil-
  ★ lage museums from this magnificent Queen Anne–style Victorian on
a quiet residential street. The meticulously decorated rooms include
Island Cottage, with a whirlpool tub and doors that open onto a private deck overlooking the backyard garden, and Grand Manan, which
has a fireplace, a whirlpool tub, and a four-poster king-size bed. ⊠ *96
Limerock St., 04841,* ☎ *207/594–2257 or 800/546–3762,* FAX *207/594–
1846. 8 rooms. Croquet, bicycles. Full breakfast. MC, V.*

Outdoor Activities and Sports

BOAT TRIPS

Bay Island Yacht Charters (⊠ 120 Tillison Ave., ☎ 207/236–2776 or
800/421–2492) operates bareboats and charters. **North End Shipyard
Schooners** (☎ 800/648–4544) operates three- and six-day cruises on
the schooners *American Eagle, Isaac H. Evans,* and *Heritage.* **Three
Cheers** (⊠ Rockland Landing, Marina Park Dr., ☎ 207/594–0900)
operates lobster-fishing and lighthouse cruises. **Vessels of Windjammer Wharf** (☎ 207/236–3520 or 800/999–7352) organizes three-
and six-day cruises on the *Pauline,* a 12-passenger motor yacht, and
the *Stephen Taber,* a windjammer. *Victory Chimes* is a 132-ft, three-
masted schooner, the largest in Maine's windjammer fleet, that takes
three- and six-day trips.

TOURS

Coastal Explorer Tours (☎ 207/594–7568) operates specialty tours for
lighthouse viewing, boat building, photography, and other interests.
Downeast Air Inc. (☎ 207/594–2171 or 800/594–2171) offers scenic
flights and lighthouse tours.

Shopping

Rockland's Main Street has experienced a quiet change in the wake of
the expansion of the Farnsworth Art Museum. Galleries are clustered
around the museums, and boutiques and antiques and specialty stores
are sprouting up along both the main and side streets. **Between the Muse**
(⊠ 8 Elm St., ☎ 207/596–6868) specializes in modern art and has a
sculpture garden. **Caldbeck Gallery** (⊠ 12 Elm St., ☎ 207/596–5935)
features contemporary Maine works by artists such as William Thon.
Maine authors frequently sign books at the **Personal Bookstore** (⊠ 78
Main St., Thomaston, ☎ 207/354–8058 or 800/391–8058). The **Read-
ing Corner** (⊠ 408 Main St., ☎ 207/596–6651) carries many cookbooks, children's books, and Maine-related titles, and has good
newspaper and magazine selections. The **Store** (⊠ 435 Main St., ☎
207/594–9246) stocks top-of-the-line cookware and table accessories
and has an outstanding card selection.

Camden

  ㉕ *8 mi north of Rockland, 19 mi south of Belfast.*

"Where the mountains meet the sea," Camden's longtime publicity slo-
gan, is an apt description, as you will discover when you step out of
your car and look up from the harbor. The town is famous not only
for geography but for its large fleet of windjammers—relics and repli-
cas from the age of sail. At just about any hour during warm months
you're likely to see at least one windjammer tied up in the harbor. The
best shopping in the region can be found in the busy downtown. The
district's compact size makes it perfect for exploring on foot: Shops,

restaurants, and galleries line Main Street (U.S. 1) and Bayview, as well as side streets and alleys around the harbor.

If you're accustomed to the Rockies or the Alps, you may not be impressed with heights of not much more than 1,000 ft, yet the hills in **Camden Hills State Park** are lovely landmarks for miles along the low, rolling reaches of the Maine coast. The 5,500-acre park contains 20 mi of trails, including the easy Nature Trail up Mt. Battie. Hike or drive to the top for a magnificent view over Camden and island-studded Penobscot Bay. The 112-site camping area, open from mid-May to mid-October, has flush toilets and hot showers. The entrance is 2 mi north of Camden. ⊠ *U.S. 1,* ☎ *207/236–3109.* ⛫ *Trails and auto road up Mt. Battie $2.* ⊙ *Daily dawn–dusk.*

Merry Spring Gardens is a 66-acre retreat with herb, rose, rhododendron, hosta, and children's gardens as well as woodland trails. ⊠ *Off U.S. 1 on the Conway Rd.,* ☎ *207/236–2239.* ⛫ *Free.* ⊙ *Daily dawn–dusk.*

⛁ **Kelmscott Farm** is a rare-breed animal farm (sheep, pigs, horses, poultry, goats, and cows) with displays, a nature trail, children's activities, a picnic area, heirloom gardens, and frequent special events. ⊠ *Rte. 52, Lincolnville,* ☎ *207/763–4088.* ⛫ *$5.* ⊙ *May–Nov., Tues.–Sun., 10–5; Nov.–May. Tues.–Sun., 10–3.*

Dining and Lodging

$$-$$$ ✕ **Waterfront Restaurant.** A ringside seat on Camden Harbor can be had here; the best view is from the outdoor deck, open in warm weather. The fare is primarily seafood: boiled lobster, scallops, bouillabaisse, seafood risotto. Lunchtime highlights include lobster and crabmeat rolls. ⊠ *Bay View St.,* ☎ *207/236–3747. Reservations not accepted. MC, V.*

$$$ ✕🏨 **Whitehall Inn.** One of Camden's best-known inns, just north of town, is an 1843 white clapboard sea captain's home with a wide porch and a turn-of-the-century wing. The Millay Room, off the lobby, preserves memorabilia of the poet Edna St. Vincent Millay, who grew up in the area. The sparsely furnished rooms have dark-wood bedsteads, white bedspreads, and claw-foot tubs. The dining room, which serves traditional and creative American cuisine, is open to the public for dinner. ⊠ *Box 558, 52 High St., 04843,* ☎ *207/236–3391 or 800/789–6565,* ℻ *207/236–4427. 44 rooms, 40 with bath. Restaurant, tennis court, shuffleboard. MAP. AE, MC, V. Closed mid-Oct.–mid-May.*

$$-$$$ ✕🏨 **Youngtown Inn.** Inside this white Federal farmhouse are a French-inspired country retreat and a well-respected French restaurant ($$$). The country location guarantees quiet, and the inn is a short walk to the Fernald Neck Preserve on Lake Megunticook. Simple, airy rooms open to decks with views of the rolling countryside. Two have fireplaces. The restaurant, open to the public for dinner, serves entrées such as lobster ravioli and pan-seared breast of pheasant with foie gras mousse. ⊠ *Rte. 52 at Youngtown Rd., Lincolnville 04849,* ☎ *207/763–4290 or 800/291–8438,* ℻ *207/763–4078. 6 rooms, 1 suite. Full breakfast. AE, MC, V.*

$$$$ 🏨 **Inn at Ocean's Edge.** Perched on the ocean's edge, this shingle-style
★ inn looks as if it has been here for decades. In actuality, it's brand-new and built with modern-day comforts in mind. Every room has a king-size bed, an ocean view, a fireplace, and a whirlpool for two, and all have TVs, VCRs, and individually controlled heat and air-conditioning. The Lincolnville setting is private, yet minutes from Camden. ⊠ *U.S. 1, Lincolnville; mailing address: Box 704, Camden 04843,* ☎ *207/236–0945,* ℻ *207/236–0609. 14 rooms, 1 suite. Exercise room, meeting room. Full breakfast. AE, MC, V.*

$$$–$$$$ 🏨 **Victorian Inn.** It's less than 10 minutes from downtown Camden,
★   but with a quiet waterside location well off U.S. 1, the Victorian Inn
feels a world away. Most rooms and the wraparound porch have magnificent views over island-studded Penobscot Bay. Romantic touches
include canopy and brass beds, braided rugs, white wicker furniture,
and floral wallpapers. Six guest rooms have fireplaces, and there are
four more in common rooms, including the glass-enclosed breakfast
room in the turret, where a full breakfast is served. ⊠ *Sea View Dr.,
Lincolnville; mailing address: Box 1385, Camden 04843,* ☎ *207/236–
3785 or 800/382–9817,* 🆅 *207/236–0017. 5 rooms, 2 suites. Full breakfast. AE, MC, V.*

$$ 🏨 **Camden Maine Stay.** This 1802 clapboard inn within walking dis
★   tance of shops and restaurants is on the National Register of Historic
Places. The grounds are classic and inviting, from the colorful flowers
lining the granite walk in summer to the snow-laden bushes in winter.
The equally fresh and colorful rooms contain many pieces of Eastlake
furniture; six have fireplaces. ⊠ *22 High St., 04842,* ☎ *207/236–9636,*
🆅 *207/236–0621. 5 rooms, 3 suites. Full breakfast. AE, MC, V.*

Nightlife and the Arts

Bay Chamber Concerts (⊠ Rockport Opera House, 6 Central St.,
Rockport, ☎ 207/236–2823 or 888/707–2770) presents chamber
music on Thursday and Friday night during July and August; concerts
are given once a month from September to May. **Gilbert's Public House**
(⊠ 12 Bay View St., ☎ 207/236–4320) has dancing and live entertainment. **Sea Dog Tavern & Brewery** (⊠ 43 Mechanic St., ☎ 207/236–
6863), a popular brew pub in a converted woolen mill, has live entertainment in season. The **Whale's Tooth Pub** (⊠ U.S. 1, Lincolnville
Beach, ☎ 207/236–3747) has low-key entertainment on weekends.

Outdoor Activities and Sports

Maine Sport (⊠ U.S. 1, Rockport, ☎ 207/236–8797 or 800/722–
0826), the best sports outfitter north of Freeport, rents bikes, camping and fishing gear, canoes, kayaks, cross-country skis, ice skates, and
snowshoes. It also conducts skiing and kayaking clinics and trips.

The **Betselma** (⊠ Camden Public Landing, ☎ 207/236–4446) offers
one- and two-hour powerboat trips.

Windjammers create a stir whenever they sail into Camden harbor, and
a voyage around the bay on one of them, whether for an afternoon or
a week, is unforgettable. The season for the excursions is from June
to September. Excursion boats also provide an opportunity for getting
afloat on the waters of Penobscot Bay. Eggemoggin Reach is a famous
cruising ground for yachts, as are the coves and inlets around Deer Isle
and the Penobscot Bay waters between Castine and Camden.

The **Maine Windjammer Association** (⊠ Box 1144, Blue Hill 04614,
☎ 800/807–9463) represents the Camden-based windjammers *Angelique, Grace Bailey, J & E Riggin, Lewis R. French, Mary Day, Mercantile, Nathaniel Bowditch, Roseway,* and *Timberwind,* which sail on
cruises that last from three to eight days.

Shopping

Shops and galleries line Camden's Bay View and Main streets and the
alleys that lead to the harbor. **Maine Coast Artists** (⊠ 162 Russell
Ave., Rockport, ☎ 207/236–2875) specializes in contemporary Maine
art. **Maine's Massachusetts House Galleries** (⊠ U.S. 1, Lincolnville, ☎
207/789–5705) display regional art, including bronzes, carvings, sculptures, and landscapes and seascapes in pencil, oil, and watercolor. The
Owl and Turtle Bookshop (⊠ 8 Bay View St., ☎ 207/236–4769) sells
books, CDs, cassettes, and cards. The two-story shop has rooms de-

voted to marine and children's books. The **Pine Tree Shop & Bayview Gallery** (✉ 33 Bay View St., ☎ 207/236–4534) specializes in original art, prints, and posters, almost all with Maine themes. The **Windsor Chairmakers** (✉ U.S. 1, Lincolnville, ☎ 207/789–5188 or 800/789–5188) sells custom-made, handcrafted beds, chests, china cabinets, dining tables, highboys, and chairs.

Skiing and Snow Sports

CAMDEN SNOW BOWL

The Maine coast isn't known for skiing, but this small, lively park has downhill skiing as well as magnificent views over Penobscot Bay. ✉ *Box 1207, Hosmer Pond Rd., 04843,* ☎ *207/236–3438.*

Downhill. In a Currier & Ives setting the park has a 950-ft-vertical mountain, a small lodge with cafeteria, a ski school, and ski and toboggan rentals. Camden Snow Bowl has 11 trails accessed by one double chair and two T-bars. It also has night skiing.

Other activities. Camden Snow Bowl has a small lake that is cleared for ice-skating, a snow-tubing park, and a 400-ft toboggan run that shoots sledders out onto the lake.

CROSS-COUNTRY SKIING

There are 16 km (10 mi) of cross-country skiing trails at **Camden Hills State Park** (✉ U.S. 1 ☎ 207/236–9849). **Tanglewood 4-H Camp** (✉ U.S. 1 ☎ 207/789–5868), about 5 mi away in Lincolnville, has 20 km (12½ mi) of trails.

En Route Queen Anne cottages with freshly painted porches and exquisite architectural details dot the community of Bayside, a section of Northport off U.S. 1 on the way to Belfast. Some of these homes line the main one-lane thoroughfare, George Street; others are on bluffs with water views around town greens complete with flagpoles and swings; and yet others are on the shore.

Belfast

26 *27 mi north of Rockland, 46 mi east of Augusta.*

Like many other Maine towns, Belfast has ridden the tides of affluence and depression. A shipbuilding center in the 1800s and home to many sea captains, the city fell on hard times, only to be rescued by the chicken-processing industry. In the 1980s, that moved south. This time it's high tech, namely credit-card giant MBNA, that has helped rescue the city economically. The upswing in the economy promises well for visitors, who'll find an old-fashioned redbrick Victorian downtown and a lively waterfront, as well as affordable lodging and dining. The houses on Church Street are a veritable glossary of 19th-century architectural styles; pick up a map with a walking tour at the visitor center at the foot of Main Street.

A ride on the **Belfast & Moosehead Lake Railroad** (✉ One Depot Sq., Unity, ☎ 207/948–5500 or 800/392–5500), which operates from mid-June to December ($14), is especially enjoyable in the fall after the leaves begin to change colors. During the run between Belfast and Waldo Station, the notorious Waldo Station Gang "robs" the train. The railroad's timetable coordinates with a **cruise boat**; a discount applies if you travel on both.

Moose Point State Park (✉ U.S. 1 between Belfast and Searsport, ☎ 207/548–2882) is ideal for easy hikes and picnics overlooking Penobscot Bay.

Dining and Lodging

$$ ✕ **90 Main.** Young chef-owner Sheila Costello is at the helm of this family-run restaurant. Using Pemaquid oysters, Maine blueberries, organic vegetables grown on a nearby farm, and other local ingredients, Costello creates flavorful dishes that delight the senses. The chalkboard of specials includes a macrobiotic option, or you can start with the smoked seafood and pâté sampler or the spinach salad with sautéed chicken, sweet peppers, hazelnuts, and a warm raspberry vinaigrette. Entrées include rib-eye steak and seafood linguine. The adjacent deli and bakery sells sandwiches and delicious homemade breads and treats. ✉ *90 Main St.,* ☎ *207/338–1106. AE, MC, V.*

$–$$ 🏨 **Jeweled Turret Inn.** Turrets, columns, and gables embellish this inn, originally built in 1898 as the home of a local attorney. The magnificent woodwork is oak, maple, fir, and pine, and elegant Victorian pieces furnish the rooms. The inn is named for the jewel-like stained-glass windows in the stairway turret; the gem theme continues in the den, where the ornate rock fireplace is said to include rocks from every state in the Union. ✉ *40 Pearl St., 04915,* ☎ *207/338–2304 or 800/696–2304. 7 rooms. Full breakfast. MC, V.*

$–$$ 🏨 **The White House.** New owners have poured their hearts and purses into renovating this fine example of Greek Revival architecture, an 1840–1842 landmark by architect Calvin Ryder. An eight-sided cupola tops the house; inside are ornate plaster ceiling medallions, rare Italian marble fireplaces, an elliptical flying staircase, and intricate moldings. Crystal chandeliers, Asian rugs, and antiques and reproduction pieces elegantly decorate the spacious rooms. Two guest rooms have whirlpool tubs. You can relax in the English garden, in the gazebo, or under the enormous copper beech tree. ✉ *1 Church St., 04915,* ☎ *207/338–1901 or 888/290–1901,* ℻ *207/338–5161. 4 rooms, 2 suites. Full breakfast. D, MC, V.*

Searsport

㉗ *11 mi north of Belfast, 57 mi east of Augusta.*

Searsport, Maine's second-largest deepwater port (after Portland), bills itself as the antiques capital of Maine. The town's stretch of U.S. 1 has many antiques shops and a large weekend flea market in summer. A former shipbuilding center, Searsport also holds homes built by the many sea captains who made their homes here; some are now bed-and-breakfasts.

★ The fine holdings within the nine historic and four modern buildings of the **Penobscot Marine Museum** provide fascinating documentation of the region's seafaring way of life. These buildings, including a church (still active) and a sea captain's house, have not been moved but remain where they were built in town. Included are display photos of 284 sea captains, artifacts of the whaling industry (lots of scrimshaw), navigational instruments, treasures collected by seafarers around the globe, an outstanding collection of marine art, and models of famous ships. Plan to spend about two hours here. ✉ *U.S. 1 at Church St.,* ☎ *207/548–2529.* 🎫 *$6.* ☉ *Memorial Day–late-Oct., Mon.–Sat. 10–5, Sun. noon–5.*

Dining and Lodging

$$$ ✕ **Rhumb Line.** The upscale restaurant in this 18th-century sea captain's home delivers fine dining, although the service and decor need some fine-tuning. The servers are formally attired but may perform unevenly, and the light pine chairs don't seem the best choice with the Asian rugs and gleaming hardwood floors. Still, the artfully presented food does shine. Pepper-glazed pork tenderloin, barbecued duck with

potato pancakes, and horseradish-crusted salmon are typical entrées.
⊠ *U.S. 1,* ☎ *207/548–2600. MC, V. No lunch.*

$–$$ ☷ **Homeport Inn.** This 1861 inn, a former sea captain's home, provides
an opulent Victorian environment that might put you in the mood to
rummage through the nearby antiques and treasure shops. The back
rooms downstairs have private decks and views of the bay. Families
often stay in the two-bedroom housekeeping cottage. ⊠ *U.S. 1,* ☎ *207/
548–2259 or 800/742–5814. 10 rooms, 7 with bath; 1 2-bedroom cottage. Full breakfast. AE, D, MC, V.*

Shopping

Along U.S. 1 you'll see several dozen shops and, in season, outdoor
flea markets. More than 70 dealers show their wares in the two-story
Searsport Antique Mall (⊠ 149 E. Main St./ U.S. 1, ☎ 207/548–2640);
look for everything from linens and silver to turn-of-the-century oak.
Pumpkin Patch Antiques (⊠ 15 W. Main St./U.S. 1, ☎ 207/548–6047)
displays such items as quilts, nautical items, and painted and wood furniture from about 20 dealers. It's open April through Thanksgiving or
by appointment.

Castine

❷❽ *30 mi southeast of Searsport.*

The French, the British, the Dutch, and the Americans fought over Castine from the 17th century to the War of 1812. Present-day Castine's
many attributes include its lively harborfront, Federal and Greek Revival houses, and town common; there are two museums and the ruins
of a British fort to explore. For a nice stroll, park your car at the landing and walk up Main Street past the two inns and on toward the white
Trinitarian Federated Church, which has a tapering spire.

Among the white clapboard buildings that ring the town common are
the Ives House (once the summer home of the poet Robert Lowell),
the Abbott School, and the Unitarian Church, capped by a whimsical
belfry.

Castine's **Soldiers and Sailors Monument** (⊠ Castine Town Common)
is typical of many town memorials that honor the state's participation
in the Civil War. It was dedicated in May 1887 to the veterans of that
conflict.

Dining and Lodging

$$ ✕☷ **Castine Inn.** Amy and Tom Gutrow have taken this well-respected
★ inn and infused it with youthful, contemporary flair. Upholstered easy
chairs and fine prints and paintings are typical of the furnishings in
this inn's airy rooms. The third floor has the best views: the harbor
over the formal gardens on one side, the village on the other. The din-
ing room ($$$), decorated with a wraparound mural of Castine and
its harbor, is open to the public for breakfast and dinner; the creative
menu features local ingredients and entrées such as Kalamata-olive–
crusted salmon with a yellow-pepper–grapefruit sauce. There's a snug,
English-style pub off the lobby. ⊠ *Box 41, Main St., 04421,* ☎ *207/
326–4365,* ⑆ *207/326–4570. 15 rooms, 4 suites. Restaurant, pub,
sauna. Full breakfast. MC, V. Restaurant hrs limited mid-Oct.–mid-
Dec. Inn closed mid-Dec.–Apr.*

Shopping

Chris Murray Waterfowl Carver (⊠ Upper Main St., ☎ 207/326–
9033) sells award-winning wildfowl carvings. **H.O.M.E.** (⊠ U.S. 1,
Orland, ☎ 207/469–7961) is a cooperative crafts village with a crafts
and pottery shop, weaving shop, flea market, market stand, and wood-

working shop. **McGrath-Dunham Gallery** (⊠ Main St., ☎ 207/326–9938) carries fine art.

Blue Hill

㉙ *19 mi east of Castine.*

Blue Hill has a dramatic perch over the harbor. It is renowned for its pottery and has good shops and galleries.

Dining and Lodging

$$–$$$ ✕ **Jonathan's.** The downstairs room at nautically themed Jonathan's has captain's chairs, linen tablecloths, and local art; in the post-and-beam upstairs, there's wood everywhere, plus high-back chairs and candles with hurricane globes. Fresh fish and meat entrées are always on the menu. The lengthy wine list has French, Italian, Californian, and Maine-produced vintages. ⊠ *Main St.,* ☎ *207/374–5226. MC, V.*

$$–$$$ ✕ **The Landing.** There's a great view over boat-filled Bucks Harbor from
★ this second-floor restaurant in sleepy South Brooksville. Tasty starters include the roasted corn and crab cakes and the rabbit and shiitake ravioli, which you can follow with grilled medallions of halibut, pan-seared breast of Long Island duckling, or penne with grilled tiger shrimp. ⊠ *Steamboat Wharf Rd., South Brooksville,* ☎ FAX *207/326–8483. MC, V. Closed mid-Sept.–mid-June.*

$$$–$$$$ ✕🏠 **Blue Hill Inn.** Rambling and antiques-filled, this inn is a comfort-
★ ing place to relax after exploring nearby shops and galleries; four rooms have fireplaces. The multicourse, candlelighted dinners at the renowned dining room ($$$; reservations essential) are prepared with organically raised produce and herbs, local meats, and seafood. An hors d'oeuvres hour in the garden, or by the living-room fireplace, precedes dinner. ⊠ *Box 403, Union St./Rte. 177, 04614,* ☎ *207/374–2844 or 800/826–7415,* FAX *207/374–2829. 11 rooms, 1 apartment. Restaurant. MAP. D, MC, V. Closed Dec.–Apr. and midweek in Nov.*

$ 🏠 **Bucks Harbor Inn.** The spirit and decor are those of a traditional B&B (shared baths, friendly hosts, nothing too fancy), but owners Peter and Anne Eberling, unlike many other innkeepers, welcome children. Breezes off the water cool the large corner rooms. A full cooked-to-order breakfast is served on the porch. ⊠ *Box 268, Rte. 176, South Brooksville 04617,* ☎ *207/326–8660,* FAX *207/326–0730. 6 rooms without bath. Full breakfast. MC, V.*

Nightlife and the Arts

Kneisel Hall Chamber Music Festival (⊠ Kneisel Hall, Rte. 15, ☎ 207/374–2811) has concerts on Sunday and Friday in summer. **Left Bank Bakery and Café** (⊠ Rte. 172, ☎ 207/374–2201) presents musical talent from across the nation. **Surry Opera Co.** (⊠ Morgan Bay Rd., Surry, ☎ 207/667–2629) stages operas throughout the area in summer.

Outdoor Activities and Sports

Holbrook Island Sanctuary (⊠ Off Cape Rosier Rd., Brooksville, ☎ 207/326–4012) has a gravelly beach with a splendid view, a picnic area, and hiking trails. The **Phoenix Centre** (⊠ Rte. 175, Blue Hill Falls, ☎ 207/374–2113) operates sea-kayaking tours of Blue Hill Bay and Eggemoggin Reach.

Shopping

Big Chicken Barn (⊠ U.S. 1, Ellsworth, ☎ 207/374–2715) has three floors filled with books, antiques, and collectibles. **Handworks Gallery** (⊠ Main St., ☎ 207/374–5613) carries unusual crafts, jewelry, and clothing. **Leighton Gallery** (⊠ Parker Point Rd., ☎ 207/374–5001) shows oil paintings, lithographs, watercolors, and other contemporary art in the gallery, and sculpture in its garden. **North Country Textiles** (⊠ Main St., ☎ 207/374–2715) specializes in fine woven shawls, place mats, throws, baby blankets, and pillows in subtle patterns and color schemes. **Old Cove Antiques** (⊠ Rte. 15, Sargentville, ☎ 207/359–2031) has folk art, quilts, and hooked rugs.

Rackliffe Pottery (⊠ Rte. 172, ☎ 207/374–2297) is famous for its vivid blue pottery, including plates, tea and coffee sets, pitchers, casseroles, and canisters. **Rowantrees Pottery** (⊠ Union St., ☎ 207/374–5535) has an extensive selection of styles and patterns in dinnerware, tea sets, vases, and decorative items.

En Route   Scenic Route 15 south from Blue Hill passes through Brooksville and on through the graceful suspension bridge that crosses Eggemoggin Reach to Deer Isle. The turnout and picnic area at **Caterpillar Hill,** 1 mi south of the junction of Routes 15 and 175, commands a fabulous view of Penobscot Bay, hundreds of dark green islands, and the Camden Hills across the bay. From this perspective the hills look like a faraway mountain range, although they are less than 25 mi away.

Deer Isle Village

③⓪ *16 mi south of Blue Hill.*

In Deer Isle Village, thick woods give way to tidal coves. Stacks of lobster traps populate the backyards of shingled houses, and dirt roads lead to summer cottages.

Haystack Mountain School of Crafts attracts internationally renowned glassblowers, potters, sculptors, jewelers, blacksmiths, printmakers, and weavers to its summer institute. You can attend evening lectures or visit artists' studios (by appointment only). ⊠ *South of Deer Isle Village on Rte. 15, turn left at Gulf gas station and follow signs for 6 mi,* ☎ *207/348–2306.* ▨ *Free.* ☉ *June–Sept.*

Dining and Lodging

$$$$ ✕▥ **Goose Cove Lodge.** This heavily wooded property at the end of a back road has a fine stretch of ocean frontage, a sandy beach, and a long sandbar that leads to a nature preserve. Cottages and suites are in secluded woodlands and on the shore. Some are attached, some have a single large room, and still others have one or two bedrooms. All but three units have fireplaces. Dinner at the restaurant (reservations essential) is always superb and includes at least one vegetarian entrée; complimentary hors d'oeuvres precede the meal. On Friday night, there's a lobster feast on the inn's private beach. ⊠ *Box 40, Goose Cove Rd., Sunset 04683,* ☎ *207/348–2508 or 800/728–1963,* ☏ *207/ 348–2624. 2 rooms, 9 suites, 13 cottages. 2 restaurants, hiking, volleyball, beach, boating. MAP. AE, D, MC, V. All but 4 units closed mid-Oct.–mid-May.*

$$$ ✕▥ **Pilgrim's Inn.** A deep-red, four-story gambrel-roof house, the Pil-
★   grim's Inn dates from about 1793 and overlooks a mill pond and harbor in Deer Isle Village. The library has wing chairs and Oriental rugs; a downstairs taproom has a huge brick fireplace and pine furniture. Guest rooms have English fabrics and carefully selected antiques. The dining room (reservations essential; no lunch) is in the attached barn, a rustic yet elegant space with farm implements, French oil lamps, and tiny windows. The five-course menu changes nightly but might include rack of lamb or fresh seafood. ⊠ *Rte. 15A, 04627,* ☎ *207/348–6615,* ☏ *207/348–7769. 13 rooms, 10 with bath; 2 seaside cottages. Restaurant, bicycles. Full breakfast; MAP available. MC, V. Closed mid-Oct.–mid-May.*

Shopping

Blue Heron Gallery & Studio (⊠ Church St., ☎ 207/348–6051) sells the work of the Haystack Mountain School of Crafts faculty. **Harbor Farm** (⊠ Rte. 15, Little Deer Isle, ☎ 207/348–7737) carries wonderful products for the home, such as pottery, artworks, furniture, dinnerware, linens, and folk art. **Old Deer Isle Parish House Antiques** (⊠ Rte. 15, ☎ 207/348–9964) is a place for poking around in jumbles of old kitchenware, glassware, books, and linens. **Turtle Gallery** (⊠ Rte. 15, ☎ 207/348–9977) shows contemporary painting and sculpture.

Stonington

③① *7 mi south of Deer Isle.*

Stonington is an emphatically ungentrified community that tolerates summer visitors but makes no effort to cater to them. Main Street holds gift shops and galleries, but this is a working port town—the principal activity is at the waterfront, where fishing boats arrive with the day's catch. At night, the town can be rowdy. The high, sloped island that rises beyond the archipelago known as Merchants Row is Isle au Haut (☞ Isle au Haut, *below*), accessible by mail boat from Stonington, which contains a remote section of Acadia National Park.

Dining and Lodging

$$–$$$ ✕ **The Cafe Atlantic.** Whether you want ice cream, lobster, or a nice meal, you'll find it at this harborfront eatery. Country linens and antiques decorate the restaurant, which serves fresh seafood as well as chicken and steak. For lobster-in-the-rough, head to the deck overhanging the water. For a quick snack, visit the ice cream window. ⊠ *Main St.,* ☎ *207/367–6373. AE, D, MC, V.*

$$–$$$ ⊡ **Inn on the Harbor.** From the front, this inn composed of four 100-year-old Victorian buildings is as plain and unadorned as Stonington itself. But out back it opens up, with an expansive deck over the harbor. Many guests take breakfast here in the morning. Rooms on the harbor side have views, and some have fireplaces and private decks. Those on the street side lack the views and can be noisy at night. ⊠ *Box 69, Main St., 04681,* ☎ *207/367–2420 or 800/942–2420,* 𝔽𝔸𝕏 *207/367–5165. 13 rooms, 1 suite. Espresso bar. Continental breakfast. AE, D, MC, V.*

Shopping

Dockside Books & Gifts (⊠ W. Main St., ☎ 207/367–2652) stocks an eclectic selection of books, crafts, and gifts in a harborfront shop. **Eastern Bay Gallery** (⊠ Main St., ☎ 207/367–5006) carries contemporary Maine crafts; summer exhibits highlight the works of specific artists.

Isle au Haut

③② *14 mi south of Stonington.*

Isle au Haut thrusts its steeply ridged back out of the sea south of Stonington. Accessible only by **passenger mail boat** (☎ 207/367–5193 or 207/367–6516), the island is worth visiting for the ferry ride itself, a half-hour cruise amid the tiny islands of Merchants Row, where you might see terns, guillemots, and harbor seals.

More than half the island is part of **Acadia National Park:** 17½ mi of trails extend through quiet spruce and birch woods, along beaches and seaside cliffs, and over the spine of the central mountain ridge. (For more information on the park, *see* Bar Harbor *and* Acadia National Park *in* Mount Desert Island, *below.*) From mid-June to mid-September, the mail boat docks at **Duck Harbor** within the park. The small campground here, with five Adirondack-type lean-tos, is open from mid-May to mid-October and fills up quickly. Reservations, which are essential, can be made after April 1 by writing to Acadia National Park (⊠ Box 177, Bar Harbor 04609).

Lodging

$$$$ ⊡ **The Keeper's House.** Thick spruce forest surrounds this converted lighthouse-keeper's house on a rock ledge. There is no electricity, but every guest receives a flashlight upon registering; guests dine by candlelight on seafood or chicken and read in the evening by kerosene lantern. Trails link the inn with Acadia National Park's Isle au Haut trail network, and you can walk to the village. The spacious rooms contain simple, painted-wood furniture and local crafts. A separate cottage, the Oil House, has no indoor plumbing. Access to the island is via the mail boat from Stonington. ⊠ *Box 26, Lighthouse Rd., 04645,* ☎ *207/367–2261. 4 rooms share 2 baths, 1 cottage. Dock, bicycles. AP. No credit cards. BYOB. Closed Nov.–Apr.*

Penobscot Bay A to Z

Arriving and Departing

See Arriving and Departing *in* Maine A to Z, *below.*

Getting Around

BY CAR

U.S. 1 follows the west coast of Penobscot Bay, linking Rockland, Rockport, Camden, Belfast, and Searsport. On the east side of the bay, Route 175 (south from U.S. 1) takes you to Route 166A (for Castine) and Route 15 (for Blue Hill, Deer Isle, and Stonington). A car is essential for exploring the bay area.

Contacts and Resources

B&B RESERVATION AGENCY

Camden Accommodations (☎ 207/236–6090 or 800/236–1920, FAX 207/236–6091) provides assistance for reservations in and around Camden.

BOAT TRIPS AND TOURS

See Outdoor Activities and Sports *in* Rockland *and* Camden, *above.*

The **Maine Windjammer Association** (⊠ Box 1144, Blue Hill 04614, ☎ 800/807–9463) represents 12 windjammers.

EMERGENCIES

Blue Hill Memorial Hospital (⊠ Water St., Blue Hill, ☎ 207/374–2836). **Island Medical Center** (⊠ Airport Rd., Stonington, ☎ 207/367–2311). **Penobscot Bay Medical Center** (⊠ U.S. 1, Rockport, ☎ 207/596–8000). **Waldo County General Hospital** (⊠ 56 Northport Ave., Belfast, ☎ 207/338–2500).

VISITOR INFORMATION

Belfast Area Chamber of Commerce (⊠ Box 58, 1 Main St., Belfast 04915, ☎ 207/338–5900). **Blue Hill Chamber of Commerce** (⊠ Box 520, Blue Hill 04614, ☎ no phone). **Castine Town Office** (⊠ Emerson Hall, Court St., Castine 04421, ☎ 207/326–4502). **Deer Isle–Stonington Chamber of Commerce** (⊠ Box 459, Stonington 04681, ☎ 207/348–6124). **Rockland–Thomaston Area Chamber of Commerce** (⊠ Harbor Park, Box 508, Rockland 04841, ☎ 207/596–0376 or 800/562–2529). **Rockport-Camden-Lincolnville Chamber of Commerce** (⊠ Public Landing, Box 919, Camden 04843, ☎ 207/236–4404 or 800/223–5459). **Waldo County Regional Chamber of Commerce** (⊠ School St., Unity 04988, ☎ 207/948–5050 or 800/870–9934).

MOUNT DESERT ISLAND

Acadia is the informal name for the area east of Penobscot Bay that includes Mount Desert Island (pronounced "dessert") as well as Blue Hill Bay and Frenchman Bay. Mount Desert, 13 mi across, is Maine's largest island, and it encompasses most of Acadia National Park, an astonishingly beautiful preserve with rocky cliffs, crashing surf, and serene mountains and ponds. Maine's number one tourist attraction, it draws more than 4 million visitors a year. The 40,000 acres of woods and mountains, lake and shore, footpaths, carriage roads, and hiking trails that make up the park extend to other islands and some of the mainland. Outside the park, on Mount Desert's eastern shore, Bar Harbor has become a busy tourist town. Less commercial and congested are the smaller island towns, such as Southwest Harbor and Northeast Harbor, and the outlying islands.

Bar Harbor

㉝ *160 mi northeast of Portland, 22 mi southeast of Ellsworth on Rte. 3.*

An upper-class resort town in the 19th century, Bar Harbor now serves visitors to Acadia National Park with inns, motels, and restaurants. Most of its grand mansions were destroyed in a fire that devastated the island in 1947, but many surviving estates have been converted into inns and restaurants. Motels abound, yet the town retains the beauty of a commanding location on Frenchman Bay. Shops, restaurants, and hotels are clustered along Main, Mt. Desert, and Cottage streets.

The **Bar Harbor Historical Society Museum** displays photographs of Bar Harbor from the days when it catered to the very rich. Other exhibits document the fire of 1947. ⊠ *33 Ledgelawn Ave.,* ☎ *207/288–3807 or 207/288–0000.* ⌷ *Free.* ☉ *June–Oct., Mon.–Sat. 1–4 or by appointment.*

☾ The small **Natural History Museum** at the College of the Atlantic has wildlife exhibits, a hands-on discovery room, interpretive programs, and a self-guided nature trail. ⊠ *Rte. 3,* ☎ *207/288–5015.* ⌷ *$2.50.* ☉ *Mid-June–Labor Day, Mon.–Sat. 10–5; Labor Day–Columbus Day, Thurs.–Mon. 10–4.*

☾ The **Acadia Zoo** has pastures, streams, and woods that shelter about 45 species of wild and domestic animals, including reindeer, wolves, monkeys, and a moose. A barn has been converted into a rain-forest habitat for monkeys, birds, reptiles, and other Amazon creatures. ⊠ *Rte. 3, Trenton, north of Bar Harbor,* ☎ *207/667–3244.* ⌷ *$6.* ☉ *May–Dec., daily 9:30–dusk.*

On Frenchman Bay but off Mount Desert Island, the 55-acre **Lamoine State Park** (⊠ Rte. 184, Lamoine, ☎ 207/667–4778) has a boat-launching ramp, a fishing pier, a children's playground, and a 61-site campground that's open from mid-May to mid-October.

Dining and Lodging

$$$ ✕ **The Burning Tree.** Fresh is the key word at this casual restaurant just outside town. The menu emphasizes seafood and organic produce and chicken; some typical items are pan-sautéed monkfish, Cajun lobster, crab au gratin, and chicken pot roast. There are always two or three vegetarian choices. Local contemporary art adorns the walls in the two dining rooms and porch. ⊠ *Rte. 3, Otter Creek,* ☎ *207/288–9331. MC, V. Closed Tues. and mid-Oct.–late May.*

$$$ ✕ **George's.** Candles, flowers, and linens grace the tables, and art fills
★ the walls of the four small dining rooms in this old house. The menu's

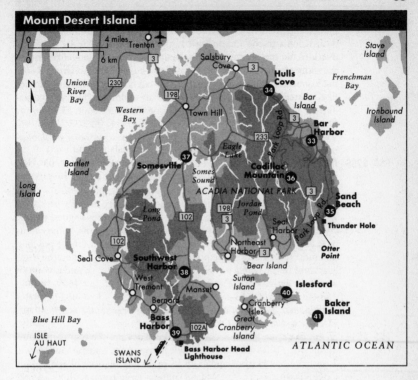

Mediterranean influences can be tasted in the phyllo-wrapped lobster; the lamb and wild-game entrées are superb. The prix-fixe menu includes an appetizer, an entrée, and dessert. Jazz musicians perform nightly in peak season. ⊠ *7 Stephen's La.,* ☎ *207/288–4505. AE, D, DC, MC, V. Closed Nov.–mid-June. No lunch.*

$$$ ✕ **Porcupine Grill.** This restaurant, named for a cluster of islets in Frenchman Bay, has a menu that changes regularly but might include starters such as pan-roasted mussels or citrus barbecued quail and main courses like grilled lobster, twin Portobello fillets, or filet mignon. Soft green walls, antique furnishings, and Villeroy & Boch porcelain create an ambience that complements the cuisine. ⊠ *123 Cottage St.,* ☎ *207/288–3884. AE, MC, V. Closed Sun. and Mar.–Apr.; closed weekdays Oct.–Feb. and May–June. No lunch.*

$$–$$$ ✕ **Café This Way.** Jazz, unmatched tables and chairs, and a few couches provide a relaxing background for the creative, internationally inspired menu at this restaurant tucked in a back street in Bar Harbor. You might begin with crab cakes with tequila-lime sauce and then move on to cashew-crusted chicken over sautéed greens with sesame-ginger aioli or perhaps butternut squash ravioli with roasted red peppers, broccoli, and a rosemary maple cream sauce. Save room for the homemade desserts. ⊠ *14½ Desert St.,* ☎ *207/288–4483. MC, V.*

$–$$$ ✕ **Galyn's.** The upstairs dining rooms at this casual restaurant have a ★ limited view of the harbor, but most people come for the well-crafted dishes and affordable prices. The dinner menu lists fish, chicken, lobster, seafood, beef, and vegetarian dishes. Sandwiches, salads, and entrées like quiche, jambalaya, ribs, and stir-fries are served at lunch. ⊠ *17 Main St.,* ☎ *207/288–9706. AE, D, MC, V.*

$$$–$$$$ ✕🏨 **Bar Harbor Inn.** The roots of this genteel inn date from the 1880s. Rooms are spread out over three buildings on nicely landscaped waterfront property, just a short walk to town. The main inn was completely renovated in 1998. Most rooms have balconies, hot tubs, fireplaces, and great views. The two-level suites are a good choice for families. Rooms in the Oceanfront Lodge offer private decks or patios overlooking the ocean, while those in the Newport Lodge, behind it, are more simply furnished and smaller. The formal waterfront Reading Room serves mostly Continental fare but has some Maine specialties like lobster pie and a scrumptious Indian pudding. The more casual Terrace Grill is an outdoor restaurant on the waterfront. ⊠ *Newport Dr., 04609,* ☎ *207/288–3351 or 800/248–3351,* ℻ *207/288–5296. 153 rooms. 2 restaurants, no-smoking rooms, exercise room, pool, business services. Continental breakfast. AE, D, DC, MC, V.*

$$$–$$$$ ▥ **Balance Rock Inn.** This grand summer cottage built in 1903 commands a prime, secluded location on the water but is only two blocks from downtown. The atmosphere is a bit stuffy, but service is thorough and thoughtful. Rooms are spacious and meticulously furnished with reproduction pieces—four-poster and canopy beds in guest rooms, crystal chandeliers and a grand piano in common rooms. Some rooms have fireplaces, saunas, steam rooms, whirlpool tubs, or private porches, and most have views of the pool and well-tended gardens on the front lawn and to the water beyond. From the bar on the veranda, you can watch the activity in the harbor. ⊠ *21 Albert Meadow, 04609,* ☎ *207/ 288–2610 or 800/753–0494,* ℻ *207/288–5534. 13 rooms, 1 suite, 3 apartments. Bar, pool, exercise room, concierge. Full breakfast. AE, D, MC, V. Closed late Oct.–early May.*

$$$–$$$$ ▥ **Inn at Canoe Point.** Seclusion and privacy are the main attributes
★ of this snug, 100-year-old Tudor-style house on the water at Hulls Cove, 2 mi from Bar Harbor and ¼ mi from Acadia National Park's Hulls Cove Visitor Center. The Master Suite, a large room with a gas fireplace, has French doors that open onto a waterside deck. The inn's living room has huge windows that look out on the water, a granite fireplace, and a waterfront deck where breakfast is served on summer mornings. ⊠ *Box 216, Rte. 3, 04609,* ☎ *207/288–9511,* ℻ *207/ 288–2870. 3 rooms, 2 suites. Full breakfast. D, MC, V.*

$$–$$$$ ▥ **Ullikana.** Inside the stucco-and-timber walls of this traditional Tudor
★ cottage, the riotous decor juxtaposes antiques with contemporary country pieces, vibrant color with French country wallpapers, and abstract art with folk creations. The combination not only works—it shines. Rooms are large, most have at least a glimpse of the water, many have fireplaces, and some have decks. Breakfast is an elaborate multicourse affair. The owners have refurbished the Yellow House across the drive, with an additional six rooms decorated in traditional Old Bar Harbor style. Ullikana is a short walk to downtown shops, yet it's a private location with pretty gardens. ⊠ *16 The Field, 04609,* ☎ *207/288–9552,* ℻ *207/288–3682. 16 rooms. Full breakfast. MC, V. Closed Nov.–May.*

$–$$ ▥ **Bass Cottage in the Field.** What a bargain! Anna Jean Turner began welcoming guests to this former summer estate when she came here as a young girl in 1928. She continues to operate the inn with the help of her niece. Behind Bar Harbor's Main Street and a short walk from the Shore Path, Bass Cottage is a step back in time in both decor and price. The rooms could use a face-lift, but most likely you'll spend your time on the glassed-in wraparound porch, which is furnished with antique white wicker. ⊠ *In the Field, 04609,* ☎ *207/288–3705,* ℻ *207/ 288–2005. 10 rooms, 6 with baths. No credit cards. Closed mid-Oct.– late May.*

Nightlife and the Arts

For dancing, try **Carmen Verandah** (⊠ 119 Main St., upstairs, ☎ 207/ 288–2766). **Geddy's Pub** (⊠ 19 Main St., ☎ 207/288–5077) has live entertainment early in the evening followed by a DJ spinning discs. At the **Lompoc Cafe & Brewpub** (⊠ 30 Rodick St., ☎ 207/288–9513) you can relax in a garden setting and play a game of bocce. You can sink into an easy chair with a pizza and a beer and watch a flick at **Reel Pizza Cinerama** (⊠ 33B Kennebec Pl., ☎ 207/288–3811).

Arcady Music Festival (☎ 207/288–3151) schedules concerts (primarily classical) at locations around Mount Desert Island and at some off-island sites, year-round. **Bar Harbor Music Festival** (⊠ 59 Cottage St., ☎ 207/288–5744) arranges recitals, jazz, chamber music, string-orchestra, and pop concerts by young professionals from July to early August.

Outdoor Activities and Sports

BICYCLING

Acadia Bike & Canoe (⊠ 48 Cottage St., ☎ 207/288–9605) and **Bar Harbor Bicycle Shop** (⊠ 141 Cottage St., ☎ 207/288–3886) rent bicycles.

BOATING AND WHALE-WATCHING

For canoe rentals try **Acadia Bike & Canoe** (☞ Bicycling, *above*). For guided kayak tours, try **National Park Kayak Tours** (⊠ 39 Cottage St., ☎ 207/288–0342) or **Coastal Kayaking Tours** (⊠ 48 Cottage St., ☎ 207/288–9605).

Acadian Whale Watcher (⊠ Golden Anchor Pier, West St., ☎ 207/288–9794 or 800/421–3307) runs 3½-hour whale-watching cruises from June to mid-October. **Downeast Windjammer & Lighthouse Cruises** (⊠ Bar Harbor Inn Pier, ☎ 207/288–4585) offers 1½- to 2-hour tours aboard the four-masted schooner *Margaret Todd* and the historic 1911 fishing schooner *Sylvia W. Beal* between mid-May and October. **Whale Watcher Inc.** (⊠ 1 West St., ☎ 207/288–3322 or 800/508–1499) operates the windjammer *Bay Lady,* the nature-sightseeing cruise vessel *Acadian,* and the 300-passenger *Atlantis* in summer.

Shopping

Bar Harbor in summer is prime territory for browsing for gifts, T-shirts, and novelty items. For bargains, head for the outlets that line Route 3 in Ellsworth, which have good discounts on shoes, sportswear, cookware, and more.

Ben and Bill's Chocolate Emporium (⊠ 66 Main St., ☎ 207/288–3281) is a chocolate lover's nirvana, and the adventurous can try lobster ice cream here. **Birdsnest Gallery** (⊠ 12 Mt. Desert St., ☎ 207/288–4054) sells fine art, paintings, and sculpture. The **Eclipse Gallery** (⊠ 12 Mt. Desert St., ☎ 207/288–9048) carries handblown glass, ceramics, art photography, and wood furniture. **Island Artisans** (⊠ 99 Main St., ☎ 207/288–4214) is a crafts cooperative. The **Lone Moose–Fine Crafts** (⊠ 78 West St., ☎ 207/288–4229) has art glass and works in clay, pottery, wood, and fiberglass.

Acadia National Park

4 mi northwest of Bar Harbor (to Hulls Cove).

There is no one Acadia. The park holds some of the most spectacular and varied scenery on the eastern seaboard: a rugged coastline of surf-pounded granite and an interior graced by sculpted mountains, quiet ponds, and lush deciduous forests. Cadillac Mountain, the highest point of land on the eastern coast, dominates the park. Although it's rugged,

★ **Acadia National Park** is also a land of graceful stone bridges, horse-drawn carriages, and the elegant Jordan Point Tea House. The 27-mi Park Loop Road provides an excellent introduction, yet to truly appreciate the park you must get off the main road and experience it by walking or taking a carriage ride on the carriage trails, by hiking or perhaps sea kayaking. If you get off the beaten path, you'll find places in the park that you can have practically to yourself, despite the millions of visitors who descend in summer.

㉞ The popular **Hulls Cove** approach to Acadia National Park, northwest of Bar Harbor on Route 3, brings you to the start of the **Park Loop Road**. Even though it is often clogged with traffic in summer, the road provides the best introduction to the park. You can drive it in an hour, but allow at least half a day or more to explore the many sites along the route. At the start of the loop, the **visitor center** shows a free 15-minute orientation film. Also available at the center are the *Acadia Beaver Log* (the park's free newspaper detailing guided hikes and other ranger-led programs), books, maps of hiking trails and carriage roads, the schedule for naturalist-led tours, and cassettes for drive-it-yourself tours. Traveling south on the Park Loop Road, you'll reach a small ticket booth where you pay the $10-per-vehicle entrance fee, good for seven consecutive days. Take the next left to the parking area for Sand Beach. ⊠ *Visitor center, Park Loop Rd. off Rte. 3,* ☎ *207/288–3338.* ☉ *Park daily. Visitor center late June–Aug., daily 8–6; mid-Apr.–mid-June and Sept.–Oct., daily 8–4:30.*

㉟ **Sand Beach** is a small stretch of pink sand backed by the mountains of Acadia and the odd lump of rock known as the Beehive. The **Ocean Trail,** which runs alongside the Park Loop Road from Sand Beach to the Otter Point parking area, is an easily accessible walk with some of the most spectacular scenery in Maine: huge slabs of pink granite heaped at the ocean's edge, ocean views unobstructed to the horizon, and **Thunder Hole,** a natural seaside cave into which the ocean rushes and roars.

★ ㊱ **Cadillac Mountain,** at 1,532 ft, is the highest point on the eastern seaboard. From the smooth, bald summit you have an awesome 360-degree view of the ocean, islands, jagged coastline, and woods and lakes of Acadia and its surroundings. You can drive or hike to the summit.

The Sieur de Monts Spring exit off the Park Loop offers two enticing sites. The **Abbé Museum** holds a treasure trove of Maine's Native American history, including arrowheads, moccasins, tools, jewelry, and a well-documented collection of baskets. A new museum, planned for downtown Bar Harbor, will open in 2000 or 2001. ⊠ *Sieur de Mont Spring exit from Rte. 3 or Acadia National Park Loop Rd.,* ☎ *207/288–3519.* 🎟 *$2.* ☉ *July–Aug., daily 9–5; mid-May–June and Sept.–mid-Oct., daily 10–4.*

The **Wild Gardens of Acadia** present a miniature view of the plants that grow on Mt. Desert Island. ⊠ *Rte. 3 at the Sieur de Mont Spring exit,* ☎ *207/288–3400.* 🎟 *Free.* ☉ *Paths 24 hrs.*

Dining and Lodging

$$–$$$ ✕ **Jordan Pond House.** The restaurant's setting overlooking Jordan Pond is magnificent and serene, but the loudspeaker blaring out the names of parties to be seated is jarring. Come for tea and the oversize popovers with homemade strawberry jam and ice cream, a century-old tradition. If you choose to sit on the terrace or lawn, be forewarned that bees are more than a nuisance. The menu offers lunch and dinner items, including lobster stew, but these get mixed reviews. ⊠ *Park Loop Rd.,* ☎ *207/276–3316. AE, D, MC, V. Closed late Oct.–mid-May.*

$ △ **Blackwoods and Seawall.** These two campgrounds with a total of 530 campsites fill up quickly during the summer. Space at Seawall is allocated on a first-come, first-served basis, starting at 8 AM. Between mid-June and mid-September, reserve a Blackwoods site within five months of a visit. No reservations are required in the off-season. *Blackwoods:* ⊠ *Rte. 3, Northeast Harbor,* ☎ *800/365–2267.* ☉ *Year-round.*

*Seawall: ⊠ Rte. 102A, Northeast Harbor, ☎ 207/244–3600. Closed
late Sept.–late May.*

Outdoor Activities and Sports

BIKING

The carriage roads that wind through the woods and fields of Acadia
National Park are ideal for biking (☞ Bar Harbor for rentals) and jog-
ging when the ground is dry and for cross-country skiing in winter. The
Hulls Cove visitor center has maps.

CARRIAGE RIDES

Wildwood Stables (⊠ Park Loop Rd., near Jordan Pond House, ☎
207/276–3622) gives romantic tours in horse-drawn carriages on the
51-mi network of carriage roads designed and built by philanthropist
John D. Rockefeller, Jr. There are three two-hour trips and three one-
hour trips daily, including a "tea-and-popover ride" that stops at Jordan Pond House (☞ Dining and Lodging, *above*) and a sunset ride to
the summit of Day Mountain.

HIKING

Acadia National Park maintains nearly 200 mi of foot and carriage
paths, from easy strolls along flatlands to rigorous climbs that involve
ladders and handholds on rock faces. Among the more rewarding
hikes are the Precipice Trail to Champlain Mountain, the Great Head
Loop, the Gorham Mountain Trail, and the path around Eagle Lake.
The Hulls Cove visitor center has trail guides and maps and will help
you match a trail with your interests and abilities.

Around Acadia

On completing the 27-mi Park Loop Road, you can continue an auto
tour of the island by heading west on Route 233 for the villages on
Somes Sound, a true fjord—the only one on the East Coast—which
③⑦ almost bisects Mount Desert Island. **Somesville,** the oldest settlement
on the island (1621), is a carefully preserved New England village of
white clapboard houses and churches, neat green lawns, and bits of
blue water visible behind them.

③⑧ **Southwest Harbor,** south from Somesville on Route 102, combines the
salty character of a working port with the refinements of a summer
resort community. From the town's Main Street (Route 102), turn left
onto Clark Point Road to reach the harbor.

☾ **Mount Desert Oceanarium** has exhibits in two locations on the fishing
and sea life of the Gulf of Maine, a live-seal program, a lobster hatch-
ery, and hands-on exhibits such as a touch tank. *⊠ Clark Point Rd.,
Southwest Harbor, ☎ 207/244–7330; ⊠ Rte. 3, Thomas Bay, Bar Harbor, ☎ 207/288–5005. ⊞ Call for admission fees (combination tickets available for both sites). ☉ Mid-May–mid-Oct., Mon.–Sat. 9–5.*

Wendell Gilley Museum of Bird Carving showcases bird carvings by Gilley,
presents carving demonstrations and workshops and natural-history programs, and exhibits wildlife art. *⊠ 4 Herrick Rd., Southwest Harbor,
☎ 207/244–7555. ⊞ $3.25. ☉ July–Aug., Tues.–Sun. 10–5; June and
Sept.–Oct., Tues.–Sun. 10–4; May and Nov.–Dec., Fri.–Sun. 10–4.*

③⑨ In **Bass Harbor,** 4 mi south of Southwest Harbor (follow Route 102A
when Route 102 forks), visit the **Bass Harbor Head lighthouse,** which
clings to a cliff at the eastern entrance to Blue Hill Bay. It was built in
1858. The tiny lobstering village has cottages for rent, inns, a restaurant, and a gift shop. Also here is the **Maine State Ferry Service**'s car-
and-passenger ferry (☎ 207/244–3254) to Swans Island. The ferry has
six daily runs June to mid-October, fewer the rest of the year.

Dining and Lodging

$–$$ ✕ **Beal's Lobster Pier.** You can watch lobstermen bringing in their catch at this working lobster pound, where you can order lobster at one take-out window, fried foods, burgers, and dessert at another. ⊠ *End of Clark Point Rd., Southwest Harbor,* ☎ *207/244–3202 or 207/244–7178 or 800/245–7178. Closed mid-Oct.–mid-May.*

$–$$ ✕ **Keenan's.** Come early, and don't be put off by the exterior of this shack housing a casual restaurant; the food is considered among the best on the island. Specialties are seafood gumbo, shrimp étouffée, and baby back ribs. Children can order burgers. ⊠ *Corner of Rte. 102A and Flatiron Rd., Bass Harbor,* ☎ *207/244–3403. Reservations not accepted. No credit cards. No lunch.*

$$–$$$$ ✕🖫 **Claremont Hotel.** Built in 1884 and operated continuously as an inn, the Claremont calls up memories of the long, leisurely vacations of days gone by. The yellow clapboard structure commands a view of Somes Sound. Croquet is played on the lawn, and cocktails and lunch are served at the Boat House in summer. The cottages have not been updated as much as the inn's rooms; some guests complain about the facilities in them. The old-style dining room ($$$), open to the public for breakfast and dinner, has picture windows overlooking the sound. The menu changes weekly and always includes fresh fish and at least one vegetarian entrée; reservations are essential, and a jacket is required for dinner. ⊠ *off Clark Point Rd., Box 137, Southwest Harbor 04679,* ☎ *207/244–5036 or 800/244–5036,* ℻ *207/244–3512. 29 rooms, 1 suite, 13 cottages. Restaurant, tennis court, croquet, dock, boating, bicycles. Full breakfast; MAP available. No credit cards. Hotel and restaurant closed mid-Oct.–mid-June; cottages closed Nov.–mid-May.*

$$ 🖫 **Island House.** This sweet B&B on the quiet side of the island has four simple and bright rooms in the main house. The carriage-house suite comes complete with a sleeping loft and a kitchenette. ⊠ *Box 1006, 121 Clark Point Rd., Southwest Harbor 04679,* ☎ *207/244–5180. 4 rooms, 1 suite. Full breakfast. MC, V.*

$–$$ 🖫 **The Moorings Inn & Cottages.** Nothing is fancy here except the jaw-dropping view of Somes Sound. The roots of the Maine House date back to the late 18th century; the cottages and a small motel are more recent. Rooms in the Maine House are decorated with antiques and country charm; the motel rooms lack the atmosphere but have sliding glass doors onto decks. The homey cottage rooms offer the most privacy and have cooking facilities. Lookout Front has a fireplace, screened porch, and king-size bed. ⊠ *Box 744, 135 Shore Rd., Manset 04679,* ☎ *207/244–5523, 207/244–3210, or 800/596–5523. 13 rooms, 5 cottages, 1 apartment. Dock. Continental breakfast. No credit cards. Closed late Oct.–late Apr.*

Nightlife and the Arts

A lively boating crowd frequents the lounge at the **Moorings Restaurant** (⊠ Shore Rd., Manset, ☎ 207/244–7070), which is accessible by boat and car. The lounge stays open until after midnight from mid-May to October.

Outdoor Activities and Sports

BICYCLING

Southwest Cycle (⊠ Main St., Southwest Harbor, ☎ 207/244–5856) rents bicycles.

BOATING

Manset Yacht Service (⊠ Shore Rd., Manset, ☎ 207/244–4040) rents power boats and sailboats. **National Park Canoe Rentals** (⊠ Pretty Marsh Rd., Somesville, at the head of Long Pond, ☎ 207/244–5854) rents canoes.

The *Rachel B. Jackson* (⊠ Manset Town Wharf, Manset, ☎ 207/244–7813), a Maine-built windjammer, takes passengers on 2½-hour sails around Somes Sound and the Cranberry Isles.

Shopping

E. L. Higgins (⊠ Bernard Rd., off Rte. 102, Bernard, ☎ 207/244–3983) carries antique wicker as well as antique furniture and glassware. **Marianne Clark Fine Antiques** (⊠ Main St., Southwest Harbor, ☎ 207/244–9247) has formal and country furniture, American paintings, and accessories from the 18th and 19th centuries. **Port in a Storm Bookstore** (⊠ Main St., Somesville, ☎ 207/244–4114) is a book lover's nirvana.

Excursions to the Cranberry Isles

Off the southeast shore of Mount Desert Island at the entrance to Somes Sound, the five Cranberry Isles—Great Cranberry, Islesford (or Little Cranberry), Baker Island, Sutton Island, and Bear Island—escape the hubbub that engulfs Acadia National Park in summer. Great Cranberry and Islesford are served by the **Beal & Bunker passenger ferry** (☎ 207/244–3575) from Northeast Harbor and by **Cranberry Cove Boating Company** (☎ 207/244–5882) from Southwest Harbor. Baker Island is reached by the summer cruise boats of the **Islesford Ferry Company** (☎ 207/276–3717) from Northeast Harbor; Sutton and Bear islands are privately owned.

40 **Islesford** comes closest to having a village: a collection of houses, a church, a fishermen's co-op, a market, and a post office near the ferry dock.

The **Islesford Historical Museum,** run by Acadia National Park, has displays of tools, documents relating to the island's history, and books and manuscripts of the poet Rachel Field (1894–1942), who summered on Sutton Island. ⊠ *Isleford,* ☎ *207/288–3338.* ⊡ *Free.* ☉ *Mid-June–late Sept., daily 10:30–noon and 12:30–4:30.*

41 The 123-acre **Baker Island,** the most remote of the Cranberry Isles, looks almost black from a distance because of its thick spruce forest. The Islesford Ferry cruise boat from Northeast Harbor conducts a 4½-hour narrated tour, during which you are likely to see ospreys nesting on a sea stack off Sutton Island, harbor seals basking on ledges, and cormorants flying low over the water. Because Baker Island has no natural harbor, the boat ties up offshore, and you take a fishing dory to get to shore.

Mount Desert Island A to Z

Arriving and Departing

See Arriving and Departing *in* Maine A to Z, *below.*

Getting Around

BY CAR

North of Bar Harbor, the scenic 27-mi Park Loop Road leaves Route 3 to circle the eastern quarter of Mount Desert Island, with one-way traffic from Sieur de Monts Spring to Seal Harbor and two-way traffic between Seal Harbor and Hulls Cove. Route 102, which serves the western half of Mount Desert, is reached from Route 3 just after it enters the island or from Route 233 west from Bar Harbor. All these island roads pass through the precincts of Acadia National Park.

Contacts and Resources

CAR RENTAL

Avis (⊠ Bangor International Airport, 299 Godfrey Blvd., ☎ 207/947–8383 or 800/331–1212). **Budget** (⊠ Hancock County Airport, Rte. 3,

Trenton, ☎ 207/667–1200 or 800/527–0700). **Hertz** (✉ Bangor International Airport, 299 Godfrey Blvd., ☎ 207/942–5519 or 800/654–3131). **Thrifty** (✉ Bangor International Airport, 357 Odlin Rd., ☎ 207/942–6400 or 800/367–2277).

EMERGENCIES

Mount Desert Island Hospital (✉ 10 Wayman La., Bar Harbor, ☎ 207/288–5081). **Maine Coast Memorial Hospital** (✉ 50 Union St., Ellsworth, ☎ 207/667–5311). **Southwest Harbor Medical Center** (✉ Herrick Rd., Southwest Harbor, ☎ 207/244–5513).

GUIDED TOURS

Bar Harbor Taxi and Tours (☎ 207/288–4020) conducts half-day historic and scenic tours of the area. **National Park Tours** (☎ 207/288–3327) operates a 2½-hour bus tour of Acadia National Park, narrated by a naturalist. The bus departs twice daily, from May to October, across from Testa's Restaurant at Bayside Landing on Main Street in Bar Harbor.

Acadia Air (☎ 207/667–5534), on Route 3 in Trenton, between Ellsworth and Bar Harbor at Hancock County Airport, rents aircraft and flies seven aerial sightseeing routes, from spring to fall.

VISITOR INFORMATION

Acadia National Park (✉ Box 177, Bar Harbor 04609, ☎ 207/288–3338). **Bar Harbor Chamber of Commerce** (✉ 93 Cottage St., Box 158, Bar Harbor 04609, ☎ 207/288–3393, 207/288–5103, or 800/288–5103). **Southwest Harbor/Tremont Chamber of Commerce** (✉ Box 1143, Main St., Southwest Harbor 04679, ☎ 207/244–9264 or 207/423–9264).

WAY DOWN EAST

East of Ellsworth on U.S. 1 is a different Maine, a place pretty much off the beaten path that seduces with a rugged, simple beauty. Red-hued blueberry barrens dot the landscape, and scraggly jack pines hug the highly accessible shoreline. The quiet pleasures here include hiking, birding, and going on whale-watching and puffin cruises. Many artists live in the region; you can often purchase works directly from them.

Hancock

㊷ *9 mi east of Ellsworth.*

As you approach the small town of Hancock and the summer colony of cottages at Hancock Point, stunning views await, especially at sunset, over Frenchman Bay toward Mt. Desert.

Dining and Lodging

$$$ ✕🏠 **Le Domaine.** Owner-chef Nicole L. Purslow whips up classic haute cuisine, the perfect accompaniments to which can be found amid the more than 40,000 bottles of French wine in the restaurant's cellar. Le Domaine is known primarily for its food, but its small French-country-style guest rooms are also inviting. Ask for a room in the rear, overlooking the lawns and gardens and away from the noise of U.S. 1. ✉ *HC 77, Box 496, U.S. 1, 04640, ☎ 207/422–3395 or 800/554–8498, FAX 207/422–2316. 7 rooms. Restaurant, hiking. Full breakfast; MAP available. AE, D, MC, V. Closed late Oct.–mid-May.*

$$–$$$ ✕🏠 **Crocker House Inn.** Set amid tall fir trees, this century-old shingle-style cottage is a mere 200 yards from the water and holds comfortable rooms decorated with antiques and country furnishings. The accommodations in the Carriage House, which also has a TV room

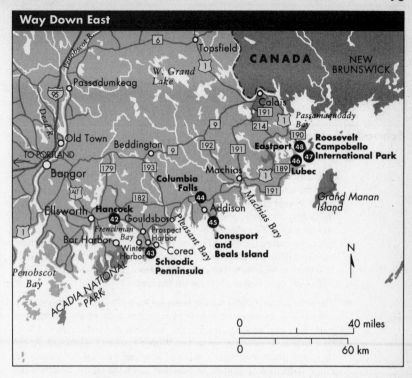

and a hot tub, are best for families. The inn's dining room draws Maine residents from as far away as Bar Harbor for meals that might include poached salmon or rack of lamb. ⊠ *HC 77, Box 171, Hancock Point Rd., 04640,* ☎ *207/422–6806,* ℻ *207/422–3105. 11 rooms. Restaurant, hot tub, bicycles. Full breakfast; MAP available. AE, D, MC, V.*

\$\$ 🏠 **Island View Inn.** Noted Maine architect John Calvin Stevens is rumored to have designed this waterfront shingle-style cottage, which has a wraparound porch and views of Frenchman's Bay and Cadillac Mountain. All the rooms have decks, but the nicest (and quietest) accommodations are in the rear. ⊠ *HC 32, Box 24, U.S. 1, Sullivan Harbor, 04664,* ☎ *207/422–3031. 6 rooms. Beach, boating. Full breakfast. D, MC, V. Closed mid-Oct.–late May.*

\$\$ 🏠 **Sullivan Harbor Farm.** Antiques and country pieces decorate this simple bed-and-breakfast in an 1829 farmhouse built by Captain James Urann, a shipbuilder who launched his boats across the road. The house, set well back from the road, has nice views of Frenchman Bay and Mount Desert Island. You can relax on the pretty grounds or take a canoe or kayak to the cove across the way. Even if you don't stay here, stop by to purchase some of the award-winning salmon cold-smoked here in the traditional Scottish manner. ⊠ *Box 96, U.S. 1, 04664,* ☎ *207/422–3735 or 800/422–4014,* ℻ *207/422–8229. 4 rooms, 3 with bath; 2 cottages available by week. Boating. Full breakfast. D, MC, V. Closed late Oct.–May.*

Nightlife and the Arts

Pierre Monteux School for Conductors (⊠ Off U.S. 1, ☎ 207/422–3931) presents orchestral and chamber concerts from mid-June through July. The **Monteux Opera Festival** (⊠ Off U.S. 1, ☎ 207/422–3931) stages works in the Forest Studio of the Pierre Monteux Memorial Foundation from mid-July to mid-August.

Shopping

Hog Bay Pottery (⊠ Rte. 200, Franklin, ☏ 207/565–2282) sells pottery by Charles Grosjean and handwoven rugs by Susanne Grosjean. **Spring Woods Gallery** (⊠ Rte. 200, Sullivan, ☏ 207/422–3006) carries contemporary art by Paul and Ann Breeden and other artists, as well as Native American pottery, jewelry, and instruments. The sculpture garden is a delight. **Sugar Hill Gallery** (⊠ U.S. 1, ☏ 207/422–8207) offers high-quality Maine crafts.

Schoodic Peninsula

㊸ *23 mi southeast of Hancock; 32 mi east of Ellsworth.*

The landscape of the Schoodic Peninsula makes it easy to understand why the overflow from Bar Harbor's wealthy summer population settled in Winter Harbor: the views over Frenchman's Bay to Mount Desert, the craggy coastline, and the towering evergreens. A drive through the community of Grindstone Neck shows what Bar Harbor might have been like before the Great Fire of 1947. Artists and craftspeople have opened galleries in and around Winter Harbor, to which no visit would be complete without a stop at **Gerrish's Store** (⊠ Main St. ☏ 207/963–5575), an old-fashioned ice cream counter.

★ The Schoodic section of **Acadia National Park** (⊠ Off Rte. 186, ☏ 207/288–3338), 2 mi east of Winter Harbor, has a scenic 6½-mi one-way loop that edges around the tip of the peninsula and yields views of Winter Harbor, Grindstone Neck, and Winter Harbor Lighthouse. At the tip of the point, you'll get a sense of how unforgiving the sea can be: Huge slabs of pink granite lie jumbled along the shore, thrashed unmercifully by the crashing surf, and jack pines cling to life amid the rocks. The Fraser Point Day-Use Area at the beginning of the loop is an ideal place for a picnic. Work off your lunch with a hike up Schoodic Head for the panoramic views up and down the coast. Admission is free, but there is no visitor center here.

Prospect Harbor, on Route 186 northeast of Winter Harbor, is a small fishing village nearly untouched by tourism. There's little to do in **Corea**, at the tip of Route 195, other than watch the fishermen at work, pick your way over stone beaches, or gaze out to sea—and that's what makes it so special.

Dining and Lodging

$$$ ✕ **Kitchen Garden.** This restaurant just off U.S. 1 in an old Cape-style house is a wonderful surprise. The six-course, fixed-price menu emphasizes organic foods, home-grown produce, and Jamaican specialties. Bring your own wine or beer. ⊠ *335 Village Rd., Steuben,* ☏ *207/546–2708. Reservations essential. No credit cards. Closed Mon.–Tues. June–Nov., and Sun.–Thurs. in winter.*

$$–$$$ ✕ **Fisherman's Inn.** The wide-ranging menu at the two pine-panel dining rooms here includes straightforward seafood, Italian, and beef dishes. Service can be frightfully slow. ⊠ *7 Newman St., Winter Harbor,* ☏ *207/963–5585. AE, D, MC, V. Closed Nov.–Mar.*

$–$$ ✕ **West Bay Lobsters in the Rough.** Lobsters, steamers, corn-on-the-cob, coleslaw, baked beans, and homemade blueberry pie are among the offerings here. Eat at picnic tables or picnic on nearby Schoodic Point. ⊠ *Rte. 186, Prospect Harbor,* ☏ *207/963–7021. AE, D, DC, MC, V. Closed Nov.–May.*

$$$ ▥ **Oceanside Meadows.** Inspired by the ocean out the front door; fields, ★ woods, and a salt marsh out back; and moose, eagles and other wildlife, the owners have created an environmental center here with lectures, musical performances, and other events held weekly in the barn.

Rooms, furnished with antiques, country pieces, and family treasures, are spread out among two white clapboard buildings, and many have ocean views. Breakfast is an extravagant multicourse affair. In the off-season, the inn is open by special arrangement. ⊠ *Box 90, Rte. 195/ Corea Rd., Prospect Harbor 04669,* ☎ *207/963–5557,* ☎ *207/963– 5928. 13 rooms, 1 suite. No-smoking rooms, croquet, horseshoes, hiking, beach. Full breakfast. MC, V. Closed Nov.–Apr.*

$$ ☷ **Black Duck.** This small bed-and-breakfast has comfortable public areas and guest rooms. Two tiny cottages perch on the harbor. ⊠ *Crowley Island Rd., Corea 04624,* ☎ *207/963–2689,* ☎ *207/963–7495. 4 rooms, 2 with bath; 2 cottages. MC, V.*

$ ☷ **The Pines.** The rooms may be small and undistinguished, but this motel's location, right at the beginning of the Schoodic Point Loop, makes it a good value. Six units have kitchenettes. ⊠ *Rte. 186, 04693,* ☎ *207/963–2296. 3 rooms, 4 cottages, 2 cabins. Snack bar. MC, V.*

Outdoor Activities and Sports
Moose Look Guide Service (⊠ Rte. 186, Gouldsboro, ☎ 207/963–7720) provides kayak tours and rentals, rowboat and canoe rentals, and bike rentals and conducts guided fishing trips.

Shopping
The wines sold at the **Bartlett Maine Estate Winery** (⊠ off Rte. 1, Gouldsboro, ☎ 207/546–2408) are produced from locally grown apples, pears, blueberries, and other fruit. The **Harbor Shop** (⊠ Newman St., Winter Harbor, ☎ 207/963–4117) has handmade gifts by American artisans. **Lee Art Glass Studio** (⊠ Main St., Winter Harbor, ☎ 207/ 963–7004) carries fused-glass tableware and other items. Whimsical and serious metal sculptures can be found at **McDavid Sculpture** (⊠ 177 Main St., Winter Harbor, ☎ 207/963–5990). **Pyramid Glass** (⊠ Rte. 186, South Gouldsboro, ☎ 207/963–2027) sells stained-glass artwork and mosaics. **U.S. Bells** (⊠ Rte. 186, Prospect Harbor, ☎ 207/ 963–7184) carries hand-cast bronze wind and door bells.

Columbia Falls

④ *41 mi east of Ellsworth, 78 mi west of Calais.*

Columbia Falls, founded in the late 18th century, is a small, pretty village on the Pleasant River.

★ Judge Thomas Ruggles, a wealthy lumber dealer, store owner, postmaster, and Justice of the Court of Sessions, built **Ruggles House** in 1818. The house's distinctive Federal architecture, flying staircase, Palladian window, and woodwork—supposedly crafted over a period of three years by one man with a penknife—are worth making the ¼-mi detour off U.S. 1. ⊠ *Main St.,* ☎ *no phone.* ☷ *Donation requested.* ☉ *June 1– Oct. 15, weekdays 9:30–4:30, Sun. 11–4:30.*

Lodging
$ ☷ **Pleasant Bay Inn and Llama Keep.** This Cape-style inn takes advantage of its riverfront location. You can stroll the nature paths on the property, which winds around a peninsula and out to Pleasant Bay, and you can even take a llama with you for company. The rooms, all with water views, are decorated with antiques and have country touches. ⊠ *Box 222, West Side Rd., Addison 04606,* ☎ *207/483–4490. 3 rooms, 1 with bath. Full breakfast. MC, V.*

Shopping
Columbia Falls Pottery (⊠ Main St., ☎ 207/483–4075) stocks stoneware and a sampling of Maine foods.

Jonesport and Beals Island

㊺ *12 mi south of Columbia Falls, 20 mi southwest of Machias.*

Jonesport and Beals Island, two fishing communities joined by a bridge over the harbor, are less polished than the towns on the Schoodic Peninsula (☞ *above*). The birding here is superb.

Norton of Jonesport (☎ 207/497–5933) takes passengers on day trips to Machias Seal Island, where there's a large puffin colony.

Great Wass Island Preserve (☎ 207/729–5181) a 1,540-acre nature conservancy at the tip of Beals Island, protects rare plants, stunted pines, and raised peat bogs. Trails lead through the woods and emerge onto the undeveloped, raw coast, where you can make your way along the rocks and boulders before retreating into the forest. To get to the preserve from Jonesport, cross the bridge over Moosabec Reach to Beals Island. Go through Beals to Great Wass Island. Follow the road, which eventually becomes unpaved, to Black Duck Cove, about 3 mi from Beals, where there is a parking area on the left. Admission is free.

Dining and Lodging

$$ ✕ **Seafarer's Wife and Old Salt Room.** These two restaurants share a central kitchen. Allow at least a couple of hours to dine at the Seafarer's Wife, where a five-course meal (hors d'oeuvres, soup, salad, entrée, and dessert) is presented at a leisurely pace in a candlelighted dining room. The casual Old Salt Room, open for lunch and dinner, specializes in fresh fish and seafood. Bring your own wine—neither restaurant has a liquor license. ⊠ *Rte. 187, Jonesport,* ☎ *207/497–2365. MC, V. No lunch at the Seafarer's Wife.*

$$ ✕🏠 **Harbor House.** The first floor of this three-story waterfront building houses an antiques shop and a lobster-in-the-rough restaurant ($–$$; closed late October–April). You can eat on the porch overlooking the water or on picnic tables on the lawn. Upstairs, two rooms face the water. ⊠ *Box 468, Sawyer Sq., Jonesport 04649,* ☎ *207/497–5417,* FAX *207/497–3211. 2 rooms. Restaurant, no-smoking rooms. Full breakfast. MC, V.*

$ 🏠 **Raspberry Shores.** This comfortably furnished Victorian sits on Main Street, but its backyard slopes down to a small beach on Jonesport Harbor. Rooms in the back of the house share the view, but the nicest room is in the turret and right on the road, which can be noisy. ⊠ *Box 217, Rte. 187, Jonesport 04649,* ☎ *207/497–2463. 3 rooms without bath. Beach. Full breakfast. MC, V. Closed Nov.–Apr.*

Lubec

㊻ *28 mi east of Machias.*

Lubec is the first town in the United States to see the sunrise. Once a thriving shipbuilding and sardine packing site, it now attracts residents and visitors with its rural beauty.

★ **Quoddy Head State Park,** the easternmost point of land in the United States, is marked by candy-striped West Quoddy Head Light. The mystical, magical, 2-mi path along the cliffs here yields magnificent views of Canada's Grand Manan island. Whales can often be sighted offshore. The 483-acre park has a picnic area. ⊠ *S. Lubec Rd. off Rte. 189,* ☎ *no phone.* 🎫 *$1 donation requested.* ☉ *Memorial Day–mid-Oct., daily 8 AM–sunset; Apr.–early May and mid-Oct.–Dec., weekends 9 AM–sunset.*

㊼ **Roosevelt Campobello International Park,** a joint project of the American and Canadian governments, has hiking trails and history. It can be reached by land only by crossing the International Bridge from Lubec. Stop at the information booth for an update on tides—specifically, when you will be able to walk out to East Quoddy Head Lighthouse—as well as details on walking and hiking trails. Keep in mind that once you've crossed the bridge, you're in the Atlantic time zone. Neatly manicured, preening itself in the bay, Campobello Island has always had a special appeal to the wealthy and the famous. It was here that the Roosevelt family spent its summers. The 34-room **Roosevelt Cottage**, which is open for touring, was presented to Eleanor and Franklin as a wedding gift. ✉ *Rte. 774, Welshpool, Campobello Island, New Brunswick, Canada,* ☎ *506/752–2922.* 🎫 *Free.* ☉ *House mid-May–mid-Oct., daily 10–6; grounds daily.*

Dining and Lodging

$–$$ ✗🏨 **Home Port Inn.** The grandest accommodations in Lubec are in this 1880 Colonial atop a hill. The spacious rooms, some with water views, are furnished with antiques and family pieces. The large living room has a fireplace and a television, and there are two sitting areas. The dining room ($$), the best in town, is open to the public for dinner. The menu emphasizes seafood. ✉ *45 Main St., 04652,* ☎ *207/733–2077 or 800/457–2077. 7 rooms. Restaurant. Continental breakfast. D, MC, V. Closed mid-Oct.–late-May.*

$–$$ 🏨 **Peacock House.** Four generations of the Peacock family lived in this 1860 Victorian before it was converted into an inn. The Maine hospitality of owners Chet and Veda Childs comes with a southern accent. A few of the simply furnished rooms have water views through lace-curtained windows; rooms on the first floor have air-conditioning. ✉ *27 Summer St., 04652,* ☎ 📠 *207/733–2403. 5 rooms. Full breakfast. MC, V. Closed mid-Oct.–mid-May.*

$ 🏨 **Bayviews.** This unfussy waterfront B&B welcomes families and musicians; there are pianos in the living room and one guest room. Some rooms have water views. ✉ *6 Monument St., 04652,* ☎ *207/733–2181. 4 rooms, 1 with bath; 1 suite. Continental breakfast. No credit cards. Closed Oct.–June.*

Outdoor Activities and Sports

East Coast Charters (✉ Peacock Canning, 72 Water St., ☎ 800/853–3999) operates whale-watching trips and sea-kayaking tours.

En Route The road to Eastport leads through the Pleasant Point Indian Reservation, where the **Waponahki Museum and Resource Center** explains the culture of the Passamaquoddy, or "People of the Dawn." Tools, baskets, beaded artifacts, historic photos, and arts and crafts are displayed. ✉ *Rte. 190, Perry,* ☎ *207/853–4001.* 🎫 *Free.* ☉ *Weekdays 8:30–11 and noon–4.*

Eastport

48 *39 mi from Lubec, 102 mi east of Ellsworth.*

The town of Eastport is actually a small island, connected to the mainland by a granite causeway. In the late 19th century, 14 sardine canneries operated in Eastport. The decline of that industry in the 20th century has left the city economically depressed, though a new port facility, growing aquaculture, and an increase in tourism bode well for the future. From the waterfront, you can take a ferry to Deer Island and Campobello.

The **National Historic Waterfront District** extends from the Customs House, down Water Street to Bank Square and the Peavey Library. Pick up a walking map at the **Chamber of Commerce** (✉ 78 Water St., ☎ 207/853–4644) and wander through streets lined with historic homes

and buildings. You can also take the waterfront walkway to watch the
fishing boats and freighters. The tides fluctuate as much as 28 ft,
which explains the ladders and steep gangways necessary to access boats.

Raye's Mustard Mill is the only remaining mill in the U.S. producing
stone-ground mustard. Historically, this mill served the sardine-pack-
ing industry. You can purchase mustards made on the premises at the
mill's Pantry Store; local crafts are also for sale. ⊠ *85 Washington St.,*
☎ *207/853–4451 or 800/853–1903.* ⊠ *Free.* ☉ *Jan.–Mar., weekdays
8–5; Apr.–Dec., daily 10–5. Tours on the hr Memorial Day–Labor Day;
rest of year subject to guide availability.*

The short hike to **Shakford Head** (⊠ Behind Washington County
Technical College on Deep Cove Rd.) affords views over Passamaquoddy
Bay to Campobello. From here you can see the pens for Eastport's growing salmon-farming industry as well as the construction site of the new
port facility.

Cobscook Bay State Park is one of Maine's prettiest and least- crowded
parks. More than 200 species of birds, including the American bald
eagle, have been identified in and around the park, which has picnic
grounds, a playground, a nature trail, and campsites ($12–$16) with
showers. ⊠ *RR1 off Rte. 1, Dennysville,* ☎ *207/726–4412.* ⊠ *$1.* ☉
Mid-May–mid-Oct.

Dining and Lodging

$$–$$$ ✕ **Eastport Lobster and Fish.** Fish and seafood don't come much fresher
than they do at this restaurant, where the lobsters weigh as much as
2½ pounds. You can eat in the dining room, the downstairs pub, or
out on the dock. Service can be frustratingly slow. ⊠ *167 Water St.,*
☎ *207/853–9669. MC, V. Call ahead Oct.–mid-May.*

$–$$ ✕ **La Sardina Loca.** Bright lights and Christmas decorations are among
the festive touches at the easternmost Mexican restaurant in the United
States. ⊠ *28 Water St.,* ☎ *207/853–2739. MC, V. Closed Mon. No
lunch.*

$$ ☗ **Motel East.** Rooms at this waterfront motel are spacious; many
have kitchenettes, and most have private balconies overlooking the water.
⊠ *23A Water St., 04631,* ☎ ℻ *207/853–4747. 14 rooms, 1 cottage.
AE, D, DC, MC, V.*

$–$$ ☗ **Brewer House.** In 1827, Captain John Nehemiah Marks Brewer built
an ornate Greek Revival house across from one of his shipyards. Now
a B&B, the house, which is on the National Register of Historic Places,
is distinguished by details like carved Grecian moldings, Ionic pilasters,
marble fireplaces, silver doorknobs, and an elliptical staircase. ⊠ *Box
94, U.S. 1, Robbinston 04671,* ☎ *207/454–2385 or 800/821–2028.
4 rooms, 2 with bath; 1 apartment. Full breakfast. MC, V.*

$ ☗ **Weston House.** A Federal-style home built in 1810, the antiques-filled
★ Weston House overlooks Eastport and Passamaquoddy Bay from a prime
in-town location. An elegant multicourse breakfast is served in the formal dining room. The family room, with a fireplace and a TV, is a casual place to plan the day's activities. Naturalist John J. Audubon
stayed here in 1833. Dinner is available by advance reservation. ⊠ *26
Boynton St., 04631,* ☎ *207/853–2907 or 800/853–2907,* ℻ *207/856–
0981. 5 rooms share 2½ baths. Full breakfast. No credit cards.*

Outdoor Activities and Sports

East Coast Ferries, Ltd. (☎ 506/747–2159) provides ferry service between Eastport and Deer Island and Deer Island and Campobello from
late June to mid-September. **Harris Whale Watching** (⊠ Harris Point
Rd., Eastport, ☎ 207/853–2940 or 207/853–4303) operates three-hour
tours. **Tidal Trails** (⊠ Water St., ☎ 207/853–7373) operates boat char-

ters, natural-history tours, and guided bird-watching, canoeing, sea-kayaking, and saltwater-fishing trips.

Shopping
Dog Island Pottery (⊠ 224 Water St., ☎ 207/853–4775) stocks stoneware pottery and local crafts. The **Eastport Gallery** (⊠ 69 Water St., ☎ 207/853–4166) displays works by area artists. **Jim's Smoked Salmon** (⊠ 37 Washington St., ☎ 207/853–4831) sells Atlantic salmon, mussels, and roe hot-smoked in apple wood. **Joe's Basket Shop** (⊠ Rte. 190, Pleasant Point, ☎ 207/853–2840) sells fancy and course (work) baskets and jewelry made by the Passamaquoddy.

Way Down East A to Z

Arriving and Departing
See Arriving and Departing *in* Maine A to Z, *below.*

Getting Around
BY CAR

U.S. 1 is the primary coastal route, with smaller roads leading to the towns on the long fingers of land in this region. Route 182 is a pleasant inland route; Route 186 loops through the Schoodic Peninsula. The most direct route to Lubec is Route 189, but Route 191, between East Machias and West Lubec, is a scenic coastal drive.

BY FERRY

East Coast Ferries, Ltd. (☎ 506/747–2159) provides ferry service between Eastport and Deer Island and Deer Island and Campobello from late June to mid-September.

Contacts and Resources
GUIDED TOURS

Quoddy Air (⊠ Eastport Municipal Airport, County Rd., Eastport, ☎ 207/853–0997) operates scenic flights. **Scenic Island Tours** (⊠ 37 Washington St., Eastport, ☎ 207/853–2840) offers guided tours of Eastport in a 1947 Dodge Woody bus that once transported workers to sardine factories. Picnic lunches featuring smoked salmon are available.

VISITOR INFORMATION

Eastport Area Chamber of Commerce (⊠ Box 254, 78 Water St., 04631, ☎ 207/853–4644). **Lubec Area Chamber of Commerce** (⊠ Box 123, 04652, ☎ 207/733–4522). **Machias Bay Area Chamber of Commerce** (⊠ Box 606, 378 Main St., 04654, ☎ 207/255–4402). **Quoddy Coastal Tourism Association of New Brunswick and Maine** (⊠ Box 1171, St. Andrews, New Brunswick, Canada E0G 2X0, ☎ 800/377–9748). **Schoodic Peninsula Chamber of Commerce** (⊠ Box 381, Winter Harbor 04693, ☎ no phone).

WESTERN LAKES AND MOUNTAINS

Less than 20 mi northwest of Portland and the coast, the sparsely populated lake and mountain areas of western Maine stretch north along the New Hampshire border to Québec. In winter this is ski country; in summer the woods and waters draw vacationers.

The Sebago–Long Lake region has antiques stores and lake cruises on a 42-mi waterway. Kezar Lake, tucked away in a fold of the White Mountains, has long been a hideaway of the wealthy. Children's summer camps dot the region. Bethel, in the Androscoggin River valley, is a classic New England town, its town common lined with historic homes. The far more rural Rangeley Lake area brings long stretches of pine, beech, spruce, and sky—and stylish inns and bed-and-breakfasts with easy access to golf, boating, fishing, and hiking.

Sebago Lake

49 *17 mi northwest of Portland.*

Sebago Lake, which provides all the drinking water for Greater Portland, is Maine's best-known lake after Moosehead (☞ The North Woods, *below*). Many camps and year-round homes surround Sebago, which is popular with water-sports enthusiasts. At the north end of the lake, the **Songo Lock** (☎ 207/693–6231), which permits the passage of watercraft from Sebago Lake to Long Lake, is the one surviving lock of the Cumberland and Oxford Canal. Built of wood and masonry, the original lock dates from 1830 and was expanded in 1911; today it sees heavy traffic in summer.

The 1,300-acre **Sebago Lake State Park** on the north shore of the lake provides opportunities for swimming, picnicking, camping (250 sites), boating, and fishing (salmon and togue). ⊠ *11 Park Access Rd., Casco,* ☎ *207/693–6615 May–mid-Oct.; 207/693–6231 at other times.* 🎫 *$2.50.* ☉ *Daily 9–8.*

The **Jones Museum of Glass & Ceramics** houses more than 7,000 objects of glass, pottery, stoneware, and porcelain from around the world. Also on the premises are a research library and gift shop. ⊠ *35 Douglas Mountain Rd. off Rte. 107,* ☎ *207/787–3370.* 🎫 *$5.* ☉ *Mid-May–mid-Nov., Mon.–Sat. 10–5, Sun. 1–5.*

OFF THE
BEATEN PATH

SABBATHDAY LAKE SHAKER MUSEUM – Established in the late 18th century, this is the last active Shaker community in the United States. Members continue to farm crops and herbs, and you can see the meetinghouse of 1794—a paradigm of Shaker design—and the ministry shop with 14 rooms of Shaker furniture, folk art, tools, farm implements, and crafts from the 18th to early 20th centuries. There is also a small gift shop, but don't expect to find furniture or other large Shaker items. On the busy road out front, a farmer usually has summer and fall vegetables for sale. In autumn, he sells cider, apples, and pumpkins. On Sunday, the Shaker day of prayer, the community is closed to visitors. ⊠ *Rte. 26, New Gloucester (20 mi north of Portland, 12 mi east of Naples),* ☎ *207/926–4597.* 🎫 *Tour $5, extended tour $6.50.* ☉ *Memorial Day–Columbus Day, Mon.–Sat. 10–4:30.*

Naples

50 *16 mi northwest of North Windham, 32 mi northwest of Portland.*

Naples swells with seasonal residents and visitors in summer. The town occupies an enviable location between Long Lake and Sebago Lake.

The **Naples Historical Society Museum** has a jailhouse, a bandstand, a 1938 Dodge fire truck, a coach, and information about the Cumberland and Oxford Canal and the Sebago–Long Lake steamboats. ⊠ *Village Green, U.S. 302,* ☎ *207/693–4297.* 🎫 *Free.* ☉ *July–Aug., Fri. 10–3; call for additional hrs.*

☺ ***Songo River Queen II,*** a 92-ft stern-wheeler, takes passengers on hour-long cruises on Long Lake and longer voyages down the Songo River and through Songo Lock. ⊠ *U.S. 302, Naples Causeway,* ☎ *207/693–6861.* 🎫 *Long Lake cruise $7, Songo River ride $10.* ☉ *July–Labor Day, daily at 9:45, 1, 2:30, 3:45, 7; call for schedule of reduced spring and fall hrs.*

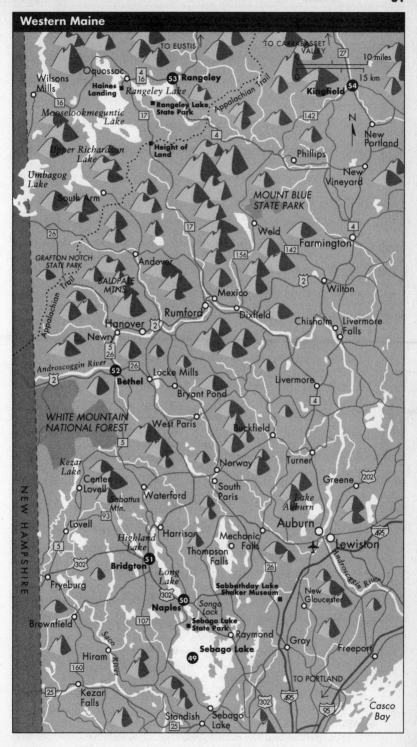

Western Maine

TO EUSTIS

TO CARRABASSET VALLEY

27

10 miles

15 km

N

Wilsons Mills

Oquossoc

4 16

53 **Rangeley**

Rangeley Lake

Haines Landing

Rangeley Lake State Park

Mooselookmeguntic Lake

17

4

Height of Land

Kingfield 54

142

New Portland

Phillips

New Vineyard

Upper Richardson Lake

Umbagog Lake

South Arm

26

GRAFTON NOTCH STATE PARK

Andover

17

MOUNT BLUE STATE PARK

Weld

156

142

Farmington

4

BALDPATE MTNS

Appalachian Trail

Mexico

Rumford

Dixfield

Chisholm

Wilton

2

Livermore Falls

Hanover

2

Newry

5 26

Androscoggin River

2

52 **Bethel**

26

Locke Mills

Bryant Pond

Livermore

4

WHITE MOUNTAIN NATIONAL FOREST

West Paris

Buckfield

5

Kezar Lake

Center Lovell

Sabattus Mtn.

Waterford

Norway

South Paris

Turner

Lake Auburn

Greene

202

93

Lovell

5

Highland Lake

Harrison

Mechanic Falls

Thompson Falls

Auburn

Lewiston

495

Androscoggin River

51 **Bridgton**

302

Fryeburg

Long Lake

302

Naples 50

107

Songo Lock

Sabbathday Lake Shaker Museum

26

New Gloucester

Brownfield

Saco River

Sebago Lake State Park

Raymond

Gray

Freeport

Hiram

160

49 **Sebago Lake**

TO PORTLAND

Kezar Falls

25

Standish

25

Sebago Lake

302

495

95

Casco Bay

NEW HAMPSHIRE

Dining and Lodging

$$$$ ✕ **Bistro du Lac.** This casual restuarant inside a big red farmhouse across from Sebago Lake has a perhaps-too-ambitious country-French menu. Though entrées like salmon with caramelized leeks and rack of lamb don't quite live up to their potential, the food is good and the prix-fixe menu ($47) fairly reasonable. Sunday brunch is also served. ⊠ *U.S. 302 and Rte. 85, Raymond,* ☎ *207/655–4100. MC, V. Closed Tues.– Wed. No lunch.*

$$$$ 🏨 **Migis Lodge.** The lodge's pine-panel cottages, scattered among 100 shorefront acres, have fieldstone fireplaces and are handsomely furnished with braided rugs and handmade quilts. A warm, woodsy feeling pervades the main inn. The deck has views (marvelous at sunset) of Sebago Lake. Though you may be tempted just to gaze out on the lake, the lodge provides plenty of outdoor and indoor activities, all of which are included in the room rate. Guests gather in the main dining room for three fancy meals daily. ⊠ *Box 40, Migis Lodge Rd., off U.S. 302, South Casco 04077,* ☎ *207/655–4524,* 𝔽𝔸𝕏 *207/655–2054. 29 cottages, 6 rooms. Dining room, tennis court, exercise room, beach, boating, waterskiing, fishing, playground. AP. No credit cards.*

$$–$$$ 🏨 **Augustus Bove House.** Built as the Hotel Naples in the 1820s, this rambling brick B&B sits across from the Naples Causeway and has views down Long Lake. Rooms are furnished with antiques and a television. ⊠ *Box 501, R.R. 1, U.S. 302, 04055,* ☎ *207/693–6365. 10 rooms, 7 with bath; 1 suite. Hot tub. Full breakfast. AE, D, MC, V.*

Nightlife and the Arts

Deertrees Theater and Cultural Center (⊠ Deertrees Rd. off Rte. 117, Harrison, ☎ 207/583–6747) hosts musicals, dramas, dance performances, shows for children, concerts, and other events from late June through Labor Day.

Outdoor Activities and Sports

U.S. 302 cuts through Naples, and in the center at the Naples Causeway are rental craft for fishing or cruising. Sebago, Long, and Rangeley lakes are popular areas for sailing and motorboating. For rentals, try **Mardon Marine** (⊠ U.S. 302, ☎ 207/693–6264), **Naples Marina** (⊠ U.S. 302 and Rte. 114, ☎ 207/693–6254; motorboats only), or **Sun Sports Plus** (⊠ U.S. 302, ☎ 207/693–3867).

Shopping

The **Shops of South Casco Village** (⊠ U.S. 302, South Casco, ☎ 207/ 655–5060) include a gift shop, an antiques shop, and an art gallery with a sculpture garden.

Bridgton

51 *8 mi north of Naples, 16 mi east of Fryeburg, 30 mi south of Bethel.*

In and around the drab town of Bridgton, between Long and Highland Lakes, are antiques shops, a museum, and the Shawnee Peak ski resort. The **Bridgton Historical Society Museum** is in a former fire station that was built in 1902. On display are artifacts of the area's history and materials on the local narrow-gauge railroad. ⊠ *Gibbs Ave.,* ☎ *207/647–3699.* 🎫 *$2.* ☉ *July–Aug., Tues.–Fri. 10–4.*

Dining and Lodging

$$–$$$ ✕ **Tom's Homestead.** An 1821 house holds two quiet dining rooms and a spacious bar. The international-style menu includes a wide selection of choices, from Louisiana frog legs Provençale to Wiener schnitzel. ⊠ *U.S. 302,* ☎ *207/647–5726. AE, D, MC, V. Closed Mon.*

$–$$$ ✕ **Black Horse Tavern.** A Cape Cod cottage more than 200 years old houses this country-style restaurant with a shiny bar, horse blankets, and stirrups for decor. On the menu are steaks, seafood, soups, salads, and burgers. ⊠ *8 Portland St.,* ☎ *207/647–5300. Reservations not accepted. D, MC, V.*

$$$$ ✕⛢ **Quisisana.** Music lovers may think they've found heaven on earth at this delightful resort on Kezar Lake, about 14 mi northwest of Bridgton. After dinner, the staff, students, and graduates of some of the finest music schools in the country perform at the music hall—everything from Broadway tunes to concert piano pieces. White cottages have pine interiors and cheerful decor. One night you might have a typical New England dinner of clam chowder, lobster, and blueberry pie; the next night the choice might be saddle of lamb with a black-olive tapenade or salmon-and-leek roulade with a roasted-red-pepper sauce. All meals and activities are included in the rates (except for a nominal fee for the use of the motorboats). For most of the resort's season, a one-week stay beginning Saturday is required. ⊠ *Pleasant Point Rd., Center Lovell 04016,* ☎ *207/925–3500,* ℻ *207/925–1004 in season. 11 rooms in 2 lodges, 32 cottages. Restaurant, 3 tennis courts, windsurfing, boating, waterskiing. AP. Closed Sept.–mid-June.*

$$ ⛢ **Bear Mountain Inn.** After swimming at the private beach on Bear Lake or hiking up Bear Mountain (across the street), it's nice to return to this rambling farmhouse inn, which the owner has meticulously decorated in a woodsy theme. A country breakfast with an emphasis on organic ingredients is served in the dining room, which has a fieldstone fireplace and views over the lake. ⊠ *Rte. 35, South Waterford 04081,* ☎ *207/583–4404. 9 rooms, 5 with bath; 1 suite; 1 cottage. Badminton, croquet, horseshoes, volleyball, beach, boating, fishing, ice-skating, cross-country skiing, snowmobiling. Full breakfast. MC, V.*

$$ ⛢ **Bridgton House.** It's an easy walk from this white clapboard cottage to village shops and restaurants or to Highland Lake. When the weather's nice, breakfast is served on the fine wraparound porch. The rooms in the back of the house are quieter than those on the U.S. 302 side of the house. ⊠ *2 Main St./U.S. 302, 04009,* ☎ *207/647–0979. 6 rooms, 3 with bath. Full breakfast. No credit cards. Closed Nov.–Apr.*

$–$$ ⛢ **Waterford Inne.** This gold-painted house on a hilltop provides a good home base for trips to lakes, ski trails, and antiques shops. The bedrooms have lots of nooks and crannies. The Nantucket, with a whale motif, and the Chesapeake, with a private porch and a fireplace, are the nicest. A converted woodshed holds five additional rooms, and though they have less character than the rooms in the inn, four have sunny decks. ⊠ *Box 149, Chadbourne Rd., Waterford 04088,* ☎ ℻ *207/583–4037. 9 rooms, 6 with bath; 1 suite. Badminton, ice-skating, cross-country skiing. Full breakfast. AE. Closed Apr.*

Outdoor Activities and Sports

Two scenic canoeing routes on the Saco River (near Fryeburg) are the gentle stretch from Swan's Falls to East Brownfield (19 mi) and from East Brownfield to Hiram (14 mi). For rentals, try **Canal Bridge Canoes** (⊠ U.S. 302, Fryeburg Village, ☎ 207/935–2605) or **Saco River Canoe and Kayak** (⊠ Rte. 5, Fryeburg, ☎ 207/935–2369). **Sporthaus** (⊠ 61 Main St., Bridgton, ☎ 207/647–5100) rents bicycles, canoes, sailboats, sailboards, skis, and snowshoes.

Shopping

Craftworks (⊠ Main St., ☎ 207/647–5436) carries American crafts, Maine foods, women's clothing, and gifts. The **Maine Theme** (⊠ Main St., ☎ 207/647–2161) specializes in handcrafted wares from throughout New England.

Skiing and Snow Sports

SHAWNEE PEAK

On the New Hampshire border, Shawnee Peak draws many skiers from the North Conway, New Hampshire, area (18 mi away) and from Portland (45 mi). Popular with families, this facility is being upgraded. There's also snowshoeing. ⊠ *Box 734, U.S. 302, 04009,* ☎ *207/647–8444.*

Downhill. Shawnee Peak has a 1,300-ft vertical and perhaps the most night-skiing terrain in New England. Most of the 36 runs are pleasant cruisers for intermediates, with some beginner slopes, a few pitches suitable for advanced skiers, and a few gladed runs. Lifts include one quad, one double, and two triple chairs and one surface lift.

Child care. The area's nursery takes children from age 6 months to 6 years. The SKIwee program is for children between ages 4 and 6; those between 7 and 12 also have a program. Children under 6 ski free when accompanied by a parent. The Youth Ski League has instruction for aspiring racers.

En Route   From Bridgton, the most scenic route to Bethel is along U.S. 302 west, across Moose Pond to Knight's Hill Road, turning north to Lovell and Route 5, which will take you on to Bethel. It's a drive that lets you admire the jagged crests of the White Mountains outlined against the sky to the west and the rolling hills that alternate with brooding forests at roadside. At Center Lovell you can barely glimpse the secluded Kezar Lake to the west, the retreat of wealthy and very private people; Sabattus Mountain, which rises behind Center Lovell, has a public hiking trail and stupendous views of the Presidential Range from the summit.

Bethel

 66 mi north of Portland, 22 mi east of Gorham, NH.

Bethel is pure New England, a town with white clapboard houses and white-steeple churches and a mountain vista at the end of every street. The architecture here is something to behold. In winter this is ski country: Bethel is midway between Sunday River in Newry and Mt. Abram in Locke Mills. Sunday River (☞ Skiing and Snow Sports, *below*) has plenty of action in summer, too.

A stroll in Bethel should begin at the **Moses Mason House and Museum,** a Federal home of 1813. The museum, on the town common across from the Bethel Inn and Country Club, has nine period rooms and a front hall and stairway wall decorated with murals by Rufus Porter. You can pick up materials here for a walking tour of Bethel Hill Village, most of which is on the National Register of Historic Places. ⊠ *14 Broad St.,* ☎ *207/824–2908.* ☎ *$2.* ☉ *July–Labor Day, Tues.–Sun. 1–4; Labor Day–June, by appointment.*

The **Major Gideon Hastings House** on Broad Street has a columned-front portico typical of the Greek Revival style. The severe white **West Parish Congregational Church** (1847), with an unadorned triangular pediment and a steeple supported on open columns, is on Church Street, around the common from the Major Gideon Hastings House. The campus of **Gould Academy** (⊠ Church St., ☎ 207/824–7777), a preparatory school, opened its doors in 1835; the dominant style of the school buildings is Georgian.

White Mountain National Forest straddles New Hampshire and Maine. Although the highest peaks are on the New Hampshire side, the Maine section has magnificent rugged terrain, camping and picnic areas, and hiking opportunities from hour-long nature loops to a 5½-hour scramble up Speckled Mountain. ⊠ *Evans Notch Visitation Center, 18 Mayville Rd., 04217,* ☎ *207/824–2134.* 🅿 *Parking $3.* ☉ *Center daily 8–4:30 in summer; closed Wed. in winter.*

At **Grafton Notch State Park** (⊠ Rte. 26, 14 mi north of Bethel, ☎ 207/824–2912) you can take an easy nature walk to Mother Walker Falls or Moose Cave and see the spectacular Screw Auger Falls, or you can hike to the summit of Old Speck Mountain, the state's third-highest peak. If you have the stamina and the equipment, you can pick up the Appalachian Trail here, hike over Saddleback Mountain, and continue on to Katahdin. The **Maine Appalachian Trail Club** (⊠ Box 283, Augusta 04330) publishes a map and trail guide.

Dining and Lodging

$$–$$$$ ✕🖬 **Bethel Inn and Country Club.** Bethel's grandest accommodation is a full-service resort that includes 36 km (22 mi) of cross-country ski trails. Although not very large, the rooms in the main inn, sparsely furnished with Colonial reproductions, are the most desirable: The choice rooms have fireplaces and face the mountains that rise over the golf course. All 40 two-bedroom condos on the fairway face the mountains; they are clean, even a bit sterile. A formal dining room ($$–$$$; reservations essential) serves elaborate dinners of roast duck, prime rib, lobster, and swordfish. The room rates include a full breakfast and dinner. ⊠ *Box 49, Village Common, 04217,* ☎ *207/824–2175 or 800/654–0125,* 🅵🅰🆇 *207/824–2233. 48 rooms, 9 suites, 40 condo units. Restaurant, bar, pool, 18-hole golf course, tennis court, health club, cross-country skiing, conference center. MAP. AE, D, DC, MC, V.*

$$ ✕🖬 **Victoria Inn.** It's hard to miss this turreted inn, with its beige-, mauve-, and teal-painted exterior and massive attached carriage house topped with a cupola. Inside, Victorian details include ceiling rosettes, stained-glass windows, elaborate fireplace mantels, and gleaming oak trim. Guest rooms vary in size and decor; most are furnished with antiques. The one-bedroom-with-loft units in the carriage house are perfect for families. The restaurant, open to the public for dinner ($$–$$$), has three rooms, one with a wraparound mural of Italian scenes. Chef Eric Botka's menu lists entrées such as beef tenderloin au poivre and rack of lamb. A children's menu is available. ⊠ *Box 249, 32 Main St., 04217,* ☎ *207/824–8060 or 888/774–1235,* 🅵🅰🆇 *207/824–3926. 15 rooms. Restaurant. Full breakfast. MC, V. Restaurant closed Mon.–Tues.*

$$–$$$$ 🖬 **Jordan Grand Resort Hotel.** A hit with Sunday River skiers, this condominium hotel provides ski-in, ski-out access to the Jordan Bowl trails. Most units have kitchenettes, and there's a heated outdoor pool to relax in after a day on the slopes. ⊠ *Box 450, 1 Grand Circle, off Skiway Rd. and off U.S. 2, Newry 04217,* ☎ *207/824–5000 or 800/543–2754,* 🅵🅰🆇 *207/824–5399. 195 condominiums. Two restaurants, pool, tennis court, health club, baby-sitting, meeting rooms. AE, D, MC, V.*

$$$ 🖬 **Sunday River Inn.** This modern chalet on the Sunday River ski-area access road has private rooms for families and dorm rooms (bring your sleeping bag) for groups and students, all within easy access of the slopes. A hearty breakfast and dinner are served buffet-style, and a stone hearth dominates the comfortable living room. The inn operates an excellent ski-touring center. ⊠ *19 Skiway Rd., Newry 04261,* ☎ *207/824–2410,* 🅵🅰🆇 *207/824–3181. 3 rooms with bath, 12 rooms share 2 baths, 5 dorms share 2 baths, 4 rooms in separate building share 2 baths. Hot tub, sauna, cross-country skiing. MAP. AE, MC, V. Closed Apr.–late-Nov.*

$$ 🖬 **Chapman Inn.** New owners are renovating and updating this circa-1865 Colonial inn on Bethel's town green. Inn rooms are comfortably furnished with antiques and country pieces, and there are dorm ac-

commodations in the barn. Guests have use of a game room and a kitchen. The huge country-style breakfast will fuel skiers and others for an active morning. ⊠ *Box 1067, Bethel Common, 04217,* ☎ *207/824–2657 or 877/359–1398,* FAX *207/824–7152. 7 rooms, 5 with bath; 1 efficiency; 24-bed dormitory. Saunas, hot tub, ice-skating, coin laundry. Full breakfast. AE, D, MC, V.*

\$\$ ✕🛏 **Sudbury Inn.** Value and location are the chief attributes of this white clapboard inn, whose guest rooms and dining room have country charm. Prime rib, sirloin au poivre, broiled haddock, lasagna, and other standards are on the menu. The pub, which offers a large selection of microbrews and weekend entertainment, is a popular hangout. The huge breakfast includes omelets, eggs Benedict, pancakes, and homemade granola. ⊠ *Box 369, 151 Main St., 04217,* ☎ *207/824–2174 or 800/395–7837,* FAX *207/824–2329. 10 rooms, 7 suites. Restaurant, pub. Full breakfast. AE, MC, V.*

Nightlife and the Arts

Sunday River nightlife is spread out between the mountain and downtown Bethel. For a quiet evening, head to the piano bar at the **Bethel Inn** (⊠ The Common, ☎ 207/824–2175). At the mountain, try the **Bumps Pub** (⊠ Whitecap Lodge, ☎ 207/824–5269) for après-ski and evening entertainment—Tuesday night is comedy night, ski movies are shown on Wednesday, and bands play on weekends and holidays. **Sunday River Brewing Company** (⊠ U.S. 2, ☎ 207/824–4253) has pub fare and live entertainment—usually progressive rock bands—on weekends. The **Sudbury Inn** (⊠ 151 Main St., ☎ 207/824–2174) is popular for après-ski and has music that tends toward the blues.

Outdoor Activities and Sports

Mahoosuc Guide Service (⊠ Bear River Rd., Newry, ☎ 207/824–2073) leads day and multiday dog-sledding expeditions on the Maine–New Hampshire border. Lifts at **Sunday River Mountain Bike Park** (⊠ Sunday River Rd., Newry, ☎ 207/824–3000) bring cyclists to the trails. **Telemark Inn & Llama Treks** (⊠ King's Hwy., Mason Township, ☎ 207/836–2703) operates one- to six-day llama-supported hiking trips in the White Mountain National Forest.

Shopping

Bonnema Potters (⊠ 146 Lower Main St., ☎ 207/824–2821) sells plates, lamps, tiles, and vases in colorful modern designs. The **Lyons' Den** (⊠ U.S. 2, Hanover, ☎ 207/364–8634), a great barn of a place near Bethel, stocks antique glass, china, tools, prints, rugs, hand-wrought iron, and some furniture. **Mt. Mann Jewelers** (⊠ 57 Maine St. Pl., ☎ 207/824–3030) carries contemporary jewelry with unusual gems.

Skiing and Snow Sports

MT. ABRAM

This ski area has a rustic Maine feeling and is known for its snow grooming, home-style cooking, and family atmosphere. Skiers here prefer the low-key attitude and wallet-friendly rates. Night skiing and snow tubing are available. Many skiers stay in the reasonably priced condominiums on the mountain road. ⊠ *Box 120, Rte. 26, Locke Mills 04255,* ☎ *207/875–5003.*

Downhill. The mountain reaches just over 1,000 vertical ft. The majority of the terrain is intermediate, with fall-line steep runs and two areas for beginning and novice skiers. The area has two double chairlifts and three T-bars. Plans for the 1999–2000 season include a new base lodge and the replacement of one of the T-bars with a chairlift. In addition to learn-to-ski classes, there are improvement clinics for all ability levels and age groups. Facilities include two base lodges, a children's terrain garden, a halfpipe for snowboarders, a snowboard park, and a snow-tubing park.

Child care. The Mt. Abram's Day Care Center takes children from age 6 months to 6 years. Children between 3 and 6 who are enrolled in the center can take lessons on weekends and during vacation weeks. For juniors from 6 to 16 there are individual classes plus a series of 10 two-hour lessons on weekends.

SUNDAY RIVER

In the 1980s, Sunday River was a sleepy little ski area with minimal facilities. Today it is among the best-managed ski areas in the East and the flagship of the owner Les Otten's American Skiing Company empire. Spread throughout the valley are three base areas, two condominium hotels, trailside condominiums, town houses, and a ski dorm. Sunday River is home to the Maine Handicapped Skiing program, which provides lessons and services for skiers with disabilities. In summer, Sunday River's Adventure Park attracts families with its water slides, climbing wall, BMX park, and in-line skating park, as well as hiking and mountain biking. ⊠ *Sunday River Rd. off U.S. 2, Newry, mailing address: Box 450, Bethel 04217, ☎ 207/824–3000; 207/824–5200 for snow conditions; 800/543–2754 for reservations.*

Downhill. White Heat has gained fame as the steepest, longest, widest lift-served trail in the East; but skiers of all abilities will find plenty of suitable terrain, from a 5-km (3-mi) beginner run to steep glades and in-your-face bumps. The area has 126 trails, the majority of them in the intermediate range. Expert and advanced runs are grouped from the peaks, and most beginner slopes are near the base. Trails spreading down from eight peaks have a total vertical descent of 2,340 ft and are served by nine quads, four triples, and two double chairlifts and three surface lifts.

Other activities. Within the housing complexes are indoor pools, outdoor heated pools, saunas, and hot tubs. Sunday River also has a snowboard park. The Entertainment Center at White Cap has a lighted halfpipe, a lighted ice-skating rink, a tubing area, a teen center, and a nightclub with live music.

Child care. Sunday River operates three licensed day-care centers for children from ages 6 weeks to 6 years. Coaching for children from ages 3 to 18 is available in the Children's Center at the South Ridge base area.

En Route   The routes north from Bethel to the Rangeley district are all scenic, particularly in the autumn when the maples are aflame with color. In the town of Newry, make a short detour to the **Artist's Bridge** (turn off Route 26 onto Sunday River Road and drive about 3 mi), the most painted and photographed of Maine's eight covered bridges. Route 26 continues on to **Grafton Notch State Park,** about 12 mi from Bethel. Here you can hike to stunning gorges and waterfalls and into the Baldpate Mountains. Past the park, Route 26 continues to Errol, New Hampshire, where Route 16 will return you east around the north shore of Mooselookmeguntic Lake, through Oquossoc, and into Rangeley. A more direct route (if marginally less scenic) from Bethel to Rangeley still allows a stop in Newry. Follow U.S. 2 north and east from Bethel to the twin towns of Rumford and Mexico, where Route 17 continues north to Oquossoc, about an hour's drive. When you've driven for about 20 minutes beyond Rumford, the signs of civilization all but vanish and you pass through what seems like untouched territory—though the lumber companies have long since tackled the virgin forests—and sporting camps and cottages are tucked away here and there. The high point of this route is **Height**

of Land, about 30 mi north of Rumford, with its unforgettable views of range after range of mountains and the island-studded blue mass of Mooselookmeguntic Lake directly below. Turnouts on both sides of the highway allow you to pull over for a long look. **Haines Landing** on Mooselookmeguntic Lake lies 7 mi west of Rangeley. Here you can stand at 1,400 ft above sea level and face the same magnificent scenery you admired at 2,400 ft from Height of Land on Route 17. Boat and canoe rentals are available at Mooselookmeguntic House.

Rangeley

🛞 *67 mi north of Bethel.*

Rangeley, north of Rangeley Lake on Route 4/16, has lured fisherfolk, hunters, and winter-sports enthusiasts for a century to its more than 40 lakes and ponds and 450 square mi of woodlands. Equally popular in summer or winter, Rangeley has a rough, wilderness feel to it. Lodgings are in the woods, around the lake, and along the golf course.

On the south shore of Rangeley Lake, **Rangeley Lake State Park** (⊠ Off Rte. 17, ☎ 207/864–3858) has superb lakeside scenery, swimming, picnic tables, a boat ramp, showers, and 50 campsites.

The **Wilhelm Reich Museum** interprets the life and work of controversial physician-scientist Wilhelm Reich, who believed that a force called orgone energy was the source of neurosis. The Orgone Energy Observatory, designed for Reich in 1948, exhibits biographical materials, inventions, and the equipment used in his experiments. Also on view are Reich's library, personal memorabilia, and artwork. Trails lace the 175-acre grounds, and the observatory deck has magnificent views of the countryside. ⊠ *Dodge Pond Rd.,* ☎ *207/864–3443.* 🖾 *$3.* ⏱ *July–Aug., Tues.–Sun. 1–5; Sept., Sun. 1–5.*

OFF THE BEATEN PATH

SANDY RIVER & RANGELEY LAKES RAILROAD – You can ride a mile through the woods along a narrow-gauge railroad on a century-old train drawn by a replica of the *Sandy River No. 4* locomotive. ⊠ *Bridge Hill Rd., Phillips (20 mi southeast of Rangeley),* ☎ *207/639–3352.* 🖾 *$3.* ⏱ *June–Oct., 1st and 3rd Sun. each month; rides at 11, 1, and 3.*

Dining and Lodging

$$–$$$ ✕ **Gingerbread House.** A big fieldstone fireplace, well-spaced tables, and an antique marble soda fountain, all with views to the woods beyond, make for a comfortable atmosphere at this gingerbread-trim house, which is open for breakfast, lunch, and dinner. The ambitious dinner menu doesn't quite deliver, but the portions are huge. ⊠ *Rtes. 17 and 4, Oquossoc,* ☎ *207/864–3602. Reservations essential on summer weekends. AE, D, DC, MC, V. Closed Mon.–Tues. No dinner Sun.*

$–$$ ✕ **Porter House Restaurant.** This popular restaurant, seemingly in the middle of nowhere, draws diners from Rangeley, Kingfield, and Canada with its good service, excellent food, and casual atmosphere. Of the 1908 farmhouse's four dining rooms, the front one downstairs, which has a fireplace, is the most intimate and elegant. The broad Continental-style menu includes entrées for diners with light appetites. On the heavier side are porterhouse steak and roast duckling. Try the boneless lamb loin and lobster Brittany casserole if they're on the menu. ⊠ *Rte. 27, Eustis, 20 mi north of Rangeley,* ☎ *207/246–7932. Reservations essential on weekends. AE, D, MC, V.*

$$ ✕🔛 **Country Club Inn.** Built in the 1920s on the Mingo Springs Golf Course, this retreat enjoys a secluded hilltop location and sweeping lake and mountain views. The inn's baronial living room has a cathedral ceiling, a fieldstone fireplace at each end, and game trophies. The

rooms downstairs in the main building and in the motel-style wing added in the 1950s are cheerfully if minimally decorated. The glassed-in dining room—open to nonguests by reservation only—has linen-draped tables set well apart. The menu includes roast duck, veal, fresh fish, and filet mignon. ⊠ *Box 680, Mingo Loop Rd., 04970,* ☎ *207/864–3831. 19 rooms. Restaurant, pool. Full breakfast; MAP available. AE, MC, V. Closed Apr.–mid-May and mid-Oct.–late-Dec.*

$$$$ 🏨 **Grant's Kennebago Camps.** People rough it in comfort at this traditional Maine sporting camp on Kennebago Lake. "Sports" and families have been coming here for more than 85 years, lured by the fresh water, mountain views, excellent fly-fishing, and hearty home-cooked meals. The wilderness setting, between the Kennebago Mountains, is nothing less than spectacular. The cabins, whose screened porches overlook the lake, have woodstoves and are finished in knotty pine. Meals (included in the price) are served in the cheerful waterfront dining room. Motorboats, canoes, sailboats, Windsurfers, and mountain bikes are available. Float-plane rides and fly-fishing instruction can be arranged. ⊠ *Box 786, off Rte. 16, 04970,* ☎ *207/864–3608 in summer; 207/282–5264 in winter; 800/633–4815. 19 cabins. Dining room, lake, hiking, boating, fishing, mountain bikes, baby-sitting, playground. AP. MC, V. Closed Oct.–late May.*

$$–$$$ 🏨 **Hunter Cove on Rangeley Lake.** These lakeside cabins, which sleep from two to six people, provide all the comforts of home in a rustic setting. The interiors are unfinished knotty pine and include kitchens, full baths, and comfortable, if plain, living rooms. Cabin No. 1 has a fieldstone fireplace, and others have wood-burning stoves. Cabins No. 5 and No. 8 have hot tubs. Summer guests can take advantage of a sand swimming beach, boat rentals, and a nearby golf course. In winter, snowmobile right to your door or ski nearby (cross-country and downhill). ⊠ *Mingo Loop Rd.,* ☎ *207/864–3383. 8 cabins. Beach, boating. AE.*

$$ 🏨 **Rangeley Inn and Motor Lodge.** From Main Street you see only the three-story, blue inn building (circa 1907), but behind it is a newer motel wing with views of Haley Pond, a lawn, and a garden. Some of the inn's sizable rooms have iron-and-brass beds and subdued wallpaper, some have claw-foot tubs, and others have whirlpool tubs. The motel units contain Queen Anne reproduction furniture and velvet chairs. ⊠ *Box 160, 51 Main St., 04970,* ☎ *207/864–3341 or 800/666–3687,* FAX *207/864–3634. 36 inn rooms, 15 motel rooms, 2 cabins. Restaurant, bar, meeting room. MAP available. AE, D, MC, V.*

Nightlife and the Arts

Rangeley Friends of the Arts (⊠ Box 333, 04970, ☎ no phone) sponsors musical theater, fiddlers' contests, rock and jazz, classical, and other summer fare, mostly at Lakeside Park.

Outdoor Activities and Sports

BOATING

Rangeley and Mooselookmeguntic lakes are good for canoeing, sailing, and motorboating. For rentals, call **Oquossoc Cove Marina** (⊠ Oquossoc, ☎ 207/864–3463), **Dockside Sports Center** (⊠ Town Cove, ☎ 207/864–2424), or **River's Edge Sports** (⊠ Rte. 4, Oquossoc, ☎ 207/864–5582).

FISHING

Fishing for brook trout and salmon is at its best in May, June, and September; the Rangeley area is especially popular with fly-fishers. Nonresident anglers over the age of 12 must have a fishing license. The **Department of Inland Fisheries and Wildlife** (⊠ 284 State St., Augusta 04333, ☎ 207/287–2871) can provide further information.

If you'd like a fishing guide, try **Clayton (Cy) Eastlack** (☎ 207/864–3416) or **Westwind Charters and Guide Service** (☎ 207/864–5437).

SNOWMOBILING

This is a popular mode of winter transportation in the Rangeley area, with more than 100 mi of maintained trails linking lakes and towns to wilderness camps. The **Maine Snowmobile Association** (☞ Contacts and Resources *in* Maine A to Z, *below*) has information about Maine's nearly 8,000-mi Interconnecting Trail System.

Skiing and Snow Sports

SADDLEBACK SKI AND SUMMER LAKE PRESERVE

A down-home atmosphere prevails at Saddleback, where the quiet and the absence of crowds, even on holiday weekends, draw return visitors—many of them families. The base area has the feeling of a small community. ⊠ *Box 490, Saddleback Rd. off Rte. 4, 04970,* ☎ *207/864–5671; 207/864–3380 for snow conditions; 207/864–5364 for reservations.*

Downhill. The expert terrain is short and concentrated at the top of the mountain; an upper lift makes the trails easily accessible. The middle of the mountain is mainly intermediate, with a few meandering easy trails; the beginner or novice slopes are toward the bottom. Two double chairlifts and three T-bars carry skiers to the 41 trails on the 1,830 ft of vertical.

Cross-country. Forty km (25 mi) of groomed cross-country trails spread out from the base area and circle Saddleback Lake and several ponds and rivers.

Child care. The nursery takes children from age 6 weeks to 8 years. There are ski classes and programs for kids of different levels and ages.

Kingfield

54 *33 mi east of Rangeley, 15 mi west of Phillips, 21 mi north of Farmington.*

In the shadows of Mt. Abraham and Sugarloaf Mountain, Kingfield has everything a "real" New England town should have: a general store, historic inns, and a white clapboard church. Don't ignore Sugarloaf/USA in summer: The ski resort has an 18-hole golf course and six tennis courts for public use in warmer months.

The **Stanley Museum** houses a collection of original Stanley Steamer cars built by the Stanley twins, Kingfield's most famous natives. ⊠ *School St.,* ☎ *207/265–2729.* ☞ *$2.* ⊙ *May–Oct., Tues.–Sun. 1–4; Nov.–Apr. by appointment.*

Nowetah's American Indian Museum displays an extensive collection of baskets as well as artifacts from native peoples of North and South America. This small museum is part of a store. ⊠ *Rte. 27, New Portland,* ☎ *207/628–4981.* ☞ *Free.* ⊙ *Daily 10–5.*

Dining and Lodging

$$$–$$$$ ✕🏨 **Sugarloaf Inn Resort.** This lodge provides ski-on access to Sugarloaf/USA, a complete health club, and rooms that range from king-size on the fourth floor to dorm-style (bunk beds) on the ground floor. A greenhouse section of the Seasons Restaurant ($$–$$$) affords views of the slopes; "ski-in" lunches are served here. At breakfast the sunlight pours into the dining room, and at dinner you can watch the snow-grooming machines prepare your favorite run. ⊠ *Box 5000, R.R. 1, Sugarloaf Access Rd., Carrabassett Valley 04947,* ☎ *207/237–6814* *or 800/843–5623,* FAX *207/237–3773. 38 rooms, 4 dorm-style rooms. Restaurant, health club, meeting rooms. AE, D, MC, V.*

$ ✕🍴 **One and Three Stanley Avenue.** These sister properties, a gourmet restaurant and a simple B&B, are in adjacent Victorian houses. The quiet neighborhood is a few minutes' walk from downtown Kingfield and about a 20-minute drive from Sugarloaf/USA. Both are decorated with period furnishings. The restaurant specializes in creative Continental fare and emphasizes fresh Maine ingredients. ✉ *Box 169, 3 Stanley Ave., 04947,* ☎ *207/265–5541. 6 rooms, 3 with bath. Full breakfast. MC, V. Restaurant closed May–Nov.*

$$$$ 🍴 **Grand Summit.** A six-story brick structure at the base of the lifts on Sugarloaf, this hotel combines New England ambience with European-style service. Oak and redwood paneling in the main rooms is enhanced by contemporary furnishings. Valet parking, ski tuning, lockers, and mountain guides are available through the concierge. The Double Diamond Pub has a lively après-ski scene. ✉ *R.R. 1, Box 2299, Carrabassett Valley 04947,* ☎ *207/237–2222 or 800/527–9879,* FAX *207/ 237–2874. 100 rooms, 19 suites. Restaurant, pub, hot tub, massage, sauna, spa. AE, D, DC, MC, V.*

Nightlife and the Arts

At Sugarloaf, nightlife is concentrated at the mountain's base village. Monday is blues night at the **Bag & Kettle** (☎ 207/237–2451), which is the best choice for pizza and burgers. In the base village you'll find **Gepetto's** (☎ 207/237–2953), a popular après-ski hangout that serves American-style food. A microbrewery on the access road called the **Sugarloaf Brewing Company** (☎ 207/237–2211) pulls in revelers who come for après-ski brewskies. **Widowmaker Lounge** (☎ 207/237–6845) frequently presents live entertainment in the base lodge.

Outdoor Activities and Sports

T.A.D. Dog Sled Services (✉ Rte. 27, Carrabassett Valley, ☎ 207/246–4461) conducts short 1½-mi rides near Sugarloaf/USA. Sleds accommodate up to two adults and two children.

Skiing and Snow Sports

SUGARLOAF/USA

Abundant natural snow, a huge mountain, and the only above-tree-line skiing in the East have made Sugarloaf one of Maine's best-known ski areas. Improvements by the American Skiing Company have resulted in increased snowmaking, new lifts, and new trails. Sugarloaf skiers like the nontrendy Maine atmosphere and the base village, which has restaurants and shops. Two slopeside hotels and hundreds of slopeside condominiums provide ski-in/ski-out access. Once you are here, a car is unnecessary—a shuttle connects all mountain operations. Summer is much quieter than winter, but you can bike, hike, golf, and fish. ✉ *R.R. 1, Box 5000, Sugarloaf Access Rd., Carrabassett Valley 04947,* ☎ *207/237–2000; 207/237–6808 for snow conditions; or 800/843–5623.*

Downhill. With a vertical of 2,820 ft, Sugarloaf is taller than any other New England ski peak except Killington in Vermont. The advanced terrain begins with the steep snowfields on top, wide open and treeless. Coming down the face of the mountain, there are black-diamond runs everywhere, often blending into easier terrain. Many intermediate trails can be found down the front face, and a couple more come off the summit. Easier runs are predominantly toward the bottom, with a few long, winding runs that twist and turn from higher elevations. Serving the resort's 126 trails are two high-speed quad, two quad, one triple, and eight double chairlifts and one T-bar.

Cross-country. The Sugarloaf Ski Outdoor Center has 95 km (62 mi) of cross-country trails that loop and wind through the valley. Trails connect to the resort.

Other Activities. Snowboarders will find two snowboard parks and a halfpipe, the largest in the Northeast. The **Sugarloaf Sports and Fitness Club** (☎ 207/237–6946) has an indoor pool, six indoor and outdoor hot tubs, racquetball courts, full fitness and spa facilities, and a beauty salon. Use of club facilities is included in all lodging packages. Snowshoeing and ice skating are available at the Outdoor Center.

Child care. A nursery takes children from age 6 weeks to 6 years. Children's ski programs begin at age 3. A night nursery is open on Thursday and Saturday from 6 to 10 PM by reservation. Instruction is provided on a half-day or full-day basis for children from ages 4 to 14. Nightly children's activities are free. The teen club, Avalanche, is in the base lodge.

Western Lakes and Mountains A to Z

Arriving and Departing
See Arriving and Departing *in* Maine A to Z, *below.*

Getting Around
BY CAR

A car is essential to tour the western lakes and mountains. To travel from town to town in the order described in this section, take U.S. 302 to Route 26 to U.S. 2 to Route 17 to Route 4/16 to Route 142.

BY PLANE

Mountain Air Service (✉ Rangeley, ☎ 207/864–5307) provides air access to remote areas, scenic flights, and charter fishing trips. **Naples Flying Service** (✉ Naples Causeway, Naples, ☎ 207/693–6591) operates sightseeing flights over the lakes in summer.

Contacts and Resources
EMERGENCIES

Bethel Area Health Center (✉ Railroad St., Bethel, ☎ 207/824–2193). **Mt. Abram Regional Health Center** (✉ Depot St., Kingfield, ☎ 207/265–4555). **Northern Cumberland Memorial Hospital** (✉ S. High St., Bridgton, ☎ 207/647–8841). **Rangeley Regional Health Center** (✉ Main St., Rangeley, ☎ 207/864–3303).

RESERVATION SERVICES

Condominium lodging at Shawnee Peak is available through the **Bridgton Group** (☎ 207/647–2591). Bethel's **Chamber of Commerce** (☎ 207/824–3585 or 800/442–5826) has a reservations service. For reservations at Sugarloaf/USA, contact **Sugarloaf Area Reservations Service** (☎ 800/843–2732).

VISITOR INFORMATION

Bethel Area Chamber of Commerce (✉ Box 439, 30 Cross St., Bethel 04217, ☎ 207/824–2282 or 800/442–5526). **Bridgton–Lakes Region Chamber of Commerce** (✉ Box 236, U.S. 302, Bridgton 04009, ☎ 207/647–3472). **Greater Windham Chamber of Commerce** (✉ Box 1015, U.S. 302, Windham 04062, ☎ 207/882–8265). **Naples Business Association** (✉ Box 412, Naples 04055, ☎ 888/627–5379). **Rangeley Lakes Region Chamber of Commerce** (✉ Box 317, Main St., Rangeley 04970, ☎ 207/864–5571 or 800/685–2537). **Sugarloaf Area Chamber of Commerce** (✉ R.R.1, Box 2151, Kingfield 04947, ☎ 207/235–2100).

THE NORTH WOODS

Maine's North Woods, the vast area in the north-central section of the state, is best experienced by canoe or raft, hiking trail, or on a fishing trip. Some great theaters for these activities are Moosehead Lake, Baxter State Park, and the Allagash Wilderness Waterway—as well as the summer resort town of Greenville, dramatically situated Rockwood, and the no-frills outposts that connect them. For outfitters, *see* Contacts and Resources *in* North Woods A to Z, *below*.

Rockwood

⑤⑤ *180 mi north of Portland, 91 mi northwest of Bangor.*

Rockwood, on Moosehead Lake's western shore, is a good starting point for a wilderness trip or a family vacation on the lake. Moosehead Lake, Maine's largest, supplies more in the way of rustic camps, restaurants, guides, and outfitters than any other northern locale. Its 420 mi of shorefront, three-quarters of which is owned by paper manufacturers, is virtually uninhabited. Though it doesn't possess many amenities, Rockwood has the most striking location of any town on Moosehead: The dark mass of **Mt. Kineo,** a sheer cliff that rises 789 ft above the lake and 1,789 ft above sea level, looms just across the narrows (you get an excellent view just north of town on Route 6/15).

East Outlet of the Kennebec River, a popular Class II and III white-water run for canoeists and white-water rafters, is about 10 mi from Rockwood on Route 6/15 south. You'll come to a bridge with a dam to the left. The outlet ends at the Harris Station Dam at Indian Pond, headwaters of the Kennebec.

OFF THE
BEATEN PATH

KINEO - Once a thriving summer resort, the original Mount Kineo Hotel (built in 1830 and torn down in the 1940s) was accessed primarily by steamship. An effort to renovate the remaining buildings in the early 1990s failed, but Kineo still makes a pleasant day trip from Rockwood. You can rent a motorboat in Rockwood and make the journey across the lake in about 15 minutes. There's a small marina on the shore, in the shadow of Mt. Kineo, and a half dozen buildings dot the land. Some are for sale and others are being restored, but there is no real town here. A tavern sells cold libations to drink there or take with you. A walkway laces the perimeter of the mountain.

Lodging

$$$$ 🏨 **Attean Lake Lodge.** The Holden family has owned and operated this island lodge about an hour west of Rockwood since 1900. The 18 log cabins, which sleep from two to six people, provide a secluded environment. The tastefully decorated central lodge has a library and games. ⊠ *Box 457, off Rte. 201, Birch Island, Jackman 04945,* ☎ *207/ 668–3792,* 📠 *207/668–4016. 18 cabins. Beach, boating, recreation room, library. AP. AE, MC, V. Closed Oct.–May.*

$–$$ 🏨 **The Birches.** This family-oriented resort supplies the full north-country experience: Moosehead Lake, birch woods, log cabins, and boats. The century-old main lodge has four guest rooms, a lobby with a trout pond, and a living room dominated by a fieldstone fireplace. The 15 cottages have wood-burning stoves or fireplaces and sleep from 2 to 15 people. The dining room (closed in December and April) overlooking the lake is open to the public for breakfast and dinner; the fare at dinner is pasta, seafood, and steak. ⊠ *Box 41, off Rte. 6/15, on Moosehead Lake, 04478,* ☎ *207/534–7305 or 800/825–9453,* 📠 *207/534–*

The North Woods

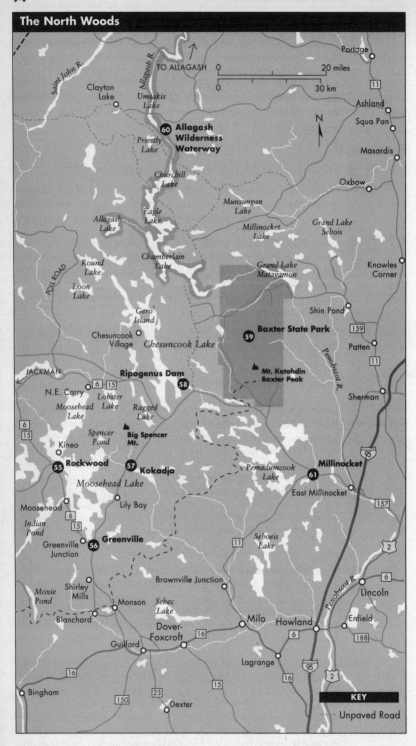

TO ALLAGASH

0   20 miles
0   30 km

N

Saint John R.

Allagash R.

Clayton
Lake

Umsakis
Lake

60 **Allagash
Wilderness
Waterway**

Priestly
Lake

Churchill
Lake

Munsungan
Lake

Millinocket
Lake

Grand Lake
Sebois

Allagash
Lake

Eagle
Lake

Chamberlain
Lake

Grand Lake
Matagamon

Round
Lake

TOLL ROAD

Loon
Lake

Gero
Island

Knowles
Corner

Chesuncook
Village

Chesuncook Lake

59 **Baxter State Park**

Shin Pond

159

Patten

Penobscot R.

JACKMAN

Ripogenus Dam

58

▲ **Mt. Katahdin
Baxter Peak**

Sherman

N.E. Carry

6 15

Lobster
Lake

Ragged
Lake

Moosehead
Lake

Spencer
Pond

▲ **Big Spencer
Mt.**

6
15

Kineo

55 **Rockwood**

57 **Kokadjo**

Moosehead Lake

Pemadumcook
Lake

Millinocket

61

East Millinocket

95

157

Moosehead

Lily Bay

6
15

Indian
Pond

Greenville
Junction

56 **Greenville**

11

Seboeis
Lake

Penobscot R.

2

6

Lincoln

Moxie
Pond

Shirley
Mills

Monson

Brownville Junction

Enfield

188

Blanchard

Sebec
Lake

Dover-
Foxcroft

16

Milo

Howland

6

95

Guilford

Lagrange

2

Bingham

16

150

23

Dexter

15

16

KEY

Unpaved Road

8835. 4 lodge rooms share bath, 15 cottages. Dining room, hot tub, sauna, boating. AE, D, MC, V.

$ 🖫 **Rockwood Cottages.** These eight white cottages on Moosehead Lake, off Route 15 and convenient to the center of Rockwood, have screened porches and fully equipped kitchens and sleep from two to seven people. There is a one-week minimum stay in July and August. ⊠ *Box 176, Rte. 15, 04478,* ☎ FAX *207/534–7725. 8 cottages. Sauna, dock, boating. D, MC, V. Closed Dec.–Apr.*

Outdoor Activities and Sports

Mt. Kineo Cabins (⊠ Rte. 6/15, ☎ 207/534–7744) rents canoes and larger boats on Moosehead Lake for the trip to Kineo. Rent a boat or take a shuttle operated by **Rockwood Cottages** (☎ 207/534–7725) or **Old Mill Campground** (☎ 207/534–7333) and hike one of the trails to the summit of Mt. Kineo for a picnic lunch and panoramic views. The **Birches** (☎ 207/534–7305) operates a moose cruise.

Greenville

🟠 *20 mi south of Rockwood, 160 mi northeast of Portland.*

Greenville has a smattering of shops, restaurants, and hotels. The largest town on Moosehead Lake, it is home to the Big Squaw Mountain Resort (☞ Skiing and Snow Sports, *below*), a ski area that in summer runs a recreation program for children and has two tennis courts, hiking, and lawn games.

Moosehead Marine Museum has exhibits on the local logging industry and the steamship era on Moosehead Lake, plus photographs of the Mount Kineo Hotel. ⊠ *Main St.,* ☎ *207/695–2716.* 🎫 *Free.* ☉ *Late May–early Oct., daily 10–4.*

The Moosehead Marine Museum offers three-hour and six-hour trips
★ on Moosehead Lake aboard the **Katahdin**, a 1914 steamship (now diesel). The 115-ft *Katahdin,* fondly called *The Kate,* carried passengers to Kineo until 1942 and then was used in the logging industry until 1975. ⊠ *Main St. (boarding is on the shoreline by the museum),* ☎ *207/695–2716.* 🎫 *$9–$24.* ☉ *Late May–Columbus Day.*

Lily Bay State Park (⊠ Lily Bay Rd., ☎ 207/695–2700), 8 mi northeast of Greenville, has a good swimming beach, two boat-launching ramps, and a 93-site campground.

Dining and Lodging

$–$$ ✕ **Kelly's Landing.** This family-oriented restaurant on the Moosehead shorefront has indoor and outdoor seating, excellent views, and a dock for boaters. The fare includes sandwiches, burgers, lasagna, seafood dinners, and prime rib. ⊠ *Rte. 6/15, Greenville Junction,* ☎ *207/695–4438. MC, V.*

$$$–$$$$ ✕🖫 **Greenville Inn.** Built more than a century ago, this rambling structure is a block from town on a rise over Moosehead Lake. The ornate cherry and mahogany paneling, Oriental rugs, and leaded glass create an aura of masculine ease. Cottages have mountain and lake views, and some have decks. The restaurant ($$$; reservations essential; no lunch) has water views. The menu, revised daily, reflects the owners' Austrian background: shrimp with mustard-dill sauce, salmon marinated in olive oil and basil, a veal cutlet with a mushroom cream sauce. ⊠ *Box 1194, Norris St., 04441,* ☎ *207/695–2206 or 888/695–6000,* FAX *207/695–0335. 4 rooms and 1 suite in main inn, 1 suite in carriage house, 6 cottages. Restaurant. Full breakfast. D, MC, V.*

$$$$ 🏨 **Lodge at Moosehead Lake.** This mansion overlooking Moosehead
★ Lake is about as close as things get to luxury in the North Woods. All
rooms have whirlpool baths, fireplaces, and hand-carved four-poster
beds; most have lake views. The restaurant, where breakfast is served,
has a spectacular view of the water. ⊠ *Lily Bay Rd., 04441,* ☎ *207/
695–4400,* FAX *207/695–2281. 5 rooms, 3 suites. Restaurant. D, MC,
V. Closed late Oct.–mid-Jan.; mid-Mar.–mid-May; mid-Jan.–mid-Mar.,
Tues.–Wed.*

$–$$ 🏨 **Devlin House.** You get nearly the same sweeping views over Moose-
head Lake at this small bed-and-breakfast as you do from the more exclusive and expensive Lodge at Moosehead Lake (☞ *above*). Rooms have
king-size beds. ⊠ *Box 1102, Lily Bay Rd., 04441,* ☎ *207/695–2229.
3 rooms. Full breakfast. Open year-round, but call ahead in winter.*

$ 🏨 **Chalet Moosehead.** Fifty yards off Route 6/15 and right on Moose-
head Lake, this accommodation holds efficiencies (with two double beds,
a living room, and a kitchenette), motel rooms, and cabins, all with
picture windows to capture the view. The attractive grounds include
a private beach and dock. ⊠ *Box 327, Rte. 6/15, Greenville Junction
04442,* ☎ *207/695–2950 or 800/290–3645. 8 efficiencies, 7 motel
rooms, 2 cabins. Horseshoes, beach, dock, boating. AE, D, MC, V.*

Outdoor Activities and Sports

Kineo Kayak Guide Service (☎ 207/474–3945 or 207/695–2896) offers guided kayak tours and moose safaris throughout the Moosehead
Lake and Kennebec Valley area. **Moose Country Safaris and Dogsled
Trips** (☎ 207/876–4907) leads moose safaris, dogsled trips, and canoe
and kayak trips.

FISHING

Togue, landlocked salmon, and brook and lake trout lure thousands
of anglers to the region from ice-out in mid-May until September; the
hardiest return in winter to ice-fish. For up-to-date **information** on water
levels, call ☎ 207/695–3756 or 800/322–9844.

RAFTING

The Kennebec and Dead rivers and the West Branch of the Penobscot
River offer thrilling white-water rafting (guides are strongly recommended). These rivers are dam-controlled, so trips run rain or shine
daily from May to October (day and multiday trips are conducted).
Most guided raft trips on the Kennebec and Dead rivers leave from
the Forks, southwest of Moosehead Lake, on Route 201; Penobscot
River trips leave from either Greenville or Millinocket. Many rafting
outfitters operate resort facilities in their base towns. **Raft Maine** (☎
800/723–8633) has lodging and rafting packages and information
about outfitters.

Shopping

Indian Hill Trading Post (⊠ Rte. 6/15, ☎ 207/695–2104) stocks just
about anything you might need for a North Woods vacation, including sporting and camping equipment, canoes, and fishing licenses;
there's even an adjacent grocery store. You enter **Moosehead Traders**
(⊠ Moosehead Center Mall, Rte. 6/15, ☎ 207/695–3806) through an
antler archway; inside are books, clothing, and antiques and artifacts.

Skiing and Snow Sports

BIG SQUAW MOUNTAIN RESORT

The management is modernizing this remote but pretty resort overlooking
Moosehead Lake. The emphasis is on affordable family skiing—prices
are downright cheap compared with those at other in-state areas. New
snowmaking, new grooming equipment, and a new attitude make this

a wonderful place for skiers longing to escape crowds. ⊠ *Box D, Rte. 6/15, 04441,* ☎ *207/695–1000.*

Downhill. Trails are laid out according to difficulty, with the easy slopes toward the bottom, intermediate trails weaving from midpoint, and steeper runs high up off the 1,750-vertical-ft peak. The 22 trails are served by one triple and one double chairlift and two surface lifts.

Child care. The nursery takes children from infants through age 6. The ski school has daily lessons and racing classes for children of all ages.

Kokadjo

57 *22 mi northeast of Greenville.*

Kokadjo, population "not many," has a sign that reads "Keep Maine green. This is God's country. Why set it on fire and make it look like hell?" This is the last outpost before you enter the North Woods. As you leave Kokadjo, bear left at the fork and follow signs to Baxter State Park. A drive of 5 mi along this road (now dirt) brings you to the Bowater/Great Northern Paper Company's Sias Hill checkpoint, where from June to November you must sign in and pay a user fee ($8 per car for nonresidents, valid for 24 hours) to travel the next 40 mi. Access is through a forest where you're likely to encounter logging trucks (which have the right of way), logging equipment, and work in progress. At the bottom of the hill after you pass the checkpoint, look to your right— there's a good chance you'll spot a moose.

Lodging

$$ ⊞ **Northern Pride Lodge.** North Woods–quaint with basic creature comforts is the best way to describe this lakefront lodge decorated with Victorian-era antiques and fishing and hunting trophies. Rooms are small, but the big porch is likely where you'll be spending much of your time. A huge country breakfast is served to all guests; lunch and dinner are available, too. The restaurant is open to the public for dinner. ⊠ *HC 76, Box 588, Greenville Rd., 04441,* ☎ *207/695–2890. 5 rooms without bath. Restaurant. Full breakfast; MAP and AP available. MC, V.*

Ripogenus Dam

58 *20 mi northeast of Kokadjo, 25 mins southeast of Chesuncook Village by floatplane.*

Ripogenus Dam and the granite-walled Ripogenus Gorge are on Ripogenus Lake, east of Chesuncook Lake. The gorge is the jumping-off point for the famous 12-mi West Branch of the Penobscot River whitewater rafting trip and the most popular put-in point for Allagash canoe trips. The Penobscot River drops more than 70 ft per mile through the gorge, giving rafters a hold-on-for-your-life ride. The best spot to watch the Penobscot rafters is from Pray's Big Eddy Wilderness Campground, overlooking the rock-choked **Crib Works Rapid** (a Class V rapid). To get here, follow the main road northeast and turn left on Telos Road; the campground is about 10 yards after the bridge.

En Route From the Pray's Big Eddy Wilderness Campground, take the main road (here called the Golden Road for the amount of money it took the Great Northern Paper Company to build it) southeast toward Millinocket. The road soon becomes paved. After you drive over the one-lane Abol Bridge and pass through the Bowater/Great Northern Paper Company's Debsconeag checkpoint, bear left to reach Togue Pond Gatehouse, the southern entrance to Baxter State Park.

Baxter State Park

★ ⑤⑨ *24 mi northwest of Millinocket.*

Few places in Maine are as remote or as beautiful as Baxter State Park and the Allagash Wilderness Waterway (☞ *below*). Baxter, a gift from Governor Percival Baxter, is the jewel in the crown of northern Maine, a 204,733-acre wilderness area that surrounds **Katahdin,** Maine's highest mountain (5,267 ft at Baxter Peak) and the terminus of the Appalachian Trail. There are 46 mountain peaks and ridges, 18 of which exceed an elevation of 3,000 ft. Day-use parking areas fill quickly in season; it's best to arrive early, before 8 AM. The park is intersected by about 175 mi of trails. No pets, domestic animals, oversize vehicles, or motorcycles are allowed in the park, and there are no pay phones or gas stations. The one visitor center is at Togue Pond, for which Millinocket is the nearest gateway. ⊠ *mailing address: Baxter State Park Authority, 64 Balsam Dr., Millinocket 04462,* ☎ *207/723–5140.* ⊡ *$8 per vehicle; free to Maine residents. Office closed mid-Oct.–mid-May.*

OFF THE BEATEN PATH
LUMBERMAN'S MUSEUM – This museum comprises 10 buildings filled with exhibits depicting the history of logging, including models, dioramas, and equipment. ⊠ *Shin Pond Rd./Rte. 159, Patten (22 mi southeast of Baxter State Park),* ☎ *207/528–2650.* ⊡ *$2.50.* ☉ *Memorial Day–Sept., Tues.–Sat. 9–4, Sun. 11–4.*

Camping

$ ⚠ **Baxter State Park.** Camping spaces at the 10 campgrounds here can only be reserved by mail (phone reservations not accepted). Reservations can be made beginning January 1—some sites are fully booked for midsummer weekends soon after that. The state also maintains primitive backcountry sites that are available without charge on a first-come, first-served basis. ⊠ *Baxter State Park Authority, 64 Balsam Dr., Millinocket 04462,* ☎ *207/723–5140. Closed mid-Oct.–mid-May.*

Outdoor Activities and Sports

Katahdin, in Baxter State Park (☞ *above*), draws thousands of hikers every year for the daylong climb to the summit and the stunning views of woods, mountains, and lakes from the hair-raising Knife Edge Trail along its ridge. The crowds can be formidable on clear summer days, so if you crave solitude, tackle one of the 45 other mountains in the park, all of which are accessible from a 150-mi network of trails. South Turner can be climbed in a morning (if you're fit)—it has a great view of Katahdin across the valley. On the way you'll pass Sandy Stream Pond, where moose are often seen at dusk. The Owl, the Brothers, and Doubletop Mountain are good day hikes.

Allagash Wilderness Waterway

⑥⓪ *22 mi north of Ripogenus Dam.*

The Allagash is a spectacular 92-mi corridor of lakes and rivers that cuts across 170,000 acres of wilderness, beginning at the northwest corner of Baxter and running north to the town of Allagash, 10 mi from the Canadian border. For information, contact the **Allagash Wilderness Waterway** (⊠ 106 Hogan Rd., Bangor 04401, ☎ 207/941–4014).

Outdoor Activities and Sports

The Allagash rapids are ranked Class I and Class II (very easy and easy), but that doesn't mean the river is a piece of cake; river conditions vary greatly with the depth and volume of water, and even a Class I rapid can hang your canoe up on a rock, capsize you, or spin you around. On the lakes, strong winds can halt your progress for days. The Allagash should not be undertaken lightly or without planning; the complete 92-mi course requires 7 to 10 days. The canoeing season along the Allagash is from mid-May to October, although it's wise to remember that the black-fly season ends about July 1. The best bet for a novice is to go with a guide; a good outfitter (☞ Contacts and Resources *in* North Woods A to Z, *below*) will help plan your route and provide your craft and transportation.

The Mt. Everest of Maine canoe trips is the 110-mi route on the St. John River from Baker Lake to Allagash Village, with a swift current all the way and two stretches of Class III rapids. The best time to canoe the St. John is between mid-May and mid-June, when the river level is high.

Those with their own canoe who want to go it alone can take Telos Road north from Ripogenus Dam, putting in at Chamberlain Thoroughfare Bridge at the southern tip of Chamberlain Lake, or at Allagash Lake, Churchill Dam, Bissonnette Bridge, or Umsaskis Bridge. One popular and easy route follows the Upper West Branch of the Penobscot River from Lobster Lake (just east of Moosehead Lake) to Chesuncook Lake. From Chesuncook Village you can paddle to Ripogenus Dam in a day.

The Aroostook River from Little Munsungan Lake to Fort Fairfield (100 mi) is best run in late spring. More challenging routes include the Passadumkeag River from Grand Falls to Passadumkeag (25 mi with Class I–III rapids); the East Branch of the Penobscot River from Matagamon Wilderness Campground to Grindstone (38 mi with Class I–III rapids); and the West Branch of the Pleasant River from Katahdin Iron Works to Brownville Junction (10 mi with Class II–III rapids).

Millinocket

⑥ *90 mi northwest of Greenville, 19 mi southeast of Baxter State Park, 70 mi north of Bangor.*

Millinocket, with a population of 7,000, is a gateway to Baxter State Park (☞ *above*).

OFF THE BEATEN PATH
KATAHDIN IRON WORKS – For a worthwhile day trip from Millinocket, take Route 11 west to a trailhead 5 mi north of Brownville Junction. Drive the gravel road 6 mi to Katahdin Iron Works, the site of a mining operation that employed nearly 200 workers in the mid-1800s; a deteriorated kiln, a stone furnace, and a charcoal-storage building are all that remain. From here, a hiking trail leads over fairly rugged terrain to **Gulf Hagas,** with natural chasms, cliffs, a 3-mi gorge, waterfalls, pools, exotic flora, and rock formations.

Dining and Lodging

$–$$ ✕ **Scootic Inn and Penobscot Room.** This informal restaurant and lounge has a varied menu of steak, seafood, pizza, and sandwiches. The large-screen TV is usually tuned to sports. ✉ *70 Penobscot Ave.,* ☎ *207/723–4566. AE, D, MC, V.*

$ ☶ **Atrium Motel.** Off Route 157 next to a shopping center, this motor inn has a large central atrium with facilities that make up for its unappealing location and standard motel furnishings. ✉ *740 Central St., 04462,* ☎ ℻ *207/723–4555. 72 rooms, 10 suites. Indoor pool, hot tub, health club. Continental breakfast. AE, D, DC, MC, V.*

$ 🖫 **Big Moose Inn.** There's nothing fancy about this old-fashioned inn and the cabins and campsites nestled between Ambejesus and Millinocket lakes, just 8 mi from the entrance to Baxter State Park. The inn has a big stone and brick fireplace decorated with a moose trophy and snow-shoes; inn rooms are comfortably furnished with country pieces. The popular dining room ($$), open for dinner Wednesday through Sat-urday, emphasizes seafood. Canoes and a store are other amenities. ⊠ *Box 98, Baxter State Park Rd., 04462,* ☎ *207/723–8391,* FAX *207/723–8199. 11 rooms share 3 baths, 11 cabins, 44 campsites. Restaurant, boating. Continental breakfast. MC, V. Closed mid-Oct.–May.*

Outdoor Activities and Sports

Kathadin Area Guide Service (⊠ 74 Water St., ☎ 207/723–9522 or 800/548–4355) outfits fishing, snowmobiling, canoeing, and camping expeditions. **Penobscot River Outfitters** (☎ 800/794–5267) rents ca-noes and offers a shuttle service. **New England Outdoor Center** (☎ 207/723–5438 or 800/766–7238) rents snowmobiles and offers guided trips.

North Woods A to Z

Arriving and Departing

Bangor International Airport (☞ Arriving and Departing *in* Maine A to Z, *below*) is the closest airport.

Getting Around

BY CAR

A car is essential to negotiate this vast region but may not be useful to someone spending a vacation entirely at a wilderness camp. Public roads are scarce in the north country, but lumber companies maintain pri-vate roads that are often open to the public (sometimes by permit only). When driving on a logging road, always give lumber company trucks the right of way. Be aware that loggers often take the middle of the road and will neither move over nor slow down for you.

I–95 offers the quickest access to the North Woods. U.S. 201 (Exit 36 off I–95) is the major route to Jackman and to Québec. Route 15 con-nects Jackman to Greenville and Bangor. The Golden Road is a pri-vate, paper company–operated road that links Greenville to Millinocket.

BY PLANE

Charter flights, usually by seaplane, from Bangor, Greenville, or Millinocket to smaller towns and remote lake and forest areas can be arranged with the following flying services, which will transport you and your gear and help you find a guide: **Currier's Flying Service** (⊠ Greenville Junction, ☎ 207/695–2778), **Folsom's Air Service** (⊠ Greenville, ☎ 207/695–2821), **Katahdin Air Service** (⊠ Millinocket, ☎ 207/723–8378), **Scotty's Flying Service** (⊠ Shin Pond, ☎ 207/528–2626).

Contacts and Resources

CAMPING

Reservations for state park campsites (excluding Baxter State Park) can be made through the **Bureau of Parks and Lands** (☞ Contacts and Re-sources *in* Maine A to Z, *below*). **Maine Sporting Camp Association** (☎ 800/305–3057) publishes a list of its members, with details on the facilities available at each camp.

The **Bureau of Parks and Lands** (⊠ State House Station 22, Augusta 04333, ☎ 207/287–3821) will tell you if you need a camping permit and where to obtain one. The **Maine Forest Service, Department of Con-servation** (⊠ State House Station 22, Augusta 04333, ☎ 207/287–2791) will direct you to the nearest ranger station, where you can get a fire permit (⊠ Greenville Ranger Station, Box 1107, Lakeview St., Greenville 04441, ☎ 207/695–3721). The **Maine Campground Owners Association** (⊠ 655 Main St., Lewiston 04240, ☎ 207/782–5874) publishes a helpful annual directory of its members; 18 are in the Katahdin-Moosehead area, and 25 are in the Kennebec and Moose River valleys. **Maine Tourism Association** (⊠ Box 2300, 325B Water St., Hallowell 04347, ☎ 207/623–0363; 800/533–9595 outside ME) publishes a listing of private campsites and cottage rentals. **North Maine Woods** (⊠ Box 421, Ashland 04732, ☎ 207/435–6213) maintains 500 primitive campsites on commercial forest land and takes reservations for 20 of them; early reservations are recommended.

CANOEING

Most canoe rental operations will arrange transportation, help plan your route, and provide a guide. Transport to wilderness lakes can be arranged through the flying services listed under Getting Around by Plane, *above.*

The **Bureau of Parks and Lands** (☞ Camping, *above)* provides information on independent Allagash canoeing and camping. The following outfitters serve the area:

Allagash Canoe Trips (⊠ Box 713, Greenville 04441, ☎ 207/695–3668) operates guided trips on the Allagash Waterway, plus the Moose, Penobscot, and St. John rivers. **Allagash Wilderness Outfitters/Frost Pond Camps** (⊠ Box 620, Greenville 04441, ☎ 207/695–2821) provides equipment, transportation, and information for canoe trips on the Allagash and the Penobscot rivers. **Mahoosuc Guide Service** (⊠ Bear River Rd., Newry 04261, ☎ 207/824–2073) conducts guided trips on the Penobscot, Allagash, and Moose rivers. **North Country Outfitters** (⊠ Box 41, Rockwood 04478, ☎ 207/534–2242 or 207/534–7305) operates a white-water canoeing and kayaking school, rents equipment, and sponsors guided canoe trips on the Allagash Waterway and the Moose, Penobscot, and St. John rivers. **North Woods Ways** (⊠ R.R. 2, Box 159-A, Guilford 04443, ☎ 207/997–3723) organizes wilderness canoeing trips on the Allagash, as well as on the Penobscot and St. John rivers. **Willard Jalbert Camps** (⊠ 6 Winchester St., Presque Isle 04769, ☎ 207/764–0494) has been sponsoring guided Allagash trips since the late 1800s.

EMERGENCIES

Charles A. Dean Memorial Hospital (⊠ Pritham Ave., Greenville, ☎ 207/695–2223 or 800/260–4000). **Mayo Regional Hospital** (⊠ 75 W. Main St., Dover-Foxcroft, ☎ 207/564–8401). **Millinocket Regional Hospital** (⊠ 200 Somerset St., Millinocket, ☎ 207/723–5161).

GUIDES

Fishing guides are available through most wilderness camps, sporting goods stores, and canoe outfitters. For assistance in finding a guide, contact North Maine Woods (☞ Visitor Information, *below).* A few well-established guides are **Gilpatrick's Guide Service** (⊠ Box 461, Skowhegan 04976, ☎ 207/453–6959), **Maine Guide Fly Shop and Guide Service** (⊠ Box 1202, Main St., Greenville 04441, ☎ 207/695–2266), and **Professional Guide Service** (⊠ Box 346, Sheridan 04775, ☎ 207/435–8044).

HORSEBACK RIDING

Northern Maine Riding Adventures (⊠ 64 Garland Line Rd., Dover-Foxcroft 04426, ☎ 207/564–3451), owned by registered Maine guides Judy Cross-Strehlke and Bob Strehlke, conducts one-day, two-day, and weeklong pack trips (10 people maximum) through parts of Piscataquis County. A popular two-day trip explores the Whitecap–Barren Mountain Range, near Katahdin Iron Works (☞ Millinocket, *above*).

RAFTING

Raft Maine (☎ 800/723–8633) is an association of white-water outfitters licensed to lead trips down the Kennebec and Dead rivers and the West Branch of the Penobscot River. Rafting season begins May 1 and continues through mid-October.

VISITOR INFORMATION

Baxter State Park Authority (✉ 64 Balsam Dr., Millinocket 04462, ☎ 207/723–5140). **Katahdin Area Chamber of Commerce** (✉ 1029 Central St., Millinocket 04462, ☎ 207/723–4443). **Moosehead Lake Region Chamber of Commerce** (✉ Box 581, Rtes. 6 and 15, Greenville 04441, ☎ 207/695–2702). **North Maine Woods** (✉ Box 421, Ashland 04732, ☎ 207/435–6213 for maps; a canoeing guide for the St. John River; and lists of outfitters, camps, and campsites).

MAINE A TO Z

Arriving and Departing

By Bus

Concord Trailways (☎ 800/639–3317) provides service between Boston and Bangor (via Portland); a coastal route connects towns between Brunswick and Searsport. **Vermont Transit** (☎ 207/772–6587) connects towns in southwestern Maine with cities in New England and throughout the United States. Vermont Transit is a subsidiary of **Greyhound** (☎ 800/231–2222).

By Car

Interstate 95 is the fastest route to and through the state from coastal New Hampshire and points south, turning inland at Brunswick and going on to Bangor and the Canadian border. U.S. 1, more leisurely and scenic, is the principal coastal highway from New Hampshire to Canada. U.S. 302 is the primary access to the Sebago Lake region, while Route 26 leads to the western mountains and Route 27 leads to the Rangeley and Sugarloaf regions. U.S. 201 is the fastest route to Québec and Route 9 is the inland route from Bangor to Calais.

By Ferry

Bay Ferries (☎ 888/249–7245) operates the Cat, a high-speed car-ferry service on a catamaran, between Yarmouth, Nova Scotia, and Bar Harbor from mid-May to mid-October. The crossing takes 2½ hours, and the Cat has everything from a casino to sightseeing decks. **Prince of Fundy Cruises** (☎ 800/341–7540; 800/482–0955 in Maine) operates a car ferry from May to October between Portland and Yarmouth, Nova Scotia.

By Plane

Portland International Jetport (✉ Westbrook St. off Rte. 9, ☎ 207/774–7301) is served by Business Express, Continental, Delta, United, and US Airways. **Bangor International Airport** (✉ Godfrey Blvd., Exit 47 off I–95, ☎ 207/947–0384) is served by American, Business Express, Continental, Delta, Northwest Airlink, and US Airways. **Hancock County Airport** (✉ Rte. 3, ☎ 207/667–7329), in Trenton, 8 mi northwest of Bar Harbor, is served by Continental Connection/Colgan Air. **Knox County Regional Airport** (✉ Off Rte. 73, ☎ 207/594–4131), in Owls Head, 3 mi south of Rockland, has flights to Boston and Bar Harbor on Continental Connection/Colgan Air.

See Air Travel *in* Smart Travel Tips A to Z for airline phone numbers.

Getting Around

By Car

The maximum speed limit is 65 mph, unless otherwise posted, on I–95 and the Maine Turnpike. Local municipalities post speed limits on roads within their jurisdictions. It is a state law to stop for pedestrians. Drivers can make right turns on red if no sign prohibits such turns. Note that Maine law requires drivers to turn on their lights when windshield wipers are operating.

In many areas a car is the only practical means of travel. The *Maine Map and Travel Guide,* available for a small fee from the Maine Tourism Association, is useful for driving throughout the state; it has directories, mileage charts, and enlarged maps of city areas. DeLorme's *Maine Atlas & Gazetteer,* sold at local bookstores, includes enlarged, detailed maps of every part of the state.

By Ferry

Maine State Ferry Service (☎ 207/596–2202 or 800/491–4883) provides service from Rockland, Lincolnville, and Bass Harbor to islands in Penobscot and Blue Hill bays.

By Plane

Regional flying services, operating from regional and municipal airports (☞ Arriving and Departing, *above*), provide access to remote lakes and wilderness areas as well as to Penobscot Bay islands.

Contacts and Resources

Antiques

For a directory of members of the **Maine Antique Dealer Association,** send a self-addressed, stamped envelope to MADA (⊠ Box 604, North Turner 04266). You can send $3 to receive a copy of the **Maine Antique Dealer Directory** (⊠ R.R. 3, Box 1290, Winslow 04901).

Camping

Reservations for state park campsites (excluding Baxter State Park) can be made from January until August 23 through the **Bureau of Parks and Lands** (☎ 207/287–3824; 800/332–1501 in ME). Make reservations as far ahead as possible (at least seven days in advance), because sites go quickly. The **Maine Campground Owners Association** (⊠ 655 Main St., Lewiston 04240, ☎ 207/782–5874, FAX 207/782–4497) has a statewide listing of private campgrounds.

Car Rental

Alamo (⊠ Rear 9 Johnson St., ☎ 207/775–0855; 800/327–9633 in Portland). **Avis** (⊠ Portland International Jetport, ☎ 207/874–7501 or 800/331–1212). **Budget** (⊠ Portland International Jetport, ☎ 207/772–6789 or 800/527–0700). **Hertz** (⊠ 1049 Westbrook St., Portland International Jetport, ☎ 207/774–4544 or 800/654–3131). **Thrifty** (⊠ 1000 Westbrook St., Portland International Jetport, ☎ 207/772–4628 or 800/367–2277).

Fishing

For information about fishing and licenses, contact the **Department of Inland Fisheries and Wildlife** (☎ 207/287–8000).

Kayaking

Maine Island Kayak Co. (⊠ 70 Luther St., Peaks Island, ☎ 800/796–2373) provides sea-kayaking instruction and conducts tours along the Maine coast.

Rafting

Raft Maine (⊠ Box 3, Bethel 04217, ☎ 800/723–8633) provides information on whitewater rafting on the Kennebec, Penobscot, and Dead rivers.

Skiing

For information on alpine skiing, contact **Ski Maine** (⊠ Box 7566, Portland 04112, ☎ 207/622–6983, 207/761–3774 or 888/624–6345 for ski conditions). For information on cross-country skiing, contact the **Maine Nordic Ski Council** (⊠ Box 645, Bethel 04217, ☎ 800/754–9263).

Snowmobiling

The **Maine Snowmobile Association** (⊠ Box 77, Augusta 04332, ☎ 207/622–6983 or 207/626–5717 for trail conditions) offers an excellent state-wide trail map of about 8,000 mi of trails.

Visitor Information

Maine Innkeepers Association (⊠ 305 Commercial St., Portland 04101, ☎ 207/773–7670). **Maine Tourism Association** (⊠ Box 2300, 325B Water St., Hallowell 04347, ☎ 207/623–0363; 800/533–9595 outside ME).

The **Maine Tourism Association** operates wlcome centers on U.S. 2 in Bethel and U.S. 302 in Fryeburg. **State of Maine Visitor Information Centers** are located on I–95 in Hampden, I–95 and U.S. 1 in Kittery, and on U.S. 1 in Yarmouth, off Exit 17 of I–95.

3 VERMONT

Southern Vermont has manicured landscapes, immaculate villages, and summer theaters, as well as a surprisingly large chunk of wilderness in the Green Mountain National Forest. Central Vermont offers the state's largest ski resort, Killington, along with the rolling farmland vistas of the lower Lake Champlain valley. Up north, Vermont attractions include the state's largest city, cosmopolitan and collegiate Burlington; the nation's smallest state capital, Montpelier; the legendary slopes of Stowe; and the leafy back roads of the Northeast Kingdom.

EVERYWHERE YOU LOOK AROUND VERMONT, the evidence is clear: This is not the state it was 30 years ago. That may be true for the rest of New England as well,

Revised and updated by Kay and Bill Scheller

but the contrasts between the present and recent past seem all the more sharply drawn in the Green Mountain State, if only because an aura of timelessness has always been at the heart of the Vermont image. Vermont was where all the quirks and virtues outsiders associate with up-country New England were supposed to reside. It was where the Yankees were Yankee-est and where there were more cows/than people.

Not that you should be alarmed, if you haven't been here in a while; Vermont hasn't become southern California, or even, for that matter, southern New Hampshire. This is still the most rural state in the Union (meaning that it has the smallest percentage of citizens living in statistically defined metropolitan areas), and it still turns out most of New England's milk, even though there are, finally, more people than cows. It's still a place where cars occasionally have to stop while a dairy farmer walks his herd across a secondary road; and up in Essex County, in what George Aiken dubbed the Northeast Kingdom, there are townships with zero population. And the kind of scrupulous, straightforward, plainspoken politics practiced by Governor (later Senator) Aiken for 50 years has not become outmoded in a state that still turns out on town-meeting day.

How has Vermont changed? In strictly physical terms, the most obvious transformations have taken place in and around the two major cities, Burlington and Rutland, and near the larger ski resorts, such as Stowe, Killington, Stratton, and Mt. Snow. Burlington's Church Street, once a paradigm of all the sleepy redbrick shopping thoroughfares in northern New England, is now a pedestrian mall with chic bistros; outside the city, suburban development has supplanted farms in towns where someone's trip to Burlington might once have been an item in a weekly newspaper. As for the ski areas, it's no longer enough simply to boast the latest in chairlift technology. Slopeside hotels and condos have boomed, especially in the southern part of the state, making ski areas into big-time resort destinations. And once-sleepy Manchester has become one of New England's factory-outlet meccas.

But the real metamorphosis in the Green Mountains has to do more with style, with the personality of the place, than with development. The past couple of decades have seen a tremendous influx of outsiders—not only skiers and "leaf peepers" but people who have come to stay year-round—and many of them are determined either to freshen the local scene with their own idiosyncrasies or to make Vermont even more like Vermont than they found it. On the one hand, this translates into the fact that Vermont is the only state represented in Washington by an independent socialist congressman; on the other, it means that sheep farming has been reintroduced to the state, largely to provide a high-quality product for the hand-weaving industry.

This ties in with another local phenomenon, one best described as Made in Vermont. Once upon a time, maple syrup and sharp cheddar cheese were the products that carried Vermont's name to the world. The market niche that they created has since been widened by Vermonters—a great many of them refugees from more hectic arenas of commerce—offering a dizzying variety of goods with the ineffable cachet of Vermont manufacture. There are Vermont wood toys, Vermont apple wines, Vermont chocolates, even Vermont gin. All of it is marketed with the tacit suggestion that it was made by Yankee elves in a shed out back on a bright autumn morning.

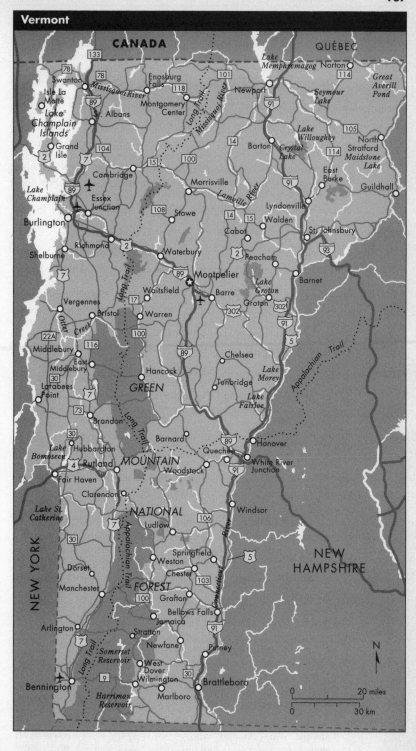

Vermont

CANADA · QUÉBEC

Lake Memphremagog · Norton

133

78 · Swanton · 78
Isle La Motte · 118 · Enosburg Falls · 101 · Newport · 114
89 · Missisquoi River · Montgomery Center · Long Trail · Missisquoi River · Seymour Lake · Great Averill Pond

Lake Champlain Islands · St. Albans · 100 · 14 · Barton · Crystal Lake · Lake Willoughby · 105 · North Stratford
104 · 15 · Morrisville · Lamville River · 91 · East Burke · 114 · Maidstone Lake
Grand Isle · Cambridge · Lyndonville · Guildhall
2 · 7 · 89 · 108 · Stowe · 14 · Walden
Essex Junction · 15 · Cabot · St. Johnsbury
Burlington · Lake Champlain · Waterbury · 2 · Peacham · 93
Shelburne · Richmond · 2 · 89 · Montpelier · Lake Groton · Barnet
7 · Long Trail · Waitsfield · Barre · 302 · Groton · 302
Vergennes · 17 · Warren · 302 · 5
Bristol · 100 · 89 · 91
Otter Creek
22A · Chelsea · Appalachian Trail
Middlebury · 116 · Hancock · Lake Morey
East Middlebury · GREEN · Tunbridge
30 · Larabees Point · 7 · Lake Fairlee
73 · Brandon · Long Trail · Barnard · 89 · Hanover
30 · Hubbardton · Quechee
Lake Bomoseen · 4 · Rutland · MOUNTAIN · Woodstock · White River Junction
Fair Haven · 91
Clarendon · Windsor
Lake St. Catherine · NATIONAL · 106
30 · 7 · Ludlow
Dorset · Weston · Springfield · 5 · NEW HAMPSHIRE
Manchester · Chester · 103
100 · FOREST · Grafton
Arlington · Jamaica · Bellows Falls · 91
7 · Stratton · Newfane · Putney
Long Trail · Somerset Reservoir · West Dover · 30
Bennington · 9 · Wilmington · Brattleboro
Harriman Reservoir · Marlboro

NEW YORK

Connecticut River

Appalachian Trail

N

0 ——— 20 miles
0 ——— 30 km

The most successful Made in Vermont product is Ben & Jerry's ice cream. Neither Ben nor Jerry comes from old Green Mountain stock, but their product has benefited immensely from the magical reputation of the place where it is made. Along the way, the company (which started in Burlington under the most modest circumstances in 1979) has become the largest single purchaser of Vermont milk.

Pleasures and Pastimes

Biking

Vermont is great bicycle-touring country, especially the often deserted roads of the Northeast Kingdom. Many companies lead weekend tours and weeklong trips throughout the state. If you'd like to go it on your own, most chambers of commerce have brochures highlighting good cycling routes in their area, including *Vermont Life* magazine's "Bicycle Vermont" map and guide, and many bookstores sell *25 Bicycle Tours in Vermont* by John Freidin.

Dining

Over the past few years, Vermont chefs have been working hard to live up to two distinct responsibilities. One is the need to honor the home-and-hearth traditions of Yankee cooking, the realm of pot roast and Indian pudding, sticky buns and homemade corn relish. But as travelers and residents have become more sophisticated, there has been a demand for the ethnic cuisines, lighter adaptations of classics, and new American treatments of seasonal ingredients that now characterize urban menus.

The more ambitious restaurants and inn kitchens have not only managed to balance these two gastronomic imperatives but have often succeeded in combining them. The trick is to take an innovative hand with Vermont game and local produce, introduce fresh herbs and other seasonings, and change menus to suit the season. Look for imaginative approaches to native New England foods like fiddlehead ferns (available only for a short time in the spring), maple syrup (Vermont is the largest U.S. producer), dairy products (especially cheese), native fruits and berries that are often transformed into jams and jellies, "new Vermont" products such as salsa and salad dressings, and venison, quail, pheasant, and other game.

Your chances of finding a table for dinner vary with the season: Many restaurants have lengthy waits during peak seasons (when it's always a good idea to make a reservation) and then shut down during the slow months of April and November. Some of the best dining is found at country inns.

Fishing

Central Vermont is the heart of the state's warm-water lake and pond fishing. Harriman and Somerset reservoirs have both warm- and cold-water species; Harriman has a greater variety. Lake Dunmore produced the state-record rainbow trout; Lakes Bomoseen and St. Catherine are good for rainbows and largemouth bass. In the east, Lakes Fairlee and Morey hold bass, perch, and chain pickerel, while the lower part of the Connecticut River contains smallmouth bass, walleye, and perch; shad are returning via the fish ladders at Vernon and Bellows Falls.

In northern Vermont, rainbow and brown trout inhabit the Missisquoi, Lamoille, Winooski, and Willoughby rivers, and there's warm-water fishing at many smaller lakes and ponds. Lakes Seymour, Willoughby, and Memphremagog and Great Averill Pond in the Northeast Kingdom are good for salmon and lake trout. The Dog River near Montpelier has one of the best wild populations of brown trout in the state.

Good news is that landlocked Atlantic salmon are returning to the Clyde River following removal of a controversial dam.

Lake Champlain, stocked annually with salmon and lake trout, has become the state's ice-fishing capital; walleye, bass, pike, and channel catfish are also taken. Ice fishing is also popular on Lake Memphremagog.

Lodging

Vermont's largest hotels are in Burlington and near the major ski resorts. There's a dearth of inns and bed-and-breakfasts in Burlington, though chain hotels provide dependable accommodations. Elsewhere you'll find a range of inns, B&Bs, and small motels. The many lovely and sometimes quite luxurious inns and B&Bs provide what many people consider the quintessential Vermont lodging experience. Rates are highest during foliage season, from late September to mid-October, and lowest in late spring and November, when many properties close. Many of the larger hotels offer package rates. Some quiet, romantic inns discourage bringing children.

National Forests

The two sections of the 355,000-acre Green Mountain National Forest (GMNF) are central and southern Vermont's primary stronghold of woodland and high mountain terrain. Like all national forests, it contains sections on which timber leases are sometimes granted, but it's possible to travel through much of this preserve without seeing significant evidence of human intrusion. In addition to the paved public highways that traverse the GMNF, many of the occasional logging roads are maintained for public use, and although unpaved, these are kept in good condition during snow-free times of the year.

The Forest Service maintains a number of picnic areas and primitive campgrounds; complete information is available from the Forest Supervisor (☞ Contacts and Resources *in* Vermont A to Z, *below*). Fishing, subject to state laws and seasonal closings and limits, is allowed throughout the GMNF. Canoeing, cross-country skiing, and hiking are also popular; the Appalachian and Long trails run the length of the forest. Snowmobiles and other forms of motorized transportation, such as all-terrain vehicles, are permitted on marked trails, except within roadless areas designated as wilderness.

Skiing

The Green Mountains run through the middle of Vermont like a bumpy spine, visible from almost every point in the state; generous accumulations of snow make the mountains an ideal site for skiing. Increased snowmaking capacity and improved, high-tech computerized equipment at many areas virtually assure a good day on the slopes. Vermont has 26 alpine ski resorts with nearly 1,000 trails and some 5,000 acres of skiable terrain. Combined, the resorts operate nearly 200 lifts and have the capacity to carry some 215,000 skiers per hour. Though grooming is sophisticated at all Vermont areas, conditions usually run to a typically Eastern hard pack, with powder a rare luxury and ice a bugbear after January thaw. The best advice for skiing in Vermont is to keep your skis well tuned.

Route 100 is also known as "Skier's Highway," passing by 13 of the state's ski areas. Vermont's major resorts are Stowe, Jay Peak, Sugarbush, Killington, Okemo, Mt. Snow, and Stratton. Midsize, less hectic areas to consider include Ascutney, Bromley, Smugglers' Notch, Pico, Mad River Glen, and Burke Mountain. At press time, Bolton Valley Ski Resort—long a favorite because of its proximity to Burlington and ample intermediate terrain—was scheduled to reopen for the 1999–

2000 season under a new owner. For information, call the **Vermont Ski Area Association** at ☎ 802/223–2439.

Exploring Vermont

Vermont can be divided into three regions. The southern part of the state, flanked by Bennington on the west and Brattleboro on the east, played an important role in Vermont's Revolutionary War–era drive to independence (yes, there was once a Republic of Vermont) and its eventual statehood. The central part is characterized by rugged mountains and the gently rolling dairy lands near Lake Champlain. Northern Vermont is the site of the state's capital, Montpelier, and its largest city, Burlington, yet it is also home to Vermont's most rural area, the Northeast Kingdom.

Numbers in the text correspond to numbers in the margin and on the Southern Vermont, Central Vermont, and Northern Vermont maps.

Great Itineraries

There are many ways to take advantage of Vermont's beauty—skiing or hiking its mountains, biking or driving its back roads, fishing or sailing its waters, shopping for local products, visiting its museums and sights, or simply finding the perfect inn and never leaving the front porch. Distances in Vermont are relatively short, yet the mountains and many back roads will slow a traveler's pace. You can see a representative north–south section of Vermont in a few days; if you have up to a week you can hit the highlights around the state.

IF YOU HAVE 3 DAYS

Spend a few hours in historic **Bennington** ⑤ in the southern part of Vermont; then travel north to see Hildene and stay in 🏨 **Manchester** ⑦. On your second day take Route 100 through Weston and travel north through the Green Mountains to Route 125, where you turn west to explore 🏨 **Middlebury** ㉔. On day three, enter the Champlain Valley, which has views of the Adirondack Mountains to the west. Stop at Shelburne Farms and carry on to **Burlington** ㉞; catch the sunset from the waterfront and take a walk on Church Street.

IF YOU HAVE 5 TO 7 DAYS

You can make several side trips off Route 100 and also visit the Northeast Kingdom on a trip this length. Visit **Bennington** ⑤ and 🏨 **Manchester** ⑦ on day one. Spend your second day walking around the small towns of **Chester** ⑪ and 🏨 **Grafton** ⑫. On day three head north to explore **Woodstock** ⑲ and 🏨 **Quechee** ⑱, stopping at either the Billings Farm Museum and Marsh-Billings National Park or the Vermont Institute of Natural Science. Head leisurely on your fourth day toward 🏨 **Middlebury** ㉔, along one of Vermont's most inspiring mountain drives, Route 125 west of Route 100. Between Hancock and Middlebury, you'll pass nature trails and the picnic spot at Texas Falls Recreation Area, then traverse a moderately steep mountain pass. Spend day five in 🏨 **Burlington** ㉞. On day six head east to **Waterbury** ㉙ and then north to 🏨 **Stowe** ㉚ and Mount Mansfield for a full day. Begin your last day with a few hours in **Montpelier** ㉘ on your way to **Peacham** ㉟, **St. Johnsbury** ㊳, 🏨 **Lake Willoughby** ㊱, and the serenity and back roads of the Northeast Kingdom. Especially noteworthy are U.S. 5, Route 5A, and Route 14.

When to Tour Vermont

The number of visitors and the rates for lodging reach their peaks along with the color of the leaves during foliage season, from late September to mid-October. But if you have never seen a kaleidoscope of autumn colors, it is worth braving the slow-moving traffic and paying the extra money. In summer the state is lush and green. Winter, of course, is high season at Vermont's ski resorts. Rates are lowest in late spring and November, although many properties close during these times.

SOUTHERN VERMONT

The Vermont tradition of independence and rebellion began in southern Vermont. Many towns founded in the early 18th century as frontier outposts or fortifications were later important as trading centers. In the western region the Green Mountain Boys fought off both the British and the claims of land-hungry New Yorkers—some say their descendants are still fighting. In the 19th century, as many towns turned to manufacturing, the farmers here retreated to hillier regions and, as the modern ski and summer-home booms got under way, retreated even farther.

The first thing you'll notice upon entering the state is the conspicuous lack of billboards along the highways and roads. The foresight back in the 1960s to prohibit them has made for a refreshing absence of aggressive visual clutter that allows unencumbered views of working farmland, fresh-as-paint villages, and quiet back roads—but does not hide the reality of abandoned dairy barns, bustling ski resorts, and strip-mall sprawl.

The towns are listed in counterclockwise order, beginning in the east, south of the junction of I–91 and Route 9 in Brattleboro, and following the southern boundary of the state toward Bennington, then north up to Manchester and Weston and south back to Newfane.

Brattleboro

❶ *60 mi south of White River Junction.*

Its downtown bustling with activity, Brattleboro, with about 13,000 inhabitants, is the center of commerce for southeastern Vermont. This town at the confluence of the West and Connecticut rivers originated as a frontier scouting post and became a thriving industrial center and resort town in the 1800s. More recently, the area has become a home to political activists and a raft of earnest counterculturists.

A former railroad station, the **Brattleboro Museum and Art Center** has replaced locomotives with art and historical exhibits. The museum's organs were made in Brattleboro between 1853 and 1961, when the city was home to the Estey Organ Company, one of the world's largest organ manufacturers. ✉ *Vernon and Main Sts.,* ☎ *802/257–0124.* 🔳 *$3.* ☉ *Mid-May–early Nov., Tues.–Sun. noon–6.*

Larkin G. Mead, Jr., a Brattleboro resident, stirred 19th-century America's imagination with an 8-ft snow angel he built at the intersection of Routes 30 and 5. **Brooks Memorial Library** has a replica of the angel as well as exhibits of Vermont art. ✉ *224 Main St.,* ☎ *802/254–5290.* ☉ *Labor Day–Memorial Day, Mon.–Wed. 9–9, Thurs.–Fri. 9–6, Sat. 9–5; Memorial Day–Labor Day, Sat. 9–noon.*

Dining and Lodging

$$$ ✕ **Peter Havens.** In a town better known for tofu than toniness, this chic little bistro knows just what to do with a filet mignon—serve it with Roquefort walnut butter, of course. Look for the house-cured gravlax made with lemon vodka and fresh seasonal seafood, which even includes a spring fling with soft-shelled crabs. The wine list is superb. ✉ *32 Elliot St.,* ☎ *802/257–3333. MC, V. Closed Mon. No lunch.*

Southern Vermont

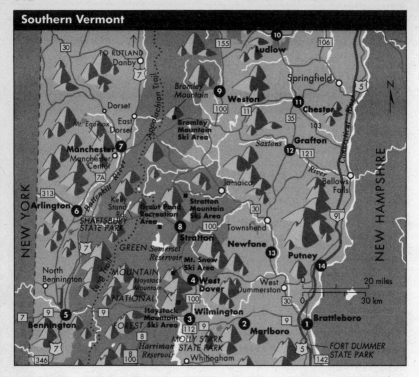

$ ✕ **Common Ground.** The political posters and concert fliers that line the staircase at Common Ground attest to Vermont's strong progressive element. The stairs lead to loftlike, rough-hewn dining rooms. Owned cooperatively by the staff, this mostly organic vegetarian restaurant serves cashew burgers, veggie stir-fries, curries, hot soup and stew, and the humble bowl of brown rice. All the desserts, including a chocolate cake with peanut butter frosting, are made without white sugar. ⊠ *25 Elliot St.,* ☏ *802/257–0855. No credit cards. Closed Mon.–Wed.*

$ ✕ **Sarkis Market.** Gail Sarkis's Lebanese grandmother gave her many of the recipes she uses to create Middle Eastern delicacies such as falafel, stuffed grape leaves, hummus, and *kibbe*—a layered meatloaf stuffed with ground lamb, pine nuts, and onions. Undecided about what to order? Go for the combination plate and finish with a wedge of homemade baklava. Bring your own bottle of wine. ⊠ *50 Eliot St.,* ☏ *802/ 258–4906. AE, MC, V. Closed Sun. except during Oct.*

$–$$ ✕🏨 **Latchis Hotel.** The current generation of Latchises run this 1938 downtown Art Deco landmark. Front rooms overlook busy—and often noisy—Main Street. All the rooms have coffeemakers and are furnished comfortably, if not in high style; the suites are a bargain. Muffins arrive outside your door in the morning, and you can catch a movie under the zodiac ceiling of the adjoining Latchis Theater. The Latchis Grille (closed on Monday and Tuesday in winter; no lunch on weekdays) serves pub food as well as more creative fare like chicken and watercress roulade and is home to the Windham Brewery, which brews rich ales and lagers. ⊠ *50 Main St., 05301,* ☏ *802/254–6300,* 𝔽𝔸𝕏 *802/ 254–6304. 30 rooms. Restaurant. Continental breakfast. AE, MC, V.*

$$–$$$ 🏨 **40 Putney Road.** Joan Broderick welcomes guests to her antiques-filled French château–style estate with a glass of port and a smile and leaves handmade chocolates on the pillow at night. In warm weather, breakfast is served on the patio of the formally landscaped grounds, which lead to the shores of the West River. Rooms have antiques, phones,

and a TV/VCR; the suite has a gas fireplace and sleeps four. ✉ *40 Putney Rd., 05301,* ☎ *802/254–6268 or 800/941–2413,* 𝕱𝕬𝕏 *802/258–2673. 3 rooms, 1 suite. Full breakfast. AE, D, MC, V.*

Nightlife and the Arts

Common Ground (✉ 25 Elliot St., ☎ 802/257–0855) often presents folk music or performance art on weekends, especially during Sunday brunch. **Mole's Eye Cafe** (✉ 4 High St., ☎ 802/257–0771) hosts musical performers: acoustic or folk on Wednesday, open mike on Thursday, danceable R&B or blues on weekends. There's a cover charge on Friday and Saturday.

Outdoor Activities and Sports

CANOEING

Connecticut River Safari (✉ U.S. 5, ☎ 802/257–5008) has guided and self-guided tours as well as canoe rentals.

SKATING

Nelson Withington Skating Rink (✉ Memorial Park, 4 Guilford St., ☎ 802/257–2311) rents skates.

STATE PARK

The hiking trails at **Fort Dummer State Park** (✉ S. Main St., 2 mi south of Brattleboro, ☎ 802/254–2610) afford views of the Connecticut River valley; campsites are available.

Shopping

The **Book Cellar** (✉ 120 Main St., ☎ 802/254–6026), with two floors of volumes, carries many travel books. **Vermont Artisan Design** (✉ 106 Main St., ☎ 802/257–7044), one of the state's best crafts shops, displays contemporary ceramics, glass, wood, clothing, jewelry, and furniture.

Marlboro

❷ *10 mi west of Brattleboro.*

Tiny Marlboro draws musicians and audiences from around the world each summer to the Marlboro Music Festival, founded by Rudolf Serkin and joined for many years by Pablo Casals. **Marlboro College,** high on a hill off Route 9, is the center of musical activity. The college's white-frame buildings have outstanding views of the valley below, and the campus is studded with apple trees.

The **Southern Vermont Natural History Museum** opened its doors in 1997 when a privately held wildlife collection with more than 500 birds in 80 small dioramas was donated to the newly formed museum. One of New England's largest collections of mounted birds, it also holds specimens of three extinct birds as well as a complete collection of mammals native to the Northeast. ✉ *Rte. 9,* ☎ *802/464–0048.* 🎫 *$2.* ☉ *Memorial Day–Oct., daily 9–5; call for hrs rest of yr.*

Nightlife and the Arts

The **Marlboro Music Festival** (✉ Marlboro Music Center, Marlboro College, ☎ 802/254–2394; 215/569–4690 Sept.–June) presents chamber music in weekend concerts in July and August. The **New England Bach Festival** (☎ 802/257–4523), with a chorus under the direction of Blanche Moyse, is held at Marlboro College in October.

Wilmington

❸ *8 mi west of Marlboro.*

Wilmington is the shopping and dining center for the Mt. Snow ski area (☞ West Dover, *below*) to the north. Main Street has a cohesive assemblage of 18th- and 19th-century buildings, many of them listed on the National Register of Historic Places. For a great stroll, pick up a self-guided tour map from the **Chamber of Commerce** (⊠ Rte. 9, W. Main St., ☎ 802/464–8092).

North River Winery, which occupies a converted farmhouse and barn, produces fruit wines such as Green Mountain Apple and Vermont Pear. ⊠ *Rte. 112, 6 mi south of Wilmington,* ☎ *802/368–7557.* ☑ *Free.* ☉ *Daily 10–5; tours late May–Dec.*

OFF THE BEATEN PATH

SCENIC TOUR – To begin a scenic (though well-traveled) 35-mi circular tour with panoramic views of the region's mountains, farmland, and abundant cow population, drive west on Route 9 to the intersection with Route 8. Turn south and continue to the junction with Route 100; follow Route 100 through Whitingham (the birthplace of the Mormon prophet Brigham Young), and stay with the road as it turns north again and takes you back to Route 9.

Lodging

$$–$$$$ ▥ **Trail's End.** A cozy and congenial four-season lodge set on 10 acres, Trail's End is 4 mi from Mt. Snow. The inn's centerpiece is its cathedral-ceiling living room with catwalk loft seating and a 21-ft fieldstone fireplace. Guest rooms are comfortable, if simple, though two suites have fireplaces, whirlpool tubs, cable TV, refrigerators, and microwaves; four other rooms also have fireplaces. Breakfast is served at immense round pine tables; dinner is prepared during the holiday season only. There's a stocked trout pond on site and cross-country ski trails are nearby. ⊠ *5 Trail's End La., 05363,* ☎ *802/464–2727 or 800/859–2585,* ℻ *802/464–5532. 15 rooms. Pool, pond, tennis court. Full breakfast. AE, D, MC, V.*

$$–$$$$ ▥ **White House of Wilmington.** The grand staircase in this Federal-style mansion leads to rooms with antique bathrooms and brass wall sconces. The newer section has more contemporary plumbing; some rooms have fireplaces, whirlpool tubs, and lofts. The leather wing chairs of the public rooms suggest formality, but the atmosphere is casual and comfortable. Although it's a 10-minute drive to Mt. Snow/Haystack, the White House is primarily a cross-country ski touring center, with a rental shop and 12 km (7 mi) of groomed trails. ⊠ *178 Rte. 9 E, 05363,* ☎ *802/464–2135 or 800/541–2135,* ℻ *802/464–5222. 23 rooms. Restaurant, bar, 1 indoor and 1 outdoor pool, sauna, cross-country skiing. Full breakfast; MAP available. AE, D, DC, MC, V.*

Nightlife and the Arts

The standard fare on weekends at **Poncho's Wreck** (⊠ S. Main St., ☎ 802/464–9320) is acoustic jazz or mellow rock. **Sitzmark** (⊠ Rte. 100, ☎ 802/464–3384) hosts rock bands on weekends.

Outdoor Activities and Sports

SLEIGH RIDES

Adams Farm (⊠ 15 Higley Hill Rd., ☎ 802/464–3762) has three double-traverse sleighs drawn by Belgian draft horses. Rides include a narrated tour and hot chocolate. A petting farm is open during the summer.

STATE PARK

Molly Stark State Park (⊠ Rte. 9, east of Wilmington, ☎ 802/464–5460) has campsites and a hiking trail that leads to a vista from a fire tower on Mt. Olga.

Lake Whitingham (Harriman Reservoir) is the largest lake in the state; there are boat launch areas at Wards Cove, Whitingham, Mountain Mills, and the Ox Bow. **Green Mountain Flagship Company** (⊠ Rte. 9, about 2 mi west of Wilmington, ☎ 802/464–2975) runs a cruise boat on Lake Whitingham and rents canoes, kayaks, surfbikes, and sailboats from May to late October.

Shopping

Quaigh Design Centre (⊠ Rte. 9, West Main St., ☎ 802/464–2780) sells New England crafts, artwork from New England and Britain, and Scottish woolens and tartans. **Wilmington Flea Market** (⊠ Rtes. 9 and 100 S, ☎ 802/464–3345) sells antiques on weekends from Memorial Day to mid-October.

West Dover

❹ *6 mi north of Wilmington.*

The Congregational church in small West Dover, a classic New England town, dates back to the 1700s. The year-round population of about 1,000 swells on winter weekends as skiers flock to Mt. Snow/Haystack Ski Resort. The many condos, lodges, and inns at the base of the mountain accommodate them.

Dining and Lodging

$$$–$$$$ ✕ **Doveberry Inn.** Rack of venison with a caper-and-fresh-tomato *demi-glace* (sauce) served over polenta, wood-grilled veal chop with wild mushrooms, and pan-seared salmon with herbed risotto are among the northern Italian dishes served in the Doveberry's intimate, candlelighted dining rooms. ⊠ *Rte. 100,* ☎ *802/464–5652 or 800/722–3204. AE, MC, V. Closed Tues. No lunch.*

$$–$$$$ ✕⌂ **Deerhill Inn and Restaurant.** The west-facing windows at this En-
★ glish-style country inn have views of the valley below and the ski slopes across the way. A huge fireplace dominates the living room, and English hand-painted yellow wallpaper, a garden-scene mural, and collections of antique plates accent the dining rooms. One guest room has an Asian bedroom set, several have hand-painted murals on the wall, and many have fireplaces. The four balcony rooms are the largest; they have great views. Longtime Deerhill Valley residents Linda and Michael Anelli enjoy sharing their wealth of information about the area with guests. In the restaurant ($$$–$$$$; closed Wednesday), Michael prepares upscale comfort food that might include fresh fish, a veal medallion with wild mushrooms in a lemon cream sauce, or a black-pepper sirloin steak. ⊠ *Box 136, Valley View Rd., 05356,* ☎ *802/464–3100 or 800/993–3379,* 𝖥𝖠𝖷 *802/464–5474. 13 rooms, 2 suites. Restaurant, pool. Full breakfast; MAP available. AE, MC, V.*

Nightlife and the Arts

Deacon's Den Tavern (⊠ Rte. 100, ☎ 802/464–9361) books bands on weekends from Thanksgiving through Easter. The **Snow Barn** (⊠ Near the base of Mt. Snow, ☎ 802/464–1100, ext. 4693) presents entertainers several days a week.

Skiing and Snow Sports

Mt. Snow, established in the 1950s, was purchased in 1996 by the American Skiing Company, which also owns Sugarbush, Killington, and Pico. Recent developments have included the 1998 opening of the year-round Grand Summit Hotel and Conference Center; the inauguration of the Learn to Ski and Ride Center at the Perfect Turn Discovery Center, complete with its own expanded terrain, triple chairlift and building; and increased snowmaking capability. Two new terrain parks are the Carnival mini-park for kids and the Inferno for advanced snowboarders. One lift ticket lets you ski at Mt. Snow and Haystack.

Haystack—the southernmost ski area in Vermont—is much smaller than Mt. Snow but has a more personal atmosphere. A modern base lodge is close to the lifts. A free shuttle connects the two ski areas. ⌧ *400 Mountain Rd., Mt. Snow 05356, ☎ 802/464–3333; 800/245–7669 for lodging; 802/464–2151 for snow conditions.*

Downhill. Mt. Snow is a remarkably well formed mountain. Most of the trails down its 1,700-ft vertical summit are intermediate, wide, and sunny. Most of the beginner slopes are toward the bottom; most of the expert terrain is on the North Face, where there's excellent fall-line skiing. Of the 134 trails, about two-thirds are intermediate. The trails are served by three high-speed quads, one regular quad, 10 triple chairs, six double chairs, and two Magic Carpets (similar to an escalator). The ski school's Perfect Turn instruction program is designed to help advanced and expert skiers.

Most of the 44 trails at Haystack are pleasantly wide with bumps and rolls and straight fall lines—good cruising, intermediate runs. The Witches, with three double-black-diamond trails—is very steep but short. A beginner section, safely tucked below the main-mountain trails, provides a haven for lessons and slow skiing. Three triple and two double chairlifts and one T-bar service Haystack's 1,400 vertical ft.

Child care. Mt. Snow's lively, well-organized child care center (reservations necessary) takes children from ages 6 weeks to 6 years. The center has age-appropriate toys and balances indoor play—including arts and crafts—with trips outdoors. The Pre-ski program is for 3-year-olds, and a Perfect Kids program for ages 4–12 teaches skiing and snowboarding.

CROSS-COUNTRY SKIING

Four cross-country-trail areas within 4 mi of Mt. Snow/Haystack provide more than 150 km (90 mi) of varied terrain. The **Hermitage** (⌧ Coldbrook Rd., Wilmington, ☎ 802/464–3511) and the **White House of Wilmington** (⌧ Rtes. 9 and 100, ☎ 802/464–2135; ☞ Wilmington, *above*) both have 50 km (30 mi) of groomed trails. **Timber Creek** (⌧ Rte. 100, north of the Mt. Snow entrance, ☎ 802/464–0999) is appealingly small with 16 km (10 mi) of thoughtfully groomed trails. **Sitzmark** (⌧ East Dover Rd., Wilmington, ☎ 802/464–3384) has 40 km (24 mi) of trails, with 12 km (7 mi) of them machine tracked.

Bennington

⑤ *21 mi west of Wilmington.*

Bennington, college town and commercial focus of Vermont's southwest corner, lies at the edge of the Green Mountain National Forest. It has retained much of the industrial character it developed in the 19th century, when paper mills, grist mills, and potteries formed the city's economic base. It was in Bennington, at the Catamount Tavern, that Ethan Allen organized the Green Mountain Boys, who helped capture Ft. Ticonderoga in 1775. Here also, in 1777, American general John Stark urged his militia to attack the British-paid Hessian troops across the New York border: "There are the redcoats; they will be ours or tonight Molly Stark sleeps a widow!"

A brochure available at the chamber of commerce (☞ Visitor Information *in* Southern Vermont A to Z, *below*) describes an interesting self-guided walking tour of **Old Bennington,** a National Register Historic District west of downtown. Impressive white-column Greek Revival and sturdy brick Federal homes stand around the village green. In the graveyard of the **Old First Church,** at Church Street and Monument Avenue, the tombstone of the poet Robert Frost proclaims, "I had a lover's quarrel with the world."

The **Bennington Battle Monument,** a 306-ft stone obelisk with an elevator to the top, commemorates General Stark's victory over the British, who attempted to capture Bennington's stockpile of supplies. The battle, which took place near Walloomsac Heights in New York State, helped bring about the surrender two months later of the British commander "Gentleman Johnny" Burgoyne. ⊠ *15 Monument Ave.,* ☎ *802/447–0550.* ⊠ *$1.50.* ◯ *Mid-Apr.–late Oct., daily 9–5.*

The **Bennington Museum**'s rich collections include vestiges of rural life, a good percentage of which are packed into towering glass cases. The decorative arts are well represented; one room is devoted to early Bennington pottery. Two rooms cover the history of American glass and contain fine Tiffany specimens. The museum displays the largest public collection of the work of Grandma Moses, who lived and painted in the area. Among the 30 paintings and assorted memorabilia is her only self-portrait and the famous painted caboose window. Also here are the only surviving automobile of Bennington's Martin company, a 1925 Wasp, and the Bennington Flag, one of the oldest versions of the Stars and Stripes in existence. ⊠ *W. Main St./Rte. 9,* ☎ *802/447–1571.* ⊠ *$6.* ◯ *Nov.–May, daily 9–5; June–Oct., daily 9–6.*

Built in 1865 and home to two Vermont governors, the **Park-McCullough House** is a 35-room classic French Empire–style mansion furnished with period pieces. Several restored flower gardens grace the landscaped grounds, and a stable houses a collection of antique carriages. A summer concert series and special events are held on the grounds each season. ⊠ *Corner of Park and West Sts., North Bennington,* ☎ *802/442–5441.* ⊠ *$5.* ◯ *Late May–late Oct., Thurs.–Mon. 10–4; last tour at 3. Call for Victorian Christmas dates.*

Contemporary stone sculpture and white-frame neo-Colonial dorms surrounded by acres of cornfields punctuate the green meadows of **Bennington College**'s placid campus. The small liberal arts college, one of the most expensive to attend in the country, is noted for its progressive program in the arts. ⊠ *Rte. 67A, off U.S. 7; look for stone entrance gate,* ☎ *800/833–6845 for tour information.*

Dining and Lodging

$ ✕ **Blue Benn Diner.** Breakfast is served all day in this authentic diner, where the eats include turkey hash and breakfast burritos with scrambled eggs, sausage, and chilies. Pancakes of all imaginable varieties are also prepared. The menu lists many vegetarian selections. Lines may be long, especially on weekends. ⊠ *U.S. 7N,* ☎ *802/442–5140. No credit cards. No dinner Sat.–Tues.*

$$–$$$ ▦ **South Shire Inn.** Canopy beds in lushly carpeted rooms, ornate plaster moldings, and a dark mahogany fireplace in the South Shire's library re-create the grandeur of the Victorian past; fireplaces and hot tubs in some rooms add warmth. Four freshly renovated rooms in the Carriage House have whirlpool baths. The furnishings are antique except for the reproduction beds. The South Shire is in a quiet residential neighborhood within walking distance of the bus depot and downtown stores. Breakfast is served in the burgundy-and-white dining room. ⊠ *124 Elm St., 05201,* ☎ *802/447–3839,* 🅵🅰🆇 *802/442–3547. 9 rooms. Full breakfast. AE, MC, V.*

$$ 🖼 **Molly Stark Inn.** This gem of a B&B may make you so comfortable
★ that you'll feel like you're staying with an old friend. Tidy blue-plaid
wallpaper, gleaming hardwood floors, antique furnishings, and a wood-
burning stove in a brick alcove of the sitting room add country charm
to this 1860 Queen Anne Victorian. Molly's Room, at the back of the
building, gets less noise from Route 9 and has a whirlpool bath; the
attic suite is the most spacious. A secluded cottage with a 16-ft ceil-
ing, a king-size brass bed, and a two-person whirlpool bath surrounded
by windows with views of the woods is the perfect spot for a roman-
tic retreat. The innkeeper's genuine hospitality and quirky charisma
delight guests, as does the full country breakfast, made with mostly
local ingredients, which has been known to include puffed-apple pan-
cakes and freshly baked cinnamon buns. ✉ *1067 E. Main St./Rte. 9,
05201,* ☎ *802/442–9631 or 800/356–3076,* 📠 *802/442–5224. 7
rooms. Full breakfast. AE, D, MC, V.*

Nightlife and the Arts
Oldcastle Theatre Co. (✉ Bennington Center for the Arts, Rte. 9 and
Gypsy La., ☎ 802/447–0564) performs from May to October.

Outdoor Activities and Sports
Cutting Edge (✉ 160 Benmont Ave., ☎ 802/442–8664) rents and re-
pairs bicycles and also sells and rents snowboards and cross-country
skis. It has one of Vermont's few skateboarding parks, open daily
from noon to 6.

HIKING

About 4 mi east of Bennington, the **Long Trail** crosses Route 9 and runs
south to the summit of Harmon Hill. Allot two or three hours for this
hike.

STATE PARKS

Lake Shaftsbury State Park (✉ Rte. 7A, 10½ mi north of Bennington,
☎ 802/375–9978) is one of a few parks in Vermont with group camp-
ing; it has a swimming beach, nature trails, boat and canoe rentals, and
a snack bar. **Woodford State Park** (✉ Rte. 9, 10 mi east of Bennington,
☎ 802/447–7169) has an activities center on Adams Reservoir, camp-
sites, a playground, boat and canoe rentals, and marked nature trails.

Shopping
The **Apple Barn and Country Bake Shop** (✉ U.S. 7S, ☎ 802/447–7780)
sells home-baked goodies, fresh cider, Vermont cheeses, and maple syrup.
The showroom at the **Bennington Potters Yard** (✉ 324 County St., ☎
802/447–7531 or 800/205–8033) stocks first-quality pottery and an-
tiques in addition to seconds from the famed Bennington Potters. Pre-
pare to get dusty digging for an almost-perfect piece of this utilitarian
stoneware at a modest discount. On the free tour you can follow the
clay through production and hear about the Potters Yard, in business
for five decades. Tours begin at 10 and 2, daily. **Hawkins House Crafts-
market** (✉ U.S. 7, 262 North St., ☎ 802/447–0488) showcases jew-
elry, woodenware, glass, pottery, rugs, and clothing from more than
450 Vermont craftspeople.

Arlington

❻ *15 mi north of Bennington.*

Don't be surprised to see familiar-looking (if considerably aged) faces
among the roughly 2,200 people of Arlington. The illustrator Norman
Rockwell lived here from 1939 to 1953, and many of the models for his
portraits of small-town life were his neighbors. Settled first in 1763, Ar-
lington was called Tory Hollow for its Loyalist sympathies—even though

a number of the Green Mountain Boys lived here, too. Smaller than Bennington and more down-to-earth than upper-crust Manchester to the north, Arlington exudes a certain Rockwellian folksiness. Dorothy Canfield Fisher, a novelist popular in the 1930s and 1940s, also lived here.

There are no original paintings at the **Norman Rockwell Exhibition,** but the exhibition rooms are crammed with reproductions of the illustrator's works, arranged in every way conceivable: chronologically, by subject matter, and juxtaposed with photos of the models—several of whom work here. ⊠ *Rte. 7A/Main St.,* ☎ *802/375–6423.* ☞ *$2.* ☉ *May–Oct., daily 9–5; Nov.–Dec. and Feb.–Apr., daily 10–4.*

Dining and Lodging

$$$$ ✕⌷ **West Mountain Inn.** A former farmhouse built in the 1840s, this
★ romantic inn has a front lawn with a spectacular view of the countryside. Its 150 acres include a llama farm. Rooms 2, 3, and 4 overlook the lawn; the three small nooks of Room 11 resemble railroad sleeper berths and are perfect for kids. A children's room, brightly painted with life-size Disney characters, is stocked with games, stuffed animals, and a TV with VCR. A low-beamed candlelighted dining room ($$$) is the setting for six-course prix-fixe dinners featuring updated Continental cuisine. Aunt Min's Swedish rye and other toothsome breads, as well as desserts, are all made on the premises. Try to get a table by the window. ⊠ *River Rd., off Rte. 313, 05250,* ☎ *802/375–6516,* ℻ *802/ 375–6553. 18 rooms, 6 suites. Restaurant, bar, hiking, cross-country skiing, meeting rooms. MAP or B&B rates available. AE, D, MC, V.*

$$–$$$ ✕⌷ **Arlington Inn.** The Greek Revival columns at the entrance to a home
★ built by a railroad magnate in 1848 lend it an imposing presence, but the atmosphere is hardly forbidding. The inn's charm is created by linens that coordinate with the Victorian-style wallpaper, claw-foot tubs in some bathrooms, and the house's original moldings and wainscoting. The carriage house, built a century ago, contains country-French and Queen Anne furnishings. Some rooms have TVs and phones. The restaurant serves French and Continental dishes and game, such as antelope from Texas. Polished wood floors, rose walls, and soft candlelight complement the food. ⊠ *Rte. 7A, 05250,* ☎ *802/375–6532 or 800/443–9442,* ℻ *802/375–6534. 16 rooms, 4 suites. Restaurant, bar, tennis court. Full breakfast. AE, D, DC, MC, V.*

$$–$$$ ⌷ **Hill Farm Inn.** This homey inn has the feel of the country farmhouse it used to be. The surrounding farmland, deeded to the Hill family by King George in 1775, is protected from development by the Vermont Land Trust. The fireplace in the informal living room, the sturdy antiques, and the spinning wheel in the upstairs hallway all convey a relaxed, friendly atmosphere. Room 7 has a beamed cathedral ceiling, and from its porch you can see Mt. Equinox. The rooms in the 1790 guest house are very private; the one- and two-bedroom cottages are charming. ⊠ *Box 2015, Hill Farm Rd., off Rte. 7A, 05250,* ☎ *802/ 375–2269 or 800/882–2545,* ℻ *802/375–9918. 11 rooms, 6 with bath; 2 suites; 4 cabins in summer. Full breakfast. AE, D, MC, V.*

Outdoor Activities and Sports
Battenkill Canoe, Ltd. (⊠ Rte. 7A, ☎ 802/362–2800 or 800/421– 5268) has rentals and day trips on the Battenkill and inn-to-inn tours.

Shopping
The shops at **Candle Mill Village** (⊠ Old Mill Rd., between U.S. 7 and Rte. 7A, East Arlington, ☎ 802/375–6068 or 800/772–3759) specialize in community cookbooks from around the country, music boxes, and candles. The mill itself was built in the 1760s by Remember Baker, a cohort of Ethan Allen and one of the Green Mountain Boys. The nearby waterfall makes a pleasant backdrop for a picnic.

Equinox Valley Nursery (✉ Rte. 7A, between Arlington and Manchester, ☎ 802/362–2610) is known for its perennials (more than 1,000 varieties) and materials for water gardens. The nursery has 17 greenhouses and a conservatory, sells 150 varieties of herbs, and carries many Vermont-made products in the large gift shop.

Manchester

★ ❼ *9 mi north of Arlington.*

Manchester, where Ira Allen proposed financing Vermont's participation in the American Revolution by confiscating Tory estates, has been a popular summer retreat since the mid-19th century. Manchester Village's tree-shaded marble sidewalks and stately old homes reflect the luxurious resort lifestyle of a century ago. Manchester Center's upscale factory outlets appeal to the affluent 20th-century ski crowd drawn by nearby Bromley and Stratton mountains. Warning: Shoppers come in droves at times, giving the place the feel of a crowded mall on the weekend before Christmas. If you're coming here from Arlington, take pretty Route 7A, which passes directly by a number of sights.

★ **Hildene,** the summer home of Abraham Lincoln's son and onetime Pullman company chairman Robert Todd Lincoln, is a beautifully preserved 412-acre estate. The 24-room mansion, with its Georgian Revival symmetry, welcoming central hallway, and grand curved staircase, is unusual in that its rooms are not roped off. When the 1,000-pipe Aeolian organ is played, the music reverberates as though from the mansion's very bones. Tours include a short film on the owner's life and a walk through the elaborate formal gardens. When snow conditions permit, you can cross-country ski on the property, which has views of nearby mountains. In December, the house is decorated for special holiday tours that include horse-drawn sleigh rides. ✉ *Rte. 7A,* ☎ *802/362–1788.* ☞ *$7.* ☉ *Mid-May–Oct., daily 9:30–5:30 (last tour at 4); Dec. tour hrs vary.*

The **American Museum of Fly Fishing,** which houses the largest collection of fly-fishing equipment in the world, displays more than 1,500 rods, 800 reels, 30,000 flies, and the tackle of famous people such as Winslow Homer, Bing Crosby, and Jimmy Carter. Its library of 2,500 books is open by appointment. ✉ *Rte. 7A at Seminary Ave.,* ☎ *802/362–3300.* ☞ *$3.* ☉ *Daily 10–4.*

The 10-room **Southern Vermont Art Center** is set on 375 acres dotted with contemporary sculpture. A popular retreat for local patrons of the arts, the nonprofit educational center has a permanent collection of 19th- and 20th-century American art and presents changing exhibits. The graceful Georgian mansion is the frequent site of concerts, performances, and films. A botany trail passes by a 300-year-old maple tree. In summer a restaurant opens for business. ✉ *West Rd.,* ☎ *802/362–1405.* ☞ *$3, $2 in winter.* ☉ *Mid-May–late Oct., Tues.–Sat. 10–5, Sun. noon–5; Dec.–early Apr., Mon.–Sat. 10–5.*

You may want to keep your eye on the temperature gauge of your car as you drive the 5-mi toll road to the top of 3,825-ft **Mt. Equinox.** Along the way you'll see the Battenkill trout stream and the surrounding Vermont countryside. Picnic tables line the drive, and there's an outstanding view down both sides of the mountain from a notch known as the Saddle. The **Equinox Mountain Inn** (☎ 802/362–1113 or 800/868–6843) is perched on top of the mountain. ✉ *Off Rte. 7A, south of Manchester,* ☎ *802/362–1114.* ☞ *$6 for car and driver, $2 each additional adult.* ☉ *May–Oct., daily 8 AM–10 PM.*

Dining and Lodging

$$$$ ✕ **Chantecleer.** Intimate dining rooms have been created in a former dairy barn that has a large fieldstone fireplace. The menu reflects the chef's Swiss background: The appetizers include *Bündnerfleisch* (air-dried Swiss beef) and frogs' legs in garlic butter; among the entrées are rack of lamb, whole Dover sole filleted tableside, and veal chops. The restaurant is 5 mi north of Manchester. ⌧ *Rte. 7A, East Dorset,* ☎ *802/362–1616. Reservations essential. AE, DC, MC, V. Closed Mon.– Tues. in winter, Tues. in summer. No lunch.*

$$–$$$ ✕ **Bistro Henry's.** This airy restaurant on the outskirts of town attracts a devoted clientele for authentic Mediterranean fare. Recently on the menu were merlot-braised lamb shank with balsamic-glazed onions and garlic mashed potatoes; eggplant, mushroom, and fontina terrine Provençal; and crispy sweetbreads in Armagnac cream. The outstanding wine list is extensive. ⌧ *Rte. 11/30,* ☎ *802/362–4982. AE, DC, MC, V. Closed Mon. No lunch.*

$$ ✕ **Quality Restaurant.** Gentrification has reached the down-home neighborhood place that was the model for Norman Rockwell's *War News* painting. Quality has Provençal wallpaper and polished wood booths, and the sturdy New England standbys of grilled meat loaf and hot roast beef or turkey sandwiches have been joined by grilled lamb chops, sautéed scallops with a vegetable medley tossed with pesto and served on fettuccine, and grilled swordfish with lemon butter. The breakfasts are popular. ⌧ *Main St.,* ☎ *802/362–9839. AE, DC, MC, V.*

$$$$ ✕🏠 **Barrows House.** Jim and Linda McGinniss's 200-year-old Federal-★ style inn is a longtime favorite with those who wish to escape the commercial hustle of Manchester (Bromley is about 8 mi away). The deep-red woodwork and library theme of the pub room make it an intimate venue for dining on country fare that might include Chesapeake crab cakes. The greenhouse room, with terra-cotta and deep-blue hues, is a pleasant summer eating spot. The rooms, spread among nine buildings on 12 acres, afford great privacy. ⌧ *Box 98, Rte. 30, Dorset (6 mi north of Manchester), 05251,* ☎ *802/867–4455 or 800/639–1620,* 📠 *802/867–0132. 18 rooms, 10 suites. Restaurant, pool, sauna, 2 tennis courts, bicycles, cross-country skiing. Full breakfast; MAP available. AE, D, DC, MC, V.*

$$$$ ✕🏠 **The Equinox.** This grand white-column resort was a fixture even before Abe Lincoln's family began summering here; it's worth a look around even if you don't stay here. The spacious, sunny rooms are furnished with reproductions of antiques. In the Marsh Tavern, richly upholstered settees, stuffed armchairs, and several fireplaces create a plush traditional ambience. The food is equally pleasing: Devonshire shepherd's pie and a woodland supper of roast duck, venison sausage, and wild mushrooms are popular. The Colonnade, where men are requested to wear jackets, is elegant. Among the many facilities here is a school for falconry. The resort is often the site of large conferences. ⌧ *Skyline Dr., off Rte. 7A, Manchester Village 05254,* ☎ *802/362– 4700 or 800/362–4747,* 📠 *802/362–1595. 119 rooms, 36 suites, 10 3-bedroom town houses. 2 restaurants, bar, 1 indoor and 1 outdoor pool, sauna, steam room, 18-hole golf course, 3 tennis courts, croquet, health club, horseback riding, fishing, mountain bikes, ice-skating, cross-country skiing. AE, D, DC, MC, V.*

$$$$ ✕🏠 **Reluctant Panther.** The large bedrooms here have goose-down duvets and Pierre Deux linens and are styled with antique, country, and contemporary furnishings. All have fireplaces, and the suites have double sunken whirlpool baths. The best views are from Rooms B and D. In Wildflowers restaurant ($$$–$$$$; reservations essential; closed Tuesday and Wednesday; from November through May, open Friday and

Saturday only), a huge fieldstone fireplace dominates the larger of the two dining rooms. The menu, which changes daily, might include rack of venison with an herbed cornmeal crust or grilled veal chop with a ragout of shiitake and wild mushrooms. ⊠ *Box 678, West Rd., 05254,* ☎ *802/362–2568 or 800/822–2331,* FAX *802/362–2586. 14 rooms, 6 suites. Restaurant, bar, meeting room. MAP. AE, MC, V.*

$$$–$$$$ 🏨 **Lake St. Catherine Inn.** If you're lucky enough to have good friends with a big, rambling house on a lake, you've got an idea of what this inn has to offer. Hosts Pat and Ray Endlich have thought of everything— snug lounges and dining overlooking the water, a lakeside deck, and plenty of watercraft. The lake is a favorite among anglers, and Ray will be happy to cook your catch. Accommodations are simple and comfortable, and the food hearty and satisfying. Reserve early: the inn, 25 mi northwest of Manchester via Route 30, has a loyal following. ⊠ *Cones Point Rd., Poultney 05764,* ☎ *802/247–6411 or 800/626– 5724 outside VT. 35 rooms, 1 housekeeping cottage. Lake, boating, fishing. MAP. No credit cards. Closed Nov.–Apr.*

$$–$$$$ 🏨 **1811 House.** The atmosphere of an English country home can be
★   experienced without crossing the Atlantic. The pub-style bar serves 63 single-malt Scotches and is decorated with horse brasses, Waterford crystal is used in the dining room, and 3 acres of lawn are landscaped in the English floral style. Rooms contain period antiques; six have fireplaces, and many have four-poster beds. Bathrooms are old-fashioned but serviceable, particularly the Robinson Room's marble-enclosed tub. ⊠ *Box 39, Rte. 7A, 05254,* ☎ *802/362–1811 or 800/432–1811,* FAX *802/362–2443. 14 rooms. Bar. Full breakfast. AE, D, MC, V.*

$$–$$$$ 🏨 **Inn at Ormsby Hill.** During the Revolutionary War, this 1774 Fed-
★   eral-style building provided refuge from the British for Ethan Allen, and it later served the same purpose for slaves heading north on the Underground Railroad. When renovating, the owners created interesting public spaces and romantic bedrooms. Furnished with antiques and canopied or four-poster beds, the rooms have fireplaces that can be viewed from the bed or the two-person whirlpool tub. Some have mountain views. Breakfasts in the conservatory—entrées may include baked, stuffed French toast with an apricot brandy sauce—are sumptuous. An optional buffet supper is served Friday night. ⊠ *1842 Main St./Rte. 7A, 05255,* ☎ *802/362–1163 or 800/670–2841,* FAX *802/362– 5176. 10 rooms. Full breakfast. D, MC, V.*

$–$$ 🏨 **Aspen Motel.** A rare find in this area, the immaculate, family-owned Aspen is set well back from the highway and is moderately priced. The spacious, tastefully decorated rooms have Colonial-style furnishings, and all have cable TV and in-room coffee; some have refrigerators. The social room has a fireplace. ⊠ *Rte. 7A N, 05255,* ☎ *802/362–2450,* FAX *802/362–1348. 24 rooms, 2 2-bedroom suites. Pool, playground. AE, D, MC, V.*

Nightlife and the Arts

The two pre–Revolutionary War barns of the **Dorset Playhouse** (⊠ Off town green, ☎ 802/867–5777) host a community group in winter and a resident professional troupe in summer. The **Marsh Tavern** (☎ 802/ 362–4700) at the Equinox (☞ Dining and Lodging, *above*) has cabaret music and jazz from Wednesday to Sunday in summer and on weekends in winter. **Mulligan's** (⊠ Rte. 7A, ☎ 802/362–3663), which serves American cuisine, is a popular hangout in Manchester Village, especially for après-ski; DJs program the music on weekends.

Outdoor Activities and Sports

BIKING

The 20-mi Dorset–Manchester trail runs from Manchester Village north on West Street to Route 30, turns west at the Dorset village green onto West Road, and heads back south to Manchester. **Battenkill Sports** (✉ Exit 4 off U.S. 7, at Rte. 11/30, ☎ 802/362–2734 or 800/340–2734) rents and repairs bikes and provides maps and route suggestions.

FISHING

Battenkill Anglers (☎ 802/362–3184) teaches the art and science of fly-fishing. It has both private and group lessons. The **Orvis Co.** (✉ Rte. 7A, Manchester Center, ☎ 800/235–9763) hosts a nationally known fly-fishing school on the Battenkill, the state's most famous trout stream, with three-day courses given weekly between April and October.

HIKING

One of the most popular segments of the **Long Trail** starts at Route 11/30 west of Peru Notch and goes to the top of Bromley Mountain. The round-trip trek takes about four hours.

The **Mountain Goat** (✉ Rte. 7A south of Rte. 11/30, ☎ 802/362–5159) sells hiking, backpacking, and climbing equipment and rents snowshoes and cross-country and telemark skis. The shop also conducts rock- and ice-climbing clinics.

STATE PARK

Emerald Lake State Park (✉ Rte. 7, East Dorset, ☎ 802/362–1655), 9 mi north of Manchester, has campsites, a marked nature trail, an on-site naturalist, boat and canoe rentals, and a snack bar.

Shopping

ART AND ANTIQUES

Carriage Trade (✉ Rte. 7A north of Manchester Center, ☎ 802/362–1125) contains room after room of Early American antiques and has a fine collection of ceramics. **Danby Antiques Center** (✉ ⅛ mi off U.S. 7, Danby, ☎ 802/293–5990), 13 mi north of Manchester, has 11 rooms and a barn filled with furniture and accessories, folk art, textiles, and stoneware. **Gallery North Star** (✉ Rte. 7A, ☎ 802/362–4541) shows oils, watercolors, lithographs, and sculptures by Vermont artists. **Tilting at Windmills Gallery** (✉ Rte. 11/30, ☎ 802/362–3022) exhibits the works of well-known artists like Douglas Flackman of the Hudson River School.

BOOKS

Northshire Bookstore (✉ Main St., ☎ 802/362–2200 or 800/437–3700), a community bookstore for more than 20 years, carries many travel and children's books and sponsors readings year-round.

CLOTHING

Orvis Sporting Gifts (✉ Union St., ☎ 802/362–6455), a discount outlet that carries discontinued items from the popular outdoor clothing and home furnishings mail-order company, is housed in what was Orvis's shop in the 1800s. Anne Klein, Liz Claiborne, Donna Karan, Levi Strauss, Giorgio Armani, and Jones New York are among the shops on Route 11/30 and U.S. 7 South—a center for **designer outlet stores.**

FISHING GEAR

Orvis Retail Store (✉ Rte. 7A, ☎ 802/362–3750), an outdoor specialty store that is one of the largest suppliers of fishing gear in the Northeast, also carries clothing, gifts, and hunting supplies.

MALLS AND MARKETPLACES

Manchester Commons (✉ U.S. 7 and Rte. 11/30, ☎ 802/362–3736 or 800/955–7467), the largest and spiffiest of three large factory-direct minimalls, has such big-city names as Joan and David, Baccarat, Coach, Ralph Lauren, Calvin Klein, and Cole-Haan. **Manchester Square** (✉ Rte. 11/30 and Richville Rd.) has stores such as Giorgio Armani, Emporio Armani, Tommy Hilfiger, Brooks Brothers, Levis, and Escada.

Skiing and Snow Sports

BROMLEY MOUNTAIN

The first trails at Bromley were cut in 1936. Many families appreciate the resort's convivial atmosphere. The area has a comfortable red-clapboard base lodge, built when the ski area first opened more than 60 years ago and recently expanded. The resort has a large ski shop and a condominium village adjacent to the slopes. A reduced-price, two-day lift pass is available, as is a snowboard park–only lift ticket. Kids 6 and under ski free when accompanied by an adult. Eighty-four percent of the area is covered by snowmaking. ⊠ *Box 1130, Rte. 11, Manchester Center 05255,* ☎ *802/824–5522 for snow conditions; 802/865–4786; 800/865–4786 for lodging.*

Downhill. Most ski areas are laid out to face the north or east, but Bromley faces south, making it one of the warmer spots to ski in New England. Its 41 trails are equally divided into beginner, intermediate, and advanced terrain; the last is serviced by the Blue Ribbon quad chair on the east side. The vertical drop is 1,334 ft. Four double chairlifts, two quad lifts, a J-bar, and two surface lifts for beginners provide transportation. The high-speed quad lift takes skiers from the base to the summit in just six minutes.

Child care. Bromley is one of the region's best places to bring children. Besides a nursery for children from ages 6 weeks to 6 years, ski instruction is provided for children from ages 3 to 14.

CROSS-COUNTRY

With 26 km (16 mi) of marked trails, the **Meadowbrook Inn** (⊠ Landgrove, ☎ 802/824–6444 or 800/498–6445) offers an idyllic setting for cross-country skiing and snowshoeing. The inn, which has eight guest rooms and a restaurant, has rental gear and provides lessons.

Stratton

8 *18 mi southeast of Manchester.*

Stratton, home to the famous Stratton Mountain Resort, has a self-contained town center with shops, restaurants, and lodgings clustered at the base of the slopes. There's plenty of activity year-round between skiing and summer sports.

Dining and Lodging

$$$$ ✕🏠 **Windham Hill Inn.** Antiques, throw blankets, and canopy beds dec-
★ orate the rooms at this exquisite retreat. Most have fireplaces or Vermont Castings stoves, and several have large soaking tubs. The barn-loft rooms are the newest and most luxurious. The Marion Goodfellow room has its own private cupola with a 360-degree view of the 160-acre grounds, and a floor-to-ceiling bay window is the signature of the Meadowlook room. The restaurant serves nouveau French fare such as grilled mustardseed-encrusted lamb loin with a rosemary merlot sauce. Sports equipment is provided free of charge. ⊠ *311 Lawrence Dr., West Townshend (10 mi east of Stratton Mountain) 05359,* ☎ *802/874–4080 or 800/944–4080,* ℻ *802/874–4702. 21 rooms. Restaurant, bar, pool, pond, tennis court, hiking, ice-skating, cross-country skiing. MAP. AE, D, MC, V. Closed during Christmas holidays.*

$$–$$$$ ✕🏠 **Stratton Mountain Inn and Village Lodge.** The complex includes a 120-room inn—the largest on the mountain—and a 91-room lodge of studio units equipped with microwaves, refrigerators, and small wet bars. The lodge is the only slopeside ski-in, ski-out hotel at Stratton. Ski packages that include lift tickets bring down room rates. ⊠ *Stratton Mountain Rd., 05155,* ☎ *802/297–2500 or 800/777–1700,* ℻ *802/*

297–1778. 211 rooms. 2 restaurants, pool, hot tub, sauna, golf course, tennis courts. AE, D, DC, MC, V.

Nightlife and the Arts

Haig's Black Angus Steak House (✉ River Rd., ☎ 802/297–1300 or 800/897–5894) in Bondville, 5 mi from Stratton, has a dance club with a DJ or a band on weekends and holidays. There's also a diverting indoor simulated golf course. Popular **Mulligan's** (✉ Mountain Rd., ☎ 802/297–9293) serves American cuisine. Bands or DJs provide entertainment in the late afternoon and on weekends. The **Red Fox Inn** (✉ Winhall Hollow Rd., ☎ 802/297–2488) in Bondville hosts musicians in the tavern on weekends.

Outdoor Activities and Sports

Summertime facilities at **Stratton Mountain** (☞ Skiing and Snow Sports, *below*) include 15 outdoor tennis courts, 27 holes of golf, horseback riding, mountain biking and hiking accessed by a gondola to the summit, and instructional programs in tennis and golf. The area also hosts summer entertainment and family activities, including a skating park and climbing wall.

Skiing and Snow Sports

STRATTON MOUNTAIN

Owned by Intrawest, the company that runs Whistler/Blackcomb and Mont Tremblant, Stratton has a new master plan that includes the only high-speed six-passenger lift in New England and an expanded village with additional lodging. Since its creation in 1961, Stratton has undergone physical transformations and upgrades, yet the area's sophisticated character has been retained. It has been the special province of well-to-do families and, more recently, young professionals from the New York–southern Connecticut corridor. Since the mid-'80s, an entire village, with a covered parking structure for 700 cars, has arisen at the base of the mountain: Adjacent to the base lodge are a condohotel, restaurants, and about 25 shops lining a pedestrian mall. Stratton is 4 mi up its own access road off Route 30 in Bondville, about 30 minutes from Manchester's popular shopping zone. ✉ *R.R. 1, Box 145, Stratton Mountain 05155,* ☎ *802/297–2200 or 800/843–6867; 802/ 297–4211 for snow conditions; 800/787–2886 for lodging.*

Downhill. Stratton's skiing is in three sectors. The first is the lower mountain directly in front of the base lodge-village-condo complex; several lifts reach mid-mountain from this entry point, and practically all skiing is beginner or low-intermediate. Above that, the upper mountain, with a vertical drop of 2,000 ft, has a high-speed, 12-passenger gondola, Starship XII. Down the face are the expert trails, and on either side are intermediate cruising runs with a smattering of wide beginner slopes. The third sector, the Sun Bowl, is off to one side with two quad chairlifts and two expert trails, a full base lodge, and plenty of intermediate terrain. Stratton hosts the U.S. Open Snowboarding championships; its snowboard park has a 380-ft halfpipe. A Ski Learning Park with 10 trails and five lifts has its own Park Packages available for novice skiers. In all, Stratton has 90 slopes and trails served by the gondola; a six-passenger lift; four quad, one triple, and three double chairlifts; and two surface lifts.

Cross-country. The Stratton area has more than 30 km (18 mi) of cross-country skiing and two Nordic centers: Sun Bowl and Country Club.

Other activities. The area's sports center contains two indoor tennis courts, three racquetball courts, a 25-meter indoor swimming pool, a hot tub, a steam room, a fitness facility with Nautilus equipment, and a restaurant.

Child care. The day-care center takes children from ages 6 weeks to 6 years for indoor activities and outdoor excursions. There is a ski school for children ages 4 to 12. A junior racing program and special instruction groups are geared toward more experienced young skiers.

Weston

❾ *20 mi northeast of Manchester.*

Although perhaps best known for the Vermont Country Store, Weston is famed as one of the first Vermont towns to have discovered its own intrinsic loveliness—and marketability. With its summer theater, pretty town green, and Victorian bandstand, as well as an assortment of shops offering variety without modern sprawl, the little village really lives up to its vaunted image.

The **Mill Museum,** down the road from the Vermont Country Store, has numerous hands-on displays depicting the engineering and mechanics of one of the town's mills. The many old tools on view kept towns like Weston running smoothly. ✉ *Rte. 100,* ☎ *802/824–3119.* 🎟 *Donations accepted.* ☉ *Late May–early Sept., daily 11–4; early Sept.–mid-Oct., weekends 11–4.*

Nightlife and the Arts

The members of the **Weston Playhouse** (✉ Village Green, off Rte. 100, ☎ 802/824–5288), the oldest professional theater in Vermont, have produced Broadway plays, musicals, and other works since 1937. Their season runs from late June to mid-October.

Shopping

The **Vermont Country Store** (✉ Rte. 100, ☎ 802/824–3184) sets aside one room of its old-fashioned emporium for Vermont Common Crackers and bins of fudge and other candy. For years the retail store and its mail-order catalog have carried nearly forgotten items like Lilac Vegetal aftershave, Monkey Brand black tooth powder, Flexible Flyer sleds, and tiny wax bottles of colored syrup, but there are also plenty of practical items such as sturdy outdoor clothing and even a manual typewriter. Nostalgia-evoking implements dangle from the store's walls and ceiling. (There's another store on Route 103 in Rockingham.) **Weston Bowl Mill** (✉ Rte. 100, ☎ 802/824–6219) stocks finely crafted wood products at mill prices.

En Route   From Weston you can head south on Route 100 through Jamaica and then down Route 30 through Townshend to Newfane, all pretty hamlets typical of small-town Vermont. South of Townshend, near the Townshend Dam on Route 30, is the state's longest single-span covered bridge, now closed to traffic.

Ludlow

❿ *9 mi northeast of Weston.*

Ludlow, a former mill town, relies on the popularity of Okemo Mountain Ski Resort to fill its shops and restaurants. A beautiful, often-photographed historic church sits on the town green. Calvin Coolidge went to school at Ludlow's Black River Academy.

Dining and Lodging

$$$–$$$$ 🏨 **Okemo Mountain Lodge.** Most rooms in this three-story brown-clapboard building have balconies and fireplaces, and the one-bedroom condominiums clustered around the base of the ski lifts are close to restaurants and shops. All have equipped kitchens, fireplaces, decks, and TVs with VCRs. Okemo Mountain Lodging Service also operates

the Kettle Brook, Winterplace, and Solitude slopeside condominiums. Ski-and-stay packages are available. ⊠ *77 Okemo Ridge Rd., off Rte. 103, 05149,* ☎ *802/228–5571, 802/228–4041, or 800/786–5366,* FAX *802/228–2079. 76 rooms, 84 condos. Restaurant, bar. AE, MC, V.*

Outdoor Activities and Sports

Cavendish Trail Horse Rides (⊠ Twenty Mile Stream Rd., Proctorsville, ☎ 802/226–7821) operates horse-drawn sleigh rides in snowy weather and wagon rides at other times, and guided trail rides from mid-May to mid-October.

Skiing and Snow Sports

OKEMO MOUNTAIN RESORT

An ideal ski area for families with children, Okemo has evolved into a major resort. The main attraction is a long, broad, gentle slope with two beginner lifts just above the base lodge. All the facilities at the bottom of the mountain are close together, so family members can regroup easily during the ski day. The Solitude Village Area has a triple chairlift, two new trails, and lodging. The resort offers numerous ski and skateboarding packages. ⊠ *Rte. 100; mailing address: 77 Okemo Ridge Rd., 05149,* ☎ *802/228–4041; 800/786–5366 for lodging; 802/ 228–5222 for snow conditions.*

Downhill. Above the broad beginner's slope at the base, the upper part of Okemo has a varied network of trails: long, winding, easy trails for beginners; straight fall-line runs for experts; and curving, cruising slopes for intermediates. The 98 trails are served by an efficient lift system of seven quads, three triple chairlifts, and three surface lifts; 95% are covered by snowmaking. From the summit to the base lodge, the vertical drop is 2,150 ft, the highest in southern Vermont. Okemo has a self-contained snowboarding area serviced by a surface lift; the mile-long park is home to the Pipe, a massive 420-ft by 40-ft halfpipe. There's also a snowboard park for beginners.

Cross-country. The **Okemo Valley Nordic Center** (⊠ Fox La., ☎ 802/ 228–8871) has 26 km (16 mi) of trails, all groomed.

Child care. The area's nursery, for children from ages 6 weeks to 8 years, has many indoor activities and supervised outings. Children ages 3 to 4 can get a one-hour introduction to skiing; there's a SKIwee Snow-Star program for kids ages 4–7. Nursery reservations are required. Okemo also offers a Kids' Night Out evening child-care program on Saturdays during the regular season and certain holiday weeks.

Chester

⓫ *11 mi east of Weston.*

Gingerbread Victorians frame Chester's town green. The local pharmacy on Main Street has been in continuous operation since the 1860s. The **stone village** on North Street on the outskirts of town, two rows of buildings constructed from quarried stone, was built by two brothers and is said to have been used during the Civil War as a station on the Underground Railroad. The **National Survey Charthouse** (⊠ Main St., ☎ 802/875–2121) is a map-lover's paradise. The store is good for a rainy-day browse even if maps aren't your passion.

In Chester's restored 1872 train station you can board the *Green Mountain Flyer* for a 26-mi, two-hour round-trip to Bellows Falls, on the Connecticut River at the eastern edge of the state. The journey, in superbly restored cars that date from the golden age of railroading, travels through scenic countryside past covered bridges and along the Brockway Mills gorge. A six-hour tour takes place in the fall. ⊠ *Rte.*

103, ☎ *802/463–3069 or 800/707–3530.* 🚂 *2-hr trip $12.* ☉ *Mid-June–mid-Sept., Tues.–Sun.; mid- Sept.–mid-Oct., daily. Train departs at 11, 12:10, 2, 3:10; also, special fall sunset trips. Call to confirm.*

Dining and Lodging

$ ✕ **Raspberries and Thyme.** Breakfast specials, homemade soups, a large selection of salads, homemade desserts, and a menu listing more than 40 sandwiches make this one of the area's most popular spots for casual dining. ⊠ *On the Green,* ☎ *802/875–4486. AE, D, MC, V. No dinner Tues.*

$$–$$$ ✕🏠 **Fullerton Inn.** In 1998 Robin and Jerry Szawerda purchased the Inn at Long Last, completely redecorated the common areas and guest rooms, and then brought in the furniture and sign from their restaurant next door—Ye Old Bradford Tavern. The inn now serves breakfast and dinner daily except Wednesday, offering morning delicacies such as lobster omelets and nightly entrées like roast duck and trout Provençal. The rooms, with country quilts and lace curtains, vary in size and amenities. Some favorites are the bright corner rooms and numbers 8 and 10, which share a private porch. A shuttle bus to local attractions and ski areas stops in front of the inn. ⊠ *40 Common St., on the Green, 05143,* ☎ *802/875–2444,* FAX *802/875–6414. 20 rooms, 2 suites. Restaurant. AE, D, MC, V.*

Outdoor Activities and Sports

A 26-mi driving or biking loop out of Chester follows the Williams River along Route 103 to Pleasant Valley Road north of Bellows Falls. At Saxtons River, turn west onto Route 121 and follow along the river to connect with Route 35. When the two routes separate, follow Route 35 north back to Chester.

Grafton

★ ⑫ *8 mi south of Chester.*

Like many Vermont villages its size, Grafton enjoyed its heyday as an agricultural community well before the Civil War, when its citizens grazed some 10,000 sheep and spun their wool into sturdy yarn for locally woven fabric. Unlike most other out-of-the-way country towns, though, Grafton was born again, following a long decline, by preservationists determined to revitalize not only its centerpiece, the Old Tavern, but many of the other commercial and residential structures in the village center as well. Beginning in 1963, the Windham Foundation—Vermont's second-largest private foundation—commenced the rehabilitation of Grafton. The town's **Historical Society** documents the town's renewal. ⊠ *Townshend Rd.,* ☎ *802/843–2255 for visitor center information.* 🎫 *$1.* ☉ *June–late Sept., weekends 1:30–4; late Sept.–Oct., daily 1:30–4.*

Dining and Lodging

$$$–$$$$ ✕🏠 **Old Tavern at Grafton.** White-column porches on both stories wrap around the main building of this commanding inn, which dates from 1801. The main building holds 14 rooms; the rest are dispersed among other buildings in town. Two dining rooms ($$$), one with formal Georgian furniture and oil portraits, the other with rustic paneling and low beams, serve inspired New England fare such as grilled choice sirloin steeped in McNeil's stout and a blend of spices. The Phelps Barn Bar is a popular hangout. ⊠ *Rte. 35, 05146,* ☎ *802/843–2231 or 800/ 843–1801,* FAX *802/843–2245. 62 rooms, 3 suites. Restaurant, bar, pond, tennis court, paddle tennis, mountain biking, ice-skating, cross-country skiing, recreation room. Full breakfast. MC, V. Closed Apr.*

Shopping

Gallery North Star (⊠ Townshend Rd., ☎ 802/843–2465) exhibits the oils, watercolors, lithographs, and sculptures of Vermont artists.

Newfane

⑬ *15 mi south of Grafton.*

With a village green surrounded by pristine white buildings, Newfane is sometimes described as the quintessential New England small town. The 1839 First Congregational Church and the Windham County Court House, with 17 green-shuttered windows and a rounded cupola, are often open. The building with the four-pointed spire is Union Hall, built in 1832.

Dining and Lodging

$$–$$$ ✕🖬 **Four Columns.** The majestic white columns of this Greek Revival mansion, built 150 years ago for a homesick southern bride, are more intimidating than the Colonial-style rooms inside. Rooms are decorated with a mix of antiques and turn-of-the-century reproductions. The third-floor room in the old section is the most private. The suites have cathedral ceilings, double whirlpool baths, and gas fireplaces. In the classy restaurant ($$$; closed Tuesdays and part of April), chef Greg Parks has introduced new American dishes like roasted young chicken with herbs served in a chardonnay and mushroom sauce. ⊠ *Box 278, West St., 05345,* ☎ *802/365–7713 or 800/787–6633,* ᖴᴬX *802/365–0022. 15 rooms. Restaurant, hiking. Continental breakfast; MAP in foliage season. AE, D, DC, MC, V.*

Shopping

The **Newfane Country Store** (⊠ Rte. 30, ☎ 802/365–7916) carries many quilts (which can also be custom ordered), homemade fudge, and other Vermont foods, gifts, and crafts. Collectibles dealers from across the state sell their wares at the **Newfane Flea Market** (⊠ Rte. 30, ☎ 802/365–7771), held every weekend during summer and fall.

Outdoor Activities and Sports

Townshend State Park (⊠ 3 mi north of Rte. 30, between Newfane and Townshend, ☎ 802/365–7500), the largest in southern Vermont, is popular for the swimming at Townshend Dam and the stiff hiking trail to the top of Bald Mountain. Campsites are available.

Putney

⑭ *7 mi east of Newfane, 9 mi north of Brattleboro.*

Putney, a Connecticut River valley town just upriver from Brattleboro, was a prime destination for many of the converts to alternative rural lifestyles who swarmed into Vermont during the late 1960s and early '70s. Those who remained maintain a tradition of progressive schools, artisanship, and organic farming.

☾ **Harlow's Sugar House** (⊠ U.S. 5, ☎ 802/387–5852), 2 mi north of Putney, has a working cider mill and sugar house, as well as berry picking in summer and apple picking in autumn. You can buy the fruits of these labors in the gift shop.

Tours are given of the **Green Mountain Spinnery,** a factory-shop where you can purchase yarn, knitting accessories, and patterns. ⊠ *Depot Rd. at Exit 4 off I–91,* ☎ *802/387–4528 or 800/321–9665.* ᖴ *Tours $2.* ☺ *Tours of yarn factory at 1:30 on the 1st and 3rd Tues. of each month.*

Dining and Lodging

$$–$$$ ✕🏠 **Putney Inn.** The main building of this inn dates from the 1790s. The building was later part of a seminary—the present-day pub was the chapel. Two fireplaces dominate the lobby, and the guest rooms have Queen Anne mahogany reproductions. The exterior of the adjacent building is not terribly appealing, but the spacious, modern rooms are 100 yards from the banks of the Connecticut River. Regionally inspired cuisine—seafood, New England potpies, a wild-game mixed grill, and burgers with Vermont cheddar—contains innovative flourishes. Locally raised meat is butchered on the premises. ✉ *Depot Rd., 05346,* ☎ *802/387–5517 or 800/653–5517,* ℻ *802/387–5211. 25 rooms. Full breakfast. AE, D, MC, V.*

$$ 🏠 **Hickory Ridge House Bed and Breakfast.** This gracious 1808 Federal mansion, listed on the National Register of Historic Places, has Palladian windows, a parlor with a Rumford fireplace, and large, comfortable guest rooms filled with antiques and country furnishings. Four rooms have wood-burning fireplaces, and one has a gas fireplace stove. A two-bedroom cottage, with a full kitchen and fireplace, can be rented as a unit, or the rooms can be rented separately. A two-night minimum stay is required on some weekends and holidays. ✉ *R.D. 3, Box 1410, Hickory Ridge Rd., 05346,* ☎ *802/387–5709 or 800/380–9218,* ℻ *802/387–4051. 6 rooms, 1 cottage. Hiking, cross-country skiing. Full breakfast. MC, V.*

Shopping
Allen Bros. (✉ U.S. 5 north of Putney, ☎ 802/722–3395) bakes apple pies, makes cider doughnuts, and sells Vermont foods and products.

Southern Vermont A to Z

Arriving and Departing
See Vermont A to Z, *below.*

Getting Around
BY BUS

Vermont Transit (☎ 802/864–6811; 800/451–3292; 800/642–3133 in VT) links Bennington, Manchester, Brattleboro, and Bellows Falls.

BY CAR

In the south the principal east–west highway is Route 9, the Molly Stark Trail, from Brattleboro to Bennington. The most important north–south roads are U.S. 7; the more scenic Route 7A; Route 100, which runs through the state's center; I–91; and U.S. 5, which runs along the state's eastern border. Route 30 from Brattleboro to Manchester is a scenic drive.

Contacts and Resources
EMERGENCIES

Brattleboro Memorial Hospital (✉ 9 Belmont Ave., ☎ 802/257–0341).

VISITOR INFORMATION

Bennington Area Chamber of Commerce (✉ Veterans Memorial Dr., Bennington 05201, ☎ 802/447–3311). **Brattleboro Chamber of Commerce** (✉ 180 Main St., Brattleboro 05301, ☎ 802/254–4565). **Chamber of Commerce, Manchester and the Mountains** (✉ 2 Main St., Manchester 05255, ☎ 802/362–2100). **Mt. Snow Valley Chamber of Commerce** (✉ Box 3, W. Main St., Wilmington 05363, ☎ 802/464–8092).

CENTRAL VERMONT

Central Vermont's economy once centered on the mills and railroad yards of Rutland and the marble quarries that honeycomb nearby towns. Vermont's "second city" is still a busy commercial hub, but today, as in much of the rest of the state, it's tourism that drives the economic engine. The center of the dynamo is the massive ski-and-stay infrastructure around Killington, the East's largest downhill resort. There's a lot more to central Vermont than high-speed chairlifts and slopeside condos, however. The protected (except for occasional logging) lands of the Green Mountain National Forest surround the spine of Vermont's central range; off to the west, the rolling dairylands of the southern Lake Champlain valley are one of the truly undiscovered corners of the state. To the east, in the Connecticut River valley, are towns as diverse as Calvin Coolidge's Plymouth, a Yankee Brigadoon; and busy, polished-to-perfection Woodstock, where upscale shops are just a short walk from America's newest national park.

The coverage of towns begins with Windsor, on U.S. 5 near I–91 at the eastern edge of the state; winds westward toward U.S. 7; then continues north before heading up and over the spine of the Green Mountains.

Windsor

⑮ *50 mi north of Brattleboro, 42 mi east of Rutland.*

Windsor justly bills itself as the birthplace of Vermont. An interpretive exhibit on Vermont's constitution, the first in the United States to prohibit slavery and establish a system of public schools, is housed in the **Old Constitution House.** The site, where in 1777 grant holders declared Vermont an independent republic, contains 18th- and 19th-century furnishings, American paintings and prints, and Vermont-made tools, toys, and kitchenware. ⊠ *N. Main St.,* ☎ *802/828–3211.* ⊑ *$1.* ☉ *Mid-May–mid-Oct., Wed.–Sun.; call for hrs.*

The firm of Robbins & Lawrence became famous for applying the "American system" (the use of interchangeable parts) to the manufacture of rifles. Although the company no longer exists, the **American Precision Museum** extols the Yankee ingenuity that created a major machine-tool industry here in the 19th century. The museum contains the largest collection of historically significant machine tools in the country and presents changing exhibits. ⊠ *196 Main St.,* ☎ *802/674–6628.* ⊑ *$5.* ☉ *Memorial Day–Oct., weekdays 9–5, weekends 10–4.*

The mission of the **Vermont State Craft Center,** in the restored 1846 Windsor House, is to advance the appreciation of Vermont crafts through education and exhibition. The center presents crafts exhibitions and operates a small museum. ⊠ *54 Main St.,* ☎ *802/674–6729.* ☉ *Mon.–Thurs. 10–5, Fri.–Sat. 9–6, Sun. 11–5.*

A British-style pale ale, an American amber ale, and a dark porter are among the beers produced at **Catamount Brewery,** one of Vermont's most popular microbreweries. You can sample beer at the company store and at the conclusion of the tour. ⊠ *Windsor Industrial Park, U.S. 5S, Exit 9 off I–91,* ☎ *802/674–6700 or 800/540–2248.* ⊑ *Free.* ☉ *Mon.–Sat. 10–6, tours at 11, 1, and 3; Sun. 1–5, tours at 1 and 3.*

At 460 ft, the **covered bridge** off U.S. 5, which spans the Connecticut River between Windsor and Cornish, New Hampshire, is the longest in the state.

Dining and Lodging

$$ ✕ **Windsor Station.** This converted main-line railroad station serves such main-line entrées as chicken Kiev, filet mignon, and prime rib. The booths, with their curtained brass railings, were created from the high-back railroad benches of the depot. Breakfast and lunch are served in the deli across the street every day except Sunday. ⊠ *Depot Ave.,* ☎ *802/674–2052. AE, MC, V. Closed Mon.*

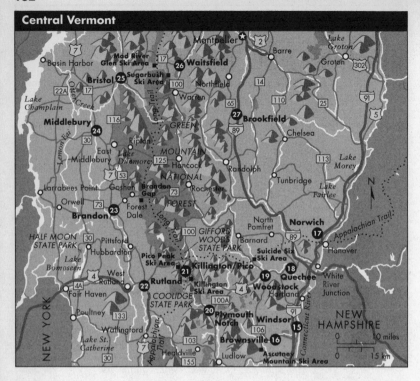

Central Vermont

$$–$$$ ✕▦ **Juniper Hill Inn.** An expanse of green lawn with Adirondack chairs and a garden of perennials sweeps up to the portico of this Greek Revival mansion, built at the turn of the century and now on the National Register of Historic Places. The central living room, with its hardwood floors, oak paneling, Oriental carpets, and thickly upholstered furniture, has a stately feel. The bedrooms are furnished with antiques; 11 have fireplaces. The four-course dinners ($$$) served in the candlelighted dining room may include herb-crusted rack of lamb or sautéed scallops with glazed garlic and champagne sauce. The inn is 7 mi from Mt. Ascutney. ⊠ *Box 79, Juniper Hill Rd., 05089,* ☎ *802/674–5273 or 800/359–2541,* ℻ *802/674–2041. 16 rooms. Restaurant, pool, hiking. Full breakfast. D, MC, V.*

Brownsville

⓰ *5 mi west of Windsor.*

Brownsville, a small village at the foot of Ascutney Mountain, has everything a village needs: country store, post office, town hall, and historic grange building. The Ascutney Mountain ski area is a self-contained four-season resort.

Dining and Lodging

$$–$$$$ ✕▦ **Ascutney Mountain Resort Hotel.** One of the big attractions of this five-building resort hotel–condo complex is the lift outside the main door. The comfortable, well-maintained suites come in different configurations and sizes—some with kitchens, fireplaces, and decks. Slopeside multilevel condos have three bedrooms, three baths, and private entrances. The Ascutney Harvest Inn ($$), which serves Continental and traditional cuisine, is within the complex. ⊠ *Box 699, Hotel Rd., off Rte. 44, 05037,* ☎ *802/484–7711 or 800/243–0011,* ℻ *802/484–*

3117. *240 suites and condos. 3 restaurants, 2 bars, pool, health club, racquetball, ice-skating, billiards. AE, MC, V.*

$–$$ ▥ **Mill Brook.** This Victorian farmhouse, built in 1880, is directly across from the Ascutney ski slopes. Making après-ski idleness easy are the four sitting rooms, decorated with antiques and contemporary furnishings. The honeymoon suite has a separate dressing room with a claw-foot bathtub; the other suites are perfect for families. ✉ *Box 410, Rte. 44, 05037,* ☎ *802/484–7283. 2 rooms, 3 suites. Hot tub. Full breakfast. AE, MC, V.*

Nightlife and the Arts

Crow's Nest Club (✉ Ascutney Mountain Resort Hotel, Rte. 33, ☎ 802/484–7711) has entertainment on weekends. **Destiny** (✉ U.S. 5, Windsor, ☎ 802/674–6671) hosts rock bands most days and has a DJ on Sunday.

Skiing and Snow Sports

ASCUTNEY MOUNTAIN RESORT

The Plausteiner family, whose patriarch, John, was instrumental in operations at Mt. Snow, in Vermont, and White Face Mountain, in Lake Placid, New York, purchased this resort in the mid-1990s and in 1998 launched a five-year expansion that will include new lifts and trails. The five buildings of the resort village include hotel suites and condominium units spread throughout. ✉ *Rte. 44, off I–91,* ☎ *802/484–7711; 800/ 243–0011 for lodging; mailing address: Box 699, Brownsville 05037.*

Downhill. Forty-six trails with varying terrain are covered by nearly 90% snowmaking. Like a stereotypical ski mountain cutout, this one reaches a wide peak and gently slopes to the bottom. Beginner and novice skiers stay toward the base, while intermediates enjoy the band that wraps the midsection. For experts, tougher black-diamond runs top the mountain. One disadvantage to Ascutney, however, is that there is no easy way down from the summit, so novice skiers should not make the trip. Trails are serviced by one double and three triple chairs. Ascutney is popular with families because it offers some of the least expensive junior lift tickets in the region.

Cross-country. The resort has 32 km (19 mi) of groomed cross-country trails; lessons, clinics, and rentals are provided.

Other activities. Ascutney Mountain Resort Hotel (☞ Dining and Lodging, *above*) has a sports-and-fitness center with full-size indoor and outdoor pools, racquetball, aerobics facilities and classes, weight training, and massage, as well as ice-skating on the pond.

Child care. Day care is available for children from ages 6 months to 10 years, with learn-to-ski options and rental equipment for toddlers and up. There are half- and full-day instruction programs for children from ages 3 to 12; a Mini-Olympians program for ages 4 to 7; and a Young Olympians program for children from ages 8 to 12. Evening baby-sitting is available.

Norwich

⑰ *6 mi north of White River Junction, 22 mi north of Brownsville.*

Norwich is home to an excellent science museum. The town is across the river from Hanover, New Hampshire, and Dartmouth College. **King Arthur Flour Baker's Store** (✉ U.S. 5, ☎ 802/649–3361), a retail outlet for all things baking oriented, sells tools and hard-to-find grains and specialty flours. The company, which has been in business since 1790, displays historic photographs of flour being delivered by horse cart.

★ ⓒ Numerous hands-on exhibits at the **Montshire Museum of Science** explore space, nature, and technology; there are also living habitats, aquariums, and many children's programs. A maze of trails winds through 100 acres of pristine woodland. An ideal destination for a rainy day, this is one of the finest museums in New England. ⊠ *Montshire Rd., Box 770,* ☎ *802/649–2200.* ☞ *$5.* ⊗ *Daily 10–5.*

Quechee

⑱ *6 mi west of White River Junction, 11 mi south of Norwich.*

Quechee is perched astride the Ottauquechee River. Quechee Gorge, 165 ft deep, is impressive, though overrun by tourists. You can see the mile-long gorge, carved by a glacier, from U.S. 4, but many people picnic nearby or scramble down one of several descents for a closer look. More than a decade ago Simon Pearce set up **Simon Pearce,** an eponymous glassblowing factory in an old mill by a waterfall here, using the water power to drive his furnace. The glass studio produces exquisite wares and houses a pottery workshop, a shop, and a restaurant (☞ Dining and Lodging, *below*); you can watch the artisans at work. ⊠ *The Mill, Main St.,* ☎ *802/295–2711 or 800/774–5277.* ⊗ *Store daily 9–9; workshop weekdays 9–9, weekends 9–5.*

Dining and Lodging

$$$ ✕ **Simon Pearce.** Candlelight, sparkling glassware from the studio downstairs, contemporary dinnerware, exposed brick, and large windows that overlook the roaring Ottauquechee River create an ideal setting for contemporary American cuisine. Sesame-crusted tuna with noodle cakes and wasabi and roast duck with mango chutney sauce are specialties of the house; the wine cellar holds several hundred vintages. ⊠ *Main St.,* ☎ *802/295–1470. AE, D, DC, MC, V.*

$$–$$$ ✕🏠 **Parker House.** The peach-and-blue rooms of this 1857 Victorian mansion are named for former residents: Emily has a marble fireplace, Walter is the smallest room, and Joseph has a view of the Ottauquechee River. All rooms on the third floor are air-conditioned. The elegant dining room ($$$) prepares sophisticated American comfort cuisine such as loin of venison with a port and balsamic vinegar sauce, and Maine crab cakes with a hint of wasabi. In warm weather, you can dine on the terrace, which has a spectacular river view. Guests have access to the Quechee Country Club's first-rate golf course, tennis courts, indoor and outdoor pool, and cross-country and downhill skiing. ⊠ *Box 0780, 16 Main St., 05059,* ☎ *802/295–6077,* 🅵🅰🆇 *802/296–6696. 7 rooms. Full breakfast; MAP available. AE, MC, V.*

$$–$$$ 🏠 **Quechee Bed and Breakfast.** Dried herbs hang from the beams in
★ the living room of this B&B, where a wood settee sits before a floor-to-ceiling fireplace that was part of the original 1795 structure. Ask for one of the rooms in the back—they're away from busy U.S. 4 and overlook the Ottauquechee River. A small, 200-year-old post-and-beam cottage that sleeps two to four perches on a cliff over the river. The inn is within walking distance of Quechee Gorge. ⊠ *Box 80, U.S. 4 at Waterman Hill, 05059,* ☎ *802/295–1776 or 800/628–8610. 8 rooms. Full breakfast. MC, V.*

Outdoor Activities and Sports

The **Vermont Fly Fishing School/Wilderness Trails** (⊠ Quechee Inn, Clubhouse Rd., ☎ 802/295–7620 or 800/235–3133) leads workshops, rents fishing gear and mountain bikes, and arranges canoe and kayak trips. In winter, the company conducts cross-country and snowshoe treks.

POLO

Quechee Polo Club (⊠ Dewey's Mill Rd., ½ mi north of U.S. 4, ☎ 802/
295–7152) draws hundreds of spectators on summer Saturdays to its
matches near the Quechee Gorge. Admission is $3 per person or $6
per carload.

Shopping

The 40 dealers at the **Hartland Antiques Center** (⊠ U.S. 4, ☎ 802/457–
4745) stock furniture, paper items, china, glass, and collectibles. More
than 350 dealers sell their wares at the **Quechee Gorge Village** (⊠ U.S.
4, ☎ 802/295–1550 or 800/438–5565), an antiques and crafts mall
in an immense reconstructed barn that also holds a country store and
the Farina Family Diner. A merry-go-round and a small-scale working railroad operate when weather permits. **Scotland by the Yard** (U.S.
4, ☎ 802/295–5351 or 800/295–5351) is the place to shop for all things
Scottish, from kilts to Harris tweed jackets and tartan ties.

Woodstock

★ ⑲ *4 mi east of Quechee.*

Perfectly preserved Federal houses surround Woodstock's tree-lined village green, and streams flow around the town center, which is anchored
by a covered bridge. The town owes much of its pristine appearance
to the Rockefeller family's interest in historic preservation and land
conservation.

The town's history of conservationism dates from the 19th century:
Woodstock native George Perkins Marsh, a congressman and diplo-
mat, wrote the pioneering book *Man and Nature* in 1864, and was
closely involved in the creation of the Smithsonian Institution in Washington, D.C. The **Billings Farm and Museum,** on the grounds of Marsh's
boyhood home, was founded by Frederick Billings in 1870 as a model
of conservation. Billings, a lawyer and businessman, put into practice
Marsh's ideas about the long-term effects of farming and grazing. Exhibits in the reconstructed Queen Anne farmhouse, school, general store,
workshop, and former Marsh homestead demonstrate the lives and skills
of early Vermont settlers. Splitting logs doesn't seem nearly so quaint
when you've watched the effort that goes into it. ⊠ *Rte. 12, ½ mi north
of Woodstock,* ☎ *802/457–2355.* ☞ *$7.* ☉ *May–late Oct., daily 10–
5; Nov.–Dec., weekends 10–4.*

The 500-acre **Marsh-Billings-Rockefeller National Park,** which opened
in 1998, is Vermont's only national park and the nation's first to focus
on conservation and stewardship of natural resources. The park encompasses the forest lands planned by Frederick Billings according to
the principles of George Perkins Marsh, as well as Billings's mansion,
gardens, and carriage roads. The entire property was the gift of Lau-
rance S. Rockefeller, who lived here with his late wife Mary, Frederick Billings's granddaughter. It is adjacent to the Billings Farm and
Museum. ⊠ *Rte. 12,* ☎ *802/457–3368.* ☞ *Free.* ☉ *Memorial Day–
Oct., daily for guided tours only; call for schedules.*

Period furnishings of the Woodstock Historical Society fill the white
clapboard **Dana House,** built circa 1807. Exhibits include the town charter, furniture, maps, and locally minted silver. The converted barn
houses the Woodstock Works exhibit, an economic portrait of the
town. ⊠ *26 Elm St.,* ☎ *802/457–1822.* ☞ *$1.* ☉ *May–late Oct., Mon.–
Sat. 10–5, Sun. noon–4; tours by appointment in winter.*

☪ The **Raptor Center** of the **Vermont Institute of Natural Science** (VINS)
houses 23 species of birds of prey, among them bald eagles, peregrine

falcons, and 3-ounce saw-whet owls. There are also ravens, turkey vultures, and snowy owls. All the caged birds have been found injured and unable to survive in the wild. This nonprofit, environmental research and education center is on a 77-acre nature preserve with walking trails. ⊠ *Church Hill Rd.,* ☎ *802/457–2779.* ⊡ *$6.* ◐ *May–Oct., daily 10–4; Nov.–Apr., Mon.–Sat. 10–4.*

Dining and Lodging

$$$–$$$$ ✕ **Prince and the Pauper.** Modern French and American fare with a
   ★   Vermont accent is the focus of this romantic restaurant in a candle-lighted Colonial setting. The grilled duck breast might have an Asian five-spice sauce; homemade lamb and pork sausage in puff pastry comes with a honey-mustard sauce. A less-expensive bistro menu is available in the lounge. ⊠ *24 Elm St.,* ☎ *802/457–1818. AE, D, MC, V. No lunch.*

$–$$$ ✕ **Bentley's.** Antique silk-fringed lamp shades, long lace curtains, and a life-size carving of a kneeling, winged knight lend a whimsical Victorian air to the proceedings here. Burgers, chili, and homemade soups are served; the entrées include roasted Maple Leaf Farm duckling with a sweet mango sauce or maple-mustard chicken coated with chopped pecans. A Sunday jazz brunch is presented from Thanksgiving through April, and there's dancing Saturday nights. ⊠ *3 Elm St.,* ☎ *802/457–3232. AE, DC, MC, V.*

$–$$ ✕ **Pane & Salute.** Authentic regional Italian breads are the specialty, but this bakery has a whole lot more to offer. You can try homemade pizzas and soups, sandwich specials, and, in season, pasta entrées such as penne with spinach, pine nuts, raisins, and Parmesan. Add a glass of Chianti and *mangia bene.* The bakery serves breakfast and lunch daily in summer, and dinner Friday and Saturday; call for winter hours. ⊠ *61 Central St.,* ☎ *802/457–4882. Reservations not accepted. MC, V. No dinner Mon.–Thurs. and Sun.*

$$$$ ✕▥ **Kedron Valley Inn.** Many rooms have a fireplace or a Franklin stove, two have decks, another has a veranda, and a fourth has a terrace overlooking the stream that runs through the inn's 15 acres. Exposed-log walls make the motel units in back more rustic than the rooms in the main inn, but they're decorated similarly, with country antiques and reproductions. The chef creates French masterpieces like fillet of Norwegian salmon stuffed with herb seafood mousse in puff pastry, and shrimp, scallops, and lobster with wild mushrooms sautéed in shallots and white wine and served with a Fra Angelico cream sauce. A terrace with views of the grounds is open in summer. ⊠ *Rte. 106, 05071,* ☎ *802/457–1473 or 800/836–1193,* ℻ *802/457–4469. 26 rooms. Restaurant, bar, pond, beach. MAP. AE, D, MC, V. Closed Apr. and 10 days before Thanksgiving.*

$$$–$$$$ ✕▥ **Jackson House Inn.** When the Florins purchased this 1890 Victorian inn in 1996, they kept the European antiques, Oriental rugs, and French-cut crystal, as well as the formal parlor and cozy library. They added two wings: one for suites with gas fireplaces, Anichini linens, down duvets, and thermal massage tubs; the other, overlooking the inn's manicured grounds, to house the cathedral-ceiling restaurant, whose focal point is a granite, open-hearth fireplace. They also brought in executive chef Brendan Nolan, previously of Aujourd'hui at Boston's Four Seasons Hotel, to oversee a menu featuring new American cuisine. The result is an elegant, full-service inn with a first-class dining room. ⊠ *37 Old Rte. 4 W, 05091,* ☎ *802/457–2065 or 800/448–1890,* ℻ *802/457–9290. 11 rooms, 6 suites. Restaurant, spa. Full breakfast. AE, MC, V.*

$$$–$$$$ ✕▥ **Woodstock Inn and Resort.** Resort entrepreneur Laurance Rockefeller, long a Woodstock resident, made this a flagship property of his Rockresorts chain. Country formality might sound like an oxymoron,

In case you want to see the world.

At American Express, we're here to make your journey a smooth one. So we have over 1,700 travel service locations in over 130 countries ready to help. What else would you expect from the world's largest travel agency?

do more

Travel

Call 1 800 AXP-3429 or visit
www.americanexpress.com/travel

In case you want to be welcomed there.

We're here to see that you're always welcomed at establishments everywhere. That's why millions of people carry the American Express® Card – for peace of mind, confidence, and security, around the world or just around the corner.

do more

Cards

In case you're running low.

We're here to help with more than 190,000 Express Cash locations around the world. In order to enroll, just call American Express at 1 800 CASH-NOW before you start your vacation.

do more AMERICAN EXPRESS

Express Cash

And in case you'd rather be safe than sorry.

We're here with American Express® Travelers Cheques. They're the safe way to carry money on your vacation, because if they're ever lost or stolen you can get a refund, practically anywhere or anytime. To find the nearest place to buy Travelers Cheques, call 1 800 495-1153. Another way we help you do more.

do more

Travelers Cheques

HORSEBACK RIDING

Kedron Valley Stables (⊠ Rte. 106, South Woodstock, ☎ 802/457–2734 or 800/225–6301) gives lessons and conducts guided trail rides and excursions in a sleigh and a wagon.

RECREATION AREA

Suicide Six (☎ 802/457–6656 for fitness center; ☞ Skiing and Snow Sports, *below*) has outdoor tennis courts, lighted paddle courts, croquet, and an 18-hole golf course that are open in the summer.

STATE PARK

Coolidge State Park (⊠ Rte. 100A, 2 mi north of Rte. 100, ☎ 802/672–3612) abuts Coolidge State Forest and has campsites (log lean-tos from the 1930s).

Shopping

The **Marketplace at Bridgewater Mills** (⊠ U.S. 4, west of Woodstock, ☎ 802/672–3332) houses shops and attractions in a three-story converted woolen mill. There's an antiques and crafts center, a bookstore, Miranda Thomas pottery, and Charles Shackleton furniture. Sample Vermont stocks gourmet foods and gifts from all over the state. **North Wind Artisans' Gallery** (⊠ 81 Central St., ☎ 802/457–4587) carries contemporary—mostly Vermont-made—crafts with sleek, jazzy designs. The **Village Butcher** (⊠ Elm St., ☎ 802/457–2756) is an emporium of Vermont comestibles. **Who Is Sylvia?** (⊠ 26 Central St., ☎ 802/457–1110), in the old firehouse, sells vintage clothing and antique linens, lace, and jewelry.

Skiing and Snow Sports

SUICIDE SIX

The site of the first ski tow in the United States (1934), this resort is owned and operated by the Woodstock Inn and Resort (☞ Dining and Lodging, *above*). The inn's package plans are remarkably inexpensive, considering the high quality of the accommodations. ⊠ *Pomfret Rd., 05091,* ☎ *802/457–6661; 800/448–7900 for lodging; 802/457–6666 for snow conditions.*

Downhill. Despite Suicide Six's short vertical of only 650 ft, the skiing is challenging: There are steep runs down the mountain's face, intermediate trails that wind around the hill, and glade skiing. Beginner terrain is mostly toward the bottom. Two double chairlifts and one surface lift service the 22 trails and slopes.

Cross-country. The **Woodstock Ski Touring Center** (☎ 802/457–2114), headquartered at the Woodstock Country Club (⊠ Rte. 106), has 60 km (37 mi) of trails. Equipment and lessons are available.

Other Activities. The resort has a snowboard area with a halfpipe. The **Woodstock Health and Fitness Center** (☎ 802/457–6656) has an indoor lap pool; indoor tennis, squash, and racquetball courts; whirlpool, steam, sauna, and massage rooms; and exercise and aerobics rooms.

Child care. The ski area has no nursery, but baby-sitting can be arranged through the Woodstock Inn if you're a guest. Lessons for children are given by the ski-school staff, and there's a children's ski-and-play park for those from ages 3 to 7.

ᴅouth Notch

⓴ *14 mi southwest of Woodstock.*

U.S. president Calvin Coolidge was born and buried in Plymouth Notch, a town that shares his character: low-key and quiet. The perfectly preserved 19th-century buildings of the **Plymouth Notch Historic**

but it best describes the relaxed yet polished atmosphere he
bies and lounges hold a grand piano, decorative quilts, a
tal fieldstone fireplace, and bowls of shiny Vermont ap
rooms are spacious, serene, and set well back from Woods
noisy main drag. The dinner fare is nouvelle New Englan
might list entrées like salmon steak with avocado beurre
Wellington, and prime rib. The resort owns Suicide Six (
Snow Sports, *below*). ⊠ *On the Green, U.S. 4, 05091,*
1100 or 800/448–7900, FAX *802/457–6699. 144 rooms. 2*
bar, 1 indoor and 1 outdoor pool, saunas, 2 18-hole golf
tennis courts, croquet, health club, racquetball, squash, c
and downhill skiing, meeting rooms. AE, MC, V.

$$$$ ⊞ **Twin Farms.** At the center of this exclusive 300-acre
★ the 1795 farmhouse where writers Sinclair Lewis and Dor
son lived. Not that Lewis and Thompson would recogni
It's been transformed into Vermont's most sumptuous—
pensive—resort. Twin Farms' rooms and cottages are
ronments, drawing their inspiration from Moorish, S
Japanese, and Adirondack design. There are fireplaces thro
with museum-quality artworks. Chef Neil Wigglesworth
contemporary cuisine that emphasizes local ingredients.
yourself at the open bar. ⊠ *Stage Rd., off Rte. 12,*
Woodstock, ☎ *802/234–9999 or 800/894–6327,* FAX *8*
Mailing address: Box 115, Barnard 05031. 6 rooms, 8 co
dining room, Japanese baths, exercise room, boating, bic
ing, cross-country and downhill skiing, recreation r
rooms. AP. AE, MC, V.

$$–$$$ ⊞ **The Woodstocker.** A short stroll from the covered
village green, this 1830s B&B offers the welcome and co
would expect from a friend's living room. Big leather c
indoor hot tub add to the casual atmosphere. The large, li
are furnished with a hodgepodge of antiques and repro
suites have kitchens. ⊠ *61 River St./U.S 4, 05091,* ☎
FAX *802/457–3897. 7 rooms, 2 suites. Full breakfast.*

$–$$$ ⊞ **Shire Motel.** Some rooms in this immaculate, in-to
decks overlooking the Ottauquechee River and the Bi
have four-poster beds, wing chairs, color TVs, and tel
plimentary coffee is served each morning. ⊠ *46 Pleas*
☎ *802/457–2211,* FAX *802/457–5836. 33 rooms. Refrig*
MC, V.

$$ ⊞ **Winslow House.** This farmhouse built in 1872 on
★ dairy farm that reached down to the Ottauquechee R
tentious place, Winslow House has only four guest ro
common area, but the two upstairs quarters are uncom
and have separate sitting rooms: Mahogany furnis
Room 3, and the English oak bed, armoire, and Missi
4 are a cut above what most small bed-and-breakfa
have phones and TVs. ⊠ *38 U.S. 4, 05091,* ☎ *802/45*
457–1820. 4 rooms. Refrigerators. Full breakfast. D

Outdoor Activities and Sports

BIKING
Cyclery Plus (⊠ 36 U.S. 4 W, West Woodstock, ☎ 802/4
rents, sells, and services equipment, has a free touring n

GOLF
Robert Trent Jones, Sr., designed the 18-hole, par-69
stock Country Club (⊠ South St., ☎ 802/457–6674)
the Woodstock Inn. Greens fees are $32–$75; cart r

Ply

District look more like a large farm than a town; in addition to the homestead there's the general store once run by Coolidge's father, a visitor center, a cheese factory, and a one-room schoolhouse. Coolidge's grave is in the cemetery across Route 100A. The Aldrich House, which mounts changing historical exhibits, is open on some weekdays during the off-season. ⊠ *Rte. 100A, 6 mi south of U.S. 4, east of Rte. 100,* ☎ *802/672–3773.* ⌑ *$5.* ⊙ *Late May–mid-Oct., daily 9:30–5.*

Killington/Pico

㉑ *11 mi (Pico) and 15 mi (Killington) east of Rutland.*

The intersection of U.S. 4 and Route 100 is the heart of central Vermont's ski country, with the Killington, Pico, and Okemo (☞ Ludlow *in* Southern Vermont, *above*) resorts nearby. Strip development characterizes the Killington access road, but the views from the top of the mountain are worth the drive.

Dining and Lodging

$$$$ ✕ **Hemingway's.** With a national reputation reinforced by major
★ awards and a loyal clientele, Hemingway's is as good as dining gets in central Vermont. You can tuck into the celebrated cream of garlic soup and a seasonal kaleidoscope of dishes based on native game, fresh seafood, and prime meats. Recent offerings on the prix-fixe menu have included autumn vegetable strudel with hazelnuts, Arctic char with flageolet beans, and Vermont venison with pumpkin sage pudding and parsnip crisps. Desserts are spectacular, as is the five-course wine tasting menu ($75), which matches each dish with an appropriate glass of wine. Request seating in either the formal, vaulted dining room or the intimate wine cellar. ⊠ *U.S. 4, Killington,* ☎ *802/422–3886. AE, MC, V. Closed most Mon. and Tues., and early Nov. and mid-Apr.–mid-May. No lunch.*

$$$–$$$$ ✕▥ **Inn at Long Trail.** This 1938 lodge is ¼ mi from the Pico ski slopes and even closer to the Appalachian and Long trails. The unusual decor—including massive indoor boulders—has nature as a prevailing theme. Irish music, darts, and Guinness always on tap are all part of the Irish hospitality, which is extended particularly to end-to-end hikers (who get a substantial break in the rates). Meals in the restaurant, open from Thursday to Sunday during peak season, might include roast duckling or mushroom and risotto strudel. The pub has live music Thursday and Saturday nights in winter and during foliage season. ⊠ *Box 267, U.S. 4, Killington 05751,* ☎ *802/775–7181 or 800/325–2540,* ℻ *802/747–7034. 22 rooms, 5 suites. Restaurant, pub. Full breakfast; MAP on winter and foliage weekends. AE, MC, V. Inn and restaurant closed mid-Apr.–mid-June; call for exact dates.*

$$$ ▥ **Cortina Inn.** This large lodge and mini-resort is comfortable and its location prime. About two-thirds of the rooms have private balconies, though the views from them aren't spectacular. Horseback riding, sleigh rides, ice-skating, and guided snowmobile, fly-fishing, and mountain biking tours are among the off-the-slopes activities. A breakfast buffet is served daily. ⊠ *U.S. 4, Mendon 05751,* ☎ *802/773–3333 or 800/451–6108,* ℻ *802/775–6948. 97 rooms. Restaurant, bar, indoor pool, hot tub, sauna, 8 tennis courts, health club. Full breakfast. AE, D, DC, MC, V.*

$$–$$$ ▥ **Summit Lodge.** Three miles from Killington Peak, this rustic two-story country lodge caters to a varied crowd of ski enthusiasts, who are warmly met by the lodge's mascots—a pair of Saint Bernards. Country decor and antiques blend with modern conveniences to create a relaxed atmosphere. Dining is formal at one of the restaurants and informal at the other. ⊠ *Killington Rd., Killington 05751,* ☎ *802/422–3535 or 800/635–6343,* ℻ *802/422–3536. 45 rooms, 2 suites. 2*

restaurants, bar, pool, pond, hot tub, massage, sauna, ice-skating, nightclub, recreation room. Full breakfast. AE, DC, MC, V.

Nightlife and the Arts

The pub at the **Inn at Long Trail** (☞ Dining and Lodging, *above*) hosts Irish music on weekends. The **Pickle Barrel** (⊠ Killington Rd., ☎ 802/422–3035), a favorite with the après-ski crowd, presents up-and-coming acts and can get pretty rowdy. The **Wobbly Barn** (⊠ Killington Rd., ☎ 802/422–3392), with dancing to blues and rock, is open during ski season.

Outdoor Activities and Sports

Cortina Inn (☞ Dining and Lodging, *above*) has an ice-skating rink with rentals and offers sleigh rides; you can also skate on Summit Pond. **Gifford Woods State Park**'s Kent Pond (⊠ Rte. 100, ½ mi north of U.S. 4, ☎ 802/775–5354) is a terrific fishing hole. Campsites are available.

Skiing and Snow Sports

KILLINGTON

"Megamountain," "Beast of the East," and plain "huge" are apt descriptions of Killington. The American Skiing Company operates Killington and its neighbor Pico—and over the past three years has spent $60 million to improve lifts, snowmaking capabilities, and lodging options. A project is under way to join Pico and Killington by interconnecting trails and lifts. The mountain has also developed numerous snowboarding parks. Lines on weekends (especially holiday weekends) can be downright dreadful—the resort has the longest ski season in the East and some of the best package plans. The area has been top rated for après-ski activities by several national ski magazines. With a single telephone call, skiers can select the price, date, and type of ski week they want; choose accommodations; book air or railroad transportation; and arrange for rental equipment and ski lessons. Ticket holders can also ski at Pico. ⊠ *400 Killington Rd., 05751,* ☎ *802/422–3333; 800/621–6867 for lodging; 802/422–3261 for snow conditions.*

Downhill. It would probably take several weeks to test all 205 trails on the six mountains of the Killington complex, even though everything interconnects. About 72% of the 1,200 acres of skiing terrain can be covered with machine-made snow. Transporting skiers to the peaks of this complex are three gondolas plus 12 quads (including six high-speed express quads), six triples, and five double chairlifts, as well as eight surface lifts (including a Magic Carpet). Several of the lifts reach the area's highest elevation, at 4,241 ft off Killington Peak, and a vertical drop of 3,150 ft to the base of the gondola. You can ride the Skyeship, the world's fastest and first heated eight-passenger lift, complete with piped-in music. The Skyeship base station has a rotisserie, food court, and a coffee bar. The skiing includes everything from Outer Limits, one of the steepest and most challenging trails anywhere in the country, to the 16-km-long (10-mi-long), super-gentle Juggernaut Trail. In the Fusion Zones, underbrush and low branches have been cleared away to provide tree skiing.

Child care. Nursery care is available for children from 6 weeks to 6 years old. There's a one-hour instruction program for youngsters from ages 3 to 8; those from 6 to 12 can join an all-day program.

PICO SKI RESORT

Although it's only 5 mi down the road from Killington, Pico has long been a favorite among people looking for uncrowded, wide-open cruiser skiing. When modern lifts were installed and a village square was constructed at the base, some feared a change in atmosphere might occur, but the condo-hotel, restaurants, and shops have not altered the essential nature of the area. Watch for big changes as the American Skiing Company brings Pico up to par with its other major resorts, Sugarbush and Killington. ⊠ *2 Sherburne Pass, Rutland 05701,* ☎ *802/422–3333; 800/ 621–6867 for lodging; 802/422–3261 for snow conditions.*

Downhill. Many of the 42 trails are advanced to expert, with two intermediate bail-out trails for the timid. The rest of the mountain's 2,000 ft of vertical terrain is mostly intermediate or easier. The mountain has nine lifts including two high-speed quads, two triples, and three double chairs, and has 85% snowmaking coverage. Snowboarders are welcome and have their own area, Triple Slope. For instruction of any kind, head to the Alpine Learning Center.

Other activities. A **sports center** (☎ 802/773–1786) at the base of the mountain has fitness facilities, a 75-ft pool, whirlpool tub, saunas, and a massage room.

Child care. Pico's nursery takes children from ages 6 months to 6 years and provides indoor activities and outdoor play. The ski school has full- and half-day instruction programs for children from ages 3 to 12.

CROSS-COUNTRY SKIING

Mountain Meadows (⊠ Thundering Brook Rd., Killington, ☎ 802/775–7077) has 57 km (34½ mi) of groomed trails and 10 km (6 mi) of marked outlying trails. You can also access 500 acres of backcountry skiing. **Mountain Top Inn and Resort** (☞ Rutland, *below*; ☎ 802/483–6089 or 800/445–2100) is mammoth, with 120 km (72 mi) of trails, 80 km (49 mi) of which are groomed.

Rutland

22 *15 mi west of Killington, 32 mi south of Middlebury, 31 mi west of Woodstock, 47 mi west of White River Junction.*

On and around U.S. 7 in Rutland are strips of shopping centers and a seemingly endless row of traffic lights, although the mansions of the marble magnates who made the town famous still command whatever attention can be safely diverted from the traffic. Rutland's compact downtown, one of only a handful of urban centers in Vermont, has experienced a modest revival and is worth an hour's stroll. The area's traditional economic ties to railroading and marble, the latter an industry that became part of such illustrious structures as the central research building of the New York Public Library in New York City, have been rapidly eclipsed by the growth of the Pico and Killington ski areas to the east.

The **Chaffee Center for the Visual Arts** (⊠ 16 S. Main St., ☎ 802/775–0356) exhibits and sells the output of more than 200 Vermont artists who work in various media. It's closed Tuesday.

OFF THE BEATEN PATH

VERMONT MARBLE EXHIBIT – The highlight of the Rutland area is this exhibit and store 4 mi north of town. A sculptor-in-residence transforms stone into finished works of art or commerce (you can choose first-hand the marble for a custom-built kitchen counter). The gallery illustrates the many industrial and artistic applications of marble—there's a hall of presidents and a replica of Leonardo da Vinci's *Last Supper* in marble—and depicts the industry's history via exhibits and a video. Factory seconds and foreign and domestic marble items are for sale. ⊠ *62 Main St., Proctor (follow signs off Rte. 3),* ☎ *802/459–2300 or 800/427–1396.* ⬚ *$5.* ☺ *Memorial Day–Oct., daily 9–5:30.*

Dining and Lodging

$$–$$$ ✕ **Royal's 121 Hearthside.** Long a local favorite for a big night out, the institution built by the late Ernie Royal still turns out the best prime rib in town, accompanied by tasty hot popovers. Also look for rack of lamb with strawberry-mint sauce and pan-roasted salmon with dill hollandaise. ⊠ *37 N. Main St.,* ☎ *802/775–0856. AE, MC, V.*

$$ ✕ **The Palms.** This restaurant has been in the Sabataso family since it opened its doors on Palm Sunday, 1933; it was the first in the state to serve pizza. The menu is primarily southern Italian, with specialties such as fried mozzarella; antipasto Neapolitan (with provolone, pepperoni, mild peppers, anchovies, and house dressing); and the chef's personal creation, veal à la Palms—veal scallops topped with mushrooms, two kinds of cheese, and a special tomato sauce. The dessert choices are fairly pedestrian. ⊠ *36 Strongs St.,* ☎ *802/773–2367. AE, DC, MC, V. Closed Sun. in summer. No lunch.*

$–$$ ✕ **Back Home Café.** Wood booths, black-and-white linoleum tile, and exposed brick lend this second-story café the feel of a New York City hole-in-the-wall. Dinner might be chicken breast stuffed with roasted red peppers and goat cheese or tortellini Alfredo primavera. Soup-and-entrée lunch specials can cost less than $5. The large bar in the back of the restaurant is occasionally the site of weekend entertainment. ⊠ *21 Center St.,* ☎ *802/775–9313. AE, MC, V.*

$$$$ ✕🏠 **Mountain Top Inn and Resort.** Just minutes from Rutland, one of the state's three or four most spectacular family resorts occupies 500 lofty acres overlooking secluded Chittenden Reservoir and the Green Mountain National Forest. The Mountain Top is essentially an out-doorperson's inn, with an equestrian center, swimming and canoeing, fishing, trap and skeet shooting, and a golf school with a 5-hole pitch-and-putt course and driving range. Winter brings cross-country skiing on more than 70 mi of trails, sleigh rides, and skating. The dinner menu ($$$) runs to satisfying, uncomplicated American fare such as rack of lamb and roast pork tenderloin and unadventurous French fare such as sole meunière. A tip: Opt for the somewhat more expensive deluxe rooms, which are larger and have spectacular views. ⊠ *195 Mountaintop Rd., Chittenden 05737,* ☎ *802/483–2311 or 800/445–2100,* 𝔽𝔸𝕏 *802/483–6373. 35 rooms, 6 cottages, 12 chalets. Restaurant, pool, driving range, horseback riding, beach, boating, fishing, cross-country skiing. MAP available. AE, MC, V. Closed Nov. and Apr.*

$$–$$$ 🏠 **Inn at Rutland.** One alternative to Rutland's chain motel and hotel accommodations is this renovated Victorian mansion. The ornate oak staircase lined with heavy embossed gold and leather wainscoting leads to rooms that blend modern bathrooms with late-19th-century touches such as elaborate ceiling moldings and frosted glass. The two large common rooms, one with a fireplace, have views of surrounding mountains and valleys. ⊠ *70 N. Main St., 05701,* ☎ *802/773–0575 or 800/808–0575,* 𝔽𝔸𝕏 *802/775–3506. 12 rooms. Mountain bikes. Full breakfast fall and winter; Continental breakfast spring and summer. AE, D, DC, MC, V.*

$$ 🏠 **Comfort Inn.** Rooms at this chain hotel are a cut above the standard, with upholstered wing chairs and blond-wood furnishings. This place is popular with bus tours in foliage season. ⊠ *19 Allen St., 05701,* ☎ *802/775–2200 or 800/432–6788,* 𝔽𝔸𝕏 *802/775–2694. 104 rooms. Restaurant, indoor pool, hot tub, sauna. Continental breakfast. AE, D, DC, MC, V.*

Nightlife and the Arts

Crossroads Arts Council (⊠ 39 E. Center St., ☎ 802/775–5413) presents music, opera, dance, jazz, and theater.

Outdoor Activities and Sports

Half Moon State Park's principal attraction is Half Moon Pond (⊠ Town Rd., 3½ mi off Rte. 30, west of Hubbardton, ☎ 802/273–2848). The park has nature trails, campsites, and boat and canoe rentals.

Shopping

An anthropologist opened **East Meets West** (⊠ U.S. 7 at Sangamon Rd., Pittsford, ☎ 802/443–2242 or 800/443–2242), which carries carvings, masks, statues, textiles, pottery, baskets, and other crafts of native peoples from around the world. **Tuttle Antiquarian Books** (⊠ 28 S. Main St., ☎ 802/773–8229) has a large collection of books on Asia. The store stocks rare and out-of-print books, genealogies, local histories, and miniature books.

Brandon

㉓ *15 mi north of Rutland.*

Straddling busy U.S. 7, Brandon nevertheless has broad side streets lined with gracious Victorian houses, lodging at the landmark Brandon Inn or at smaller B&Bs, and ready access to the mountain scenery and recreation of nearby Brandon Gap.

The **Stephen A. Douglas Birthplace** commemorates the "Little Giant" (he stood only 5 ft, 2 in tall), best known for his debates with Abraham Lincoln in 1858. Douglas, who became a U.S. representative and senator from Illinois, was born here on April 23, 1813. His boyhood home and a monument to his memory are just north of the village, next to the Baptist church. ⊠ *U.S. 7.* ☎ *Free.* ☉ *June–Labor Day, Thurs. 2–5, or by appointment (call the Nelsons at 802/247–6569 or the Martins at 802/247–6332).*

Maple syrup is Vermont's signature product, and the **New England Maple Museum and Gift Shop** explains the history and process of turning maple sap into syrup with murals, exhibits, and a slide show. ⊠ *U.S. 7, Pittsford (9 mi south of Brandon),* ☎ *802/483–9414.* ☎ *$1.25.* ☉ *May–Oct., daily 8:30–5:30; Nov.–Dec. and Mar.–Apr., daily 10–4.*

Dining and Lodging

$$ ✕🏨 **Blueberry Hill Inn.** If you're looking for total peace and quiet, this is the place. In the Green Mountain National Forest and 5½ mi off a mountain pass on a dirt road, Blueberry Hill is an idyllic spot with lush gardens, a stream, an apple orchard, and a pond with a wood-fired sauna on its bank. Many rooms have views of the surrounding mountains; all are furnished with antiques, quilts, and hot-water bottles to warm winter beds. Three rooms have lofts (good for families), and the Moosalamoo Room is in a private cottage. The restaurant menu has listed dishes such as garlic fish soup with mussels and venison fillet with cherry sauce. Tony Clark, innkeeper for more than 20 years, often joins guests for cocktails (bring your own liquor). Blueberry Hill's ski-touring center focuses on mountain biking in the summer. Hikers can take advantage of the 50 mi of marked trails. ⊠ *Rte. 32, Goshen 05733,* ☎ *802/247–6735 or 800/448–0707,* 📠 *802/247–3983. 12 rooms. Restaurant, sauna, hiking, volleyball, mountain biking, cross-country skiing. MAP; B&B plan available. MC, V.*

$$–$$$$ 🏨 **Lilac Inn.** The bridal suite at this Greek Revival mansion, which bills itself as a romantic retreat, is one of the most elegant inn rooms in Vermont, with a pewter canopy bed, whirlpool bath for two, and fireplace. The other rooms, all uniquely furnished and with claw-foot tubs and hand-held European shower heads, are also charming. A full breakfast is served on the patio or in the bright, gleaming dining room, both of which overlook the lovely gardens with 15 varieties of lilacs. Own-

ers Michael and Melanie Shane host musical and cultural events in the ballroom. The inn is home to three cats. ⊠ *53 Park St./Rte. 73, 05733,* ☎ *802/247–5463 or 800/221–0720,* ⒻⒶⓍ *802/247–5499. 9 rooms. Full breakfast. Restaurant. AE, D, MC, V. Restaurant closed Nov.–Apr.*

Outdoor Activities and Sports

Moosalamoo (☎ 800/448–0707) is the name given by a partnership of public and private entities to a 20,000-acre chunk of Green Mountain National Forest land (along with several private inholdings) just northeast of Brandon. More than 60 mi of trails take hikers, mountain bikers, and cross-country skiers through some of Vermont's most gorgeous mountain terrain. Attractions include Branbury State Park, on the shores of Lake Dunmore; secluded Silver Lake, a trout-fishing mecca; and sections of both the Long Trail and Catamount Trail (the latter is a Massachusetts-to-Québec ski trail). Both the Blueberry Hill Inn (☞ Dining and Lodging, *above*) and Churchill House Inn (☎ 802/247–3078) offer direct public access to trails.

GOLF

Neshobe Golf Club (⊠ Rte. 73, east of Brandon, ☎ 802/247–3611) has 18 holes of par-72 golf on a bent-grass course totaling nearly 6,500 yards. The Green Mountain views are terrific. Several local inns offer golf packages.

HIKING

About 8 mi east of Brandon on Route 73, a trail that takes an hour to hike starts at Brandon Gap and climbs steeply up **Mt. Horrid.** South of Lake Dunmore on Route 53, a large turnout marks a trail (a hike of about two hours) to the **Falls of Lana.** Four other trails—two short ones of less than a mile each and two longer ones—lead to the old abandoned Revolutionary War fortifications at **Mt. Independence**; to reach them, take the first left turn off Route 73 west of Orwell and go right at the fork. The road will turn to gravel and once again will fork; take a sharp left-hand turn toward a small marina. The parking lot is on the left at the top of the hill.

Shopping

The **Warren Kimble Gallery & Studio** (⊠ Off Rte. 73 E, ☎ 802/247–3026) is the workplace, gallery, and gift shop of the nationally renowned folk artist.

Middlebury

★ ㉔ *17 mi north of Brandon, 34 mi south of Burlington.*

In the late 1800s Middlebury was the largest Vermont community west of the Green Mountains: an industrial center of river-powered wool, grain, and marble mills. This is Robert Frost country; Vermont's late poet laureate spent 23 summers at a farm east of Middlebury. Otter Creek, the state's longest river, traverses the town center. Still a cultural and economic hub amid the Champlain Valley's serene pastoral patchwork, the town and countryside invite a day of exploration.

Smack in the middle of town, **Middlebury College** (☎ 802/443–5000), founded in 1800, was conceived as a more godly alternative to the worldly University of Vermont. The college has no religious affiliation today, however. The early 19th-century stone buildings contrast provocatively with the postmodern architecture of the Center for the Arts and the sports center. Music, theater, and dance performances take place throughout the year at the **Wright Memorial Theatre** and **Center for the Arts.**

The **Middlebury College Museum of Art** has a permanent collection of paintings, photography, works on paper, and sculpture. ⊠ *Center for*

*the Arts, Rte. 30, ☎ 802/443–5007. ☞ Free. ☉ Tues.–Fri. 10–5, week-
ends noon–5. Closed college holidays and last 2 weeks of Aug. and Dec.*

The **Vermont Folklife Center** has exhibits of photography, antiques, folk
paintings, manuscripts, and other artifacts and contemporary works
that examine facets of Vermont life. The center is in the basement of
the restored 1801 home of Gamaliel Painter, the founder of Middlebury College. ⊠ *2 Court St., ☎ 802/388–4964. ☞ Donations accepted.
☉ Nov.–Apr., weekdays 9–5; May–Oct., weekdays 9–5, Sat. noon–4.*

The **Sheldon Museum,** an 1829 marble merchant's house, is the oldest community museum in the country. The period rooms contain Vermont-made textiles, furniture, toys, clothes, kitchen tools, and paintings.
⊠ *1 Park St., ☎ 802/388–2117. ☞ $2; guided tour $4. ☉ June–Oct.,
Mon.–Sat. 10–5; Nov.–May, weekdays 10–5 (but call to make sure museum is open).*

More than a crafts store, the **Vermont State Craft Center at Frog Hollow** displays the work of more than 300 Vermont artisans. The center sponsors classes taught by some of those artists. There are other
centers in Burlington and Manchester. ⊠ *1 Mill St., ☎ 802/388–3177.
☉ Call for hrs.*

The Morgan horse—the official state animal—has an even temper, good
stamina, and slightly truncated legs in proportion to its body. The University of Vermont's **Morgan Horse Farm,** about 2½ mi west of Middlebury, is a breeding and training center where in summer you can
tour the stables and paddocks. ⊠ *74 Battell Dr. off Horse Farm Rd
(follow signs off Rte. 23), Weybridge, ☎ 802/388–2011. ☞ $4. ☉ May–
Oct., daily 9–5: last tour at 4:30.*

About 10 mi east of town on Route 125 (1 mi west of Middlebury College's Breadloaf campus), the easy ¾-mi **Robert Frost Interpretive Trail**
winds through quiet woodland. Plaques along the way bear quotations
from Frost's poems. A picnic area is across the road from the trailhead.

OFF THE
BEATEN PATH

LAKE CHAMPLAIN MARITIME MUSEUM – A replica of Benedict Arnold's
Revolutionary War gunboat is part of this museum, which documents
centuries of activity on the historically significant lake. The museum commemorates the days when steamships sailed along the coast of northern
Vermont carrying logs, livestock, and merchandise bound for New York
City. Among the 11 exhibit buildings is a blacksmith's shop. A one-room
stone schoolhouse built in the late 1810s houses historic maps, nautical
prints, and maritime objects. Also on site are a nautical archaeology
center and a conservation laboratory. ⊠ *Basin Harbor Rd., Basin Harbor (14 mi west of Bristol, 7 mi west of Vergennes), ☎ 802/475–2022.
☞ $7. ☉ Early May–late Oct., daily 10–5.*

Dining and Lodging

$$–$$$ ✕ **Fire & Ice.** A 55-item salad bar (with peel-and-eat shrimp), prime
rib, steak, fish, and a house specialty—homemade mashed potatoes—
are all choices at a family-friendly spot that just celebrated its 25th an-
niversary. Although large, the space is divided into several rooms (each
with a different theme) as well as numerous intimate nooks and crannies for diners who wish privacy. Families with small children may want
to request a table next to the "children's corner," which is outfitted
with cushions and a VCR. Sunday dinner begins at 1 and includes crab
legs and soup or the salad bar. ⊠ *26 Seymour St., ☎ 802/388–7166
or 800/367–7166. AE, D, DC, MC, V. No lunch Mon.*

$$–$$$ ✕ **Roland's Place.** Chef Roland Gaujac prepares classic French and
★ American dishes, elegantly served on Villeroy & Boch china, in a house

built in 1796. He opened his restaurant overlooking the Adirondacks after working as a chef in various parts of the world, including the French dining room in Los Angeles's Four Seasons Hotel. Some dishes use locally raised lamb, turkey, and venison; shrimp with chipotle and roasted garlic vinaigrette on fried ravioli is one entrée. A prix-fixe menu is available, and a special menu served daily from 5 to 6 lists numerous à la carte dishes for just $9. The restaurant has three guest rooms upstairs that are moderately priced and include a full breakfast. ⊠ *U.S. 7, New Haven,* ☎ *802/453–6309. AE, DC, MC, V. Closed Mon. No dinner Sun. Nov.–Apr.*

$$–$$$ ✕ **Woody's.** In addition to cool jazz, diner-deco light fixtures, and abstract paintings, Woody's has a view of Otter Creek below. Seafood and Vermont lamb are the restaurant's specialties—some folks say the Caesar salad is the best in the state. ⊠ *5 Bakery La.,* ☎ *802/388–4182. AE, MC, V. Closed Tues.*

$$$–$$$$ ✕🏠 **Swift House Inn.** The main building at Swift House, the Georgian
  ★   home of a 19th-century governor and his philanthropist daughter, contains white-panel wainscoting, elaborately carved mahogany and marble fireplaces, and cherry paneling in the dining room. The rooms—most with Oriental rugs and nine with fireplaces—have period reproductions such as canopy beds, curtains with swags, and claw-foot tubs. Some bathrooms have double whirlpool tubs. Rooms in the gatehouse suffer from street noise but are charming; a carriage house holds six luxury accommodations. The dining room ($$$) offers entrées like herb-crusted rack of lamb with rosemary and Madeira sauce and creamy risotto with seasonal vegetables and maple syrup. A vegetarian menu is also available. ⊠ *25 Stewart La., 05753,* ☎ *802/388–9925,* ℻ *802/388–9927. 21 rooms. Restaurant, pub, sauna, steam room. Continental breakfast. AE, D, DC, MC, V.*

$$–$$$$ 🏠 **Middlebury Inn.** Gracious New England–style hospitality is served up along with traditional Yankee fare in this three-story, brick Georgian building, which has been an inn since 1827. The property now encompasses a contemporary motel (decorated, like the rooms in the inn, with Early American–style furnishings) and the Victorian-era Porter House Mansion. Rooms have phones, TVs, and hair dryers; those facing the lovely town green are subject to the noise of passing traffic. Plan to arrive between 3 and 4 for the inn's complimentary afternoon tea, served daily except holidays. In nice weather, you can eat lunch on the wicker-furnished porch. ⊠ *14 Courthouse Sq., 05753,* ☎ *802/ 388–4961 or 800/842–4666,* ℻ *802/388–4563. 80 rooms. Two restaurants. Continental breakfast; MAP available. AE, D, MC, V.*

$–$$ 🏠 **Lemon Fair.** This tidy, unfussy bed-and-breakfast occupies a building dating from 1796; it was tiny Bridport's first church before it was moved to its present location overlooking the town green in 1819. Furnishings are Early American in style, the grounds are spacious, and the entire establishment is kid-friendly. The B&B is just 8 mi from downtown Middlebury and 4 mi from Lake Champlain. The owners live next door and will rent out the entire house. ⊠ *Crown Point Rd., Bridport 05734,* ☎ *802/758–9238,* ℻ *802/758–2135. 3 rooms without bath, 1 suite. Full breakfast. No credit cards.*

Outdoor Activities and Sports

The **Bike and Ski Touring Center** (⊠ 74 Main St., ☎ 802/388–6666) offers rentals and repairs.

BOATING

Chipman Point Marina (⊠ Rte. 73A, Orwell, ☎ 802/948–2288), where there is dockage for 60 boats, rents houseboats, sailboats, and pontoon fishing boats.

HIKING

On Route 116, about 5½ mi north of East Middlebury, a U.S. Forest Service sign marks a dirt road that forks to the right and leads to the start of the hike (about two to three hours) to **Abbey Pond,** which has a fantastic beaver lodge and dam in addition to a view of Robert Frost Mountain.

Shopping

Historic Marble Works (⊠ Maple St., ☎ 802/388–3701), a renovated marble manufacturing facility, is a collection of unique shops set amid quarrying equipment and factory buildings. One shop, De Pasquale's (☎ 802/388–3385), prepares subs and fresh fried fish platters for take-out and sells imported Italian groceries and wines. **Holy Cow** (⊠ 44 Main St., ☎ 802/388–6737) is where Woody Jackson creates and sells his Holstein cattle–inspired T-shirts, memorabilia, and paintings.

Bristol

㉕ *13 mi north of Middlebury.*

At the northeastern threshold of the Green Mountain National Forest, where the rolling farmlands of the Champlain Valley meet the foothills of Vermont's main mountain chain, Bristol has a redbrick 19th-century Main Street that reflects the town's prosperous heyday as the center of a number of wood-products industries. Almost overshadowing the still-busy little downtown are the brooding heights of the Bristol Cliffs Wilderness Area, a section of national forest that has been assured permanent status as a primitive, roadless tract.

Dining and Lodging

$–$$ ✕▥ **Mary's at Baldwin Creek.** This restaurant ($$–$$$) and B&B in a 1790 farmhouse provides a truly inspired culinary experience. The "summer kitchen" has a fireplace and rough-hewn barn-board walls, and the main dining room is done in pastels. The innovative fare includes a superb garlic soup, Vermont rack of lamb with a rosemary-mustard sauce, and duck cassis smoked over applewood. Farmhouse dinners on Tuesdays in summer highlight Vermont products; Sunday brunch is a local ritual. Guests rooms, right above the restaurant, have simple, comfortable furnishings. ⊠ *Rte. 116, 05443,* ☎ *802/453–2432 or 877/453–2432,* ℻ *802/453–4825. 5 rooms without bath. Full breakfast. AE, MC, V. Closed Mon. in winter. No lunch.*

Outdoor Activities and Sports

A challenging 32-mi bicycle ride starts in Bristol: Take North Street from the traffic light in town and continue north to Monkton Ridge and on to Hinesburg. To return, follow Route 116 south through Starksboro and back to Bristol.

Shopping

Folkheart (⊠ 18 Main St., ☎ 802/453–4101) carries unusual jewelry, toys, and crafts from around the world.

En Route From Bristol, Route 17 winds eastward up and over the **Appalachian Gap,** one of Vermont's most panoramic mountain passes. The views from the top and on the way down the other side toward the ski town of Waitsfield are a just reward for the challenging drive.

Waitsfield

㉖ *20 mi east of Bristol, 55 mi north of Rutland, 32 mi northeast of Middlebury, 19 mi southwest of Montpelier.*

Although in close proximity to Sugarbush and Mad River Glen ski areas, the Mad River valley towns of Waitsfield and Warren have maintained a decidedly low-key atmosphere. The gently carved ridges cradling the valley and the swell of pastures and fields lining the river seem to keep further notions of ski-resort sprawl at bay. With a map from the Sugarbush Chamber of Commerce you can investigate back roads off Route 100 that have exhilarating valley views.

Dining and Lodging

$$–$$$ ✕ **American Flatbread.** For ideologically and gastronomically sound pizza, you won't find a better place in the Green Mountains than this modest haven on the grounds of the Lareau Farm Country Inn between Waitsfield and Warren. Organic flour and produce fuel mind and body, and Vermont hardwood fuels the earth-and-stone oven. The "punctuated equilibrium flatbread," made with olive-pepper goat cheese and rosemary, is a dream, as are more traditional pizzas. This place is open Monday–Thursday 7:30 AM–8 PM for takeout, and Friday and Saturday for dinner as well. ⊠ *Rte. 100,* ☎ *802/496–8856. Reservations not accepted. MC, V. Closed Sun.*

$$–$$$ ✕ **Chez Henri.** Tucked in the shadows of Sugarbush ski area, this romantic slopeside bistro has garnered a year-round following with traditional French dishes: onion soup, cheese fondue, rabbit in red-wine sauce, and rack of lamb with rosemary-garlic sauce. Locals frequent the congenial bar and dine alfresco next to a stream. ⊠ *Sugarbush Village,* ☎ *802/583–2600. AE, MC, V.*

$$$$ ✕🏠 **Pitcher Inn.** In 1997, four years after burning to the ground, this ★ Mad River Valley institution was reborn in an incarnation of *haute luxe.* Designed by architect David E. Sellers, each guest room has its own motif: In the Mallard, a curved ceiling gives the illusion of a duck blind, and the windows are etched and frosted in the likeness of the banks of a marsh. The Mountain Suite has a mountain mural, and a unique slate and mirror combination renders the effect of a waterfall. Rooms have stereos and a TV/VCR; most have fireplaces. The formal dining room, under the direction of chef Tom Bivins, focuses on locally grown produce and wild game. The inn has one of the state's finest wine cellars. ⊠ *Box 347, 275 Main St., Warren 05674,* ☎ *802/496–6350 or 888/867–4824,* ℻ *802/496–6354. 8 rooms, 2 2-bedroom suites. 2 restaurants, in-room data ports. Full breakfast. AE, MC, V.*

$$ ✕🏠 **Tucker Hill Lodge.** Pine paneling and otherwise simple furnishings suffice at this 1940s lodge—most guests are more interested in skiing all day than enjoying in Victorian frills. Giorgio's Café occupies two dining rooms: one upstairs, with red tablecloths and a deep blue ceiling; and one downstairs, with a bar, open stone oven, and fireplace. Both have a warm Mediterranean feel. *Pettini a la Veneziana* (stone-seared scallops with raisins and pine nuts), and saltimbocca *alla Valdostana* (roulades of beef with fontina cheese and prosciutto) are two specialties. ⊠ *Rte. 17, 05673,* ☎ *802/496–3983 or 800/543–7841,* ℻ *802/496–3203. 21 rooms, 15 with bath. Restaurant, bar, pool, tennis court, hiking, game room. Full breakfast; MAP available. AE, MC, V.*

$$–$$$$ 🏠 **Inn at the Round Barn Farm.** Art exhibits have replaced cows in the big round barn here (one of only eight in the state), but the Shaker-style building still dominates the farm's 85 acres. The inn's guest rooms are in the 1806 farmhouse, where books line the walls of the cream-color library. The rooms are sumptuous, with eyelet-trimmed sheets, elaborate four-poster beds, rich-colored wallpapers, and brass wall lamps for easy bedtime reading. Six have fireplaces, three have whirlpool tubs, and four have steam showers. ⊠ *Box 247, E. Warren Rd., R.R. 1, 05673,* ☎ *802/496–2276,* ℻ *802/496–8832. 11 rooms. Indoor pool, cross-country skiing, recreation room. Full breakfast. AE, D, MC, V.*

$$ ☆ **Beaver Pond Farm Inn.** This small 1840 farmhouse less than a mile from Sugarbush overlooks rolling meadows, a golf course, and cross-country ski trails. Guest rooms are decorated simply, and bathrooms are ample; the inn's focal point is the huge deck. The full breakfast might include orange-yogurt pancakes. The four-course dinner (served with MAP) features entrées such as rack of lamb or pork à l'orange; vegetarian meals will be served on request. Dinner is open to nonguests by reservation only. The inn has a limited practice driving range and is next door to the Sugarbush Golf Course. The innkeeper is building a reputation as a fly-fishing guide. ⊠ *Box 306, Golf Course Rd., 05674,* ☎ *802/583–2861,* FAX *802/583–2860. 5 rooms (1 can sleep up to 4). Dining room, cross-country skiing. Full breakfast; MAP available Tues., Thurs., Sat. MC, V. Closed Jan.–mid-May.*

Nightlife and the Arts

The **Back Room at Chez Henri** (⊠ Sugarbush Village, ☎ 802/583–2600) has a pool table and is popular with the après-ski and late-night dance crowd. Local bands play danceable music at **Gallaghers** (⊠ Rtes. 100 and 17, ☎ 802/496–8800). **Giorgio's Café** (Tucker Hill Lodge, ☞ Dining and Lodging, *above*) is a cozy spot to warm yourself by the fire to the sounds of soft folk and jazz on weekends.

The **Green Mountain Cultural Center** (⊠ Inn at the Round Barn, E. Warren Rd., ☎ 802/496–7722), a nonprofit organization, brings concerts and art exhibits, as well as educational workshops, to the Mad River valley. The **Valley Players** (⊠ Rte. 100, ☎ 802/496–9612) present musicals, dramas, follies, and holiday shows.

Outdoor Activities and Sports

BIKING

The popular 14-mi Waitsfield–Warren loop begins when you cross the covered bridge in Waitsfield. Keep right on East Warren Road to the four-way intersection in East Warren; continue straight, then bear right, riding down Brook Road to the village of Warren; return by turning right (north) on Route 100 back toward Waitsfield.

GOLF

Great views and challenging play are the trademarks of the Robert Trent Jones–designed 18-hole, par-72 course at **Sugarbush Resort** (⊠ Golf Course Rd., ☎ 802/583–6727). The greens fee runs from $32 to $52; a cart (sometimes mandatory) costs $17.

ICE-SKATING

At the **Skadium** (⊠ Rte. 100, ☎ 802/496–8845 rink; 802/496–9199 recorded message), an outdoor rink, you can ice-skate in the winter and rollerblade or skateboard in warmer weather.

SLEIGH RIDES

The 100-year-old sleigh of the **Lareau Farm Country Inn** (⊠ Rte. 100, ☎ 802/496–4949) cruises along the banks of the Mad River.

Shopping

ART AND ANTIQUES

Luminosity Stained Glass Studios (⊠ Rte. 100, ☎ 802/496–2231), inside a converted church, specializes in stained glass, custom lighting, and art glass.

CRAFTS

All Things Bright and Beautiful (⊠ Bridge St., ☎ 802/496–3997) is a 12-room Victorian house jammed to the rafters with stuffed animals of all shapes, sizes, and colors as well as folk art, prints, and collectibles. **Warren Village Pottery** (⊠ Main St., Warren, ☎ 802/496–4162) sells handcrafted wares from its retail shop and specializes in functional stoneware pottery.

Skiing and Snow Sports

MAD RIVER GLEN

In 1995, Mad River Glen became the first ski area to be owned by a cooperative formed by the skiing community. The hundreds of shareholders are dedicated, knowledgeable skiers devoted to keeping skiing what it used to be—a pristine alpine experience. Mad River's unkempt aura attracts rugged individualists looking for less-polished terrain: The area was developed in the late 1940s and has changed relatively little since then. The single chairlift may be the only lift of its vintage still carrying skiers. Most of Mad River's trails (85%) are covered only by natural snow. ⊠ *Rte. 17, 05673, ☎ 802/496–3551; 800/850–6742 for cooperative office; 802/496–2001 for snow conditions.*

Downhill. Mad River is steep, with natural slopes that follow the contours of the mountain. The terrain changes constantly on the 44 interconnected trails, of which 30% are beginner, 30% are intermediate, and 40% are expert. Intermediate and novice terrain is regularly groomed. Four chairs service the mountain's 2,037-ft vertical drop. There is no snowboarding on the mountain, but telemarkers will find many compatriots. Mad River sponsors the North American Telemark Festival in early March.

Child care. The **nursery** (☎ 802/496–2123) takes children from ages 6 weeks to 6 years. The ski school has classes for children from ages 4 to 12. Junior racing is available weekends and during holidays.

SUGARBUSH

In the Warren-Waitsfield ski world, Sugarbush is Mad River Glen's alter ego. Sugarbush's current owner, the American Skiing Company, has spent $28 million to keep the resort on the cutting edge. The new Slide Brook Express quad connects the two mountains, Sugarbush South and Sugarbush North. A computer-controlled system for snowmaking has increased coverage to nearly 70%. At the base of the mountain is a village with condominiums, restaurants, shops, bars, and a sports center. ⊠ *Box 350, Sugarbush Access Rd., accessible from Rte. 100 or Rte. 17, Warren 05674, ☎ 802/583–2381; 800/537–8427 for lodging; 802/583–7669 for snow conditions.*

Downhill. Sugarbush is two distinct, connected mountain complexes. The Sugarbush South area is what old-timers recall as Sugarbush Mountain: With a vertical of 2,400 ft, it is known for formidable steeps toward the top and in front of the main base lodge. Sugarbush North offers what South has in short supply—beginner runs. North also has steep fall-line pitches and intermediate cruisers off its 2,600 vertical ft. There are 112 trails in all: 23% beginner, 48% intermediate, 29% expert. The resort has 18 lifts: seven quads (including four high-speed versions), three triples, four doubles, and four surface lifts.

Other activities. The **Sugarbush Health and Racquet Club** (☎ 802/583–6700), near the ski lifts, has Nautilus and Universal equipment; tennis, squash, and racquetball courts; a whirlpool, a sauna, and steam rooms; one indoor pool; and a 30-ft-high climbing wall.

Child care. The Sugarbush Day School accepts children from ages 6 weeks to 6 years; older children have indoor play areas and can go on outdoor excursions. There's half- and full-day instruction available for children from ages 4 to 11. Kids have their own Magic Carpet lift. Sugarbear Forest, a terrain garden, has fun bumps and jumps.

CROSS-COUNTRY SKIING

Blueberry Lake cross-country ski area (⊠ Plunkton Rd., Warren, ☎ 802/496–6687) has 30 km (18 mi) of groomed trails through thickly wooded glades. **Ole's** (⊠ Airport Rd., Warren, ☎ 802/496–3145) runs a cross-country center and small restaurant out of the tiny Warren airport; it has 60 km (37 mi) of groomed European-style trails that span out into the surrounding woods from the landing strips.

Brookfield

㉗ *15 mi south of Montpelier.*

The residents of secluded Brookfield have voted several times to keep its roads unpaved and even turned down an offered I–89 exit when the interstate highway was being built in the '60s. Crossing the nation's only **floating bridge** (⊠ Rte. 65 between Rtes. 12 and 14) still afloat feels like driving on water. The bridge, supported by nearly 400 barrels, sits at water level. It's the scene of the annual ice-harvest festival in January. The bridge is closed in winter.

Dining and Lodging

$$ ✕🏠 **Autumn Harvest Inn.** You'll be tempted to spend the whole day on the porch that graces the front of this casual inn, which was built in 1790. The inn, atop a knoll, has views of a 46-acre workhorse farm and the surrounding valley. Rooms in the older part of the house have more character; all have phones and TVs with VCRs. Prime rib and veal dishes are among the highlights of the seasonal country menu at the restaurant ($–$$; no lunch). ⊠ *R.F.D. 1, Box 1540, Clark Rd., Williamstown 05679,* ☎ *802/433–1355,* FAX *802/433–5501. 18 rooms. Restaurant, bar, pond, horseback riding, cross-country skiing. MAP and B&B plan available. AE, MC, V.*

$$ 🏠 **Green Trails Inn.** The enormous fieldstone fireplace that dominates
★ the living and dining area at Green Trails is symbolic of the stalwart hospitality of the innkeepers. Antique clocks fill the common areas, and the comfortably elegant rooms have antiques and Oriental rugs. One two-room suite has a fireplace, and two rooms have whirlpool tubs. Vegetarians are happily accommodated. This is a tranquil place for a walk down a tree-shaded country road. ⊠ *Main St., 05036,* ☎ *802/276–3412 or 800/243–3412. 14 rooms, 8 with bath. Cross-country skiing, snowshoeing, ski shop, sleigh rides. Full breakfast; MAP available in winter. D, MC, V.*

Central Vermont A to Z

Arriving and Departing
See Vermont A to Z, *below.*

Getting Around
BY BUS

Vermont Transit (☎ 802/864–6811; 800/451–3292; 800/642–3133 in VT) links Rutland, White River Junction, Burlington, and many smaller towns.

BY CAR

The major east–west road is U.S. 4, which stretches from White River Junction in the east to Fair Haven in the west. Route 125 connects Middlebury on U.S. 7 with Hancock on Route 100; Route 100 splits the region in half along the eastern edge of the Green Mountains. Route 17 travels east–west from Waitsfield over the Appalachian Gap through Bristol and down to the shores of Lake Champlain. I–91 and the parallel U.S. 5 follow the eastern border; U.S. 7 and Route 30 are the north–

south highways in the west. I–89 links White River Junction with Montpelier to the north.

Contacts and Resources

EMERGENCIES

Porter Hospital (⊠ South St., Middlebury, ☎ 802/388–7901). **Rutland Medical Center** (⊠ 160 Allen St., Rutland, ☎ 802/775–7111 or 800/ 649–2187 in Vermont).

GUIDED TOURS

Country Inns Along the Trail (⊠ R.R. 3, Box 3115, Brandon 05733, ☎ 802/247–3300 or 800/838–3301) leads skiing, hiking, and biking trips from inn to inn in Vermont. The **Vermont Icelandic Horse Farm** (⊠ N. Fayston Rd., Waitsfield 05673, ☎ 802/496–7141) conducts year-round guided riding expeditions on easy-to-ride Icelandic horses. Full-day, half-day, and hourly rides, weekend tours, and inn-to-inn treks are available.

LODGING REFERRAL SERVICES

Sugarbush Reservations (☎ 800/537–8427) and the **Woodstock Area Chamber of Commerce** (☎ 802/457–3555 or 888/496–6378) provide lodging referral services.

VISITOR INFORMATION

Addison County Chamber of Commerce (⊠ 2 Court St., Middlebury 05753, ☎ 802/388–7951 or 800/733–8376). **Quechee Chamber of Commerce** (⊠ Box 106, 15 Main St., Quechee 05059, ☎ 802/295–7900 or 800/295–5451). **Rutland Region Chamber of Commerce** (⊠ 256 N. Main St., Rutland 05701, ☎ 802/773–2747). **Sugarbush Chamber of Commerce** (⊠ Box 173, Rte. 100, Waitsfield 05673, ☎ 802/496– 3409 or 800/828–4748). **Woodstock Area Chamber of Commerce** (⊠ Box 486, 4 Central St., Woodstock 05091, ☎ 802/457–3555 or 888/ 496–6378).

NORTHERN VERMONT

Vermont's northernmost tier reveals the state's greatest array of contrasts. To the west, along Lake Champlain, Burlington and its Chittenden County suburbs have grown so rapidly that rural wags now say that Burlington's greatest advantage is that it's "close to Vermont." The north country also harbors Vermont's tiny capital, Montpelier, and its highest mountain, Mt. Mansfield, site of the famous Stowe ski slopes. To the northeast of Burlington and Montpelier spreads a sparsely populated and heavily wooded territory, the domain of loggers as much as farmers, where French spills out of the radio and the last snows melt toward the first of June.

You'll find plenty to do in the region's cities (Burlington, Montpelier, St. Johnsbury, and Barre), in the bustling resort area of Stowe, in the Lake Champlain Islands, and—if you like the outdoors—in the wilds of the Northeast Kingdom.

The coverage of towns in this area begins in the state capital, Montpelier; moves west towards Waterbury, Stowe, and Burlington; then north through the Lake Champlain Islands; east along the boundary with Canada toward Jay Peak and Newport; and south into the heart of the Northeast Kingdom before completing the circle in Barre.

Montpelier

28 *38 mi east of Burlington, 115 mi north of Brattleboro.*

With only about 8,000 residents, Montpelier is the country's least populous state capital. The intersection of State and Main streets is the city hub, bustling with the activity of state and city workers during the day. It's a pleasant place to spend an afternoon shopping and browsing; in true small-town Vermont fashion, though, the streets become deserted at night.

The **Vermont State House**—with a gleaming gold dome and granite columns 6 ft in diameter (plucked from the ground in nearby Barre)—is impressive for a city this size. The goddess of agriculture tops the dome. The Greek Revival building dates to 1836, although it was rebuilt after a fire in 1859; the latter year's Victorian style was adhered to in a lavish 1994 restoration. Interior paintings and exhibits make much of Vermont's sterling Civil War record. ⊠ *115 State St.,* ☎ *802/ 828–2228.* ☞ *Free.* ☉ *Weekdays 8–4; tours July–mid-Oct. weekdays every ½ hr 10–3:30, also Sat. 11–3.*

Perhaps you're wondering what the last panther shot in Vermont looked like? Why New England bridges are covered? What a niddy-noddy is? Or what Christmas was like for a Bethel boy in 1879? ("I skated on my new skates. In the morning Papa and I set up a stove for Gramper.") The **Vermont Museum,** on the ground floor of the Vermont Historical Society offices in Montpelier, satisfies the curious with intriguing and informative exhibits. ⊠ *109 State St.,* ☎ *802/828–2291.* ☞ *$3.* ☉ *Tues.–Fri. 9–4:30, Sat. 9–4, Sun. noon–4.*

Dining and Lodging

$$–$$$ ✕ **Chef's Table.** Nearly everyone working here is a student at the New
★ England Culinary Institute. Although this is a training ground, the quality and inventiveness are anything but beginner's luck. The menu changes daily. The atmosphere is more formal than that of the sister operation downstairs, the Main Street Bar and Grill (open daily). A 15% gratuity is added to the bill. ⊠ *118 Main St.,* ☎ *802/229–9202; 802/ 223–3188 for Grill. AE, D, MC, V. Closed Sun. No lunch weekends.*

$$–$$$ ✕ **Sarducci's.** Legislative lunches have been a lot more leisurely ever since Sarducci's came along to fill the trattoria void in Vermont's capital. These bright, cheerful rooms alongside the Winooksi River are a great spot for pizza fresh from wood-fired ovens, wonderfully textured homemade Italian breads, and imaginative pasta dishes such as pasta pugliese, which marries penne with basil, black olives, roasted eggplant, Portobello mushrooms, and sun-dried tomatoes. ⊠ *3 Main St.,* ☎ *802/ 223–0229. Reservations not accepted. AE, MC, V. No lunch Sun.*

$–$$ ✕ **Horn of the Moon.** The bulletin board plastered with notices of local events and political gatherings hints at Vermont's prominent progressive contingent. This vegetarian restaurant's cuisine includes a little Mexican, a little Italian, a lot of flavor, and not too much tofu. ⊠ *8 Langdon St.,* ☎ *802/223–2895. No credit cards. Closed Mon.*

$$–$$$ 🏠 **Inn at Montpelier.** This inn built in the early 1800s was renovated with the business traveler in mind, but the architectural detailing, antique four-poster beds, Windsor chairs, and the classical guitar on the stereo attract the leisure trade as well. The formal sitting room has a Federal feel to it, and the wide wraparound Colonial Revival porch is perfect for reading a good book or watching the townsfolk stroll by. The rooms in the annex are equally spiffy. ⊠ *147 Main St., 05602,* ☎ *802/223–2727,* 𝔽𝔸𝕏 *802/223–0722. 19 rooms. Meeting rooms. Continental breakfast. AE, D, DC, MC, V.*

Waterbury

㉙ *12 mi northwest of Montpelier.*

Waterbury's compact downtown consists of several brick business blocks, a state office complex that formerly served as a hospital, and

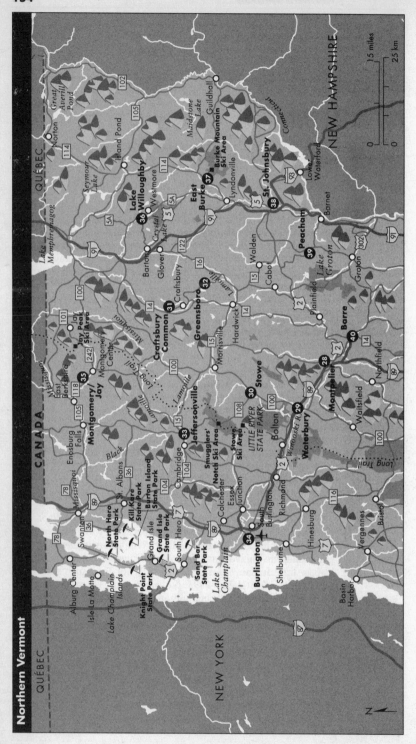

Northern Vermont

a little train station that comes to life only when Amtrak's *Vermonter* stops in town, once a day in each direction. The principal draws for visitors are north of I–89, along Route 100.

Waterbury holds one of Vermont's best-loved attractions: **Ben & Jerry's Ice Cream Factory,** the mecca, nirvana, and Valhalla for ice cream lovers. Ben and Jerry began selling ice cream from a renovated gas station in Burlington in the 1970s. Famous for their social and environmental consciousness, the boys do good works while living off the butterfat of the land. The tour only skims the surface of the behind-the-scenes goings-on at the plant—a flaw forgiven when the free samples are offered. ⊠ *Rte. 100, 1 mi north of I–89,* ☎ *802/244–8687.* ⛺ *Tour $2.* ⊙ *June, daily 9–5; July–Aug., daily 9–8; Sept.–Oct., daily 9–6; Nov.–May, daily 10–5. Tours every ½ hr in winter, more frequently in summer.*

Dining and Lodging

$$$–$$$$ ✕⌂ **Thatcher Brook Inn.** There were once two sawmills across the street from this 1899 mansion, which was the residence for the sawyers and their families. Today the hub of activity is Ben & Jerry's ice cream factory, almost right next door. Twin gazebos are poised on either end of the front porch, and stands of giant white pines bolster the inn, defining its space on busy Route 100. Comfortable guest rooms have modern bathroom fixtures and Laura Ashley–style floral wallpaper; some have fireplaces and whirlpool tubs. Pine paneling, a fireplace, framed *Life* magazine covers, and tables painted with backgammon boards make the pub a popular socializing spot. Classic French cuisine, which might include pheasant, rack of lamb, or seafood, is served in the dining room. ⊠ *Rte. 100, 05676,* ☎ *802/244–5911 or 800/292–5911,* 𝖥𝖠𝖷 *802/ 244–1294. 24 rooms. Restaurant, pub. Full breakfast; MAP available. AE, D, DC, MC, V.*

$$–$$$ ✕⌂ **Black Bear Inn.** Teddy bears in all shapes and sizes decorate this mountaintop inn overlooking the Green Mountains. Many of the rooms have glass-door woodstoves and balconies, and Rooms 10R and 16R have private hot tubs and fireplaces. Grilled Atlantic salmon with a maple–Dijon mustard glaze is a typical dish at the inn's restaurant. ⊠ *Bolton Access Rd., Bolton 05477,* ☎ *802/434–2126 or 800/395– 6335,* 𝖥𝖠𝖷 *802/434–5161. 24 rooms. Restaurant, pool, outdoor hot tub. Full breakfast. MC, V.*

Outdoor Activities and Sports

Mt. Mansfield State Forest and Little River State Park (⊠ U.S. 2, 1½ mi west of Waterbury, ☎ 802/244–7103) have extensive trail systems for hiking, including one that reaches the headquarters of the Civilian Conservation Corps unit that was stationed here in the 1930s. At Little River State Park, there are campsites, boat rentals, and trails leading to Mt. Mansfield and Camel's Hump.

Shopping

Green Mountain Chocolate Complex (⊠ Rte. 100, 2½ mi north of I–89, ☎ 802/244–1139) houses several gourmet and specialty shops including the Cabot Cheese Annex Store (☎ 802/244–6334) and Shimmering Glass Studio and Gallery (☎ 802/244–8134). **Cold Hollow Cider Mill** (⊠ Rte. 100, 3 mi north of I–89, ☎ 802/244–8771 or 800/327–7537) sells cider, baked goods, Vermont produce, and specialty foods. Tastes of fresh-pressed cider are offered while you watch how it is made.

Stowe

★ ③⓪ *8 mi north of Waterbury, 22 mi northwest of Montpelier, 36 mi northeast of Burlington.*

To many, Stowe rings a bell as the place where the von Trapp family, of *Sound of Music* fame, chose to settle after fleeing Austria. Set amid acres of pastures that fall away and allow for wide-angle panoramas of the mountains beyond, the **Trapp Family Lodge** (⊠ Luce Hill Rd., ☎ 802/253–8511 or 800/826–7000) is the site of a popular outdoor music series in summer and an extensive cross-country ski-trail network in winter.

For more than a century the history of Stowe has been determined by the town's proximity to **Mt. Mansfield,** at 4,393 ft the highest elevation in the state. As early as 1858, visitors were trooping to the area to view the mountain, which has a shape that suggests the profile of the face of a man lying on his back. If hiking to the top isn't your idea of a good time, in summer you can take the 4½-mi **toll road** to the top for a short scenic walk and a magnificent view. ⊠ *Mountain Rd., 7 mi from Rte. 100,* ☎ *802/253–3000.* ⊡ *Toll road $12.* ☉ *Late May–late Oct., daily 10–5.*

Mt. Mansfield's upper reaches are accessible by the eight-seat **gondola** that shuttles continuously up to the area of "the Chin" and the **Cliff House Restaurant** (☎ 802/253–3665; reservations essential). ⊠ *Mountain Rd., 8 mi from Rte. 100,* ☎ *802/253–3000.* ⊡ *$10.* ☉ *Mid-June–mid-Oct., daily 10–5; early Dec.–late Apr., daily 8–4 for skiers.*

When you tire of shopping on Stowe's Main Street and on Mountain Road, head for the **recreational path** that begins behind the Community Church in the center of town and meanders for 5⅓ mi along the river valley. There are many entry points along the way; whether you're on foot, skis, bike, or in-line skates, it's a tranquil means of enjoying the outdoors.

Dining and Lodging

$$–$$$ ✕ **Foxfire Inn.** A restored Colonial building might seem an unusual place to find Italian delicacies like veal rollatini, steak saltimbocca, and *tartufo* (vanilla and chocolate gelato in a chocolate cup with a raspberry center). Nonetheless, this old farmhouse just north of Stowe proper blends the two well. ⊠ *Rte. 100,* ☎ *802/253–4887. AE, D, MC, V. Closed Nov. No lunch.*

$$–$$$ ✕ **Villa Tragara.** Romance reigns in this intimate and creative north-
★ ern Italian restaurant, which consistently wins recognition as one of the state's best dining spots. Besides entrées such as *risotto con quaglie* (roast quail stuffed with toasted bread, prosciutto, sun-dried tomatoes, sage, and Asiago cheese and topped with a sauce of sherry and dried mixed fruit), the owner-chef prepares a five-course tasting menu for $40. The newest treat is the Italian tapas—smaller portions of many of the Villa's most popular offerings, moderately priced to allow patrons to pick and share dishes. (There's a $12 minimum charge per person for the tapas.) The restaurant has live entertainment Friday evenings and a popular dinner theater several Monday evenings throughout the year. ⊠ *Rte. 100, south of Stowe,* ☎ *802/244–5288. AE, MC, V. Restaurant closed Mon. No lunch.*

$–$$ ✕ **Miguel's Stowe Away.** In a little café just the other side of the border . . . actually, just the other side of Smugglers' Notch, Miguel's serves up all the Tex-Mex standards along with tasty surprises such as coconut-fried shrimp, Cajun lamb fajitas, and a Yankee-flavored maple flan. Steaks and burgers round out the gringo menu. The cozy front room has a pool table (no quarters required) and a bar stocked with frosty Corona beer. Miguel's has an outpost on the Sugarbush Access Road in Warren (☎ 802/583–3858). ⊠ *3148 Mountain Rd.,* ☎ *802/ 253–7574 or 800/245–1240. AE, D, MC, V. No lunch spring and fall.*

$$$$ ✕🛏 **Edson Hill Manor.** This French-Canadian–style manor built in 1940 sits atop 225 acres of rolling hills. Oriental rugs accent the dark wide-board floors, and a tapestry complements the burgundy-patterned sofas that face the huge stone fireplace in the living room. The guest rooms are pine paneled and have fireplaces, canopy beds, and down comforters. The dining room ($$$; no lunch; closed from Sunday to Thursday in April and May) is really the heart of the place: The walls of windows allowing contemplation of the inspiring view compete for your attention with wildflower paintings and vines climbing to the ceiling. The highly designed, sculpted food might include rack of lamb or pan-seared salmon. ✉ *1500 Edson Hill Rd., 05672,* ☎ *802/253–7371 or 800/621–0284,* 🖷 *802/253–4036. 25 rooms. Restaurant, pool, hiking, horseback riding, cross-country skiing, sleigh rides. Full breakfast; MAP available. AE, D, MC, V.*

$$$$ ✕🛏 **Topnotch at Stowe Resort and Spa.** This resort on 120 acres overlooking Mt. Mansfield, and just 3 mi from the base of the mountain, is one of the state's poshest. Floor-to-ceiling windows, a freestanding circular stone fireplace, and cathedral ceilings make the lobby an imposing setting. Rooms have thick carpeting, a small shelf of books, and accents such as painted barn-board walls or Italian prints. The minimum stay is two nights on weekends. The large European spa offers 20 massage-treatment rooms and a fitness program. Maxwell's restaurant serves Continental cuisine. ✉ *Mountain Rd., 05672,* ☎ *802/253–8585 or 800/451–8686,* 🖷 *802/253–9263. 77 rooms, 13 suites, 20 1- to 3-bedroom town homes. 2 restaurants, bar, 1 indoor and 1 outdoor pool, 14 tennis courts (4 indoor), health club, horseback riding, cross-country skiing, sleigh rides. Full breakfast; MAP available. AE, D, DC, MC, V.*

$$–$$$$ 🛏 **Inn at the Brass Lantern.** Home-baked cookies in the afternoon, a basket of logs by your fireplace, and stenciled hearts along the wainscoting reflect the care taken in turning this 18th-century farmhouse into a place of welcome. All rooms have country antiques and locally made quilts; most are oversize and some have fireplaces and whirlpool tubs. This B&B is next door to a Grand Union supermarket, but its breakfast room has a terrific view of Mt. Mansfield, a sight some guest rooms share. ✉ *Rte. 100, ½ mi north of Stowe, 05672,* ☎ *802/253–2229 or 800/729–2980,* 🖷 *802/253–7425. 9 rooms. Breakfast room. Full breakfast. AE, MC, V.*

$–$$ 🛏 **Sunset Motor Inn.** Strategically located among northern Vermont's big-three ski areas, this family-owned, family-friendly motel has clean and comfortable accommodations. Rooms numbered 70–87 in the newer section are larger and have whirlpool baths and refrigerators; the best are the ones facing the back of the motel. There's a restaurant next door. ✉ *Junction of Rtes. 15 and 100, Morrisville 05661,* ☎ *802/888–4956 or 800/544–2347,* 🖷 *802/888–3698. 55 rooms. Pool. AE, D, MC, V.*

Nightlife and the Arts

The **Matterhorn Night Club** (✉ Mountain Rd., ☎ 802/253–8198) has live music and dancing on weekends, DJs during the week. Live weekend entertainment takes place at **Stoweflake Inn** (✉ Mountain Rd., ☎ 802/253–7355). Entertainers perform at the **Topnotch at Stowe** (☞ Dining and Lodging, *above*) lounge on weekends.

Stowe Performing Arts (☎ 802/253–7792) sponsors a series of classical and jazz concerts during July in the Trapp Family Concert meadow. **Stowe Theater Guild** (✉ Town Hall Theater, Main St., ☎ 802/253–3961 summer only) performs musicals in July and August.

Outdoor Activities and Sports

BIKING

The junction of Routes 100 and 108 is the start of a 21-mi tour with scenic views of Mt. Mansfield; the course takes you along Route 100 to Stagecoach Road, to Morristown, over to Morrisville, and south on Randolph Road. The **Mountain Bike Shop** (⊠ Mountain Rd., ☎ 802/253–7919) supplies equipment and rents bicycles.

CANOEING

Umiak Outdoor Outfitters (⊠ 849 S. Main St./Rte. 100, just south of Stowe Village, ☎ 802/253–2317) specializes in canoes and kayaks, rents them for day trips, and leads guided overnight excursions. The store also operates a rental outpost at Waterbury State Park, just off Route 100.

FISHING

The **Fly Rod Shop** (⊠ Rte. 100, 3 mi south of Stowe, ☎ 802/253–7346 or 800/535–9763) provides a guiding service; gives fly-tying, casting, and rod-building classes in winter; rents fly tackle; and sells equipment, including classic and collectible firearms.

HIKING

For the two-hour climb to **Stowe Pinnacle,** go 1½ mi south of Stowe on Route 100 and turn east on Gold Brook Road opposite the Nichols Farm Lodge; turn left at the first intersection, continue straight at an intersection by a covered bridge, turn right after 1.8 mi, and travel 2.3 mi to a parking lot on the left. The trail crosses an abandoned pasture and takes a short, steep climb to views of the Green Mountains and Stowe Valley.

ICE-SKATING

Jackson Arena (⊠ Park St., ☎ 802/253–6148) is a public ice-skating rink that rents skates.

SLEIGH RIDES

Charlie Horse Sleigh and Carriage Rides (⊠ Mountain Rd., ☎ 802/253–2215) operates rides daily from 11 to 7; reservations are suggested for evening rides.

TENNIS

Topnotch at Stowe Resort and Spa (☞ Dining and Lodging, *above*) has 10 outdoor and 4 indoor courts. Public courts are located at Stowe's elementary school.

Shopping

The **Mountain Road** is lined with shops from town up toward the ski area.

Skiing and Snow Sports

STOWE MOUNTAIN RESORT

To be precise, the name of the village is Stowe and the name of the mountain is Mt. Mansfield, but to generations of skiers, the area, the complex, and the region are just plain Stowe. The resort is a classic that dates from the 1930s. Even today the area's mystique attracts as many serious skiers as social skiers. In recent years, on-mountain lodging, improved snowmaking, new lifts, and free shuttle buses that gather skiers from lodges, inns, and motels along the Mountain Road have added convenience to the Stowe experience. Yet the traditions remain: the Winter Carnival in January, the Sugar Slalom in April, ski weeks all winter. Three base lodges provide the essentials, including two on-mountain restaurants. ⊠ *5781 Mountain Rd., 05672,* ☎ *802/253–3000; 800/ 253–4754 for lodging; 802/253–3600 for snow conditions.*

Downhill. Mt. Mansfield, with a vertical drop of 2,360 ft, is one of the giants among Eastern ski mountains and the highest in Vermont. It was the only area in the East featured in Warren Miller's 1995 film, *Endless Winter.* The mountain's symmetrical shape allows skiers of all abilities long, satisfying runs from the summit. The famous Front Four runs (National, Liftline, Starr, and Goat) are the intimidating centerpieces for tough, expert runs, yet there is plenty of mellow intermediate skiing and one long beginner trail from the top that ends at the Toll House, where there is easier terrain. Mansfield's satellite sector is a network of intermediate and one expert trail off a basin served by a gondola. Spruce Peak, separate from the main mountain, is a teaching hill and a pleasant experience for intermediates and beginners; it also has a mountaintop trail that connects with slopes at neighboring resort Smugglers' Notch. In addition to the high-speed, eight-passenger gondola, Stowe has one quad, one triple, and six double chairlifts, plus one handle tow and poma, to service its 47 trails. Night-skiing trails are accessed by the gondola. The resort has 73% snowmaking coverage. Snowboard facilities include a halfpipe, quarterpipe, and two terrain parks—one for beginners, at the base of Spruce Peak, and one for experts on the Mt. Mansfield side.

Cross-country. The resort has 35 km (22 mi) of groomed cross-country trails and 40 km (24 mi) of backcountry trails. There are four interconnecting cross-country ski areas with more than 150 km (90 mi) of groomed trails within the town of Stowe.

Child care. The child-care center takes children from ages 6 weeks to 6 years, with kids' ski-school programs for ages 6 to 12. A center on Spruce Peak is headquarters for programs for children from ages 3 to 12, and there's another program for teenagers 13 to 17.

En Route Northwest of Stowe, an exciting and scenic if indirect route leads to Burlington: **Smugglers' Notch,** the narrow pass between Mt. Mansfield and Madonna Peak that is said to have sheltered 18th-century outlaws in its rugged, bouldered terrain. Weaving around the huge stones that shoulder the road, you'd hardly know you're on state highway Route 108. There are parking spots and picnic tables at the top. The notch road is closed in winter.

Craftsbury Common

③ *27 mi northeast of Stowe.*

The three villages of Craftsbury—Craftsbury Common, Craftsbury, and East Craftsbury—are among Vermont's finest and oldest towns. Handsome white houses and barns, the requisite common, a classic general store, and the Craftsbury Outdoor Center make them well worth the drive. The rolling farmland hints at the way Vermont used to be: The area's sheer distance from civilization and its rugged weather have kept most of the state's development farther south.

Lodging

$$$$ ⊞ **Inn on the Common.** Craftsbury Common is a perfect hamlet amid remote countryside, and the three white Federal-style buildings of this inn aptly represent the town's civility. All rooms contain antique reproductions and contemporary furnishings; deluxe rooms have generous seating areas and fireplaces. Cocktails and hors d'oeuvres are offered in one house's cozy library. Five-course dinners ($$$; open to nonguests by reservation) are served at a communal table in the dining room, which overlooks the inn's gardens. Guests have access to the facilities at the Craftsbury Sports Center and Albany's Wellness Barn, which has a lap pool, aerobic machines, a sauna, and a whirlpool. ⊠ *On the common, 05827,* ☎ *802/586–9619 or 800/521–2233,* 𝔽𝔸𝕏 *802/ 586–2249. 15 rooms, 1 suite. Dining room, lounge, pool, tennis court. MAP. AE, MC, V.*

$$\text{\$\$-\$\$\$}$$ **🏕 Craftsbury Outdoor Center.** Outside of town and surrounded by lakes and hills, this outdoor enthusiasts' haven has standard accommodations and sporting packages. Because of a long season of snowcover—it's white here when the rest of Vermont is green—the cross-country skiing is terrific on the 160 km (99 mi) of trails (96 km/60 mi groomed) on the property and through local farmland. During the rest of the year, sculling and running camps are held; among the other activities are mountain biking and canoeing. Nonguests can ski, mountain bike, and canoe at day-use rates; equipment rental is available. The buffet-style meals include soups, stews, and homemade breads and desserts. ⊠ *Box 31, Lost Nation Rd., 05827,* ☎ *802/586–7767 or 800/729–7751,* ℻ *802/586–7768. 29 rooms, 3 with bath; 3 cottages; 2 efficiencies. Dining room, boating, mountain bikes, cross-country skiing. AP. MC, V.*

Greensboro

㉜ *10 mi southeast of Craftsbury Common.*

Greensboro is an idyllic small town with a long history as a vacation destination. **Willey's Store** (⊠ Main St., ☎ 802/533–2621), with wooden floors and tin ceilings, warrants exploration. You never know what you'll find—foodstuffs, baskets, candy, kitchen paraphernalia—in this packed-to-the-rafters emporium.

Dining and Lodging

$$\text{\$\$\$\$}$$ **✕🏕 Highland Lodge.** Tranquillity defined: an 1860 house that overlooks a pristine lake, with 120 acres of rambling woods and pastures laced with hiking and skiing trails (ski rentals available). Widely known for its great front porch, this quiet family resort is part refined elegance and part casual country of the summer-camp sort. The comfortable guest rooms have Early American furnishings. Most rooms have views of the lake; the one- to three-bedroom cottages are more private (four with gas stoves stay open in winter). The traditional dinner menu, which incorporates Vermont foods, might include entrées such as roasted leg of lamb and grilled Black Angus sirloin. ⊠ *E. Craftsbury Rd., 05841,* ☎ *802/533–2647,* ℻ *802/533–7494. 11 rooms, 11 1- to 3-bedroom cottages. Restaurant, lake, tennis court, hiking, boating, cross-country skiing, recreation room, children's programs. MAP. D, MC, V. Closed mid-Mar.–late May and mid-Oct.–mid-Dec.*

$$\text{\$-\$\$}$$ **🏕 Brick House Guests and Perennial Pleasures Nursery.** Out of a handsome brick home flows an abundance of homespun entrepreneurship. British-born proprietor Judith Kane runs an eclectic B&B with large, antiques-filled bedrooms and a cozy library complete with fireplace, sherry, and books on everything from crystal healing to architectural history. The breakfasts, served on charmingly mismatched china, are sumptuous. Judith's daughter Rachel runs the nursery (closed on Monday and from mid-September to April), which specializes in heirloom plants and herbs. In summer you can sit for a spell in the gardens and enjoy traditional English cream tea (reservations advised). ⊠ *Box 128, 2 Brick House Rd., East Hardwick 05836,* ☎ *802/472–5512. 3 rooms, 1 with bath. Full breakfast. MC, V.*

Jeffersonville

㉝ *18 mi north of Stowe, 28 mi northeast of Burlington.*

Mt. Mansfield and Madonna Peak tower over Jeffersonville, whose activities are closely linked with those of Smugglers' Notch Ski Resort.

Boyden Valley Winery (⊠ Junction of Rtes. 15 and 104, Cambridge, ☎ 802/644–8151) conducts tours of its micro-winery and also showcases an excellent selection of Vermont specialty products and local handicrafts, including fine furniture. The winery is closed Monday.

Lodging

$$$$ 🏨 **Smugglers' Notch Resort.** Most of the condos at this large year-round resort (☞ Skiing and Snow Sports, *below*) have fireplaces and decks. The resort is known for its many family programs. Rates include lift tickets and ski lessons in season. ⊠ *Rte. 108, 05464,* ☎ *802/644–8851 or 800/451–8752,* ℻ *802/644–1230. 375 condos. 3 restaurants, bar, indoor pool, hot tub, sauna, 10 tennis courts (2 indoors), exercise room, ice-skating, recreation room, baby-sitting, children's programs, nursery, playground. AE, DC, MC, V.*

$–$$ 🏨 **Highlander Motel.** The rooms are clean and tidy and just 2½ mi from Smugglers' Village. You can enjoy breakfast (the only meal the restaurant serves) by the fire. Pets are welcome. ⊠ *Rte. 108 S, 05464,* ☎ *802/644–2725 or 800/367–6471,* ℻ *802/644–2725. 12 rooms. Restaurant, pool, recreation room. MC, V.*

Nightlife and the Arts

Most après-ski action in the Smugglers' Notch area revolves around the afternoon bonfires and nightly live entertainment in the **Meeting House** (⊠ The Village, Rte. 108, ☎ 802/644–8851).

Outdoor Activities and Sports

Smugglers' Notch State Park (⊠ Rte. 108, 10 mi north of Mt. Mansfield, ☎ 802/253–4014) is good for picnicking and hiking on wild terrain among large boulders.

Northern Vermont Llamas (⊠ 766 Lapland Rd., Waterville, ☎ 802/644–2257) offers half- and full-day treks from May through October along the cross-country ski trails of Smugglers' Notch. The llamas carry everything, including snacks and lunches.

Vermont Horse Park (⊠ Rte. 108, ☎ 802/644–5347) conducts rides on authentic horse-drawn sleighs. Indoors are tennis courts, a pool, and a hot tub.

Shopping

ANTIQUES

The **Buggy Man** (⊠ Rte. 15, 7 mi east of Jeffersonville, ☎ 802/635–2100) and **Mel Siegel** (⊠ Rte. 15, 7 mi east of Jeffersonville, ☎ 802/635–7838) stock affordable, quality antiques.

CLOTHING

Johnson Woolen Mills (⊠ Main St., Johnson, 9 mi east of Jeffersonville, ☎ 802/635–2271) is an authentic factory store with deals on woolen blankets, yard goods, and the famous Johnson outerwear.

CRAFTS

Vermont Rug Makers (⊠ Rte. 100C, East Johnson, 10 mi east of Jeffersonville, ☎ 802/635–2434) weaves imaginative rugs and tapestries from fabrics, wools, and exotic materials. Its International Gallery displays rugs and tapestries from countries throughout the world. The shop has a branch on Main Street in Stowe.

Skiing and Snow Sports

SMUGGLERS' NOTCH RESORT

This sprawling resort complex consistently wins accolades for its family programs: Its children's ski school is one of the best in the country—and possibly *the* best. But skiers of all levels come here (in 1996, Smugglers' became the first ski area in the East to designate a triple-black-diamond run—the Black Hole). All the essentials are available at the base of the lifts. The Family Snowmaking Learning Center demonstrates the processes of state-of-the-art computer-controlled snowmaking and teaches about weather and snow crystals. A new snowboard park was added in 1998. ✉ *Rte. 108, 05464,* ☎ *802/644–8851 or 800/451–8752.*

Downhill. Smugglers' has three mountains. The highest, Madonna, with a vertical drop of 2,610 ft, is in the center and connects with a trail network to Sterling (1,500-ft vertical). The third mountain, Morse (1,150-ft vertical), is adjacent to Smugglers' "village" of shops, restaurants, and lodgings; it's connected to the other peaks by trails and a shuttle bus. The wild, craggy landscape lends a pristine, wilderness feel to the skiing experience on the two higher mountains. The tops of each of the mountains have expert terrain—a couple of double-black diamonds make Madonna memorable. Intermediate trails fill the lower sections. Morse has many beginner trails. Smugglers' 60 trails are served by five double chairlifts, including the Mogul Mouse Magic Lift, and three surface lifts. There is top-to-bottom snowmaking on all three mountains, allowing for 62% coverage.

Cross-country. The area has 37 km (23 mi) of groomed and tracked cross-country trails.

Other activities. The self-contained village has ice-skating, sleigh rides, and horseback riding.

Child care. The state-of-the-art, professional Child Care Center accepts children from ages 6 weeks to 12 years. Children from ages 3 to 17 can attend ski camps that have instruction, movies, games, and other activities.

Burlington

★ ㉞ *76 mi south of Montréal, 349 mi north of New York City, 223 mi northwest of Boston.*

The largest population center in Vermont, Burlington was named one of the country's "Dream Towns" by *Outside* magazine. The city, founded in 1763, is the center of a rapidly growing suburban area but has held its own against highway malls by cleverly positioning itself in the "festival marketplace" retail style, as well as by trading on its incomparable lakeside location. The city's eclectic population of 40,000 includes many transplants from larger urban areas as well as roughly 20,000 students from the area's five colleges. For years it was the only city in America with a socialist mayor—now the nation's sole socialist congressional representative.

The **Church Street Marketplace**—a pedestrian mall of intriguing boutiques, restaurants, sidewalk cafés, crafts vendors, and street performers—is an animated downtown focal point. Most people in central and northern Vermont come at least occasionally to the town center, if only to run errands or to see a show.

Crouched on the shores of Lake Champlain, which shimmers in the shadows of the Adirondacks to the west, Burlington's revitalized **waterfront** teems with outdoor enthusiasts who stroll along its recreation path and ply the waters in sailboats and motorcraft in summer. A 500-passenger, three-level cruise vessels, *The Spirit of Ethan Allen II,* takes people on narrated cruises on the lake and, in the evening, dinner and sunset sailings that drift by the Adirondacks and the Green Mountains. ✉ *Burlington Boat House, College St. at Battery St.,* ☎ *802/862–8300.* ☞ *$8.* ⊘ *Cruises late May–mid-Oct., daily 10–9.*

Part of the waterfront's revitalization and still a work-in-progress, the ♺ **Lake Champlain Basin Science Center** is in the perfect location to fulfill its mission to educate the public about the ecology, history, and culture of the lake region. From looking at plankton through a "kidscope" to dragging a net off the University of Vermont research boat docked on the property, there are activities for the whole family. The university's Research Lab is scheduled to open at the Science Center in late 1999. ⊠ *One College St.,* ☎ *802/864–1848.* ☞ *$2.* ☉ *Mid-June–Labor Day, daily 11–5; fall and winter, weekends and school vacations 12:30–4:30.*

Crowning the hilltop above Burlington is the campus of the **University of Vermont** (☎ 802/656–3480), known simply as UVM for the abbreviation of its Latin name, Universitas Viridis Montis—the University of the Green Mountains. With more than 10,000 students, UVM is the state's principal institution of higher learning. The most architecturally interesting buildings face the **Green**, which contains some of the grandest surviving specimens of the elm trees that once shaded virtually every street in Burlington, as well as a statue of UVM founder Ira Allen, Ethan's brother. The **Robert Hull Fleming Art Museum** (⊠ Colchester Ave., ☎ 802/656–0750), just behind the Ira Allen Chapel, houses American portraits and landscapes, including works by Sargent, Homer, and Bierstadt; two Corots and a Fragonard; and an Egyptian mummy. Contemporary Vermont works are also exhibited.

Ethan Allen, Vermont's Revolutionary-era guerrilla fighter, remains a captivating figure. Exhibits at the visitor center at the **Ethan Allen Homestead** answer questions about his flamboyant life. The house contains frontier hallmarks like rough saw-cut boards and an open hearth for cooking. A re-created Colonial kitchen garden resembles the one the Allens would have had. After the tour, you can stretch your legs on scenic trails along the Winooski River. ⊠ *North Ave., off Rte. 127, north of Burlington,* ☎ *802/865–4556.* ☞ *$4.* ☉ *Mid-May–mid-June, daily 1–5; mid-June–mid-Oct., Mon.–Sat. 10–5, Sun. 1–5.*

A few miles south of Burlington, the Champlain Valley gives way to fertile farmland, affording stunning views of the rugged Adirondacks across the lake. You can trace much of New England's history simply ★ by wandering the 45 acres and 37 buildings of the **Shelburne Museum.** The outstanding 80,000-object collection of Americana consists of 18th- and 19th-century period homes and furniture, fine and folk art, farm tools, more than 200 carriages and sleighs, Audubon prints, an old-fashioned jail, even a private railroad car from the days of steam. The museum also has an assortment of duck decoys, an old stone cottage, and a display of early toys—as well as the *Ticonderoga,* an old side-wheel steamship, grounded amid lawn and trees. ⊠ *U.S. 7, Shelburne, 5 mi south of Burlington,* ☎ *802/985–3346.* ☞ *$17.50 for 2 consecutive days, $7 in winter for 1 day.* ☉ *Late May–late Oct., daily 10–5; call ahead for limited winter hrs.*

★ ☾ **Shelburne Farms** has a history of improving the farmer's lot by developing new agricultural methods. Founded in the 1880s as a private estate, the 1,400-acre property is an educational and cultural resource center with, among other things, a working dairy farm, a Children's Farmyard, and a spot for watching the farm's famous cheddar cheese being made. Frederick Law Olmsted, co-creator of New York's Central Park, designed the magnificent grounds overlooking Lake Champlain. ⊠ *West of U.S. 7 at the junction of Harbor and Bay Rds., Shelburne, 6 mi south of Burlington,* ☎ *802/985–8686.* ☞ *Day pass $5, tour is an additional $4.* ☉ *Visitor center and shop daily 9–5; tours Memorial Day–mid-Oct., last tour at 3:30.*

☾ On the tour of the **Vermont Teddy Bear Company,** you'll hear more puns than you ever thought possible and learn how a few homemade bears, sold from a cart on Church Street, have turned into a multimillion-dollar business. A children's play tent is set up outdoors in summer, and you can wander the beautiful 57-acre property. ⊠ *2236 Shelburne Rd., Shelburne,* ☎ *802/985–3001.* ⊡ *Tour $1.* ⊙ *Tours Mon.–Sat. 9:30–4, Sun. 10:30–4; store Mon.–Sat. 9–6, Sun. 10–5.*

At the 6-acre **Vermont Wildflower Farm,** the display along the flowering pathways changes constantly: violets in the spring, daisies and black-eyed Susans for summer, and fall colors that rival that of the trees' foliage. You can buy wildflower seeds, crafts, and books here. ⊠ *U.S. 7, Charlotte, 5 mi south of the Shelburne Museum,* ☎ *802/425–3500.* ⊡ *$3.* ⊙ *Early May–late Oct., daily 10–5.*

OFF THE
BEATEN PATH

GREEN MOUNTAIN AUDUBON NATURE CENTER – Bursting with great things to do, see, and learn, this is a wonderful place to orient yourself to Vermont's outdoor wonders. The center's 300 acres of diverse habitats are a sanctuary for all things wild, and the 5 mi of trails provide an opportunity to explore and understand the workings of differing natural communities. Events at the center include dusk walks, wildflower and birding rambles, nature workshops, and educational activities for both kids and adults. The center is 18 mi southeast of Burlington. ⊠ *Huntington-Richmond Rd., Richmond,* ☎ *802/434–3068.* ⊡ *Donations accepted.* ⊙ *Grounds dawn–dusk, center weekdays 9–4:30.*

LAKE CHAMPLAIN ISLANDS – When Vermonters talk about "the islands," chances are they're not referring to the Caribbean but to a place a lot closer to home—the Lake Champlain Islands, an elongated archipelago stretching southward from the Canadian border. The islands are a center of water recreation in summer and ice fishing in winter. One of the islands' more unusual claims to fame is the summer residence of the **Royal Lippizaner Stallions,** heirs to the celebrated Austrian dressage tradition; in July and August they perform in an outdoor arena just off U.S. 7 in North Hero (☎ *802/372–5683*). A preferred islands' lodging place is **Shore Acres Inn and Restaurant** (⊠ U.S. 2, North Hero, ☎ *802/372–8722*), with a lakeside location looking west toward the Green Mountains. North of Burlington, a scenic drive through the islands on U.S. 2 begins at I–89 and travels north through South Hero, Grand Isle, and Isle La Motte to Alburg Center, 5 mi from the Canadian border. Here Route 78 will take you east to the mainland.

MISSISQUOI NATIONAL WILDLIFE REFUGE – The 6,300 acres of federally protected wetlands, meadows, and woods provide a beautiful setting for bird-watching, canoeing, or walking nature trails. ⊠ *Swanton, 36 mi north of Burlington,* ☎ *802/868–4781.*

Dining and Lodging

$$–$$$ ✕ **Isabel's.** An old lumber mill on Lake Champlain houses this restaurant, which has high ceilings, exposed-brick walls, and knockout views. The menu is seasonal; past dishes, all presented with an artistic flair, have included Thai seafood pasta and vegetable Wellington. Lunch and weekend brunch are popular, and you can dine on the outdoor patio on warm days. ⊠ *112 Lake St.,* ☎ *802/865–2522. AE, D, DC, MC, V. No dinner Sun.– Mon. Nov.–Apr.*

$$–$$$ ✕ **Trattoria Delia.** Didn't manage to rent that villa in Umbria this year?
★   The next best thing, if your travels bring you to Burlington, is this superb Italian country eatery just around the corner from City Hall Park. Local game and produce are the stars, as in roast rabbit marinated in herbs, wine, and olive oil. The chef's passion for the truly homemade extends to wild boar sausage, salami, and fresh mozzarella. Wood-grilled

items are a specialty. ⊠ *152 St. Paul St.,* ☎ *802/864–5253. AE, D, DC, MC, V.*

$$ ✕ **NECI Commons.** The initials stand for New England Culinary Institute, the respected Montpelier academy whose students and teachers run this all-under-one-roof café, bakery, market, restaurant, and bar. The deli counter can get a little pricey—are you ready for garlic mashed potatoes at $4.99 a pound?—but everything is fresh and tasty. It's open daily for breakfast, lunch, and dinner. ⊠ *25 Church St.,* ☎ *802/862–6324. AE, D, MC,V.*

$$ ✕ **Sweet Tomatoes.** The dishes cooked in the wood-fired oven of this bright and boisterous trattoria send off a mouthwatering aroma. The menu includes pizzas and *caponata* (roasted eggplant with onions, capers, olives, parsley, celery, and tomatoes), and farfalle with sweet sausage, roasted red peppers, onions, tomatoes, black olives, and rosemary in a tomato basil sauce. In warm weather you can dine at outdoor tables abutting the bustling Church Street Marketplace. ⊠ *83 Church St.,* ☎ *802/660–9533. AE, MC, V.*

$–$$ ✕ **Libby's Blue Line Diner.** The menu here is diverse—a mix of classic diner cuisine and more upscale offerings such as eggplant burgers and brook trout. Portions are generous, and the prices are right. The only problem is this place's popularity: Reservations are not accepted and the lines can be long (Sunday breakfast is particularly popular). Try to go at an off time, between standard mealtimes. ⊠ *1 Roosevelt Hwy./U.S. 7, Colchester,* ☎ *802/655–0343. Reservations not accepted. AE, MC, V. No dinner Sun. in winter.*

$$$–$$$$ ✕⌸ **Basin Harbor Club.** Owned by the Beach family since 1886, this
★ outstanding resort sprawls over 700 acres of prime real estate overlooking Lake Champlain. Luxurious accommodations, a full roster of activities including an 18-hole Geoffrey Cornish golf course, boating (including a 40-ft tour boat), and a day-long children's program make Basin Harbor a popular spot for families. Some rooms have fireplaces, decks, or porches. The restaurant menu is classic American, and the wine list excellent. Coats and ties are required in common areas after 6 PM. ⊠ *Basin Harbor Rd., Vergennes 05491,* ☎ *802/475–2311 or 800/622–4000,* 𝖥𝖠𝖷 *802/475–6545. 38 rooms in 3 guest houses, 77 cottages. 2 restaurants, pool, 18-hole golf course, 5 tennis courts, health club, bicycles, boating, children's programs (in summer and on fall weekends). MAP and AP available. MC, V. Closed mid-Oct.–mid-May.*

$$$–$$$$ ✕⌸ **Inn at Essex.** About 10 mi from downtown Burlington, near Essex Outlet Fair, is a state-of-the-art inn and conference center dressed in country clothing. Rooms with flowered wallpaper and reproduction period desks lend the place some character, and many of the rooms have fireplaces. The two restaurants—the refined Butler's and the more casual Tavern—are run by the New England Culinary Institute. The sophisticated American cuisine at Butler's includes dishes such as sweet dumpling squash with ginger-garlic basmati rice, and lobster in yellow-corn sauce with spinach pasta. Five-onion soup, burgers, and daily flat-bread pizza specials are among the highlights at the Tavern. ⊠ *70 Essex Way, off Rte. 15, Essex Junction 05452,* ☎ *802/878–1100 or 800/288–7613,* 𝖥𝖠𝖷 *802/878–0063. 97 rooms. 2 restaurants, bar, pool, billiards, library. Continental breakfast. AE, D, DC, MC, V.*

$$–$$$$ ✕⌸ **Inn at Shelburne Farms.** This is storybook land: Built at the turn
★ of the century as the home of William Seward and Lila Vanderbilt Webb, the Tudor-style inn perches on Saxton's Point overlooking Lake Champlain, the distant Adirondacks, and the sea of pastures that make up this 1,400-acre working farm. Each room is different, from the wallpaper to the period antiques. The two dining rooms ($$$–$$$$) define elegance, and the seasonal contemporary menu makes clever use of local ingredients. Sunday brunch (not served in May) is one of the

area's best. The inn's profits help support the farm's environmental education programs for local schools. ⊠ *Harbor Rd., Shelburne 05482,* ☎ *802/985–8498,* FAX *802/985–8123. 24 rooms, 17 with bath. Restaurant, lake, tennis court, hiking, boating, fishing, billiards, recreation room. AE, D, DC, MC, V. Closed mid-Oct.–mid-May.*

$$$ ✕🗊 **Radisson Hotel–Burlington.** This sleek corporate giant, which faces the lakefront, is the hotel closest to downtown shopping. Some rooms have incredible views of the Adirondack Mountains. The hotel's restaurant serves traditional but inspired Continental fare. ⊠ *60 Battery St., 05401,* ☎ *802/658–6500 or 800/333–3333,* FAX *802/658–4659. 255 rooms. 2 restaurants, bar, indoor pool, exercise room, airport shuttle. AE, D, DC, MC, V.*

$$–$$$$ 🗊 **Willard Street Inn.** High in the historic hill section of Burlington, this grand house with an exterior marble staircase and English gardens incorporates elements of Queen Anne and Colonial–Georgian Revival styles. The stately foyer, paneled in cherry, leads to a more formal sitting room with velvet drapes. The solarium is bright and sunny with marble floors, many plants, and big velvet couches to relax in while you contemplate views of Lake Champlain. All the rooms have down comforters and phones; some have lake views and canopied beds. Orange French toast is among the breakfast favorites. ⊠ *349 S. Willard St., 05401,* ☎ *802/651–8710 or 800/577–8712,* FAX *802/651–8714. 15 rooms, 12 with bath. Full breakfast. AE, D, DC, MC, V.*

Nightlife and the Arts

NIGHTLIFE

Name and local musicians come to **Higher Ground** (⊠ 1 Main St., Winooski, ☎ 802/654–8888). The music at the **Metronome** (⊠ 188 Main St., ☎ 802/865–4563) ranges from cutting-edge sounds to funk, blues, and reggae. The band Phish got its start at **Nectar's** (⊠ 188 Main St., ☎ 802/658–4771). This place is always jumping to the sounds of local bands and never charges a cover. **Vermont Pub and Brewery** (⊠ 144 College St., ☎ 802/865–0500) makes its own beer and fruit seltzers and is arguably the most popular spot in town. Folk musicians play here regularly.

THE ARTS

Burlington City Arts (☎ 802/865–7166; 802/865–9163 for 24-hr Artsline) has up-to-date arts-related information. **Flynn Theatre for the Performing Arts** (⊠ 153 Main St., ☎ 802/652–4500 for information; 802/863–5966 for tickets), a grandiose old structure, is the cultural heart of Burlington; it schedules the Vermont Symphony Orchestra, theater, dance, big-name musicians, and lectures. The **Lyric Theater** (☎ 802/658–1484) puts on musical productions in the fall and spring at the Flynn Theatre (☞ *above*). **St. Michael's Playhouse** (⊠ St. Michael's College, Rte. 15, Colchester, ☎ 802/654–2281 box office; 802/654–2617 administrative office) performs in the McCarthy Arts Center Theater. The **UVM Lane Series** (☎ 802/656–4455 for programs and times; 802/656–3085 for box office) sponsors classical as well as folk music concerts in the Flynn Theatre, Ira Allen Chapel, and the UVM Recital Hall.

Outdoor Activities and Sports

BEACHES

Some of the most scenic Lake Champlain beaches are on the Champlain Islands. **Knight Point State Park** (⊠ U.S. 2, North Hero, ☎ 802/372–8389) occupies a lovely spot in the Lake Champlain Islands, midway between mainland Vermont and New York State. **North Hero State Park** (⊠ Lakeview Dr. off U.S. 2, North Hero ☎ 802/372–8727) has a children's play area nearby. **Sand Bar State Park** (⊠ U.S. 2, Milton, ☎ 802/893–2825) has a great beach for small kids, with an extremely gentle drop-off. Arrive early to beat the summer crowds. Admission is $1; the park is open from mid-May to October.

The **North Beaches** are on the northern edge of Burlington: North Beach Park (⊠ Off North Ave., ☎ 802/864–0123), Bayside Beach (⊠ Rte. 127 near Malletts Bay), and Leddy Beach (⊠ Leddy Park Rd., off North Ave.), which is popular for sailboarding.

BIKING

A recreational path runs 9 mi along Burlington's waterfront. South of Burlington, a moderately easy 18½-mi trail begins at the blinker on U.S. 7 in Shelburne and follows Mt. Philo Road, Hinesburg Road, Route 116, and Irish Hill Road. **North Star Cyclery** (⊠ 100 Main St., ☎ 802/ 863–3832) and **Ski Rack** (⊠ 81 Main St., ☎ 802/658–3313) rent equipment and provide maps.

STATE PARKS

Grand Isle State Park (⊠ U.S. 2, 1 mi south of Grand Isle, ☎ 802/ 372–4300) has a fitness trail, hiking, and boat rentals. **Kill Kare State Park** (⊠ Rte. 36, on the mainland 4½ mi west of St. Albans Bay, then south on town road 3½ mi, ☎ 802/524–6021) is popular for camping, sailboarding, and hiking and also has boat rentals. There is ferry service from Kill Kare State Park to **Burton Island** (☎ 802/524–6353), a state park (with campsites) accessible only by water.

WATER SPORTS

Marina services are available north and south of Burlington. **Malletts Bay Marina** (⊠ 228 Lakeshore Dr., Colchester, ☎ 802/862–4072) and **Point Bay Marina** (⊠ 1401 Thompson's Point Rd., Charlotte, ☎ 802/425–2431) provide full service and repairs.

Burlington Community Boathouse (⊠ Foot of College St., Burlington Harbor, ☎ 802/865–3377) rents Jet Skis, sailboards, sailboats from 13 ft to 40 ft, and motorboats (some captained); the boathouse also gives lessons. **Marble Island Resort** (⊠ Colchester, ☎ 802/864–6800) has a marina and a nine-hole golf course.

Shopping

ANTIQUES

Architectural Salvage Warehouse (⊠ 212 Battery St., ☎ 802/658–5011) has claw-foot tubs, stained-glass windows, mantels, andirons, and the like. The large rhinoceros head bursting out of the **Conant Custom Brass** (⊠ 270 Pine St., ☎ 802/658–4482) storefront may tempt you in to see the custom work; the store specializes in decorative lighting and bathroom fixtures.

COUNTRY STORE

Shelburne Country Store (⊠ Village Green, off U.S. 7, Shelburne, ☎ 802/985–3657) offers a step back in time as you walk past the potbellied stove and take in the aroma emanating from the fudge neatly piled behind huge antique glass cases. Candles, weather vanes, glassware, and Vermont food products are its specialties.

CRAFTS

In addition to its popular pottery, **Bennington Potters North** (⊠ 127 College St., ☎ 802/863–2221) stocks interesting gifts, glassware, furniture, and other housewares. **Vermont State Craft Center** (⊠ 85 Church St., ☎ 802/863–6458) displays contemporary and traditional crafts by more than 200 Vermont artisans. **Yankee Pride** (⊠ Champlain Mill, E. Canal St., Winooski, ☎ 802/655–0500) has a large inventory of quilting fabrics and supplies as well as Vermont-made quilts.

MALLS AND MARKETPLACES

Burlington Square Mall (⊠ Church St., ☎ 802/658–2545) contains Porteous (the city's major department store, although at press time a new Filene's was set to open in fall 1999) and a few dozen shops. The **Champlain Mill** (⊠ U.S. 2/7, northeast of Burlington, ☎ 802/655–9477), a former woolen mill on the banks of the Winooski River, holds three floors of stores. **Church Street Marketplace** (⊠ Main St.–Pearl St., ☎ 802/863–1648), a pedestrian thoroughfare, is lined with boutiques, cafés, and street vendors. Built to resemble a ship, the **Wing Building** (⊠ Foot of King St., next to the ferry dock) houses boutiques, a café, and an art gallery.

En Route   The top of the mountain pass on Route 242 in Montgomery Center and the Jay Peak area affords vast views of Canada to the north and of Vermont's rugged Northeast Kingdom to the east.

Montgomery/Jay

③⑤   *51 mi northeast of Burlington.*

Montgomery is a small village near the Canadian border and Jay Peak ski resort. Amid the surrounding countryside are seven historic covered bridges. **Kilgore's Store** (⊠ Main St., Montgomery Center, ☎ 802/326–3058), an old-time country store with an antique soda fountain, is a great place to stock up on picnic supplies or enjoy a hearty bowl of soup and an overstuffed sandwich.

Dining and Lodging

$$ ✕📷 **Inn on Trout River.** The large stove is often the center of attention in the two-tier living and dining area of this 100-year-old inn, though the piano, the library, and the pub with a U-shape bar are also eye-catching. Guest rooms are decorated in either English country cottage style or country Victorian, and all have down quilts and flannel sheets in winter. The largest room has a Franklin potbellied stove, a dressing area, and a claw-foot tub. The back lawn rambles down to the river, and llama treks are available for groups. The restaurant ($$–$$$) specializes in American and Continental fare with a heart-healthy emphasis. ⊠ *Main St., Montgomery Center 05471,* ☎ *802/326–4391 or 800/338–7049,* FAX *802/326–3194. 10 rooms. Restaurant, pub, recreation room, library. Full breakfast; MAP available. AE, D, MC, V.*

$–$$ ✕📷 **Black Lantern.** Built in 1803 as a hotel for mill workers, the inn has been providing bed and board ever since. Though the feeling is country, touches of sophistication abound: Provençal-print wallpaper in the dining room, a subtle rag-roll finish in the rooms in the renovated building next door. All the suites have whirlpools, and most have fireplaces. An outdoor hot tub, sheltered by a gazebo, overlooks the mountains. The restaurant menu ($$–$$$) includes pan-seared salmon with a red pepper sauce and grilled lamb Margarite. ⊠ *Rte. 118, Montgomery Village 05470,* ☎ *802/326–4507 or 800/255–8661,* FAX *802/326–4077. 10 rooms, 6 suites. Restaurant. Full breakfast. AE, D, MC, V.*

$$$ 📷 **Hotel Jay & Jay Peak Condominiums.** Ski-lodge simplicity was the decorating goal at the hotel, with wood paneling in the rooms, built-in headboards, and vinyl wallpaper in the bathroom. Right at the lifts, the ski-in, ski-out hotel is convenient for skiers. Rooms on the southwest side have a view of Jay Peak, and those on the north overlook the valley; upper floors have balconies. The 120 condominiums (most slopeside) have fireplaces, one to three bedrooms, modern kitchens, and washers and dryers. In winter, a minimum two-night stay is required, and lift tickets and some meals are included in the rates. The summer rates are low. ⊠ *Rte. 242, 05859,* ☎ *802/988–2611 or 800/451–4449,* FAX *802/988–4049. 48 rooms, 120 condos. Restaurant, bar,*

pool, hot tub, sauna, 2 tennis courts, recreation room. MAP in winter, Continental breakfast in summer. AE, D, DC, MC, V.

Skiing and Snow Sports

JAY PEAK

Sticking up out of the flat farmland, Jay averages 332 in of snowfall a year—more than any other Vermont ski area. Its proximity to Québec attracts Montréalers and discourages eastern seaboarders; hence, the prices are moderate and the lift lines generally shorter than at other resorts. The area offers tram rides to the summit from mid-June through mid-September ($8) and, in season, rents mountain bikes. ⊠ *Rte. 242, Jay 05859,* ☎ *802/988–2611; 800/451–4449 outside VT.*

Downhill. Jay Peak is in fact two mountains with 64 trails, the highest reaching nearly 4,000 ft with a vertical drop of 2,153 ft, served by a 60-passenger tram (the only one in Vermont). The area also has a quad, a triple, two double chairlifts, and two T-bars. An expansion scheduled to be completed for the 1999–2000 season will include the addition of a 7,700-ft-long, high-speed quad chairlift—the longest in eastern North America; it will also add snowmaking capability to three trails. The smaller mountain has more straight-fall-line, expert terrain, and the tram-side peak has many curving and meandering trails perfectly suited for intermediate and beginning skiers. Jay, highly rated for gladed skiing by major skiing publications, has 19 gladed trails. Every morning at 9 AM the ski school offers a free tour, from the tram down one trail. The area has 80% snowmaking coverage.

Cross-country. A touring center at the base of the mountain has 32 km (20 mi) of groomed cross-country trails. A network of 200 km (124 mi) of trails is in the vicinity.

Child care. The child care center for youngsters ages 2 and older is open from 9 to 9. Guests of the Hotel Jay or the Jay Peak Condominiums receive this nursery care free, as well as free skiing for children ages 6 and under, evening care, and supervised dining at the hotel. Children from ages 5 to 12 can participate in an all-day SKIwee program, which includes lunch.

CROSS-COUNTRY SKIING

Hazen's Notch Cross Country Ski Center and B & B (Rte. 58, ☎ 802/ 326–4708), delightfully remote at any time of the year, has 50 km (31 mi) of marked and groomed trails and rents equipment and snow shoes.

En Route The descent from Jay Peak on Route 101 leads to Route 100, which can be the beginning of a scenic loop tour of Routes 14, 5, 58, and back to 100, or it can take you east to the city of **Newport** on Lake Memphremagog. Newport long neglected its waterfront but has recently constructed a handsome new marina and lakeside pavilion. Downtown, too, is on the rebound, with several new shops and factory outlets, including **Bogner Factory Outlet** (⊠ 48 Main St., ☎ 802/334–0135), which sells men's and ladies' ski-, golf-, and sportswear.

You will encounter some of the most unspoiled areas in all Vermont on the drive south from Newport on either U.S. 5 or I–91 (I–91 is faster, but U.S. 5 is prettier). This region, the Northeast Kingdom, is named for the remoteness and stalwart independence that have helped preserve its rural nature.

Lake Willoughby

㊱ *30 mi east of Montgomery (summer route; 50 mi by winter route), 28 mi north of St. Johnsbury.*

Flanking the eastern and western shores of Lake Willoughby, the cliffs of surrounding Mts. Pisgah and Hor drop to water's edge, giving this glacially carved, 500-ft-deep lake a striking resemblance to a Norwegian fjord. Some also compare the landscape to Lucerne's or Scotland's. In any case, Lake Willoughby is stunning. The lake is popular for summer and winter recreation, and the trails to the top of Mt. Pisgah reward hikers with glorious views.

The **Bread and Puppet Museum** is a ramshackle barn that houses a surrealistic collection of props used in past performances by the world-renowned Bread and Puppet Theater. The troupe, whose members live communally on the surrounding farm, have been performing social and political commentary with the towering (they're supported by people on stilts), eerily expressive puppets for about 30 years. ⊠ *Rte. 122, Glover, 1 mi east of Rte. 16,* ☎ *802/525–3031.* ▭ *Donations accepted.* ☉ *June–Oct., daily 9–5; other times by appointment.*

Lodging

$$–$$$$ ▥ **WilloughVale Inn & Restaurant.** Few Vermont inns can claim a more spectacular location than this waterfront property at the northern end of Lake Willoughby. The main building, with its cozy dining room and wraparound veranda, has rooms with a water view and one spacious but unfortunately situated suite facing the rear of the building. An even better bet are the cottages on Willoughby's shore. They come with fully equipped kitchens, fireplaces, screened porches, and private docks. ⊠ *Rte. 5A, Westmore 05860,* ☎ *802/525–4123 or 800/594–9102,* ℻ *802/ 525–4514. 7 rooms, 1 suite, 4 cottages. Boating. AE, MC, V.*

En Route If it's a moose sighting you're after, head north on Route 114 toward **Island Pond.** A word of warning: Although the great beasts are fun to watch, they can be a deadly road hazard. When you see a "Moose" sign, cut your speed and watch the roadsides.

East Burke and West Burke

㊲ *17 mi south of Lake Willoughby.*

A jam-packed general store, a post office, and a couple of great places to eat are about all you'll find in the twin towns of East Burke and West Burke.

Dining and Lodging

$$–$$$ ✕ **River Garden Café.** You can eat outdoors on the enclosed porch or the patio and view the perennial gardens that rim the grounds; the café is bright and cheerful on the inside as well. The healthful fare includes roasted rack of lamb, warm artichoke dip, bruschetta, pastas, and fresh fish. ⊠ *Rte. 114, East Burke,* ☎ *802/626–3514. AE, D, MC, V. Closed Mon., Apr., and Nov.*

$$$ ✕▥ **Wildflower Inn.** The hilltop views are great at this rambling com-
★ plex of old farm buildings on 500 acres. The rooms in the restored Federal-style main house and four other buildings are decorated simply with reproductions and contemporary furnishings. Rooms in the carriage house are somewhat dark and cramped; they have kitchenettes and bunk beds. In warm weather, the inn is family-oriented: There's a petting barn, planned children's activities, and a kid's swimming pool. At the restaurant ($–$$), homemade breads and vegetables grown in the garden accompany the country-style entrées. ⊠ *Darling Hill Rd., west of East Burke, Lyndonville 05851,* ☎ *802/626–8310 or 800/627– 8310,* ℻ *802/626–3039. 12 rooms, 8 suites. Restaurant, pool, hot tub, sauna, tennis court, soccer, fishing, ice-skating, cross-country skiing, sleigh rides, sledding, recreation room. Full breakfast. MC, V. Closed Apr. and Nov.*

$ ✕🍴 **Old Cutter Inn.** A small converted farmhouse only ½ mi from the Burke Mountain base lodge offers quaint inn rooms in the main building, as well as comfortable if less charming accommodations in an annex. The restaurant ($$–$$$) serves fare that reflects the Swiss chef-owner's heritage, as well as superb Continental cuisine including osso buco and veal piccata. ⊠ *R.R. 1, Box 62, Old Pinkham Rd., East Burke 05832,* ☎ *802/626–5152 or 800/295–1943. 9 rooms, 5 with bath; 1 suite. Restaurant, bar, pool, hiking, biking, cross-country skiing. MAP available. D, MC, V. Closed Wed., Apr., and Nov.*

$$–$$$ 🍴 **Burke Mountain Resort.** The modern accommodations at this resort range from economical digs to luxurious slopeside town houses and condominiums with kitchens and TVs. Some rooms have fireplaces, and others have wood-burning stoves. A two-night minimum stay is required during winter months, and ski and lodging packages are available. ⊠ *Box 247, Burke Mountain Rd., East Burke 05832,* ☎ *802/626–3305 or 800/541–5480,* FAX *802/626–3364. 150 condos. Restaurant. MC, V.*

Outdoor Activities and Sports

Village Sport Shop (⊠ 4 Broad St., Lyndonville, ☎ 802/626–8448) rents canoes, kayaks, bikes, rollerblades, paddleboats, snowshoes, and cross-country and downhill skis.

The **Wildflower Inn** (☞ Dining and Lodging, *above*) has 15-passenger sleighs drawn by Belgian draft horses.

Shopping

Bailey's Country Store (⊠ Rte. 114, East Burke, ☎ 802/626–3666), an institution, sells baked goods, wine, clothing, and sundries.

Skiing and Snow Sports

BURKE MOUNTAIN

This low-key, moderately priced resort draws many families from Massachusetts and Connecticut. There's plenty of terrain for beginners, but intermediate skiers, experts, racers, telemarkers, and snowboarders will find time-honored narrow New England trails. Many packages at Burke are significantly less expensive than those at other Vermont areas. Burke Mountain Academy has contributed a number of notable racers to the U.S. Ski Team. ⊠ *Mountain Rd., East Burke 05832,* ☎ *802/626–3305; 800/541–5480 for lodging; 800/922–2875 for snow conditions and special events.*

Downhill. With a 2,000-ft vertical drop, Burke is something of a sleeper among the larger Eastern ski areas. It has greatly increased its snowmaking capability (60%), which is enhanced by the mountain's northern location and exposure, assuring plenty of natural snow. In a recent expansion, a trail was developed on the east side of the mountain, and a snowboard park (with snowmaking capabilities) for all levels was created. Burke has one quad, one double chairlift, and two surface lifts. Lift lines, even on weekends and holidays, are light to nonexistent.

Cross-country. Burke Ski Touring Center has more than 95 km (57 mi) of trails (65 km/39 mi groomed); some lead to high points with scenic views. There's a snack bar at the center.

Child care. In the Children's Center, the nursery takes children from ages 6 months to 6 years. SKIwee and MINIriders lessons through the ski school are available to children from ages 4 to 16.

St. Johnsbury

38 *16 mi south of East Burke, 39 mi east of Montpelier.*

St. Johnsbury is the southern gateway to the Northeast Kingdom.

Though the town was chartered in 1786, its identity was not firmly established until 1830, when Thaddeus Fairbanks invented the platform scale, a device that revolutionized weighing methods that had been in use since the beginning of recorded history. Because of the Fairbanks family's philanthropic bent, this city with a distinctly 19th-century industrial feel has a strong cultural and architectural imprint.

Opened in 1891, the **Fairbanks Museum and Planetarium** attests to the Fairbanks family's inquisitiveness about all things scientific. The redbrick building in the squat Romanesque Revival architectural style of H. H. Richardson houses Vermont plants and animals, as well as ethnographic and natural history collections from around the globe. There's also an intimate 50-seat planetarium and a hands-on exhibit room for kids. On the third Saturday in September, the museum sponsors the annual Festival of Traditional Crafts, with demonstrations of early American household and farm skills such as candle and soap making. ⊠ *Main and Prospect Sts.,* ☎ *802/748–2372.* ☞ *$5.* ☉ *July–Aug., Mon.–Sat. 10–6, Sun. 1–5; Sept.–June, Mon.–Sat. 10–4, Sun. 1–5. Planetarium shows July–Aug., daily at 11 and 1:30; Sept.–June, weekends at 1:30.*

The **St. Johnsbury Athenaeum,** with its dark rich paneling, polished Victorian woodwork, and ornate circular staircases that rise to the gallery around the perimeter, is one of the oldest art galleries in the country. The gallery at the back of the building specializes in Hudson River School paintings and has the overwhelming *Domes of Yosemite* by Albert Bierstadt. ⊠ *30 Main St.,* ☎ *802/748–8291.* ☞ *Free.* ☉ *Mon. and Wed. 10–8; Tues. and Thurs.–Fri. 10–5:30; Sat. 9:30–4.*

OFF THE BEATEN PATH	**CABOT CREAMERY –** The biggest cheese producer in the state, a dairy cooperative, has a visitor center with an audiovisual presentation about the state's dairy and cheese industry. You can taste samples, purchase cheese, and tour the plant. The center is midway between Barre and St. Johnsbury. ⊠ *2870 Main St./Rte. 215, 3 mi north of U.S 2, Cabot,* ☎ *802/563–2231; 800/639–4031 for orders only.* ☞ *$1.* ☉ *June–Oct., daily 9–5; Nov.–Dec. and mid-Feb.–May, Mon.–Sat. 9–4.*

Dining and Lodging

$$$$ ✕🏨 **Rabbit Hill Inn.** The rooms at Rabbit Hill are all different: The Loft, with an 8-ft Palladian window, a king canopy bed, a double whirlpool bath, and a corner fireplace, is one of the most requested. Rooms toward the front of the inn have views of the Connecticut River and New Hampshire's White Mountains. The low wooden beams of the Irish pub are a casual contrast to the rest of the inn. The low-ceiling dining room ($$$) serves regional cuisine, perhaps grilled sausage of Vermont pheasant with pistachios or smoked chicken and red lentil dumplings nestled in red-pepper linguine. Meat and fish are smoked on the premises, and the herbs and vegetables often come from gardens out back. A two-night minimum stay is required on weekends. ⊠ *Rte. 18, Lower Waterford, 11 mi south of St. Johnsbury, 05848,* ☎ *802/748–5168 or 800/762–8669,* 🖷 *802/748–8342. 16 rooms, 5 suites. Restaurant, pub, hiking, cross-country skiing. MAP. AE, MC, V. Closed 1st 3 wks of Apr., 1st 2 wks of Nov.*

Nightlife and the Arts

Catamount Arts (⊠ 60 Eastern Ave., ☎ 802/748–2600) brings avant-garde theater and dance performances to the Northeast Kingdom as well as films and classical music.

Peacham

㊴ *10 mi southwest of St. Johnsbury.*

Tiny Peacham's stunning scenery and 18th-century charm have made it a favorite with urban refugees, artists seeking solitude and inspiration, and movie directors looking for the quintessential New England village. *Ethan Frome,* starring Liam Neeson, was filmed here.

Gourmet soups and hearty lamb and barley stew are among the seasonally changing take-out specialties at the **Peacham Store** (✉ Main St., ☎ 802/592–3310). You can browse through the locally made crafts while waiting for your order. The store was a location for the filming of the 1996 movie *The Spitfire Grill.*

Barre

㊵ *7 mi east of Montpelier, 35 mi south of St. Johnsbury.*

Barre has been famous as the source of Vermont granite ever since two men began working the quarries in the early 1800s; the large number of immigrant laborers attracted to the industry made the city prominent in the early years of the American labor movement. Downtown, at the corner of Maple and North Main, look for the statue of a representative Italian stonecutter of a century ago. On Route 14, just north of Barre, stop at **Hope Cemetery** to see spectacular examples of carving.

You might recognize the sheer walls of the **Rock of Ages granite quarry** from *Batman and Robin,* the film starring George Clooney and Arnold Schwarzenegger. The attractions of the site range from the awe-inspiring (the quarry resembles the Grand Canyon in miniature) to the mildly ghoulish (you can consult a directory of tombstone dealers throughout the country). At the craft center, you can watch skilled artisans sculpt monuments; at the quarries themselves, 25-ton blocks of stone are cut from sheer 475-ft walls by workers who clearly earn their pay. ✉ *Exit 6 off I–89, follow Rte. 63,* ☎ *802/476–3119.* ▨ *Tour of active quarry $4, craftsman center and self-guided tour free.* ☉ *Visitor center daily May–Oct., except July 4; narrated tours every 45 mins 9:15–3 weekdays only June–mid-Oct.*

Dining

$–$$ ✕ **A Single Pebble.** Devotees of Chinese food have been making a pilgrimage to this restaurant since it opened in 1997. Chef and co-owner Steve Bogart has been cooking Asian dishes for more than 30 years, and he emphasizes authenticity as well as creativity. He prepares traditional clay pot dishes as well as wok specialties such as sesame catfish, Ants Climbing a Tree (a Szechuan dish of pork and cellophane noodles), and kung po chicken. The dry fried green beans (sautéed with flecks of pork, black beans, preserved vegetables, and garlic), mock eel (thinly sliced shiitake mushrooms), and Spicy Three River Soup are house specialties. All dishes can be made without meat. ✉ *135 Barre-Montpelier Rd.,* ☎ *802/476–9700. D, MC, V. Closed Sun.–Mon. and Aug. No lunch.*

Nightlife and the Arts

Barre Opera House (✉ City Hall, Main St., ☎ 802/476–8188) hosts music, opera, theater, and dance performances.

Northern Vermont A to Z

Arriving and Departing
See Vermont A to Z, *below.*

Getting Around

BY BUS

Vermont Transit (☎ 802/864–6811; 800/451–3292; 800/642–3133 in VT) links Burlington, Waterbury, Montpelier, St. Johnsbury, and Newport.

BY CAR

In north-central Vermont, I–89 heads west from Montpelier to Burlington and continues north to Canada. Interstate 91 is the principal north–south route in the east, and Route 100 runs north–south through the center of the state. North of I–89, Routes 104 and 15 provide a major east–west transverse. From Barton, U.S. 5 and Route 122 south are beautiful drives. Strip-mall drudge bogs down the section of U.S. 5 around Lyndonville.

BY FERRY

Lake Champlain Ferries (☎ 802/864–9804), in operation since 1826, operates three ferry crossings during the summer months and one—between Grand Isle and Plattsburgh, New York—in winter through thick lake ice. Ferries leave from the King Street Dock in Burlington, Charlotte, and Grand Isle. This is a convenient means of getting to and from New York, as well as a pleasant way to spend an afternoon.

BY TRAIN

The *Champlain Valley Weekender* runs between Middlebury and Burlington, with stops in Vergennes and Shelburne. The views from the coach cars, which date from the 1930s, are of Lake Champlain, the valley farmlands, and surrounding mountains. ☎ *802/463–3069 or 800/707–3530.* ✆ *$12 round-trip.* ☉ *July–early Sept., weekends, 2 trips per day.*

Contacts and Resources

EMERGENCIES

Fletcher Allen Health Care (✉ 111 Colchester Ave., Burlington, ☎ 802/656–2345). For 24-hour medical health care information, call ☎ 802/656–2439.

GUIDED TOURS

P.O.M.G. Bike Tours of Vermont (✉ Richmond, ☎ 802/434–2270) leads weekend and five-day adult camping–bike tours.

True North Kayak Tours (✉ 53 Nash Pl., Burlington, ☎ 802/860–1910) operates a guided tour of Lake Champlain, a natural-history tour, and will arrange a custom multiday trip. The company also coordinates special trips for kids.

HIKING

The **Green Mountain Club** (✉ Rte. 100, Waterbury, ☎ 802/244–7037) maintains the Long Trail—the north–south border-to-border footpath that runs the length of the spine of the Green Mountains—as well as other trails nearby. The club headquarters sells maps and guides, and experts dispense advice.

LODGING REFERRAL SERVICE

The **Stowe Area Association** (☎ 800/247–8693) has a lodging referral service.

VISITOR INFORMATION

Lake Champlain Regional Chamber of Commerce (✉ 60 Main St., Suite 100, Burlington 05401, ☎ 802/863–3489). **Northeast Kingdom Chamber of Commerce** (✉ 30 Western Ave., St. Johnsbury 05819, ☎ 802/748–3678 or 800/639–6379). **Smugglers' Notch Area Chamber of Commerce** (✉ Box 364, Jeffersonville 05464, ☎ 802/644–2239).

The **Stowe Area Association** (✉ Main St., Box 1320, Stowe 05672, ☎ 802/253–7321 or 800/247–8693). **Vermont North Country Chamber of Commerce** (✉ The Causeway, Newport 05855, ☎ 802/334–7782 or 800/635–4643).

VERMONT A TO Z

Arriving and Departing

By Bus
Bonanza (☎ 800/556–3815) connects New York City and Providence with Bennington. **Vermont Transit** (☎ 802/864–6811 or 800/552–8737) connects Bennington, Brattleboro, Burlington, Rutland, and other Vermont cities and towns with Boston, Springfield, Albany, New York, Montréal, and cities in New Hampshire.

By Car
Interstate–91, which stretches from Connecticut and Massachusetts in the south to Québec in the north, reaches most points along Vermont's eastern border. I–89, from New Hampshire to the east and Québec to the north, crosses central Vermont from White River Junction to Burlington. Southwestern Vermont can be reached by U.S. 7 from Massachusetts and U.S. 4 from New York.

By Plane
Continental, Delta, United, and US Airways fly into **Burlington International Airport** (✉ Airport Dr., 4 mi east of Burlington off U.S. 2, ☎ 802/863–1889). **Rutland State Airport** (☎ 802/786–8881) has daily service to and from Boston on Colgan Air. West of Bennington and convenient to southern Vermont, **Albany–Schenectady County Airport** (☎ 518/869–3021) in New York State is served by 10 major U.S. carriers. *See* Air Travel *in* Smart Travel Tips A to Z for airline numbers.

By Train
Amtrak's (☎ 800/872–7245) *Vermonter* is a daytime service linking Washington, D.C., with Brattleboro, Bellows Falls, White River Junction, Montpelier, Waterbury, Essex Junction, and St. Albans. The *Adirondack,* which runs from Washington, D.C., to Montréal, serves Albany, Ft. Edward (near Glens Falls), Ft. Ticonderoga, and Plattsburgh, allowing relatively convenient access to western Vermont. The *Ethan Allen Express* connects New York City with Fair Haven and Rutland.

Getting Around

By Car
The official speed limit in Vermont is 50 mph, unless otherwise posted; on the interstates it's 65 mph. Right turns are permitted on a red light unless otherwise indicated. You can get a state map, which has mileage charts and enlarged maps of major downtown areas, free from the Vermont Travel Division. The *Vermont Atlas and Gazetteer,* sold in many bookstores, shows nearly every road in the state and is great for driving on the back roads.

By Plane
Aircraft charters are available at Burlington International Airport from **Valet Air Services** (☎ 802/863–3626 or 800/782–0773). **Mansfield Heliflight** (✉ Milton, ☎ 802/893–1003) provides helicopter transportation throughout New England.

Contacts and Resources

The Arts

Vermont Symphony Orchestra (☎ 802/864–5741) performs throughout Vermont.

B&B Reservation Agencies

American Country Collection of Bed and Breakfasts (⊠ 1353 Union St., Schenectady, NY 12308, ☎ 518/370–4948 or 800/810–4948). You can also try calling the chambers of commerce in many ski areas.

Camping

Call Vermont's **Department of Forests, Parks, and Recreation** (☎ 802/241–3655) for a copy of the Vermont Campground Guide, which lists state parks and other public and private camping facilities.

For **camping reservations in state parks** in southeastern Vermont, call ☎ 802/885–8891 or 800/299–3071; in southwestern Vermont, ☎ 802/483–2001 or 800/658–1622; in northwestern Vermont, ☎ 802/879–5674 or 800/252–2363; in northeastern Vermont, ☎ 802/479–4280 or 800/658–6934. These numbers are used from the second Tuesday in January through May 1; after that, call the individual parks for reservations. Between Labor Day and January, no reservations are taken.

Emergencies

Ambulance, fire, police (☎ 911). **Medical Health Care Information Center** (☎ 802/864–0454). **Vermont State Police** (☎ 800/525–5555).

Fishing

For information about fishing, including licenses, call the **Vermont Department of Fish and Wildlife** (☎ 802/241–3700).

Foliage and Snow Hot Line

Call ☎ 802/828–3239 for tips on peak viewing locations and times and up-to-date snow conditions.

Guided Tours

BIKING

Bicycle Holidays (⊠ Munger St., Middlebury, ☎ 802/388–2453 or 800/292–5388) creates custom-designed bike trips and will help you put together your own inn-to-inn tour by providing route directions and booking your accommodations. **Vermont Bicycle Touring** (⊠ Monkton Rd., Bristol, ☎ 802/453–4811 or 800/245–3868) leads numerous tours throughout the state as well as throughout the rest of the country and in Europe.

CANOEING

Umiak Outdoor Outfitters (⊠ 849 S. Main St., Stowe, ☎ 802/253–2317) has shuttles to nearby rivers for day excursions and customized overnight trips. **Vermont Canoe Trippers/Battenkill Canoe, Ltd.** (⊠ River Rd., off Rte. 7A, Arlington, ☎ 802/362–2800) organizes canoe tours (some are inn-to-inn) and fishing trips.

FISHING

Strictly Trout (☎ 802/869–3116) will arrange a fly-fishing trip on any Vermont stream or river, including the Battenkill.

HIKING

New England Hiking Holidays (⊠ North Conway, NH, ☎ 603/356–9696 or 800/869–0949) leads guided walks with lodging in country inns. **North Wind Hiking and Walking Tours** (⊠ Waitsfield, ☎ 802/496–5771 or 800/496–5771) conducts guided walking tours through Vermont's countryside.

Kedron Valley Stables (⊠ South Woodstock, ☎ 802/457–1480 or 800/ 225–6301) has one- to six-day riding tours with lodging in country inns.

Hiking

The **Green Mountain Club** (⊠ Rte. 100, Waterbury Center, ☎ 802/244–7037) publishes hiking maps and guides. The club also manages the Long Trail, the north–south trail that traverses the entire state.

Lodging Information

The **Vermont Chamber of Commerce** (☞ Visitor Information, *below*) publishes the *Vermont Travelers' Guidebook,* which is an extensive list of lodgings, and additional guides to country inns and vacation rentals. The **Vermont Travel Division** (☞ Visitor Information, *below*) has a brochure that lists lodgings at working farms.

State Parks

Vermont state parks open during the last week in May and close after the Labor Day or Columbus Day weekend, depending on location. Day-use charges are $2 per person for ages 14 and up, $1.50 for ages 4 to 13; children under 4 are free. Call individual parks or the **Department of Forests, Parks, and Recreation** (☎ 802/241–3655) for information.

Visitor Information

Forest Supervisor, Green Mountain National Forest (⊠ 231 N. Main St., Rutland 05701, ☎ 802/747–6700). **Vermont Chamber of Commerce** (⊠ Box 37, Montpelier 05601, ☎ 802/223–3443). **Vermont Travel Division** (⊠ 134 State St., Montpelier 05602, ☎ 802/828–3237 or 800/ 837–6668). There are **state information centers** on the Massachusetts border at I–91, the New Hampshire border at I–89, the New York border at Route 4A, and the Canadian border at I–89.

4 NEW HAMPSHIRE

New Hampshire's coast has a small stretch of towns with sandy beaches and ocean vistas. It's also home to the engaging city of Portsmouth. The Lakes Region is primarily a summer and fall haven for fishing, swimming, and boating. The White Mountains attract visitors who come to gaze on Mt. Washington, the tallest peak in the East, to ski and snowboard, to hike, and to shop at North Conway's outlet stores. Western and central New Hampshire have a string of cities along I-93 and a large unspoiled area of small towns, each with its own historic district and town green.

Revised and
updated by
Paula J.
Flanders

CRUSTY, INDEPENDENT NEW HAMPSHIRE is often defined more by what it is not than by what it is. It lacks the folksy charm of neighboring Vermont, nor does it have the miles of awe-inspiring rocky coast of Maine, its neighbor on its other side. And New Hampshire's politics generally range only from conservative to moderate, unlike the decidedly more liberal Massachusetts.

Whether in spite of or because of its differences, New Hampshire has been welcoming visitors for centuries. The first hiker to reach the top of Mt. Washington was Darby Field, in 1642. The first summer home appeared on one of the state's many lakes in 1763. Ralph Waldo Emerson, Henry David Thoreau, Nathaniel Hawthorne, and Louisa May Alcott all visited and wrote about the state, sparking a strong literary tradition that continues today. Filmmaker Ken Burns, writer J. D. Salinger, and poet Donald Hall all make their homes here.

New Hampshire's independent spirit nourishes other branches of the arts as well. Portsmouth has several theater groups, both cutting-edge and mainstream. New Hampshire's oldest professional theater, Tamworth's Barnstormers, claims the son of a president (Francis Cleveland) as founder. Throughout the state, a large number of stores display the work of local artisans. On back roads and in small towns, you can find makers of fine furniture and museum-quality pewter, glassblowers and potters, weavers and woodworkers. The League of New Hampshire Craftsmen operates eight stores around the state and runs the nation's oldest crafts fair each year during the first week of August.

But it was the mountain peaks, clear air, and sparkling lakes that attracted most of New Hampshire's early visitors, the same things that first attract people today. You can ski, snowboard, hike, and fish, or explore on snowmobiles, sailboats, and mountain bikes. Rock climbing and snowshoeing are popular, too. The diversity of the state's natural resources makes it a popular spot with everyone from avid adventurers to young families looking for easy access to nature.

New Hampshire natives had—and still have—no objection to others' enjoying the natural beauty of the state as long as they left some of their money behind when they returned home. The state has long resisted taxes on items other states take for granted, like sales and income, so the tourism adds much-needed revenue to the state coffers.

Taxes are only one hotly debated topic in the politically minded Granite State. New Hampshire was the first colony to declare itself independent from Great Britain, the first to adopt a state constitution, and the first to require that constitution to be referred to the people for approval. From the start, New Hampshire residents were independent-minded folk who took their hard-won freedoms seriously. Twenty years after the Revolutionary War's Battle of Bennington, New Hampshire native General John Stark, who led the troops to that crucial victory, wrote a letter to be read at the reunion he was too ill to attend. In it, he reminded his men, "Live free or die; death is not the worst of evils." The first half of that sentiment is now the state's motto, appearing even on its license plates. Nothing symbolizes those freedoms more than voting, and residents relish their role as host of the nation's earliest presidential primary.

With several of its cities consistently rated among the most livable in the nation, New Hampshire has seen considerable growth over the past decade or two. Even as growth has leveled in the rest of New England,

New Hampshire's population continues its upward trend, a trend fueled mainly by outsiders choosing to make their homes here.

Much of this population boom is located in the southern section of the state, so longtime residents worry that New Hampshire will soon take on two distinct personalities: one driven by the new cities of the south, such as Nashua, Derry, and Londonderry, and the other by the small towns and villages that make up the northern tier of the state. Only time will tell how New Hampshire will cope. But while the influx of newcomers has brought inevitable change, the independent nature of the people and the state's natural beauty continue to be embraced by newcomers and locals alike.

Pleasures and Pastimes

Beaches and Lakes

New Hampshire makes the most of its 18-mi coastline with several good beaches, among them Hampton Beach and Wallis Sands in Rye. Those who prefer warm lake waters to the bracing Atlantic can choose among some of the finest lakes in New England, such as Lake Winnipesaukee, Lake Sunapee, and Newfound Lake.

Biking

A safe, scenic route along New Hampshire's seacoast is the bike path along Route 1A, for which you can park at Odiorne Point and follow the road 14 mi south to Seabrook. Some bikers begin at Prescott Park and take Route 1B into New Castle, but beware of the traffic. Another pretty route is from Newington Town Hall to the Great Bay Estuary. The volume of traffic on the major coastal roads makes cycling dangerous for people unfamiliar with the area: Avoid U.S. 1 and 4 and Route 101. You'll find excellent routes in the White Mountains detailed in the mountain-bike guide map "The White Mountain Ride Guide," sold at area sports and book shops. There's also a bike path in Franconia Notch State Park at the Lafayette Campground and a mountain-biking center, Great Glen Trails, at the base of Mt. Washington. Many ski areas permit summer mountain biking on some trails.

Dining

New Hampshire is home to some of the best seafood in the country, not just lobster but also salmon pie, steamed mussels, fried clams, and seared tuna steaks. Each region has its share of country-French dining rooms and nouveau American kitchens, but the best advice is to eat where the locals do. That can be anywhere from a greasy-spoon diner to an out-of-the-way inn whose chef creates everything—including the butter—from scratch. Restaurants around the lakes and along the seacoast are busy in summer, so always make reservations.

Fishing

Lake trout and salmon swim in Lake Winnipesaukee, trout and bass in smaller lakes, and trout in streams all around the Lakes Region. Alton Bay has an "Ice Out" salmon derby in spring. In winter, ice fishers fish on all the lakes from huts known as "ice bobs." In the Sunapee region, you can fish for brook, rainbow, and lake trout; smallmouth bass; pickerel; and horned pout. The Monadnock region has more than 200 lakes and ponds, most with good fishing for rainbow trout, brown trout, smallmouth and largemouth bass, northern pike, white perch, golden trout, pickerel, and horned pout.

Lodging

In the mid-19th century, wealthy Bostonians would pack up and move to their grand summer homes in the countryside for two- or three-month stretches. Many of these homes have been restored and converted into

New Hampshire

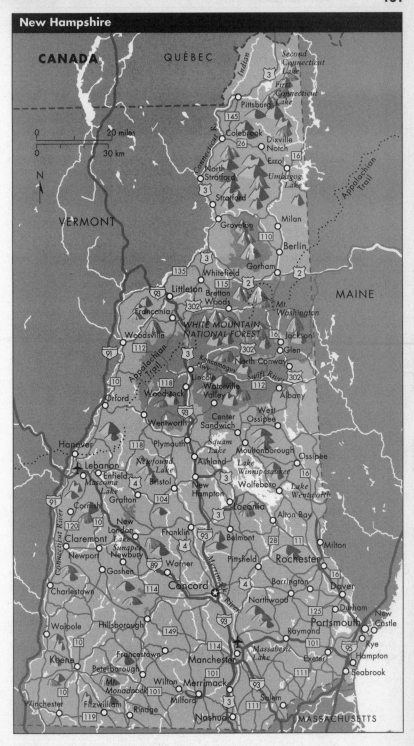

country inns. The smallest have only a couple of rooms; typically, they're done in period style. The largest contain 30 or more rooms, with private baths, fireplaces, and even hot tubs. A few of the grand old resorts still stand, with their world-class cooking staffs and tradition of top-notch service. In Manchester and Concord, as well as along major highways, chain hotels and motels dominate the lodging scene.

National and State Parks and Forests

Parklands vary widely, even within a region. The White Mountain National Forest covers 770,000 acres in northern New Hampshire. Major recreation parks are at Franconia Notch, Crawford Notch, and Mt. Sunapee. Rhododendron State Park, in Fitzwilliam in the Monadnock Region, has a singular collection of wild rhododendrons. Mt. Washington Park is on top of the highest mountain in the Northeast. Twenty-three state recreation areas offer camping, picnicking, hiking, boating, fishing, swimming, biking, and winter sports.

Shopping

Outside the state's outlet meccas of North Conway and Tilton, shopping revolves around antiques and local crafts, which are plentiful and generally high in quality. In the southern end of the Lakes Region and in Hampton Beach, shops and boutiques are all geared to summer tourists—the wares tend toward T-shirts and tacky trinkets. Many close from late October to mid-April. Summertime fairs, such as the one operated by the League of New Hampshire Craftsmen at Mt. Sunapee State Park, offer another way to see some of the state's best arts and crafts. Signs on roads throughout the state mark the locations of antiques shops, galleries, and open studios.

The densest clusters of antiques shops are along U.S. 4, between Route 125 and Concord; along Route 119, from Fitzwilliam to Hinsdale; along Route 101, from Marlborough to Wilton; and in the towns of North Conway, North Hampton, Hopkinton, Hollis, and Amherst. In the Lakes Region, most shops are along the eastern side of Winnipesaukee, near Wolfeboro and around Ossipee. Particularly in the Monadnock region, stores in barns and homes along back roads are "open by chance or by appointment." And don't ignore the summer flea markets and yard sales—deals are just waiting to happen.

Skiing and Snow Sports

Scandinavian settlers who came to New Hampshire's high, handsome, rugged peaks in the late 1800s brought their skis with them. Skiing got its modern start in the Granite State in the 1920s with the cutting of trails on Cannon Mountain; you can now ski or snowboard at nearly 20 areas, from the old, established slopes (Cannon, Cranmore, Wildcat) to more contemporary ones (Attitash, Loon, Waterville Valley). Promotional packages assembled by the ski areas allow you to sample different resorts. There's Ski 93 (referring to resorts along I–93), Ski the Mt. Washington Valley, and more.

Exploring New Hampshire

New Hampshire can be divided into four regions. The main attraction of the coast is historic Portsmouth. Inland a bit is Exeter, home of the eponymous prep school. The Lakes Region, in the east-central part of New Hampshire, has good restaurants, hiking trails, antiques shops, and, of course, water sports. People go to the White Mountains in the state's north to hike, ski, and photograph vistas and vibrant foliage. Western New Hampshire is the unspoiled heart of the state, although that beauty is bounded by the central corridor of fast-growing cities and towns along I–93.

Numbers in the text and in the margin correspond to numbers on the maps: New Hampshire Coast, New Hampshire Lakes, The White Mountains, Dartmouth–Lake Sunapee, and Monadnock Region and Central New Hampshire.

Great Itineraries

Some people come to New Hampshire to pursue a favorite sport: hiking or skiing the mountains, fishing or boating on the lakes, biking the back roads. Others prefer to drive, wandering through scenic towns and stopping to visit museums or shop for local treasures. Although New Hampshire is a small state, roads have to go around lakes and mountains, making distances longer than they appear. You can get a taste of the coast, lake, and mountain areas of the state in three to five days or so; a little more than a week gives you time to do a good loop of a number of areas around the state.

IF YOU HAVE 3 DAYS

Drive along Route 1A to see the coastline or take a boat tour of the Isles of Shoals before exploring ⛓ **Portsmouth** ⑧. On the next day, visit Lake Winnipesaukee. ⛓ **Wolfeboro** ㉑, on the eastern edge of the lake, makes a good overnight stop. On the following day, drive across the scenic Kancamagus Highway from Conway to **Lincoln** ㉕ to see the granite ledges and mountain streams for which the White Mountains are famous. Interstate 93 will take you to Route 101, on which you can return to Portsmouth or head straight south to Massachusetts.

IF YOU HAVE 5 DAYS

After visiting ⛓ **Portsmouth** ⑧ and ⛓ **Wolfeboro** ㉑, explore Squam and Ossipee lakes and the charming towns that surround them: **Moultonborough** ⑲, **Center Harbor** ⑯, and **Tamworth** ⑳. Spend your third night in the White Mountain town of ⛓ **Jackson** ㉘, which is equally beautiful in the winter, when cross-country skiing is popular, and in the summer, when hiking is the main activity. After crossing the Kancamagus Highway to **Lincoln** ㉕, tour the western part of the White Mountain National Forest by following Route 112 to Route 118. Take Route 25A and then follow Route 10 south through the upper Connecticut River valley. ⛓ **Hanover** ㊷, home of Dartmouth College, is a good overnight stop. Interstate 89 will bring you back to I–93 via **Newbury** ㊵ and the Lake Sunapee region.

IF YOU HAVE 8 DAYS

If you spend two nights in ⛓ **Portsmouth** ⑧, you'll have time to visit Strawbery Banke Museum and soak up more of the city's restaurant and cultural scene. After exploring ⛓ **Wolfeboro** ㉑ and ⛓ **Jackson** ㉘, continue north on Route 16 through Pinkham Notch to Mt. Washington, where you can hike or drive to the top. Return via U.S. 302 and U.S. 3 to ⛓ **Franconia** ㉞ and Franconia Notch State Park. Drive along Route 112 to Route 118 and take Route 25A; follow Route 10 south through the upper Connecticut River valley, where the scenery is straight out of Currier & Ives. Stop by ⛓ **Hanover** ㊷ and the Shaker Community at **Enfield** ㊶; then take either Route 12A along the Connecticut River or Route 10 south to ⛓ **Keene** ㊻. Route 119 East leads to Rhododendron State Park in **Fitzwilliam** ㊼. Continue east along Route 101 to return to the coast.

When to Tour New Hampshire

New Hampshire is a year-round destination. In summer, people flock to seaside beaches, mountain hiking trails, and lake boat ramps. In the cities, festivals bring music and theater to the forefront. Fall brings leaf-peepers, especially to the White Mountains and along the Kancamagus Highway. Skiers take to the slopes in winter, when Christmas lights and carnivals brighten the long, dark nights. April's mud season, the black fly season in late May, and unpredictable weather keep visitor numbers low in spring, but the season has its joys, not the least of which is the appearance of New Hampshire's state flower, the purple lilac, from mid-May to early June.

THE COAST

The first VIP to vacation on the New Hampshire coast was George Washington, in 1789. By all accounts he had a good time, though a bizarre fishing accident left him with a nasty black eye. Accompanied as he was by 14 generals (all in full dress uniform), he probably didn't walk barefoot along the area's sandy beaches or picnic at Odiorne Point, though he may have visited the homes of John Paul Jones and John Langdon, both of which still stand.

A visit to the coast can take an afternoon or several days. This section begins with Exeter, the first state capital; follows the coast to Portsmouth; and circles inland along the rivers to Newington and Durham.

Exeter

❶ *8 mi north of the Massachusetts border, 11 mi southwest of Portsmouth, 47 mi southeast of Concord.*

Exeter's first settlers built their homes in 1638 around the falls where the freshwater Exeter River meets the salty Squamscott. During the Revolutionary War, Exeter was the state capital, and it was here that the first state constitution and the first Declaration of Independence from Great Britain were put to paper. Phillips Exeter Academy, which opened in 1783, is still one of the nation's most- esteemed prep schools.

The **American Independence Museum,** adjacent to Phillips Exeter Academy in the Ladd-Gilman House, celebrates the birth of our nation. The story of the Revolution unfolds during each guided tour, on which you'll see drafts of the U.S. Constitution and the first Purple Heart. ✉ *1 Governor's La.,* ☎ *603/772–2622.* 🎫 *$4.* ☉ *May–Oct., Wed.–Sun. noon–5 (last tour at 4).*

Dining and Lodging

$$ ✗ **Vincent's String Bridge Cafe.** Vincent's creates veal scallopini, chicken marsala, and other Italian dishes in the heart of town. Many specials, like the shrimp in a garlic sherry sauce, incorporate fresh local ingredients. For lunch, try soup or a salad with a loaf of bread still warm from the oven. ✉ *69 Water St.,* ☎ *603/778–8219. AE, D, MC, V.*

$ ✗ **Loaf and Ladle.** Hearty chowders, soups, and stews and huge sandwiches on homemade bread are served cafeteria-style at this understated eatery. Check the blackboard for the ever-changing rotation of chef's specials, breads, and desserts, and don't miss the fresh salad bar. Overlooking the river, the café is handy to the shops, galleries, and historic houses along Water Street. ✉ *9 Water St.,* ☎ *603/778–8955. Reservations not accepted. AE, D, DC, MC, V.*

$$–$$$ ✗🏨 **Exeter Inn.** This brick Georgian-style inn on the campus of Phillips Exeter Academy has been the choice of visiting parents for the past half century. It is furnished with antique and reproduction pieces and possesses every modern amenity. Among the specialties at the Terrace Restaurant are a fillet of salmon wrapped in a pastry crust and stuffed with wild mushrooms and onions, and a napoleon of grilled vegetables with layers of Boursin cheese. On Sunday, the line forms early for a brunch with more than 40 options. ✉ *90 Front St., 03833,* ☎ *603/*

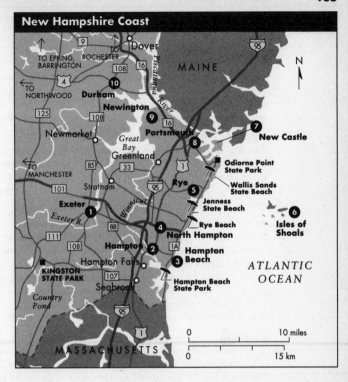

New Hampshire Coast

772–5901 or 800/782–8444, FAX 603/778–8757. 47 rooms. Restaurant, meeting rooms. AE, D, DC, MC, V.

$$–$$$$ ⊞ **Inn by the Bandstand.** Common rooms in this 1809 Federal town house, which is listed on the National Register of Historic Places, are decorated in period style. Seven guest rooms have working fireplaces; some have whirlpool baths, too. After a day of sightseeing, you can relax with a glass of the complimentary sherry found in each room. ⊠ 4 Front St., 03833, ☎ 603/772–6352, FAX 603/778–0212. 7 rooms, 2 suites. Continental breakfast. AE, D, MC, V.

$ ⛺ **Exeter Elms Family Campground.** This campground has 200 sites (some riverfront), a swimming pool, a playground, canoes for rent, and a recreation program. ⊠ 188 Court St., 03833, ☎ 603/778–7631. MC, V. Closed mid-Sept.–mid-May.

Shopping

The shop of the **Exeter League of New Hampshire Craftsmen** (⊠ 61 Water St., ☎ 603/778–8282) carries original jewelry, woodworking, and pottery. **A Picture's Worth a Thousand Words** (⊠ 65 Water St., ☎ 603/778–1991) stocks antique and contemporary prints, old maps, town histories, and rare books. **Starlight Express** (⊠ 103 Water St., ☎ 603/772–9477) sells clocks with elaborate hand-painted faces, picture frames, candles, and other accessories for the house. **Water Street Artisans** (⊠ 20 Water St., ☎ 603/778–6178) carries fine crafts.

Hampton

2 *5 mi east of Exeter, 12 mi south of Portsmouth.*

One of New Hampshire's first towns, Hampton was settled in 1638. Its name in the 17th century was Winnacunnet, which means "beautiful place of pines." The center of the early town was **Meeting House Green,** where 42 stones represent the founding families.

Tuck Museum, across from Meeting House Green, contains displays on the town's early history. ✉ *40 Park Ave.,* ☎ *603/929–0781; 603/ 926–2543 for appointments.* 🖾 *Free.* ☉ *June–Sept., Wed.–Fri. and Sun. 1–4* PM; *and by appointment.*

At **Applecrest Farm Orchards,** you can pick your own apples and berries or buy fresh fruit pies and cookies from the bakery. Fall brings cider pressing, hay rides, pumpkins, and music on weekends. In winter you can follow a cross-country ski trail through the orchard. ✉ *Rte. 88, Hampton Falls,* ☎ *603/926–3721.* ☉ *Daily 8* AM*–dusk.*

The **Raspberry Farm** has pick-your-own raspberries, strawberries, blueberries, blackberries, and other berries. The shop sells fresh- baked goods, jams, and sauces. ✉ *3 mi inland on Rte. 84, Hampton Falls,* ☎ *603/926–6604.* ☉ *Early June–late Oct., weekdays noon–5, weekends 9–5. Call for picking conditions.*

At the **Seabrook Science & Nature Center,** adjacent to the Seabrook Station nuclear power plant 4 mi south of Hampton, you can tour exhibits on the science of power, see control-room operators in training, walk through a replica of a cooling tunnel, pedal a bike to create electricity, and use interactive computer games that further explain nuclear power. The center maintains the ¾-mi Owascoag nature trail, a touch pool for kids, and several large aquariums of local sea life. ✉ *Lafayette Rd., Seabrook,* ☎ *800/338–7482.* 🖾 *Free.* ☉ *Weekdays 10–4.*

Lodging

$$ 🖾 **Hampton Falls Inn.** Intricate Burmese wall hangings and leather furniture decorate the lobby of this modern motel only a few minutes from Hampton Beach. The rooms are typical of those in chain motels, but many have a view of the neighboring farm; all have microwave ovens. An enclosed porch by the indoor pool looks out over the woods and fields. ✉ *11 Lafayette Rd./U.S. 1, 03844,* ☎ *603/926–9545,* FAX *603/ 926–4155. 33 rooms, 15 suites. Restaurant (no dinner), refrigerators, indoor pool, meeting rooms. AE, D, DC, MC, V.*

$$ 🖾 **Victoria Inn.** Built as a carriage house in 1875, this romantic bed-and-breakfast is done in the style Victorians loved best: wicker, chandeliers, and lace. One room is completely lilac; the honeymoon suite has white eyelet coverlets and a private sunroom. Innkeepers Nickie Fuller and Jason Bolduc have named one room in honor of President Franklin Pierce, who for years summered in the home next door. ✉ *430 High St. (½ mi from Hampton Beach), 03842,* ☎ *603/929–1437. 6 rooms, 3 with bath. Full breakfast. MC, V.*

$ 🖾 **Curtis Field House.** This Cape-style B&B decorated with Federal-era antiques and some reproductions occupies 10 acres between Exeter and Hampton and is only 1½ mi from I–95. Guest rooms have four-poster beds, comfortable chairs, and private baths. Relaxing on the sundeck with a good book and enjoying the fragrant gardens are favorite pastimes at this quiet property that's a short drive from Portsmouth and the beaches. ✉ *735 Exeter Rd., 03842,* ☎ *603/929– 0082. 3 rooms. Full breakfast. No credit cards. Closed Nov.–May.*

$ ⚠ **Tidewater Campground.** This camping area has 200 sites, a large playground, a pool, a game room, and a basketball court. ✉ *160 Lafayette Rd., 03842,* ☎ *603/926–5474. MC, V. Closed mid-Oct.–mid-May.*

Nightlife and the Arts

From July to September, the **Hampton Playhouse** (✉ 357 Winnacunnet Rd./Rte. 101E, ☎ 603/926–3073) brings familiar Hollywood movie and New York theater actors to the coast. Performances are held in the evening except on Monday, with matinees on Wednesday and

Friday; children's shows take place on Saturday at 11 and 2. Schedules and tickets are available at the box office or at the Chamber of Commerce Seashell on Ocean Boulevard in Hampton Beach.

Shopping

Antiques shops line U.S. 1 (Lafayette Rd.) in Hampton and neighboring Hampton Falls. The more than 50 dealers at **Antiques at Hampton Falls** (☎ 603/926–1971) have all types of antiques and collectibles. **Antiques New Hampshire** (☎ 603/926–9603) is a group shop with 35 dealers. **Antiques One** (☎ 603/926–5332) carries everything but furniture, including books and maps. The **Barn at Hampton Falls** (☎ 603/926–9003) is known for American and European furniture.

Hampton Beach

❸ *2 mi east of Hampton, 14 mi south of Portsmouth.*

An estimated 150,000 people visit Hampton Beach on the Fourth of July, and it draws plenty of people until late September, when things close up. If you like fried dough, loud music, arcade games, palm readers, parasailing, and bronzed bodies, don't miss it. The 3-mi boardwalk, where kids can play games and see how saltwater taffy is made, looks as if it was snatched out of the 1940s. Free outdoor concerts are held on many evenings in summer, and once a week there's a fireworks display. Talent shows and karaoke performances take place in the Seashell Stage, right on the beach.

Each summer locals hold a children's festival in August and celebrate the end of the season with a huge seafood feast on the weekend after Labor Day. For a quieter time, stop by for a sunrise stroll, when only seagulls and the odd jogger interrupt the serenity.

Dining and Lodging

$$–$$$$ ✕ **Ron's Landing at Rocky Bend.** Nestled in among the souvenir shops and motels is this casually elegant restaurant that prepares fresh seafood, pasta, beef, and veal dishes. Specialties include smoked Virginia oysters and filet mignon topped with fresh horseradish sauce and served with Alaskan king crab legs. In summer, dine on the second-floor screened porch, which has a sweeping view of the Atlantic. ✉ *379 Ocean Blvd., ☎ 603/929–2122. AE, D, DC, MC, V.*

$$$–$$$$ ✕🏨 **Ashworth by the Sea.** This family-owned hotel was built across the street from Hampton Beach in 1912; most rooms have private decks, and the furnishings vary from period to contemporary. The beachside rooms have breathtaking ocean views. The others look out onto the pool or the quiet street. The Ashworth Dining Room ($$–$$$) serves steaks, poultry, and fresh seafood—including seven variations on lobster. ✉ *295 Ocean Blvd., 03842, ☎ 603/926–6762 or 800/345–6736, FAX 603/926–2002. 105 rooms. 3 restaurants, in-room data ports, pool, gift shop. AE, D, DC, MC, V.*

$$–$$$ 🏨 **Oceanside Inn.** The square front and simple awnings of this oceanfront inn look much the same as those on all the other buildings lining Ocean Boulevard. Inside, though, is a hidden treasure. Carefully selected antiques and collectibles, individually decorated rooms, a cozy living room and library with a fireplace, and a second-floor veranda for watching the waves give the Oceanside the feel of a late-19th-century home. Should the resort's crush of people and noise begin to overwhelm, you'll appreciate the soundproofing that makes this inn seem like a calm port in a storm. ✉ *365 Ocean Blvd., 03842, ☎ 603/926–3542, FAX 603/926–3549. 10 rooms. Refrigerators, in-room safes. Full breakfast. AE, D, MC, V. Closed mid-Oct.–mid-May.*

Nightlife and the Arts

The **Hampton Beach Casino Ballroom** (⊠ 169 Ocean Beach Blvd., ☎ 603/926–4541; 603/929–4201 for event hot line) books name entertainment from April to October. Tina Turner, the Monkees, Jay Leno, and Loretta Lynn have all played here. Note that this is a performance venue, not a gambling casino.

North Hampton

❹ *3 mi north of Hampton, 11 mi southwest of Portsmouth.*

Factory outlets along U.S. 1 coexist in North Hampton with mansions lining the ocean along Route 1A.

Fuller Gardens, a turn-of-the-century estate garden designed in the Colonial Revival style by Arthur Shurtleff, has a 1930s addition by the Olmsted brothers. It blooms all summer long and has 2,000 rosebushes of every shade and type. Other plantings include a hosta display garden and a serenity-inspiring Japanese garden. ⊠ *10 Willow Ave.,* ☎ *603/964–5414.* ☜ *$4.50.* ☉ *Early May–mid-Oct., daily 10–6.*

Shopping

The **North Hampton Factory Outlet Center** (⊠ Lafayette Rd./U.S. 1, ☎ 603/964–9050) has tax-free goods and discounts on brand names like Famous Footwear and American Tourister. Among the center's stores are the Paper Factory, the Sports Outpost, and Bass.

En Route   On Route 1A as it winds through North Hampton and Rye sits a group of mansions known as **Millionaires' Row.** Because of the way the road curves, the drive south along this route is even more breathtaking than the drive north.

Rye

❺ *5 mi north of North Hampton, 6 mi south of Portsmouth.*

In 1623 the first European settlers landed at Odiorne Point in what is now Rye, making it the birthplace of New Hampshire. The main reasons for visiting the area are a lovely state park, oceanfront beaches, and the view from Route 1A.

★ ℭ   **Odiorne Point State Park** and the Seacoast Science Center encompass more than 350 acres of protected land. You can pick up an interpretive brochure on any of the nature trails or simply stroll and enjoy the vistas of the nearby Isles of Shoals. The tidal pools, considered the best in New England, shelter crabs, periwinkles, and sea anemones. The science center conducts guided nature walks and interpretive programs, has exhibits on the area's natural history, and traces the social history of Odiorne Point back to the Ice Age. Kids love the tide-pool touch tank and the 1,000-gallon Gulf of Maine deepwater aquarium. ⊠ *Rte. 1A north of Wallis Sands State Beach,* ☎ *603/436–8043.* ☜ *Science Center $1; park in summer, fall, and on weekends $2.50.* ☉ *Daily 10–5.*

Good for swimming and sunning, **Jenness State Beach,** on Route 1A, is a favorite with locals. The facilities include a bathhouse, lifeguards, and parking. **Wallis Sands State Beach,** on Route 1A, is a swimmers' beach with bright white sand and a bathhouse. Parking is ample and costs $8 on weekends, $5 weekdays.

Lodging

$$ ⌂ **Rock Ledge Manor.** Built out on a point, this mid-19th-century summer house with a wraparound porch was part of a resort colony and predates the houses along Millionaires' Row. All rooms have water views. Owners Stan and Sandi Smith serve breakfast in the

sunny dining room overlooking the Atlantic. This no-smoking B&B has a two-night minimum on weekends and holidays. ⊠ *1413 Ocean Blvd./Rte. 1A, 03870,* ☎ *603/431–1413. 2 rooms with bath, 2 rooms with half bath and shared shower. Full breakfast. No credit cards.*

Isles of Shoals

❻ *10 mi off the coast.*

The Isles of Shoals are nine small islands (eight at high tide). Many, like Hog Island, Smuttynose, and Star Island, retain the earthy names given them by the transient fishers who visited in the early 17th century. A colorful history of piracy, murder, and ghosts surrounds the archipelago, long populated by an independent lot who, according to one writer, hadn't the sense to winter on the mainland. Not all the islands lie within the New Hampshire border: After an ownership dispute between Maine and New Hampshire, they were divvied up between the two states (five went to Maine, four to New Hampshire).

Celia Thaxter, a native islander, romanticized these islands with her poetry in *Among the Isles of Shoals* (1873) and celebrated her garden in *An Island Garden* (1894; now reissued with the original illustrations by Childe Hassam, who loved the island). In the late 19th century, **Appledore Island** became an offshore retreat for her coterie of writers, musicians, and artists. The island is now used by the Marine Laboratory of Cornell University. **Star Island** contains a nondenominational conference center and is open to those on guided tours. For information about visiting the Isles of Shoals, *see* Guided Tours *in* The Coast A to Z, *below.*

New Castle

❼ *5 mi north of Rye, 1 mi south of Portsmouth.*

Though it consists of a single square mile of land, the small island of New Castle was once known as Great Island. The narrow roads lined with pre-Revolutionary houses make the island, which is accessible from the mainland by car, perfect for a stroll.

Wentworth by the Sea, the last of the great seaside resorts, is impossible to miss as you approach New Castle on Route 1B. Empty these days, it was the site of the signing of the Russo-Japanese Treaty in 1905, a fact that attracts many Japanese tourists. Because the current owners and the town have been unable to come to agreement on a restoration and redevelopment plan, this grand old hotel may be torn down.

Ft. Constitution was originally Ft. William and Mary, a British stronghold overlooking Portsmouth Harbor. Rebel patriots raided the fort in 1774 in one of revolutionary America's first overt acts of defiance against King George III. The rebels later used the captured munitions against the British at the Battle of Bunker Hill. Panels throughout the fort explain its history. ⊠ *Rte. 1B at the Coast Guard Station,* ☎ *no phone.* ☜ *$2.50.* ☉ *Mid-June–Labor Day, daily 9–5; Labor Day–mid-June, weekends 9–5.*

Lodging

$$ ☷ **Great Islander Bed & Breakfast.** This charming 1740 Colonial faces New Castle's Main Street and has a view of the water from the deck by the lap pool in back. Wide pine floors and exposed beams recall the pre-Revolutionary era. Antiques, quilts, and reproduction floral-patterned wallpapers decorate the rooms of this no-smoking B&B. ⊠ *Box 135, 62 Main St., 03854-0135,* ☎ *603/436–8536. 3 rooms, 1 with bath. Fans, lap pool. Continental breakfast. MC, V.*

Portsmouth

★ **8** *1 mi north of New Castle, 45 mi southeast of Concord.*

Originally settled in 1623 as Strawbery Banke, Portsmouth became a prosperous port before the Revolutionary War. The cultural epicenter of the coast, it contains some notable museums (including the collection of buildings that make up Strawbery Banke), restaurants of every stripe, plus theaters, music venues, and art galleries. Most of these attractions are in and around Market Square in the heart of the city.

The **Portsmouth Trail** passes many pre–Revolutionary War homes in the historic district. The trail breaks the city into three sections that can be explored separately or together. The walking trail can be enjoyed year-round; six houses along the way are open to visitors in summer and fall. Purchase a tour map at the information kiosk on Market Square, the Chamber of Commerce, or any of the houses.

The yellow, hip-roof **John Paul Jones House** was a boardinghouse when Jones lived here while supervising the outfitting of two ships for the Continental Navy. The 1758 structure, the headquarters of the **Portsmouth Historical Society,** contains costumes, glass, guns, portraits, and documents of the late 18th century. ⊠ *43 Middle St.,* ☎ *603/436–8420.* ⊠ *$5.* ⊙ *Memorial Day–mid-Oct., Mon.–Sat. 10–4, Sun. noon–4.*

Lining the hall staircase of the 1716 **Warner House** are the oldest-known wall murals still in place in the country. ⊠ *150 Daniel St.,* ☎ *603/436–5909.* ⊠ *$5.* ⊙ *June–mid-Oct., Mon.–Sat. 10–4, Sun. 1–4.*

The **Moffatt-Ladd House,** built in 1763, tells the story of Portsmouth's merchant class through portraits, letters, and fine furnishings. ⊠ *154 Market St.,* ☎ *603/436–8221.* ⊠ *$5.* ⊙ *June–mid-Oct., Mon.–Sat. 10–4, Sun. 2–5.*

★ The first English settlers named the area around what's now called Portsmouth for the abundant wild strawberries they found along the shore of the Piscataqua River. The city's largest museum, **Strawbery Banke Museum,** now uses the name: This 10-acre outdoor museum with period gardens, exhibits, and craftspeople holds 46 buildings that date from 1695 to 1820. Ten furnished homes represent 300 years of history in one continuously occupied neighborhood. The **Drisco House,** built in 1795, was first used as a dry-goods store, and half the house still depicts this history; the living room and kitchen, on the other hand, are decorated just as they were in the 1950s. The **Shapiro House** has been restored to reflect the life of the Russian Jewish immigrant family who lived in the home in the early 1900s. Perhaps the most opulent house is the 1860 **Goodwin Mansion,** former home of Governor Ichabod Goodwin. It is decorated in plush Victorian style. ⊠ *Marcy St.,* ☎ *603/433–1100 or 603/433–1106.* ⊠ *$12 pass for 2 consecutive days.* ⊙ *Mid-Apr.–Oct., daily 10–5; 1st 2 weekends in Dec., 4:30–9:30.*

Picnicking is popular in **Prescott Park,** on the waterfront between Strawbery Banke Museum and the Piscataqua River. A large formal garden with fountains is perfect for whiling away an afternoon. The park also contains **Point of Graves,** Portsmouth's oldest burial ground, and two warehouses that date from the early 17th century. The **Sheafe Museum** was the warehouse where John Paul Jones outfitted the USS *Ranger,* one of the U.S. Navy's earliest ships. The Strawbery Banke Museum (☞ *above*) gives boatbuilding demonstrations here. ⊠ *Marcy St.,* ☎ *603/431–1101.* ⊙ *Call for hrs and events.*

Ⓒ Nineteen hands-on exhibits at the **Children's Museum of Portsmouth** explore lobstering, sound and music, computers, space travel, and other subjects. Some programs require reservations. ⊠ *280 Marcy St.,* ☎ *603/436–3853.* ⊡ *$4.* ☉ *Tues.–Sat. 10–5, Sun. 1–5; also Mon. 10–5 in summer and during school vacations.*

The **Wentworth-Coolidge Mansion,** a National Historic Landmark, was originally the residence of Benning Wentworth, New Hampshire's first Royal Governor (1753–1770). Notable among the period furnishings in the house is the carved pine mantelpiece in the council chamber. Wentworth's imported lilac trees, believed to be the oldest in North America, bloom each May. Lectures and exhibits are presented in the visitor center. ⊠ *Little Harbor Rd., near South Street Cemetery,* ☎ *603/436–6607.* ⊡ *$2.50.* ☉ *June–Oct., Tues.–Sat. 10–3, Sun. 1–5.*

Docked at the **Port of Portsmouth Maritime Museum** in Albacore Park is the USS *Albacore,* built here in 1953. You can board this prototype submarine, which was a floating laboratory assigned to test a new hull design, dive brakes, and sonar systems for the navy. The nearby **Memorial Garden** and its reflecting pool are dedicated to those who lost their lives in submarine service. ⊠ *600 Market St.,* ☎ *603/436–3680.* ⊡ *$4.* ☉ *May–Columbus Day, daily 9:30–5:30; Columbus Day–Apr., Thurs.–Mon. 9:30–4.*

The **Redhook Ale Brewery,** visible from the Spaulding Turnpike, conducts tours that end with a beer tasting. If you don't have time to tour, you can stop in the Cataqua Public House to sample the fresh ales and have a bite to eat. ⊠ *Pease International Tradeport, 35 Corporate Dr.,* ☎ *603/430–8600.* ⊡ *$1.* ☉ *Call for tour times.*

Dining and Lodging

$$$ ✕ **Dunfey's Aboard the *John Wanamaker*.** Portsmouth's floating restaurant, aboard a restored tugboat, prepares delicacies like shitake-encrusted halibut with wild-mushroom ravioli and Black Angus beef with garlic mashed potatoes. You can watch the river from the bar, enjoy the bistro-like atmosphere of the main dining room, or relax in the romantic Captain's Room. The upper-level deck is a favorite on starry summer nights for light meals, a glass of wine, or dessert and cappuccino. ⊠ *1 Harbour Pl.,* ☎ *603/433–3111. Reservations essential on weekends. AE, MC, V.*

$$–$$$ ✕ **Blue Mermaid World Grill.** The chefs at Blue Mermaid prepare hot Jamaican-style dishes on a wood-burning grill. Specialties include smoked-scallop chowder and grilled Maine lobster with mango butter. In summer you can eat on a deck that overlooks the 13 historic houses collectively known as the Hill. Entertainers perform (outdoors in summer) on Friday and Saturday. ⊠ *409 Hanover St.,* ☎ *603/427–2583. AE, D, DC, MC, V.*

$$–$$$ ✕ **Library at the Rockingham House.** This Portsmouth landmark was a luxury hotel, but most of the building has been converted to condominiums. The restaurant retains the original atmosphere, though, with hand-carved mahogany paneling and bookcases on every wall. The food also seems to belong in a social club of another century: Don't miss the grilled rack of lamb with a port wine and rosemary *demi-glace* (sauce) or the filet mignon with béarnaise sauce. The waitstaff presents the check between the pages of a vintage best-seller. ⊠ *401 State St.,* ☎ *603/431–5202. Reservations essential. AE, DC, MC, V.*

$$–$$$ ✕ **Muddy River Smokehouse.** Red-check tablecloths and wall murals of trees and meadows make this restaurant look like an outdoor summer barbecue joint—even when the weather turns cold. Roll up your sleeves and dig into platters of ribs, homemade corn bread, and molasses baked beans. Chicken, steak, and other dishes are on the menu, but the signature dish is hickory-smoked St. Louis ribs. ⊠ *21 Congress St.,* ☎ *603/430–9582. AE, MC, V.*

$$–$$$ ✕ **Porto Bello Ristorante Italiano.** This family-run restaurant has
★ brought the tastes of Naples to downtown Portsmouth. In the second-
story dining room overlooking the harbor, you can savor daily antipasto
specials ranging from grilled calamari to stuffed baby eggplant. Pastas include spinach gnocchi and homemade ravioli. A house specialty
is veal *carciofi*—a 6-ounce cutlet served with artichokes. The tastes are
so pure and the ingredients so fresh that you won't have trouble fin-
ishing four courses. ⊠ *67 Bow St., 2nd floor,* ☎ *603/431–2989. Reservations essential. AE, D, MC, V. Closed Mon.–Tues.*

$$$ ✕🏨 **Sheraton Harborside Portsmouth Hotel.** Portsmouth's only lux-
ury hotel, this five-story redbrick building is within easy walking dis-
tance of shops and attractions. Suites have full kitchens and living rooms.
The main restaurant, Harbor's Edge ($$$–$$$$), serves fresh seafood
and American cuisine. The Krewe Orleans restaurant and bar dishes
up Cajun specialties. ⊠ *250 Market St., 03801,* ☎ *603/431–2300 or
800/325–3535,* FAX *603/433–5649. 181 rooms, 24 suites. 2 restau-
rants, bar, indoor pool, sauna, exercise room, nightclub, meeting
rooms. AE, D, DC, MC, V.*

$$$–$$$$ 🏨 **Sise Inn.** Each room at this Queen Anne town house in Portsmouth's
★ historic district is decorated in Victorian style, with special fabrics, an-
tiques, and reproductions of antiques. Some rooms have whirlpool baths.
The no-smoking inn is close to the Market Square shopping area and
within walking distance of the theater district and several restaurants.
⊠ *40 Court St., 03801,* ☎ FAX *603/433–1200 or* ☎ *800/267–0525.
26 rooms, 8 suites. In-room VCRs, meeting rooms. Continental break-
fast. AE, DC, MC, V.*

$$ 🏨 **Martin Hill Inn.** Two buildings downtown hold a charming inn
that's within walking distance of the historic district and the water-
front. Extensive perennial gardens enhance the B&B. The quiet rooms,
comfortably furnished with antiques, are decorated in formal Colonial or country-Victorian style. The Greenhouse suite has a private solarium facing the water garden. The inn is no-smoking. ⊠ *404 Islington
St.,* ☎ *603/436–2287. 4 rooms, 3 suites. Full breakfast. MC, V.*

Nightlife and the Arts

NIGHTLIFE

The **Portsmouth Gas Light Co.** (⊠ 64 Market St., ☎ 603/430–9122)
is a popular brick-oven pizzeria and restaurant by day. On summer nights,
the management opens up the back courtyard, brings in local rock bands,
and serves a special punch in plastic sand pails. By midnight, the three-
story parking garage next door has become a makeshift auditorium.
People come from as far away as Boston and Portland to hang out at
the **Press Room** (⊠ 77 Daniel St., ☎ 603/431–5186), which showcases
folk, jazz, blues, and bluegrass performers.

THE ARTS

The **Prescott Park Arts Festival** (⊠ 105 Marcy St., ☎ 603/436–2848)
presents theater, dance, and musical events outdoors during June, July,
and August.

Beloved for its acoustics, the 1878 **Music Hall** (⊠ 28 Chestnut St., ☎
603/436–2400, film line 603/436–9900) brings the best touring events
to the seacoast—from classical and pop concerts to dance and theater.
The hall also hosts an ongoing art-house film series. The **Player's Ring**
(⊠ 105 Marcy St., ☎ 603/436–8123) highlights original plays and performances by local theater groups from September through May. The
Pontine Movement Theater (⊠ 135 McDonough St., ☎ 603/436–
6660) presents dance performances in a renovated warehouse. The **Seacoast Repertory Theatre** (⊠ 125 Bow St., ☎ 603/433–4472 or 800/

639–7650) offers a year-round schedule of musicals, classic dramas, and works by up-and-coming playwrights.

Outdoor Activities and Sports

Portsmouth doesn't have any beaches, but the **Seacoast Trolley** departs from Market Square on the hour, servicing a continuous loop between Portsmouth sights and area beaches (☞ Odiorne Point State Park *and* Wallis Sands State Beach *in* Rye, *above*). You can get a schedule for the trolley, which operates from mid-June to Labor Day, at the information kiosk in Market Square. The **Urban Forestry Center** (⊠ 45 Elwyn Rd., ☎ 603/431–6774) has gardens and marked trails appropriate for short hikes on its 180 acres.

Shopping

Market Square, in the center of town, has gift and clothing boutiques, book and card shops, and exquisite crafts stores.

Kumminz Gallery (⊠ 65 Daniel St., ☎ 603/433–6488) carries pottery, jewelry, and fiber art by New Hampshire artisans. The **Museum Shop at the Dunaway Store** (⊠ 66 Marcy St., ☎ 603/433–1114) stocks quilts, crafts, candy, gifts, postcards, reproduction and contemporary furniture, and books about the area's history. **N. W. Barrett** (⊠ 53 Market St., ☎ 603/431–4262) specializes in leather, jewelry, pottery, and fiber and other art and crafts and sells furniture, including affordable steam-bent oak pieces and one-of-a-kind lamps and rocking chairs. **Pierce Gallery** (⊠ 105 Market St., ☎ 603/436–1988) has prints and paintings of the Maine and New Hampshire coasts. The **Portsmouth Bookshop** (⊠ 1 Islington St., ☎ 603/433–4406) carries old and rare books and maps. At **Salamandra Glass Studios** (⊠ 7 Commercial Alley, ☎ 603/436–1038), you'll find hand-blown glass vases, bowls, and other items. **Tulips** (⊠ 19 Market St., ☎ 603/431–9445) specializes in wood crafts and quilts.

Newington

⑨ *2 mi northwest of Portsmouth.*

With the closing of Pease Air Force Base and the conversion of that space to public lands and private industry, Newington is undergoing a transformation. The region's only malls are here, and from the highway this seems like simply a commercial town. But the original town center, hidden away from the traffic and the malls, retains an old-time New England feel.

Great Bay National Wildlife Refuge preserves one of Newington's greatest assets: its shoreline on the Great Bay Estuary (☞ Off the Beaten Path, *below*). Although not all of the refuge's 1,000 acres are open to the public, two trails for hiking, cross-country skiing, and snowshoeing loop through a section that is home to eagles in winter and herons, white-tail deer, and harbor seals year-round. ⊠ *336 Nimble Hill Rd.,* ☎ *603/431–7511.* ▨ *Free.* ☺ *Daily, dawn–dusk.*

Dining

$–$$$ ✕ **Newick's Seafood Restaurant.** Newick's might serve the best lobster roll on the New England coast, but regulars cherish the onion rings, too. This oversize shack serves seafood and atmosphere in heaping portions. Picture windows allow terrific views over Great Bay. ⊠ *431 Dover Point Rd., Dover,* ☎ *603/742–3205. AE, D, MC, V.*

Shopping

Country Curtains (⊠ Old Beane Farm, 2299 Woodbury Ave., ☎ 603/431–2315) sells curtains, bedding, furniture, and folk art from the catalog company of the same name. The huge and generic **Fox Run Mall**

(⌧ Fox Run Rd., ☎ 603/431–5911) houses Filene's, Macy's, JC Penney, Sears, and 100 other stores.

OFF THE
BEATEN PATH

GREAT BAY ESTUARY – Great blue herons, ospreys, and snowy egrets, all of which are especially conspicuous during their spring and fall migrations, can be found among the 4,471 acres of tidal waters, mud flats, and about 48 mi of inland shoreline that compose the Great Bay Estuary. New Hampshire's largest concentration of winter eagles also lives here. Access to the estuary can be tricky and parking is limited, but the Fish and Game Department's **Sandy Point Discovery Center** (⌧ Depot Rd. off Rte. 101, Greenland, ☎ 603/778–0015) distributes maps and information and has trails for walking. Nearby towns have recreation areas along the bay. Hikers will find trails at Adam's Point (in Durham) and Great Bay National Wildlife Refuge (☞ Newington, *above*). Canoeists can put in at Chapman's Landing (⌧ Rte. 108, Stratham) on the Squamscott River.

Durham

⑩ *7 mi northwest of Newington, 9 mi northwest of Portsmouth.*

Settled in 1635 and home of General John Sullivan, a Revolutionary War hero and three-time New Hampshire governor, Durham was where Sullivan and his band of rebel patriots stored the gunpowder they captured from Ft. William and Mary (☞ New Castle, *above*). Easy access to Great Bay via the Oyster River made Durham a center of maritime activity in the 19th century. Among the lures today are the water, farms that welcome visitors, and the University of New Hampshire, which occupies much of the town's center.

The **Art Gallery** at the University of New Hampshire occasionally exhibits items from a permanent collection of about 1,100 pieces but generally uses its space to host traveling exhibits of contemporary and historic art. Noted items in the collection include 19th-century Japanese woodblock prints and American landscape paintings. ⌧ *Paul Creative Arts Center, 30 College Rd.,* ☎ *603/862–3712.* ⌧ *Free.* ☉ *Sept.– May, Mon.–Wed. 10–4, Thurs. 10–8, weekends 1–5.*

Emery Farm sells fruits and vegetables in summer (including pick-your-own raspberries, strawberries, and blueberries), pumpkins in fall, and Christmas trees in December. The farm shop carries breads and pies, as well as local crafts. Children can pet the resident goats, sheep, and other furry critters. ⌧ *U.S. 4,* ☎ *603/742–8495.* ☉ *May–Dec., call for hrs.*

Several dozen American bison roam the **Little Bay Buffalo Farm.** The on-site Drowned Valley Trading Post sells bison-related gifts and top-quality bison meat. ⌧ *50 Langley Rd.,* ☎ *603/868–3300.* ☉ *Trading Post daily 10–5, observation area daily 9–dusk.*

Dining and Lodging

$$$–$$$$ ✕⌂ **Three Chimneys Inn.** This stately yellow Georgian house on more than 3 acres has graced a hill overlooking the Oyster River since 1649. Rooms in the house and the barn, mostly named after plants from the extensive gardens, are decorated with Georgian- and Federal period antiques and reproductions, canopy or four-poster beds with Edwardian bed drapes, and Oriental rugs. Specialties in the Maples dining room include New England mussel salad and roast leg of farm-raised duckling stuffed with veal and pine nuts. The ffrost-Sawyer Tavern serves simpler fare in a cozy setting. The inn is no-smoking. ⌧ *17 Newmarket Rd., 03824,* ☎ *603/868–7800 or 888/399–9777,* ⅆ *603/868–2964. 25 rooms. 2 restaurants, in-room data ports, meeting rooms. Full breakfast. AE, D, MC, V.*

$$–$$$ ✕▥ **New England Conference Center and Hotel.** In a lush wooded area on the campus of the University of New Hampshire, this hotel is large enough to be a full-service conference center but quiet enough to feel like a retreat. The Woods restaurant specializes in American regional cuisine and is a favorite place for Sunday brunch. ⊠ *15 Strafford Ave., 03824,* ☎ *603/862–2801 or 800/590–4334,* ℻ *603/862–4897. 115 rooms. 2 restaurants, bar, meeting rooms. AE, DC, MC, V.*

$ ▥ **Hickory Pond Inn.** The rooms at this no-smoking inn have fresh, flowered wallpaper and individualized color schemes. The common areas, spiffy as well, include a charming breakfast room and a reading nook with a woodstove. ⊠ *1 Stagecoach Rd., 03824,* ☎ *603/659–2227 or 800/658–0065,* ℻ *603/659–7910. 16 rooms, 14 with bath. 9-hole golf course. Continental breakfast. AE, MC, V.*

Nightlife and the Arts

The **Celebrity Series** (☎ 603/862–3227) at the University of New Hampshire brings music, theater, and dance to Durham. The **UNH Department of Theater and Dance** (☎ 603/862–2919) produces a variety of shows. The University of New Hampshire's **Whittemore Center** (☎ 603/862–4000) hosts everything from Boston Pops concerts to home shows.

Outdoor Activities and Sports

Take a picnic to **Wagon Hill Farm** (⊠ U.S. 4 across from Emery Farm, ☎ no phone), overlooking the Oyster River. The old farm wagon, sitting by itself on the top of a hill, is one of the most photographed spots in New England. Park next to the farmhouse and follow walking trails to the wagon and through the woods to the picnic area by the water. Sledding and cross-country skiing are popular winter activities.

Shopping

Durham's stores tend to cater to college students, but some interesting shops are nearby. **Calef's Country Store** (⊠ Rte. 9, Barrington, ☎ 603/664–2231 or 800/462–2118) stocks gifts and farm products. **Salmon Falls Pottery & Stoneware** (⊠ Oak St. Engine House, Dover, ☎ 603/749–1467 or 800/621–2030) produces handmade, salt-glaze stoneware using a method that was favored by early American potters. Potters are on hand should you want to place a special order or watch them work. **Tuttle's Red Barn** (⊠ Dover Point Rd., Dover, ☎ 603/742–4313) carries jams, pickles, and other farm products.

The Coast A to Z

Arriving and Departing

BY BUS

C&J (☎ 603/431–2424), **Concord Trailways** (☎ 800/639–3317) and **Vermont Transit** (☎ 603/436–0163 or 800/451–3292) provide bus service to New Hampshire's coast from other regions.

BY CAR

The main route to New Hampshire's coast from other states is I–95, which travels from the border with Maine to the border with Massachusetts.

BY PLANE

Manchester Airport (☞ Arriving and Departing *in* New Hampshire A to Z, *below*) is a one-hour drive from the coastal region.

Getting Around

BY BUS

Coast (☎ 603/862–2328) provides limited access to towns in New Hampshire's coastal section.

BY CAR
Coastal Route 1A has views of water, beaches, and summer estates. The more convenient U.S. 1 travels inland. Route 1B tours the island of New Castle. The Spaulding Turnpike (Route 16) and U.S. 4 connect Portsmouth with Dover, Durham, and Rochester. Route 108 links Durham and Exeter. The quick route along the coast is I–95.

Contacts and Resources

EMERGENCIES
New Hampshire State Police (☎ 603/679–3333 or 800/852–3411). **Portsmouth Regional Hospital** (✉ 333 Borthwick Ave., Portsmouth, ☎ 603/436–5110 or 603/433–4042). **Exeter Hospital** (✉ 10 Buzzell Ave., Exeter, ☎ 603/778–7311).

FISHING
For information about fishing and licenses, call the **New Hampshire Fish and Game Office** (☎ 603/868–1095).

Between April and October, deep-sea fishermen head out for cod, mackerel, and bluefish. There are rentals and charters aplenty, offering half- and full-day cruises, as well as some night fishing at the Hampton, Portsmouth, Rye, and Seabrook piers. Try **Al Gauron Deep Sea Fishing** (✉ Hampton Beach, ☎ 603/926–2469), **Atlantic Fishing Fleet** (✉ Rye Harbor, ☎ 603/964–5220 or 800/942–5364), **Eastman Fishing & Marine** (✉ Seabrook, ☎ 603/474–3461), and **Smith & Gilmore** (✉ Hampton Beach, ☎ 603/926–3503).

GUIDED TOURS
Clip-clop your way through Colonial Portsmouth and Strawbery Banke with **Portsmouth Livery Company** (☎ 603/427–0044), which gives narrated horse-and-carriage tours. Look for carriages in Market Square.

The **Isles of Shoals Steamship Company** (✉ Barker Wharf, 315 Market St., Portsmouth, ☎ 603/431–5500 or 800/441–4620) runs island cruises, river trips, and whale-watching expeditions from May to October. Trips on Great Bay may include foliage excursions and tours of the Little Bay Buffalo Farm in Durham. Captains Matt Brewster and John Hodges host these voyages aboard the M/V *Thomas Laighton,* a replica of a Victorian steamship. Breakfast, lunch, and light snacks are available on board, or you can bring your own. Some trips include a stopover and historic walking tour on Star Island.

New Hampshire Seacoast Cruises (✉ Rte. 1A, Rye, ☎ 603/964–5545 or 800/964–5545) conducts naturalist-led whale-watching tours and Isles of Shoals cruises aboard the M/V *Granite State* from June to Labor Day out of Rye Harbor State Marina. From May to October, **Portsmouth Harbor Cruises** (✉ Ceres Street Dock, Portsmouth, ☎ 603/436–8084 or 800/776–0915) operates tours of Portsmouth Harbor, trips to the Isles of Shoals, foliage trips on the Cocheco River, and sunset cruises aboard the M/V *Heritage.*

HIKING
An excellent 1-mi trail reaches the summit of **Blue Job Mountain** (✉ Crown Point Rd. off Rte. 202A, 1 mi from Rochester), where a fire tower has a good view. The **New Hampshire Division of Parks and Recreation** (☎ 603/271–3254) maintains the Rockingham Recreation Trail, which wends 27 mi from Newfields to Manchester and is open to hikers, bikers, snowmobilers, and cross-country skiers.

24-HOUR PHARMACY
Rite Aid (800 Islington St., Portsmouth, ☎ 603/436–2214).

VISITOR INFORMATION
Exeter Area Chamber of Commerce (✉ 120 Water St., Exeter 03833, ☎ 603/772–2411). **Greater Dover Chamber of Commerce** (✉ 299 Central Ave., Dover 03820, ☎ 603/742–2218). **Greater Portsmouth Chamber of Commerce** (✉ 500 Market St. Ext., Portsmouth 03801, ☎ 603/436–1118). **Hampton Beach Area Chamber of Commerce** (✉ 836 Lafayette Rd., Hampton 03842, ☎ 603/926–8718).

LAKES REGION

Lake Winnipesaukee, a Native American name for "Smile of the Great Spirit," is the largest of the dozens of lakes scattered across the eastern half of central New Hampshire. With 283 mi of shoreline, it's the largest in the state. Some claim Winnipesaukee has an island for each day of the year, but the total actually falls a tad short: 274.

Unlike Winnipesaukee, which hums with activity all summer long, the more secluded Squam Lake has a dearth of public-access points. Its tranquillity no doubt attracted the producers of *On Golden Pond*; several scenes of the Oscar-winning film were shot here. Nearby Lake Wentworth is named for the first Royal Governor of the state, who, in building his country manor here, established North America's first summer resort.

Well-preserved Colonial and 19th-century villages are among the region's many landmarks, and you'll find hiking trails, good antiques shops, dozens of good restaurants, several golf courses, and myriad water-oriented activities. This section begins with Alton Bay, at Lake Winnipesaukee's southernmost tip, and the area's towns are presented clockwise around the lakes, starting on Route 11.

Alton Bay

⑪ *35 mi northeast of Concord, 41 mi northwest of Portsmouth.*

Neither quiet nor secluded, Lake Winnipesaukee's southern shore is alive with visitors from the moment the first flower blooms until the last maple has shed its leaves. Two mountain ridges hold 7 mi of Winnipesaukee in Alton Bay, the name of both the inlet and the town at its tip. The lake's cruise boats dock here. There's a dance pavilion, along with miniature golf, a public beach, and a Victorian-style bandstand.

Mt. Major, 5 mi north of Alton Bay on Route 11, has a 2½-mi trail with views of Lake Winnipesaukee. At the top is a four-sided stone shelter built in 1925.

Dining

$$$$ ✕ **Crystal Quail.** The tiny (12-seat) Crystal Quail, inside an 18th-century farmhouse, is worth the drive even if you don't like quail. The prix-fixe menu might include saffron-garlic soup, a house pâté, quenelle-stuffed sole, or duck in crisp potato shreds. ✉ *Pitman Rd., Center Barnstead (12 mi south of Alton Bay),* ☎ *603/269–4151. Reservations essential. No credit cards. BYOB. Closed Mon.–Tues. No lunch.*

Gilford

⑫ *18 mi northwest of Alton Bay, 30 mi northeast of Concord.*

One of the larger public beaches on Lake Winnipesaukee is in Gilford, a resort community. When it was incorporated in 1812, the town asked its oldest resident to name it. A veteran of the Battle of the Guilford Courthouse, in North Carolina, he borrowed that town's name—though apparently he didn't know how to spell it. Quiet and peaceful,

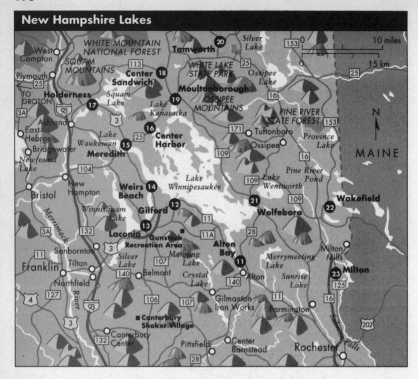

New Hampshire Lakes

Gilford remains decidedly uncommercial. The **New Hampshire Music Festival** (⊠ 88 Belknap Mountain Rd., ☎ 603/524–1000) presents award-winning orchestras from early July to mid-August.

The **Gunstock Recreation Area** has an Olympic-size pool, a children's playground, hiking trails, mountain-bike rentals and trails, horses, paddleboats, and a campground. A major downhill-skiing center (☞ Skiing and Snow Sports, *below*), it once claimed the longest rope tow lift in the country—an advantage that helped local downhill skier and Olympic silver medalist Penny Pitou perfect her craft. ⊠ *Rte. 11A,* ☎ *603/293–4341 or 800/486–7862.*

Ellacoya State Beach, on Route 11, covers just 600 ft along the southwestern shore of Lake Winnipesaukee, with views of the Ossipee and Sandwich mountain ranges.

Lodging

$$–$$$ 🏨 **B. Mae's Resort Inn.** All the rooms in this resort and conference center are large; some are suites with kitchens. Close to Gunstock ski area and within walking distance of Lake Winnipesaukee, B. Mae's is popular with skiers in winter and boaters in summer. ⊠ *Rtes. 11 and 11B, 03246,* ☎ *603/293–7526 or 800/458–3877,* FAX *603/293–4340. 58 rooms, 24 suites. 2 restaurants, bar, 1 indoor and 1 outdoor pool, hot tub, exercise room, recreation room. AE, D, DC, MC, V.*

$–$$$ 🏨 **Gunstock Country Inn.** This country-style resort and motor inn is about a minute's drive from the Gunstock Recreation Area (☞ *above*). The rooms, of various sizes and furnished with American antiques, have views of the mountains and Lake Winnipesaukee. ⊠ *580 Cherry Valley Rd./Rte. 11A, 03246,* ☎ *603/293–2021 or 800/654–0180,* FAX *603/293–2050. 25 rooms. Restaurant, indoor pool, health club. AE, MC, V.*

$ ⚠️ **Gunstock Campground.** The campground at the Gunstock Recreation Area (☞ *above*) has a pool and 300 tent and trailer sites. ✉ *Box 1307, Rte. 11A, Laconia 03247,* ☎ *603/293–4341 or 800/486–7862. AE, D, MC, V.*

Shopping
Pepi Herrmann Crystal (✉ 3 Waterford Pl., ☎ 603/528–1020) sells hand-cut crystal chandeliers and stemware. You can take a tour and watch the artists at work.

Skiing and Snow Sports
GUNSTOCK
High above Lake Winnipesaukee, this all-purpose area that dates from the 1930s attracts some skiers and snowboarders for overnight stays and others for day skiing. Gunstock allows patrons to return lift tickets for a cash refund for any reason—weather, snow conditions, health, equipment problems—within an hour and 15 minutes of purchase. Thrill Hill, a tubing park, has 10 runs, multipassenger tubes, and lift service. ✉ *Rte. 11A, 03246,* ☎ *603/293–4341 or 800/486–7862; mailing address:* ✉ *Box 1307, Laconia 03247.*

Downhill. Clever trail cutting along with grooming and surface sculpting three times daily have made this otherwise pedestrian mountain good for intermediates. That's how most of the 44 trails are rated, with a few more challenging runs and designated sections for slow skiers and learners. Lower Ramrod trail is set up for snowboarding. Gunstock, which has one quad, two triple, and two double chairlifts and two surface tows, has the largest night-skiing facility in New Hampshire, with 15 lighted trails and five lifts in operation.

Cross-country. Gunstock has 50 km (30 mi) of cross-country trails. Fifteen kilometers (9 mi) are for advanced skiers, and there are backcountry trails as well.

Child care. The nursery takes children ages 6 months and up; the ski school teaches the SKIwee system to children from age 3 to 12.

Laconia

⑬ *4 mi southwest of Gilford, 26 mi north of Concord.*

When the railroad reached Laconia—then called Meredith Bridge—in 1848, the formerly sleepy community became a manufacturing and trading center. Laconia borders both Winnisquam and Winnipesaukee lakes and is easily accessible from I–93, making it the commercial hub of the Lakes Region. The town's **Belknap Mill** (✉ Mill Plaza, ☎ 603/524–8813), the oldest unaltered, brick-built textile mill in the United States (1823), contains a knitting museum devoted to the textile industry and a year-round cultural center that sponsors concerts, exhibits, a lecture series, and workshops. Area beaches include **Bartlett Beach** (✉ Winnisquam Ave.) and **Opechee Park** (✉ N. Main St.).

Dining and Lodging
$$–$$$ ✕ **Le Chalet Rouge.** This yellow house with a modestly decorated dining room recalls a country-French bistro. To start, try the house pâté, escargots, or steamed mussels. The steak au poivre is tender and well spiced, and the duckling is prepared with seasonal sauces: rhubarb in spring, raspberry in summer, orange in fall, creamy mustard in winter. ✉ *385 W. Main St., Tilton (10 mi west of Laconia),* ☎ *603/286–4035. Reservations essential. MC, V.*

$ ✕🏠 **Hickory Stick Farm.** The 200-year-old Cape-style inn has two
★ large, old-fashioned rooms with cannonball beds, stenciled wallpaper, and lace curtains. Breakfast, served on the sunporch, might include

French toast stuffed with peaches and cream cheese. Roast duckling with herb stuffing and orange-sherry sauce is the specialty of the restaurant ($$–$$$; no lunch). Also consider the prime rib, rack of lamb, or vegetarian lasagna. ⊠ *60 Bean Hill Rd., Belmont (4 mi south of Laconia) 03220,* ☎ *603/524–3333. 2 rooms. Restaurant. Full breakfast. AE, D, MC, V. Closed Mon. Call for winter restaurant hrs.*

$$ 🔲 **Ferry Point House.** Built in the 1800s as a summer retreat for the Pillsbury family of baking fame, this red Victorian farmhouse has superb views of Lake Winnisquam. White wicker furniture and hanging baskets of flowers decorate the 60-ft veranda, and the gazebo by the water's edge may make you want to spend your whole vacation lounging and listening for loons. A paddleboat and a rowboat await those eager to get in the water. The pretty rooms have Oriental-style rugs and Victorian furniture. ⊠ *100 Lower Bay Rd., Sanbornton 03269,* ☎ *603/524–0087,* 𝔽𝔸𝕏 *603/524–0959. 6 rooms. Beach, boating, fishing. Full breakfast. No credit cards. Closed Nov.–Apr.*

Shopping

The **Belknap Mall** (⊠ U.S. 3, ☎ 603/524–5651) has boutiques, crafts stores, and a New Hampshire state liquor store. The **Bending Birch** (⊠ 569 Main St., ☎ 603/524–7589) sells local crafts, including Laconia pottery, birdhouses made in Meredith, and lap robes in New Hampshire's official tartan. The 54 stores at the **Lakes Region Factory Stores** (⊠ 120 Laconia Rd., Tilton, ☎ 603/286–7880) center include Brooks Brothers, Eddie Bauer, and Black & Decker.

OFF THE
BEATEN PATH

CANTERBURY SHAKER VILLAGE – This outdoor museum and National Historic Landmark provides insight into the world of the Shakers. A religious community founded in 1792, the Canterbury village flourished in the 1800s and practiced equality of the sexes and races, common ownership, celibacy, and pacifism. Members lived here until 1992. Shakers invented household items such as the clothespin and the flat broom and were known for the simplicity and integrity of their designs, especially furniture. Ninety-minute tours pass through some of the 694-acre property's 24 restored buildings, and crafts demonstrations take place daily. The Creamery Restaurant serves lunch daily and candlelight dinners on Friday and Saturday. A large shop sells fine Shaker reproductions. ⊠ *288 Shaker Rd., 7 mi from Exit 18 off I–93, Canterbury,* ☎ *603/783–9511 or 800/982–9511.* 🎫 *$10 for 2 consecutive days.* ☉ *May–Oct., daily 10–5; Apr. and Nov.–Dec., weekends 10–5; Fri.–Sat. 6:45 dinner and tour (reservations essential).*

Weirs Beach

⓮ *7½ mi north of Laconia, 33½ mi north of Concord.*

Weirs Beach is Lake Winnipesaukee's center for arcade activity. Anyone who loves souvenir shops, fireworks, water slides, and hordes of children will feel right at home. Several cruise boats (☞ Guided Tours *in* Lakes Region A to Z, *below*) depart from the town dock.

The period cars of the **Winnipesaukee Scenic Railroad** carry passengers along the lake's shore on one- or two-hour rides; boarding is at Weirs Beach or Meredith. ⊠ *U.S. 3, Meredith,* ☎ *603/279–5253 or 603/745–2135.* 🎫 *1-hr trip $7.50, 2-hr trip $8.50.* ☉ *July–mid-Sept., daily; weekends only Memorial Day–late June and late Sept.–mid-Oct. Call for hrs and for special Santa trains in Dec.*

☾ A giant **Water Slide** (⊠ U.S. 3, ☎ 603/366–5161) overlooks the lake. For an aquatic experience, visit **Surf Coaster** (⊠ U.S. 3, ☎ 603/366–

Finally, a travel companion that doesn't snore on the plane or eat all your peanuts.

MCI WORLDCOM   WORLDPHONE®

123 456 7891 2345
J.D. SMITH

When traveling, your MCI WorldCom Card is the best way to keep in touch. Our operators speak your language, so they'll be able to connect you back home—no matter where your travels take you. Plus, your MCI WorldCom Card is easy to use, and even earns you frequent flyer miles every time you use it. When you add in our great rates, you get something even more valuable: peace-of-mind. So go ahead. Travel the world. MCI WorldCom just brought it a whole lot closer.

You can even sign up today at www.mci.com/worldphone or ask your operator to make a collect call to 1-410-314-2938.

EASY TO CALL WORLDWIDE

1 Just dial the WorldPhone access number of the country you're calling from.
2 Dial or give the operator your MCI WorldCom Card number.
3 Dial or give the number you're calling.

Australia ✦	
To call using OPTUS	1-800-551-111
To call using TELSTRA	1-800-881-100
Bahamas/Bermuda	1-800-888-8000
British Virgin Islands	1-800-888-8000
Costa Rica ✦	0-800-012-2222
Denmark	8001-0022
Norway ✦	800 -19912
India	000-127
For collect access	000-126
United States/Canada	1-800-888-8000

For your complete WorldPhone calling guide, dial the WorldPhone access number for the country you're in and ask the operator for Customer Service. In the U.S. call 1-800-431-5402.

✦ Public phones may require deposit of coin or phone card for dial tone.

EARN FREQUENT FLYER MILES

American Airlines
A'Advantage®

Continental Airlines
OnePass

▲ **Delta Air Lines**
SkyMiles

/// **MILEAGE PLUS**®
United Airlines

US AIRWAYS
DIVIDEND MILES

MCI WorldCom, its logo and the names of the products referred to herein are proprietary marks of MCI WorldCom, Inc. All airline names and logos are proprietary marks of the respective airlines. All airline program rules and conditions apply.

MCI WORLDCOM

Fodor's

Distinctive guides packed with up-to-date expert advice and smart choices for every type of traveler.

Fodor's. For the world of ways you travel.

4991), which has seven slides, a wave pool, and a large area for young children. Day or night you can work your way through the miniature golf course, 20 lanes of bowling, and more than 500 games at **Funspot** (⊠ Rte. 11B, at U.S. 3, ☎ 603/366–4377).

Nightlife and the Arts

Moonlight dinner-and-dance cruises take place on the **M/S Mount Washington** (☎ 603/366–5531 or 888/843–6686) from Tuesday to Saturday, with two bands and a different menu each night.

Outdoor Activities and Sports

Thurston's Marina (⊠ U.S. 3 at the bridge, ☎ 603/366–4811 or 800/ 834–4812) rents pontoon boats, power boats, and personal watercraft.

Meredith

⓯ *6 mi north of Weirs Beach, 42 mi north of Concord.*

Meredith, on U.S. 3 at the western end of Lake Winnipesaukee, has a fine collection of crafts shops and art galleries. An information center is across from the Town Docks. At **Annalee's Doll Museum,** you can view a collection of the famous poseable felt dolls and learn about the woman who created them. Annalee Davis Thorndike began making the dolls after her graduation from high school in 1933. Her dolls caught on with collectors, and the Meredith Company has grown into an empire. ⊠ *Hemlock Dr. off Rte. 104,* ☎ *603/279–3333.* ☑ *Free.* ☺ *Memorial Day–Labor Day, call for hours.*

Wellington State Beach (⊠ Off Rte. 3A, Bristol, 12 mi west of Meredith), on the western shore of Newfound Lake, is one of the most beautiful area beaches. You can swim or picnic along the ½-mi shoreline or take the scenic walking trail.

Lodging

$$ ⌂ **Nutmeg Inn.** A sea captain dismantled his ship to provide the timber for this 1763 Cape-style house. Although the house has been updated over the years, the wide-board floors, wall paneling, and five fireplaces are original. All the rooms, two of which have fireplaces, are named after spices and are decorated accordingly. The no-smoking inn is on a rural side street off Route 104, the main link between I–93 and Lake Winnipesaukee. ⊠ *80 Pease Rd., 03253,* ☎ *603/279–8811,* ℻ *603/279–7703. 8 rooms. Pool, exercise room, billiards. Full breakfast. MC, V. Closed Nov., Mar.–Apr., and weekdays Dec.–Feb.*

$ ⚠ **Clearwater Campground.** This wooded tent and RV campground on Lake Pemigewasset has 153 shady sites, a large sandy beach, a recreation building, a playground, basketball and volleyball courts, and boat rentals and slips. ⊠ *26 Campground Rd., off Rte. 104, 03253,* ☎ *603/ 279–7761. Closed mid-Oct.–mid-May.*

$ ⚠ **Meredith Woods.** An indoor heated pool, a hot tub, and a game room are among the amenities at this year-round campground, whose patrons have full use of the waterfront facilities across the road at Clearwater Campground (☞ *above*). ⊠ *26 Campground Rd./Rte. 104, 03253,* ☎ *603/279–5449 or 800/848–0328. 101 sites for RVs and tents.*

Nightlife and the Arts

The **Lakes Region Summer Theatre** (⊠ Interlakes Auditorium, Rte. 25, ☎ 603/279–9933) presents Broadway musicals.

Outdoor Activities and Sports

BOATING

Meredith Marina and Boating Center (⊠ Bay Shore Dr., ☎ 603/279– 7921) rents power boats. **Wild Meadow Canoes & Kayaks** (⊠ Rte. 25

between Center Harbor and Meredith, ☎ 603/253–7536 or 800/427–7536) rents canoes and kayaks.

GOLF

Waukewan Golf Course (⊠ Off U.S. 3 and Rte. 25, ☎ 603/279–6661) is an 18-hole, par-71 course. The greens fee ranges from $22 to $28; an optional cart costs $22.

Shopping

About 170 dealers operate out of the three-floor **Burlwood Antique Center** (⊠ U.S. 3, ☎ 603/279–6387), which is open daily from May to October. The **Meredith League of New Hampshire Craftsmen** (⊠ U.S. 3, ½ mi north of Rte. 104, ☎ 603/279–7920) sells the works of area artisans. **Mill Falls Marketplace** (⊠ U.S. 3, ☎ 603/279–7006), on the bay in Meredith, contains nearly two dozen shops with clothing, gifts, and books. The **Old Print Barn** (⊠ Winona Rd.; look for LANE on the mailbox, ☎ 603/279–6479), the largest print gallery in northern New England, carries rare prints from around the world.

Center Harbor

⑯ *6 mi northeast of Meredith, 45 mi northwest of Concord.*

In the middle of three bays at the northern end of Winnipesaukee, the town of Center Harbor also borders Lakes Squam, Waukewan, and Winona. This prime location makes it popular in summer, especially with boaters who spend summer weekends on the water.

Dining and Lodging

$$–$$$ ✕▥ **Red Hill Inn.** The large bay window in the common room of this rambling inn overlooks Squam Lake. Rooms are furnished with Victorian pieces and country furniture. Twenty rooms have fireplaces, some have claw-foot tubs, and 10 have two-person whirlpool baths. For dinner, try the Vermont goat cheese bruschetta, followed by the rack of lamb encrusted in fresh rosemary and garlic. ⊠ *R.D. 1, Box 99M, Rte. 25B, 03226,* ☎ *603/279–7001 or 800/573–3445,* ℻ *603/279–7003. 18 rooms, 8 suites. Restaurant, pub, pool, outdoor hot tub, cross-country skiing. Full breakfast. AE, D, DC, MC, V.*

Outdoor Activities and Sports

Red Hill, a hiking trail on Bean Road off Route 25, northeast of Center Harbor, really does turn red in autumn. The reward at the end of the trail in any season is a view of Squam Lake and the mountains.

Shopping

Keepsake Quilting & Country Pleasures (⊠ Senter's Marketplace, Rte. 25B, ☎ 603/253–4026), reputedly America's largest quilt shop, contains 5,000 bolts of fabric, hundreds of quilting books, and countless supplies.

Holderness

⑰ *15 mi northwest of Center Harbor, 10 mi north of Meredith, 44 mi north of Concord.*

Routes 25B and 25 lead to the town of Holderness, perched between Squam and Little Squam lakes. *On Golden Pond,* starring Katharine Hepburn and Henry Fonda, was filmed on Squam, whose quiet beauty attracts nature lovers.

☾ The several trails at the 200-acre **Science Center of New Hampshire** include a ¾-mi path that passes by black bears, bobcats, otters, and other native wildlife in trailside enclosures. Educational events at the center include the "Up Close to Animals" series in July and August, at which you can study species like the red-shouldered hawk. The Children's Activity Center has interactive exhibits. ✉ *Rtes. 113 and 25,* ☎ *603/968–7194.* 🎫 *$8.* ⊙ *May–Oct., daily 9:30–4:30.*

Dining and Lodging

$$$$ ✕🏨 **Manor on Golden Pond.** Built in 1903, this dignified inn with a
★ British-manor ambience has well-groomed grounds and a private dock with canoes, paddle boats, and a boathouse. You can stay in the main inn, the cottages, or, during summer and fall, the carriage house. Sixteen rooms have wood-burning fireplaces; eight have two-person whirlpool baths. Five-course prix-fixe dinners (reservations required) may include rack of lamb, filet mignon, and apple pie. The inn is no-smoking. ✉ *U.S. 3 and Shepard Hill Rd., 03245,* ☎ *603/968–3348 or 800/ 545–2141,* 🖷 *603/968–2116. 21 rooms, 4 cottages. Restaurant, pub, pool, tennis court, beach, boating. Full breakfast. AE, MC, V.*

$$–$$$ 🏨 **Glynn House Inn.** Innkeepers Karol and Betsy Paterman restored the elegance of this three-story 1890s Queen Anne–style home but added modern touches like whirlpool baths. The two-level honeymoon suite, with a large whirlpool tub and fireplace downstairs and a four-poster bed and skylights above, is a favorite. Breakfast, served in the oval dining room, always includes fresh-baked strudel. The inn is no-smoking. ✉ *Box 719, 43 Highland St., Ashland 03217,* ☎ *603/968–3775 or 800/637–9599,* 🖷 *603/968–3129. 9 rooms, 4 suites. In-room VCRs. Full breakfast. MC, V.*

$$ 🏨 **Inn on Golden Pond.** This informal country home, built in 1879 and set on 50 wooded acres, is just across the road from Squam Lake. Rooms have a traditional country decor of hardwood floors, braided rugs, easy chairs, and calico-print bedspreads and curtains; the quietest rooms are in the rear on the third floor. The homemade jam at breakfast is made from rhubarb grown on the property. ✉ *Box 680, U.S. 3, 03245,* ☎ *603/968–7269,* 🖷 *603/968–9226. 7 rooms, 1 suite. Hiking. Full breakfast. AE, MC, V.*

$–$$ ⚠ **Yogi Bear's Jellystone Park.** Geared toward families, this camping resort has wooded, open riverfront sites as well as basic and deluxe cabins. It also has a pool, a hot tub, planned activities, miniature golf, a basketball court, river swimming, canoe and kayak rentals, and daily movies. Among the many special events are country-western-jamboree weekends and Yogi Olympics. ✉ *R.R. 1, Box 396, Rte. 132N, Ashland 03217,* ☎ *603/968–9000. 261 sites, 33 cabins.*

$ ⚠ **Squam Lakes Camp Resort and Marina.** The 119 sites at this campground have full hookups, and there's cable TV, a heated pool, a hot tub, lake frontage, a playground, restaurant, and hiking trails. ✉ *R.F.D. 1, Box 42, U.S. 3, Ashland 03217,* ☎ *603/968–7227.*

Outdoor Activities and Sports

White Mountain Country Club (✉ N. Ashland Rd., Ashland, ☎ 603/ 536–2227) has an 18-hole, par-71 golf course. The greens fee ranges from $26 to $32; an optional cart costs $22.

Center Sandwich

★ ⑱ *12 mi northeast of Holderness, 56 mi northeast of Concord.*

With Squam Lake to the west and the Sandwich Mountains to the north, Center Sandwich claims one of the prettiest settings of any town in the Lakes Region. So appealing are the town and its views that John Greenleaf Whittier used the Bearcamp River as the inspiration for his poem "Sunset on the Bearcamp." The town attracts artisans—crafts shops abound. The village center holds charming 18th- and 19th-century buildings.

The **Historical Society Museum** traces the history of Center Sandwich largely through the faces of its inhabitants. Works by mid-19th-century portraitist and town son Albert Gallatin Hoit hang alongside a local photographer's exhibit portraying the town's mothers and daughters. The museum houses a replica country store and furniture and items belonging to or made by people from Center Sandwich. ⊠ *4 Maple St.,* ☏ *603/284–6269.* ⊡ *Free.* ⊙ *June–Sept., Tues.–Sat. 11–5.*

Dining

$–$$$ ⊡ **Corner House Inn.** The restaurant, in a converted barn decorated with local arts and crafts, serves standard American fare. Before you get to the white-chocolate cheesecake with key-lime filling, try the chef's lobster-and-mushroom bisque or tasty crab cakes. On Thursday, storytellers perform in the glow of the woodstove. ⊠ *Rtes. 109 and 113,* ☏ *603/284–6219. AE, D, MC, V. Closed Mon. Nov.–May.*

Shopping

Ayottes' Designery (⊠ Rte. 113, ☏ 603/284–6915), open from Tuesday to Saturday between 10 and 5, sells weaving supplies, hand-dyed yarns, rugs, wall hangings, and place mats. **Sandwich Home Industries** (⊠ Rte. 109, ☏ 603/284–6831) presents crafts demonstrations in July and August and sells home furnishings and accessories from mid-May to October.

Moultonborough

⑲ *5 mi south of Center Sandwich, 48 mi northeast of Concord.*

Moultonborough claims 6½ mi of shoreline on Lake Kanasatka, a large chunk of Lake Winnipesaukee, and even a small piece of Squam. The highly browsable store, which is part of the **Old Country Store and Museum** (⊠ Moultonborough Corner, ☏ 603/476–5750), has been selling maple products, aged cheeses, penny candy, and other items since 1781. Much of the equipment used in the store is antique, and the museum displays antique farming and forging tools.

Construction of the **Castle in the Clouds,** the town's best-known attraction, began in 1911 and continued for three years. The odd, elaborate stone mansion, which was built without nails, has 16 rooms, eight bathrooms, and doors made of lead. Owner Thomas Gustave Plant spent $7 million, the bulk of his fortune, on this project and died penniless in 1946. A tour includes the mansion and the Castle Springs Microbrewery on the property. ⊠ *Rte. 171,* ☏ *603/476–2352 or 800/729–2468.* ⊡ *$10 with tour, $4 without tour.* ⊙ *Mid-June–mid-Oct., daily 9–5; mid-May–mid-June, weekends 10–4.*

The **Loon Center** at the **Frederick and Paula Anna Markus Wildlife Sanctuary** is the headquarters of the Loon Preservation Committee, an Audubon Society project. The loon, one of New Hampshire's most popular birds, is threatened by lake traffic, poor water quality, and habitat loss. The center presents changing exhibits about the black-and-white birds, whose calls haunt New Hampshire lakes. Two nature trails wind through the 200-acre property; vantage points on the Loon Nest Trail overlook the spot resident loons sometimes occupy in June. ⊠ *Lees Mills Rd. (follow signs from Rte. 25 to Blake Rd. to Lees Mills Rd.),* ☏ *603/476–5666.* ⊡ *Free.* ⊙ *July 4–Columbus Day, daily 9–5; rest of yr, Mon.–Sat. 9–5.*

Dining

$$–$$$ ✕ **The Woodshed.** Farm implements and antiques hang on the walls of this former barn, built in 1860. Make your way through the raw bar or try the New England section of the menu, which includes clam chowder, tender sea scallops, and Indian pudding for dessert. Another favorite is the Denver chocolate pudding, a dense pudding-cake served

warm with vanilla ice cream. ⊠ *Lee's Mill Rd.,* ☎ *603/476–2311. AE, D, DC, MC, V. Closed Mon.*

Tamworth

㉟ *11 mi northeast of Moultonborough, 59 mi northeast of Concord.*

President Grover Cleveland summered here. His son, Francis, returned to stay and founded the Barnstormers Theater. Tamworth has a clutch of villages within its borders. At one of them—Chocorua—the view through the birches of Chocorua Lake has been so often photographed that you may feel as if you've been here before. The tiny South Tamworth post office looks like a children's playhouse.

Dining and Lodging

$$$ ✕⊞ **Tamworth Inn.** Every room at this inn 1½ mi from Hemenway State
★ Forest has 19th-century American pieces and handmade quilts. Among the menu highlights in the dining room (closed on Sunday and Monday in summer, and from Sunday to Tuesday in winter) are the lobster-stuffed ravioli and the grilled pork loin chop with pomegranate and pear demi-glace. The profiterole Tamworth is big enough for two. Sunday brunch is a summer favorite. ⊠ *Main St., 03886,* ☎ *603/323–7721 or 800/642–7352,* 𝖥𝖠𝖷 *603/323–2026. 16 rooms. Restaurant, pub, pool. Full breakfast; MAP available. MC, V.*

Nightlife and the Arts

The **Arts Council of Tamworth** (☎ 603/323–8104) produces concerts—soloists, string quartets, revues, children's programs—from September to June and an arts show on the last weekend in July. **Barnstormers** (⊠ Main St., ☎ 603/323–8500), New Hampshire's oldest professional theater, performs in July and August. The box office opens in June; before June, call the Tamworth Inn (☞ *above*) for information.

Outdoor Activities and Sports

The 72-acre stand of native pitch pine at **White Lake State Park** (⊠ Rte. 16, ☎ 603/323–7350) is a National Natural Landmark. The park has hiking trails, a sandy beach, trout fishing, canoe rentals, two separate camping areas, a picnic area, and swimming.

Shopping

The many theme rooms—a Christmas room, a bride's room, a children's room, among them—at the **Country Handcrafters & Chocorua Dam Ice Cream Shop** (⊠ Rte. 16, Chocorua, ☎ 603/323–8745) contain handcrafted items. When you're done shopping, try the ice cream, coffee, or tea and scones.

En Route Route 16 between Ossipee and West Ossipee passes Lake Ossipee, known for fine fishing and swimming. Among these hamlets you'll find several antiques shops and galleries. Local craftspeople create much of the jewelry, turned wooden bowls, pewter goblets, and glassware sold at **Tramway Artisans** (⊠ Rte. 16, West Ossipee, ☎ 603/539–5700).

Wolfeboro

㉑ *28 mi south of Tamworth, 41 mi northwest of Portsmouth.*

Wolfeboro has been a resort since Royal Governor John Wentworth built his summer home on the shores of Lake Wentworth in 1763. The town borders both that lake and Lake Winnipesaukee, but the modern center of town is on the shore of Winnipesaukee. The Chamber of Commerce estimates that the population increases tenfold each June, as throngs of visitors descend upon the lake. Unlike the atmosphere in

Weirs Beach, however, the tone here is relaxed and sedate, comfortable for all ages. Wolfeboro has managed to control development and maintain a small-town feel while still offering plenty of shopping and entertainment options.

Uniforms, vehicles, and other artifacts at the **Wright Museum** illustrate the contributions of those on the home front to America's World War II effort. ⊠ *77 Center St.,* ☎ *603/569–1212.* ⊡ *$5.* ☉ *May–Oct., daily 10–4; Nov.–Apr., weekends 10–4.*

The artisans at the **Hampshire Pewter Company** (⊠ 43 Mill St., ☎ 603/ 569–4944 or 800/639–7704) use 17th-century techniques to make pewter tableware and accessories. Their Christmas ornaments are popular with collectors. Free tours are conducted at 10, 11, 1, 2, and 3 between Memorial Day and Labor Day and at 10, 11, 2, and 3 from Labor Day to Columbus Day. The gift shops on Mill Street and Main Street are open year-round.

Wentworth State Beach (⊠ Rte. 109, ☎ 603/569–3699) has good swimming and picnicking areas and a bathhouse.

Dining and Lodging

$$–$$$ ✕ **The Bittersweet.** This converted barn with an eclectic display of old quilts, pottery, sheet music, and china has the feel of a cozy crafts shop, but it's really a restaurant that locals love for the nightly specials that range from a popular lobster pie to steak Diane. The upper level has antique tables and chairs and dining by candlelight. The lower-level lounge, decorated with Victorian wicker furniture, serves lighter fare. ⊠ *Rte. 28,* ☎ *603/569–3636. AE, D, MC, V.*

$$ ✕🔲 **Wolfeboro Inn.** Built 200 years ago, this white clapboard house has 19th- and 20th-century additions with views of the waterfront of Wolfeboro Bay. The rooms have polished cherry and pine furnishings, armoires (to hide the TVs), stenciled borders, and country quilts. More than 70 brands of beer are available at Wolfe's Tavern, where fireplaces make cool evenings cozy. The main dining room ($$–$$$) serves fresh seafood and a popular slow-roasted prime rib. ⊠ *Box 1270, 90 N. Main St., 03894,* ☎ *603/569–3016 or 800/451–2389,* ℻ *603/569– 5375. 41 rooms, 3 suites, 1 1-bedroom apartment. 2 restaurants, bar, beach, boating, meeting rooms. Continental breakfast. AE, MC, V.*

Outdoor Activities and Sports

BOATING

Winnipesaukee Kayak Company (⊠ 17 Bay St., ☎ 603/569–9926) gives kayak lessons and leads group excursions on the lake.

GOLF

Kingswood Golf Course (⊠ Rte. 28, ☎ 603/569–3569) has an 18-hole, par-72 course. The greens fee ranges from $35 to $48 and in the summer includes an optional cart. At other times, a cart costs $25.

HIKING

A few miles north of town on Route 109 is the trailhead to **Abenaki Tower.** A short (¼-mi) hike to the 100-ft post-and-beam tower, followed by a more rigorous climb to the top, rewards you with a vast view of Lake Winnipesaukee and the Ossipee mountain range.

WATER SPORTS

Look for water-skiing regulations at every marina. Scuba divers can explore a 130-ft-long cruise ship that sank in 30 ft of water off Glendale in 1895. **Dive Winnipesaukee Corp.** (⊠ 4 N. Main St., ☎ 603/569–2120) runs charters out to this and other wrecks and offers rentals, repairs, scuba sales, and lessons in waterskiing and windsurfing.

Wakefield

㉒ *18 mi east of Wolfeboro, 26 mi southeast of Tamworth, 40 mi north of Portsmouth.*

East of Winnipesaukee, several laid-back villages combine to form Wakefield, a town with 10 lakes. Wakefield's registered historic district, on Wakefield Road near the Maine border, has a church, houses, and an inn that look just as they did in the 18th century.

☺ The **Museum of Childhood** displays a one-room schoolhouse, a child's room and a kitchen from 1890, model trains, antique sleds, teddy bears, 3,000 dolls, and 44 furnished dollhouses. Special events are scheduled for most Fridays. ⊠ *Wakefield Corner, off Rte. 16,* ☎ *603/522–8073.* ☜ *$3.* ☉ *Memorial Day–Labor Day, Mon. and Wed.–Sat. 11–4, Sun. 1–4.*

Lodging

$–$$ 🏨 **Wakefield Inn.** The restoration of this 1804 stagecoach inn, a high-
★ light of Wakefield's historic district, has been handled with an eye for detail. The dining-room windows retain the original panes and shutters, but the centerpiece of the building is the freestanding spiral staircase, which rises three stories. The large rooms, named for famous guests or past owners, have wide-board pine floors, big sofas, and handmade quilts. The 2-mi Wakefield Heritage Trail runs from the inn to the center of town. In late fall and early spring, you can learn how to quilt as part of the weekend Quilting Package. ⊠ *2723 Wakefield Rd., 03872,* ☎ *603/522–8272 or 800/245–0841. 7 rooms. Full breakfast. MC, V.*

Milton

㉓ *15½ mi south of Wakefield, 25 mi north of Portsmouth.*

Milton stretches alongside the Salmon Falls River, Town House Pond, Milton Pond, and Northeast Pond, all of which flow together to create a seemingly endless body of water.

The **New Hampshire Farm Museum** houses more than 60,000 artifacts recalling New Hampshire farm life from 1700 to the early 1900s. Take a guided tour through the Jones Farmhouse and then explore the Grand Barn—filled with vehicles, farm implements, and tools—the gardens, and the nature trails at your leisure. Special events demonstrating farm-related crafts take place throughout the season. ⊠ *Rte. 125 (White Mountain Hwy.),* ☎ *603/652–7840.* ☜ *$5.* ☉ *Mid-May–mid-Oct., Wed.–Sun. 10–4.*

Lakes Region A to Z

Arriving and Departing

BY BUS
Concord Trailways (☎ 800/639–3317) stops daily in Tilton, Laconia, Meredith, Center Harbor, Moultonborough, and Conway.

BY CAR
Most people driving into this region arrive via I–93 to U.S. 3 in the west or by the Spaulding Turnpike (Route 16) to Route 11 in the east.

BY PLANE
Manchester Airport (☞ Arriving and Departing *in* New Hampshire A to Z, *below*) is about an hour's drive from the Lakes Region.

Getting Around

BY BUS

See Arriving and Departing, *above.*

BY CAR

On the western side of the Lakes Region, I–93 is the principal north–south artery. Exit 20 leads to U.S. 3 and Route 11 and the southwestern side of Lake Winnipesaukee. Take Exit 23 to Route 104 to Route 25 and the northwestern corner of the region. From the coast, the Spaulding Turnpike (Route 16) heads to the White Mountains, with roads leading to the lakeside towns.

BY PLANE

Moultonborough Airport (✉ Rte. 25, Moultonborough, ☎ 603/476–8801) operates chartered flights and tours.

Contacts and Resources

BOATING

The **Lakes Region Association** (☎ 603/744–8664 or 800/925–2537) provides boating advice.

EMERGENCIES

Lakes Region General Hospital (✉ 80 Highland St., Laconia, ☎ 603/524–3211).

FISHING

The **New Hampshire Fish and Game** office (☎ 603/744–5470) has information about fishing and licenses.

GUIDED TOURS

The 230-ft **M/S Mount Washington** (☎ 603/366–5531) makes 2½-hour scenic cruises of Lake Winnipesaukee between mid-May and mid-October from Weirs Beach, Wolfeboro, Alton Bay, and Center Harbor. Evening cruises include live music and a buffet dinner.

The **M/V Sophie C.** (☎ 603/366–2628) has been the area's floating post office for more than a century. The boat departs Weirs Beach with mail and passengers daily except Sunday from mid-June until the Saturday following Labor Day; call for stops.

Sky Bright (✉ Laconia Airport, Rte. 11, ☎ 603/528–6818) operates airplane and helicopter tours and instruction on aerial photography.

From Memorial Day to late October, **Golden Pond Boat Tour** (✉ Manor on Golden Pond, U.S. 3, Holderness, ☎ 603/279–4405) visits filming sites of the movie *On Golden Pond* on Squam Lake, aboard the *Lady of the Manor,* a 28-ft pontoon craft.

From May to late October, **Squam Lake Tours** (☎ 603/968–7577) takes up to 48 passengers on a two-hour pontoon tour of "Golden Pond." The company also operates guided fishing trips and private charters.

HIKING

Contact the Alexandria headquarters of the **Appalachian Mountain Club** (☎ 603/744–8011) or the **Laconia Office of the U.S. Forest Service** (☎ 603/528–8721) for trail advice and information.

VISITOR INFORMATION

Greater Laconia Chamber of Commerce (✉ 11 Veterans Sq., Laconia 03246-3485, ☎ 603/524–5531 or 800/531–2347). **Lakes Region Association** (✉ Box 589, Center Harbor 03226, ☎ 603/253–8555 or 800/925–2537). **Squam Lakes Area Chamber of Commerce** (✉ Box 65, Ashland 03217, ☎ 603/968–4494). **Wolfeboro Chamber of Commerce** (✉ Box 547-WT7, Railroad Ave., Wolfeboro 03894, ☎ 603/569–2200 or 800/516–5324).

THE WHITE MOUNTAINS

Sailors approaching East Coast harbors frequently mistake the pale peaks of the White Mountains—the highest range in the northeastern United States—for clouds. It was 1642 when explorer Darby Field could no longer contain his curiosity about one mountain in particular. He set off from his Exeter homestead and became the first man to climb what would eventually be called Mt. Washington, the king of the Presidential Range. More than a mile high, Mt. Washington must have presented Field with formidable obstacles—its peak claims the highest wind velocity ever recorded and it may see snow every month of the year.

More than 350 years after Field's climb, curiosity about the mountains has not abated. People come by the tens of thousands to hike and climb in spring and summer, to photograph the vistas and the vibrant foliage in autumn, and to ski in winter. In this four-season vacation hub, many resorts (some of which have been in business since the mid-1800s) are destinations in themselves, with golf, tennis, swimming, hiking, cross-country skiing, and renowned restaurants.

Roughly 770,000 acres of forested mountains, valleys, and notches (deep mountain passes) in the White Mountains make up the White Mountain National Forest. Long popular with hikers, campers, and skiers, and easily accessible to Bostonians and New Yorkers, it is one of the most heavily used for recreation of the nation's protected forests. The forest includes the Presidential Range of the White Mountains: These peaks, like Mt. Washington, are all named after early presidents. Notorious for its foul weather, Mt. Washington is, nonetheless, a favorite with hikers. An auto road and a railway also lead to the top. The mountain scenery of Franconia Notch, Crawford Notch, and Pinkham Notch also fall within the forest's boundaries. Crawford and Franconia Notches are doubly protected since they are state parks as well.

This section begins in Waterville Valley, off I–93; continues to Lincoln, across the Kancamagus Highway to North Conway; and circles north on Route 16 and U.S. 302 back to the northern reaches of I–93. There is some backtracking involved because of the mountains.

Waterville Valley

24 *63 mi north of Concord.*

In 1835, visitors began arriving in Waterville Valley, a 10-mi-long cul-de-sac cut by one of New England's Mad Rivers and circled by mountains. They have come in increasing numbers ever since. First a summer resort, then more of a ski area, and now a year-round resort, Waterville Valley retains a small-town feel. There are inns, lodges, and condominiums; restaurants, cafés, and taverns; shops, conference facilities, a grocery store, and a post office. Hiking and mountain biking are the popular summer sports.

In winter, those who don't ski can ice-skate, snowboard, or snowshoe, or amuse themselves in the **White Mountain Athletic Club** (⊠ Rte. 49, ☎ 603/236–8303), a fitness center that has tennis, racquetball, and squash courts; a 25-meter indoor pool, a jogging track, exercise equipment, whirlpools, saunas, steam rooms, and a games room. The club is open to guests at many area lodgings.

Dining and Lodging

$–$$ ✕ **Chile Peppers.** Southwest-inspired Chile Peppers caters to skiers with fajitas, tacos, enchiladas, and other Tex-Mex staples. The food here may not be authentic Mexican, but it's well priced and filling. If

The White Mountains

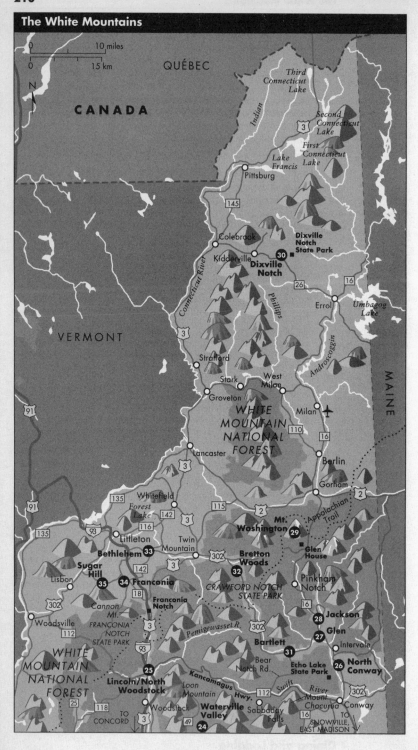

0 | 10 miles
0 | 15 km

N

QUÉBEC

CANADA

Third Connecticut Lake

[3]

Second Connecticut Lake

Lake Francis

First Connecticut Lake

Pittsburg

[145]

Indian

Colebrook

Dixville Notch State Park

Kidderville

Dixville Notch (30)

[26]

[16]

Phillips

Errol

Umbagog Lake

VERMONT

[3]

Connecticut River

Strafford

Stark

Groveton

West Milan

WHITE MOUNTAIN NATIONAL FOREST

Milan

Androscoggin

MAINE

[91]

Lancaster

[110]

[16]

Berlin

[3]

Whitefield

[135]

Forest Lake

[142] [3]

[115]

[2]

Gorham

Appalachian Trail

[2]

[91]

[135]

[93]

Littleton

[116]

Twin Mountain

Mt. Washington (29)

Bethlehem (33)

Sugar Hill (35)

[142]

Franconia (34)

[18]

[302]

Bretton Woods (32)

Glen House

Pinkham Notch

Lisbon

Cannon Mt.

FRANCONIA NOTCH STATE PARK

Franconia Notch

CRAWFORD NOTCH STATE PARK

[16]

Jackson (28)

Glen (27)

[302]

[112]

Woodsville

[3]

[93]

Pemigewasset R.

[302]

Bartlett

Intervale

North Conway (26)

WHITE MOUNTAIN NATIONAL FOREST

[25]

[118]

Lincoln/North Woodstock (25)

Bear Notch Rd.

Echo Lake State Park (31)

Kancamagus

Loon Mountain

Waterville Valley (24)

Hwy. [112]

Swift

Sabbaday Falls

[16]

River Mount Chocorua

Conway

[302]

TO CONCORD

[3]

Woodstock

[49]

TO SNOWVILLE, EAST MADISON

you're solely into Tex, the lineup includes ribs, steak, seafood, and chicken. ⊠ *Town Square,* ☎ *603/236–4646. AE, DC, MC, V.*

$$–$$$$ 🏨 **Golden Eagle Lodge.** Waterville's premier condominium property recalls the grand hotels of an earlier era. The full-service complex, which opened in 1989, has a two-story lobby and a very capable front-desk staff. Guests have access to the White Mountain Athletic Club (☞ *above*). ⊠ *Snow's Brook Rd., 03215,* ☎ *603/236–4600 or 888/703–2453,* ℻ *603/236–4947. 139 suites. Kitchenettes, indoor pool, sauna, recreation room. AE, D, DC, MC, V.*

$–$$$$ 🏨 **Black Bear Lodge.** This family-oriented all-suites hotel has one- and two-bedroom units with full kitchens. Each unit is individually owned and decorated. Children's movies are shown at night in season, and there's bus service to the slopes. Guests can use the White Mountain Athletic Club (☞ *above*). ⊠ *Box 357, Village Rd., 03215,* ☎ *603/ 236–4501 or 800/349–2327,* ℻ *603/236–4114. 107 suites. Indoor-outdoor pool, hot tub, sauna, steam room, exercise room, recreation room. AE, D, DC, MC, V.*

$–$$ 🏨 **Snowy Owl Inn.** The fourth-floor bunk-bed lofts at this inn are ideal for families; first-floor rooms, some with whirlpool tubs, are suitable for couples seeking a quiet getaway. The atrium lobby, where guests are treated to afternoon wine and cheese, contains a three-story fieldstone fireplace and many prints and watercolors of snowy owls. Four restaurants are within walking distance. Guests have access to the White Mountain Athletic Club (☞ *above*). ⊠ *Box 407, Village Rd., 03215,* ☎ *603/236–8383 or 800/766–9969,* ℻ *603/236–4890. 84 rooms. Indoor pool, hot tub. Continental breakfast. AE, D, DC, MC, V.*

Skiing and Snow Sports

WATERVILLE VALLEY

Former U.S. ski-team star Tom Corcoran designed this family-oriented resort. The lodgings and various amenities are about a mile from the slopes, but a shuttle makes a car unnecessary. ⊠ *Box 540, Rte. 49, 03215,* ☎ *603/236–8311; 603/236–4144 for snow conditions; 800/468–2553 for lodging.*

Downhill. Mt. Tecumseh, a short shuttle ride from the Town Square and accommodations, has been laid out with great care. This ski area has hosted more World Cup races than any other in the East, so most advanced skiers will be adequately challenged. Most of the 52 trails are intermediate: straight down the fall line, wide, and agreeably long. A 7-acre tree-skiing area adds variety. Snowmaking coverage of 100% ensures good skiing even when nature doesn't cooperate. The lifts serving the 2,020 ft of vertical rise include two high-speed detachable quad, two triple, three double, and four surface lifts.

Cross-country. The Waterville Valley cross-country network, with the ski center in the Town Square, has 101 km (63 mi) of trails. About two-thirds of the trails are groomed; the rest are backcountry.

Child care. The nursery takes children from age 6 months to 4 years. There are SKIwee lessons and other instruction for children ages 3 to 12. The Kinderpark, a children's slope, has a slow-running lift.

Lincoln/North Woodstock

㉕ *26 mi northwest of Waterville Valley, 65 mi north of Concord.*

Lincoln and North Woodstock, at the western end of the Kancamagus Highway and at Exit 32 off I–93, combine to make one of the state's liveliest ski-resort areas. Festivals, like the New Hampshire Scottish Highland Games in mid-September, keep Lincoln swarming with people year-round, while North Woodstock maintains more of a village feel.

A ride on the **Hobo Railroad** yields scenic views of the Pemigewasset River and the White Mountain National Forest. The narrated excursions take 1 hour and 20 minutes. ⊠ *Rte. 112, Lincoln,* ☎ *603/745–2135.* ⊡ *$8.* ⊙ *June–Labor Day, daily 11, 1, 3 (sometimes 5), and 7 (dinner train); May and Sept.–Oct., weekends 11, 1, 3 (sometimes 5), and 7 (dinner train).*

☾ In summer and fall at **Loon Mountain,** a popular ski resort, you can ride New Hampshire's longest gondola to the summit for a panoramic view of the White Mountain National Forest. Daily activities at the summit include lumberjack shows, storytelling by a mountain man, and nature tours. You can also take self-guided walks to glacial caves. Other recreational opportunities include a popular wildlife theater show, archery, horseback riding, mountain biking, and in-line skating. ⊠ *Kancamagus Hwy., Lincoln,* ☎ *603/745–8111.* ⊡ *Gondola $9.50, separate fees for other activities.* ⊙ *Daily.*

☾ At the **Whale's Tale Water Park,** you can float on an inner tube along a gentle river, careen down water slides, or body-surf in the large wave pool. ⊠ *U.S. 3, North Lincoln,* ☎ *603/745–8810.* ⊡ *$16.50.* ⊙ *Mid-June–Labor Day, daily 10–6; call for early and late-season hrs.*

Dining and Lodging

$$$ ✕⊞ **Indian Head Resort.** Views across the 180 acres of this resort motel near the Loon and Cannon Mountain ski areas are of Indian Head Rock Profile and the Franconia Mountains. Groomed cross-country ski trails and a mountain-bike trail from the resort connect to the Franconia Notch trail system. The Profile Room restaurant ($$–$$$) serves a nice selection of standard American dishes. ⊠ *U.S. 3, North Lincoln 03251,* ☎ *603/745–8000 or 800/343–8000,* 𝖥𝖠𝖷 *603/745–8414. 98 rooms, 40 cottages. Restaurant, 1 indoor and 1 outdoor pool, indoor and outdoor hot tubs, lake, sauna, tennis court, fishing, biking, ice-skating, cross-country skiing, recreation room. AE, D, DC, MC, V.*

$–$$ ✕⊞ **Woodstock Inn.** The inn's 21 rooms, spread over three buildings, are named after local geographic features. The romantic Ellsworth room comes with a whirlpool tub, a king-size canopy bed, and complimentary champagne. The Notchview, great for families, has two double beds; a ladder leads to a cozy tower with a daybed. The restaurants include the elegant Clement Room Grill; Woodstock Station ($), where everything from meat loaf to fajitas is prepared; and the Woodstock Inn Brewery. ⊠ *Box 118, U.S. 3, North Woodstock 03262,* ☎ *603/745–3951 or 800/321–3985,* 𝖥𝖠𝖷 *603/745–3701. 21 rooms, 13 with bath. 2 restaurants, bar, refrigerators, outdoor hot tub. Full breakfast. AE, D, MC, V.*

$$–$$$$ ⊞ **Mountain Club on Loon.** This first-rate slopeside resort hotel has an assortment of accommodations: suites that sleep as many as eight, studios with Murphy beds, and 117 units with kitchens. All rooms are within walking distance of the lifts, and condominiums are on-slope and nearby. Entertainers perform in the lounge on most winter weekends. ⊠ *Rte. 112, Kancamagus Hwy., Lincoln 03251,* ☎ *603/745–2244 or 800/229–7829,* 𝖥𝖠𝖷 *603/745–2317. 234 rooms. Restaurant, bar, indoor pool, massage, sauna, aerobics, health club, racquetball, squash. AE, D, MC, V.*

$$ ⊞ **Mill House Inn.** This country inn–style hotel on the western edge of the Kancamagus Highway offers free transportation to Loon Mountain during ski season. Nearby are shopping, restaurants, a cinema, and the North Country Center for the Performing Arts. ⊠ *Box 696, Rte. 112, Lincoln 03251,* ☎ *603/745–6261 or 800/654–6183,* 𝖥𝖠𝖷 *603/745–6896. 74 rooms, 21 suites. Restaurant, 1 indoor and 1 outdoor pool, indoor and outdoor hot tubs, sauna, tennis court, exercise room, nightclub. AE, D, DC, MC, V.*

Nightlife and the Arts

The **North Country Center for the Performing Arts** (⊠ Mill at Loon Mountain, Kancamagus Hwy., ☎ 603/745–6032) presents theater for children and adults and art exhibitions from July to September. Skiers head to the **Granite Bar** at the Mountain Club at the Loon Mountain resort (⊠ Kancamagus Hwy., ☎ 603/745–8111). You can dance at the **Loon Saloon** ⊠ Kancamagus Hwy., ☎ 603/745–8111) at the ski area. **Thunderbird Lounge** (⊠ Indian Head Resort, U.S. 3, North Lincoln, ☎ 603/745–8000) has nightly entertainment year-round and a large dance floor. The **Timbermill Pub** (⊠ Mill at Loon Mountain, Kancamagus Hwy., ☎ 603/745–3603) hosts bands on weekends.

Outdoor Activities and Sports

At **Lost River Reservation** (⊠ Rte. 112, North Woodstock, ☎ 603/745–8031), open from mid-May to mid-October, you can hike along the river gorge and view geological wonders like the Guillotine Rock and the Lemon Squeezer.

Shopping

CRAFTS

The **Curious Cow** (⊠ Main St., North Woodstock, ☎ 603/745–9230) is a multidealer shop selling country crafts. The **Russell Crag Gallery of Fine Crafts** (⊠ 110 Main St., North Woodstock, ☎ 603/745–8664) carries pottery, jewelry, and other items by New Hampshire artisans. **Sunburst Fashions** (⊠ 108 Main St., North Woodstock, ☎ 603/745–8745) stocks handcrafted gemstone jewelry and imported gift items.

MALL

Millfront Marketplace, Mill at Loon Mountain (⊠ I–93 and the Kancamagus Hwy., Lincoln, ☎ 603/745–6261), a former paper factory, contains restaurants, boutiques, a bookstore, and a post office.

Skiing and Snow Sports

LOON MOUNTAIN

A modern resort on the Kancamagus Highway and the Pemigewasset River, Loon Mountain opened in the 1960s and underwent serious development in the 1980s. In the base lodge and around the mountain are many food-service and lounge facilities. At night, you can try lift-serviced tubing on the lower slopes. ⊠ *Kancamagus Hwy., Lincoln 03251,* ☎ *603/745–8111; 603/745–8100 for snow conditions; 800/227–4191 for lodging.*

Downhill. Wide, straight, and consistent intermediate trails prevail at Loon. Beginner trails and slopes are set apart. Most- advanced runs are grouped on the North Peak section farther from the main mountain. Snowboarders have a halfpipe and their own snowboard park, and an alpine garden with bumps and jumps provides thrills for skiers. The vertical is 2,100 ft; a four-passenger gondola, one high-speed detachable quad, two triple and three double chairlifts, and one surface lift serve the 43 trails and slopes.

Cross-country. The touring center at Loon Mountain has 35 km (22 mi) of cross-country trails.

Child care. The day-care center takes children as young as 6 weeks old. The ski school runs several programs for children of different age groups. Children 5 and under ski free.

Kancamagus Highway

34½ mi between Lincoln and Conway.

Interstate 93 is the fastest way to the White Mountains, but it's hardly

★ the most appealing. The section of Route 112 known as the **Kancamagus Highway** passes through classic mountain vistas with some of the state's most unspoiled scenery. This stretch, punctuated by scenic overlooks and picnic areas, erupts into fiery color each fall, when photo-snapping drivers can really slow things down. Prepare yourself for a leisurely pace. There are also campgrounds off the highway. In bad weather, check with the Saco Ranger Station (☎ 603/447–5448) for road conditions.

Outdoor Activities and Sports

A couple of short hiking trails off the highway yield great rewards for relatively little effort. The **Lincoln Woods Trail** starts from the large parking lot of the Lincoln Woods Visitor Center, 4 mi east of Lincoln. You can purchase the recreation pass ($5 per vehicle, good for seven consecutive days) needed to park in any of the White Mountain National Forest lots or overlooks here; stopping to take photos or to use the rest rooms at the visitor center is permitted without a pass. The trail crosses a suspension bridge over the Pemigewasset River and follows an old railroad bed for 3 mi along the river. The parking and picnic area for **Sabbaday Falls,** about 20 mi east of Lincoln, is the trailhead for an easy ½-mi trail to the falls, a multilevel cascade that plunges through two potholes and a flume.

North Conway

㉖ *72 mi northeast of Concord, 42 mi east of Lincoln.*

North Conway is a shopper's paradise, with more than 150 outlet stores ranging from Anne Klein to Joan & David. Most of them stretch along Route 16. Before the arrival of the outlets, the town was popular with skiers and hikers, who still come for the inspiring scenery, ski resorts, and access to White Mountain National Forest.

☾ The **Conway Scenic Railroad** operates trips of varying durations in vintage coaches pulled by steam or diesel engines. The dome observation coach on the 5½-hour trip through Crawford Notch offers views of some of the finest scenery in the Northeast. Lunch is served aboard the dining car on the Valley Train to Conway or Bartlett. The 1874 Victorian train station has displays of railroad artifacts, lanterns, and old tickets and timetables. ⊠ *Rte. 16 and U.S. 302 (38 Norcross Circle),* ☎ *603/356–5251 or 800/232–5251.* ⊡ *$8.50–$52, depending on trip.* ☉ *Mid-May–late Dec., daily 9–6; Apr.–mid-May and Nov.–late Dec., weekends 10–3. Call for departure times. Reserve early during foliage season for Crawford Notch or Valley dining car.*

At **Echo Lake State Park,** you needn't be a rock climber to glimpse views from the 1,000-ft **White Horse** and **Cathedral** ledges. From the top you'll see the entire valley, in which Echo Lake shines like a diamond. An unmarked trailhead another ⁷⁄₁₀-mi on West Side Road leads to **Diana's Baths,** a spectacular series of waterfalls. ⊠ *Off U.S 302,* ☎ *603/356–2672.* ⊡ *$2.50.* ☉ *Mid-June–mid-Oct., daily dawn–dusk.*

The **Hartmann Model Railroad Museum** houses 14 operating layouts (from G to Z scales), about 2,000 engines, and more than 5,000 cars and coaches. A café, a crafts store, a hobby shop, and an outdoor ride-on train are also on site. ⊠ *U.S. 302 and Town Hall Rd., Intervale,* ☎ *603/356–9922 or 603/356–9933.* ⊡ *$5.* ☉ *Daily 10–5.*

Dining and Lodging

$–$$$ ✕ **Delaney's Hole in the Wall.** Perfect after a long day of shopping or skiing, this casual restaurant has an eclectic decor of sports and other memorabilia that includes autographed baseballs. An early photo of skiing at Tuckerman's Ravine hangs over the fireplace. The menu is varied as well, with entrées ranging from a spicy chicken and roasted red pepper quesadilla to medallions of sirloin fillet with steamed broccoli, sautéed baby shrimp, and hollandaise sauce. ⊠ *¼ mi north of North Conway on Rte. 16,* ☎ *603/356–7776. D, MC, V.*

$$$–$$$$ ✕⊞ **Darby Field Inn.** After a day of outdoor activity in the adjacent White Mountain National Forest, you can warm yourself by the fieldstone fireplace in the Darby Inn's living room or by the woodstove in the bar. Most rooms in this unpretentious 1826 converted farmhouse have mountain views. The menu at the restaurant ($$$) usually includes roast duckling with a raspberry Chambord sauce, rack of lamb with a burgundy sauce, and daily specials like Jamaican jerk pork with a mango puree. For dessert try the dark-chocolate pâté with white-chocolate sauce or the famous Darby cream pie. ⊠ *Box D, Bald Hill Rd., Conway 03818,* ☎ *603/447–2181 or 800/426–4147,* FAX *603/447–5726. 12 rooms, 3 suites. Restaurant, bar, pool, outdoor hot tub, cross-country skiing. MAP available; required during foliage season and Christmas wk. AE, MC, V. Closed Apr.*

$$–$$$$ ✕⊞ **Eastern Slope Inn Resort.** This National Historic Site on 40 acres in the heart of North Conway near Mt. Cranmore has been an operating inn for more than a century. The restaurant ($$–$$$) serves creative American fare in a glassed-in courtyard and has weekly entertainment. ⊠ *2760 Main St., 03860,* ☎ *603/356–6321 or 800/862–1600,* FAX *603/356–8732. 145 rooms. Restaurant, pub, indoor pool, hot tub, sauna, tennis courts, recreation room. AE, D, MC, V.*

$$–$$$$ ✕⊞ **Snowvillage Inn.** Journalist Frank Simonds built the main gambrel-roof house in 1916. To complement the inn's tome-jammed book-
★ shelves, guest rooms are named for famous authors. The nicest of the rooms, with 12 windows that look out over the Presidential Range, is a tribute to native son Robert Frost. Two additional buildings—the carriage house and the chimney house—also have libraries. Menu highlights in the candlelighted dining room ($$$; reservations essential) include roasted rack of lamb with herbes de Provence. Among the dessert treats are a cranberry walnut tart and a chocolate truffle cake. ⊠ *Box 68, Stuart Rd. (5 mi southeast of Conway), Snowville 03849,* ☎ *603/447–2818 or 800/447–4345,* FAX *603/447–5268. 18 rooms. Restaurant, sauna, cross-country skiing. Full breakfast; MAP available. AE, D, DC, MC, V.*

$$$ ✕⊞ **Hale's White Mountain Hotel and Resort.** The rooms at this hotel at the base of Whitehorse Ledge have mountain views. Proximity to the White Mountain National Forest and Echo Lake State Park makes you feel farther away from civilization (and the nearby outlet malls) than you actually are. Dinner at the Ledges restaurant might include farm-raised White Mountain venison in a cranberry currant sauce or beef Wellington. ⊠ *Box 1828, West Side Rd., 03860,* ☎ FAX *603/356–7100 or* ☎ *800/533–6301. 80 rooms, 13 suites. Restaurant, bar, pool, hot tub, saunas, 9-hole golf course, tennis court, health club, hiking, cross-country skiing. MAP available. AE, D, MC, V.*

$$–$$$$ ⊞ **Best Western Red Jacket Mountain View.** The Red Jacket's location atop Sunset Hill provides guests with panoramic views of the Mount Washington Valley. Many of the spacious guest rooms have balconies or decks for enjoying the view. Cozy public rooms have deep chairs and plants, and the 40-acre grounds are neatly landscaped with walking trails and gardens. ⊠ *Box 2000, Rte. 16, 03860,* ☎ *603/356–5411 or 800/752–2538,* FAX *603/356–3842. 152 rooms, 12 town houses. 2 restaurants, refrigerators, 1 indoor and 1 outdoor pool, sauna, 2 tennis courts, sleigh rides, recreation room, playground, meeting rooms. AE, D, DC, MC, V.*

$$$　🏨 **Purity Spring Resort.** In the late 1800s, Purity Spring was a farm and sawmill on a private lake. Since 1944 it's been a four-season resort with two Colonial inns, lakeside cottages, and a ski lodge. The King Pine Ski Area (☞ Skiing and Snow Sports, *below*) is right on the property. East Madison is 15 mi south of North Conway. ⊠ *HC 63 Box 40, Rte. 153, East Madison 03849,* ☎ *603/367–8896 or 800/373–3754,* 🖷 *603/367–8664. 72 rooms, 68 with bath. Restaurant, indoor pool, lake, hot tub, tennis court, hiking, volleyball, fishing. AP, MAP. AE, D, MC, V.*

$–$$　🏨 **Cranmore Inn.** This authentic country inn opened in 1863, and many of its furnishings date from the mid-1800s. Some rooms have kitchens. A mere ⅓ mi from the base of Mt. Cranmore, the inn is within easy walking distance of North Conway Village. ⊠ *Kearsarge St., 03860,* ☎ *603/356–5502 or 800/526–5502. 18 rooms. Pool. Full breakfast. AE, MC, V.*

Nightlife and the Arts

The **Best Western Red Jacket Mountain View** (⊠ Rte. 16, ☎ 603/356–5411) has weekend and holiday entertainment. **Horsefeather's** (⊠ Main St., ☎ 603/356–6862) hops on weekends. **Mt. Washington Valley Theater Company** (⊠ Eastern Slope Playhouse, Main St., ☎ 603/356–5776) presents musicals and summer theater from mid-June to Labor Day. The Resort Players, a local group, gives pre- and postseason performances.

Outdoor Activities and Sports

Snowvillage Inn (☞ Dining and Lodging, *above*) conducts a llama trek up Foss Mountain. Your picnic will include champagne and fine food. Reservations are essential.

Shopping

ANTIQUES

The **Antiques & Collectibles Barn** (⊠ 3425 Main St., ☎ 603/356–7118), 1½ mi north of the village, is a 35-dealer colony with everything from furniture and jewelry to coins and other collectibles. **North Country Fair Jewelers** (⊠ Main and Seavy Sts., ☎ 603/356–5819) carries diamonds, antique and estate jewelry, silver, watches, coins, and accessories. **Richard M. Plusch Fine Antiques** (⊠ Rte. 16/U.S. 302, ☎ 603/356–3333) deals in period furniture and accessories, including glass, sterling silver, Oriental porcelains, rugs, and paintings. **Sleigh Mill Antiques** (⊠ off Rte. 153, Snowville, ☎ 603/447–6791), an old sleigh and carriage mill 6 mi south of Conway, specializes in 19th-century oil lighting and early gas and electric lamps.

CRAFTS

The **Basket & Handcrafters Outlet** (⊠ Kearsarge St., ☎ 603/356–5332) sells gift baskets, dried-flower arrangements, and country furniture. **Handcrafters Barn** (⊠ Main St., ☎ 603/356–8996) stocks the work of 350 area artists and artisans. **League of New Hampshire Craftsmen** (⊠ 2526 Main St., ☎ 603/356–2441) carries the works of the area's best artisans. **Zeb's General Store** (⊠ Main St., ☎ 603/356–9294 or 800/676–9294) looks like an old-fashioned country store but sells up-to-the-minute food items, crafts, and other products, all made in New England.

FACTORY OUTLETS

More than 150 factory outlets—including Timberland, Pfaltzgraff, London Fog, Anne Klein, and Reebok—can be found around Route 16. The **Mount Washington Valley Chamber of Commerce** (☎ 603/356–3171) has guides to the outlets.

SPORTSWEAR

Popular stores for skiwear include **Chuck Roast** (⊠ Rte. 16, ☎ 603/

356–5589), **Joe Jones** (⊠ 2709 Main St., Conway, ☎ 603/356–9411), and **Tuckerman's Outfitters** (⊠ Norcross Circle, ☎ 603/356–3121).

Skiing and Snow Sports

KING PINE SKI AREA AT PURITY SPRING RESORT

King Pine, a little more than 9 mi south of Conway, has been a family-run ski area for more than 100 years. Some ski-and-stay packages include free skiing for midweek resort guests. Among the facilities and activities are an indoor pool and fitness complex, ice-skating, and dogsledding. ⊠ *Rte. 153, East Madison 03849,* ☎ *603/367–8896; 800/ 367–8897; 800/373–3754 for ski information.*

Downhill. King Pine's gentle slopes make it an ideal area for those learning to ski. Because most of the terrain is geared to beginner and intermediate skiers, experts won't be challenged here except for a brief pitch on the Pitch Pine trail. Sixteen trails are serviced by two triple chairs and a double chair. There's tubing on Saturday and Sunday afternoons, and night skiing and tubing on Friday and Saturday.

Cross-country. King Pine has 15 km (9 mi) of cross-country skiing.

Child care. Children up to 6 years old are welcome (from 8:30 to 4) at the nursery on the second floor of the base lodge. Children ages 4 and up can take lessons.

MT. CRANMORE

This ski area on the outskirts of North Conway opened in 1938. Two glades, one for beginners and intermediates, one for intermediates and experts, have opened more skiable terrain. The fitness center has an indoor climbing wall, tennis courts, exercise equipment, and a pool. ⊠ *Box 1640, Snowmobile Rd., 03860,* ☎ *603/356–5543; 603/356– 8516 for snow conditions; 800/786–6754 for lodging.*

Downhill. The mountain's 38 trails are well laid out and fun to ski. Most runs are naturally formed intermediates that weave in and out of glades. Beginners have several slopes and routes from the summit, but experts must be content with a few short but steep pitches. In addition to the trails, snowboarders have a terrain park and a halfpipe. One high-speed quad, one triple, and three double chairlifts carry skiers to the top. There are also two surface lifts. Night skiing is an option from Thursday to Saturday and during holiday periods. Other activities are outdoor skating, snowshoeing, and, on Fridays and Saturdays until 9 and Sundays until 4, tubing.

Child care. The nursery takes children 6 months to 5 years. There's instruction for children from age 3 to 12.

CROSS-COUNTRY

Sixty-four kilometers (40 miles) of groomed cross-country trails weave through North Conway and the countryside along the **Mt. Washington Valley Ski Touring Association Network** (⊠ Rte. 16, Intervale, ☎ 603/356–9920 or 800/282–5220).

Glen

27 *6 mi north of North Conway, 78 mi northeast of Concord.*

Glen is hardly more than a crossroads between North Conway and Jackson, but its central location has made it the home of a few noteworthy attractions and dining and lodging options.

That cluster of fluorescent buildings on Route 16 is **Story Land,** a children's theme park with life-size storybook and nursery-rhyme characters. The 16 rides and four shows include a flume ride, a Victorian-theme

river-raft ride, a farm-family variety show, and a simulated voyage to
the moon. ⊠ *Rte. 16,* ☎ *603/383–4186.* ☞ *$17.* ⊙ *Mid-June–Labor
Day, daily 9–6; Labor Day–Columbus Day, weekends 10–5.*

A trip to **Heritage New Hampshire,** next door to Story Land, is as close
as you may ever come to experiencing time travel. Theatrical sets, sound
effects, and animation usher you aboard the *Reliance* and carry you
from a village in 1634 England over tossing seas to the New World.
You will saunter along Portsmouth's streets in the late 1700s and hear
a speech by George Washington, then continue through other exhibits
to the present day. ⊠ *Rte. 16,* ☎ *603/383–9776.* ☞ *$10.* ⊙ *Mid-June–
mid-Oct., daily 9–5.*

Dining and Lodging

$–$$$ ✕ **Red Parka Pub.** Practically an institution, the Red Parka Pub has
been in downtown Glen for more than two decades. The menu has every-
thing a family could want, from an all-you-can-eat salad bar to scal-
lop pie. The barbecued ribs are local favorites. ⊠ *U.S. 302,* ☎ *603/
383–4344. Reservations not accepted. AE, D, MC, V.*

$$ ✕🏨 **Bernerhof Inn.** This Old World–style hotel is right at home in its
alpine setting. The rooms have hardwood floors with hooked rugs, an-
tiques, and reproductions. The fanciest six rooms have brass beds and
spa-size bathtubs; one suite has a Finnish sauna. The menu at the
Prince Palace restaurant ($$$) includes Swiss specialties like fondue and
Wiener schnitzel, along with new American and classic French dishes.
The Black Bear pub ($) pours many microbrewery beers. Ask the hosts
about A Taste of the Mountains cooking school. ⊠ *Box 240, U.S. 302,
03838,* ☎ *603/383–9132 or 800/548–8007,* 🖷 *603/383–0809. 9
rooms. Restaurant, pub. Full breakfast. AE, D, MC, V.*

$$–$$$ 🏨 **Best Western Storybook Resort Inn.** On a hillside near Attitash Bear
Peak, this motor inn with large rooms is well suited to families. Cop-
perfield's Restaurant has gingerbread, sticky buns, omelets, and a chil-
dren's menu. ⊠ *Box 129, intersection of U.S 302 and Rte. 16, Glen
Junction 03838,* ☎ *603/383–6800,* 🖷 *603/383–4678. 78 rooms.
Restaurant, bar, refrigerators, 1 indoor and 1 outdoor pool, indoor and
outdoor hot tubs, sauna, tennis court, playground. AE, DC, MC, V.*

Nightlife and the Arts

The **Bernerhof Inn** (☞ Dining and Lodging, *above*) is the setting for
an evening of fondue and soft music by the fireside. **Red Parka Pub**
(☞ Dining and Lodging, *above*) is a hangout for barbecue and steak
lovers. During ski season, the crowd swells to capacity in the Pub Down-
stairs when musical entertainers perform on Sunday afternoons and
Thursday evenings.

Jackson

★ ㉘ *4 mi north of Glen, 82 mi northeast of Concord.*

The village of Jackson on Route 16 has retained its storybook New
England character. Art and antiques shopping, tennis, golf, fishing, and
hiking to waterfalls are among the draws. When the snow falls, Jack-
son becomes the state's cross-country skiing capital. The village's prox-
imity to four downhill areas makes it popular with alpine skiers, too.

Dining and Lodging

$$$–$$$$ ✕🏨 **Christmas Farm Inn.** Despite its winter-inspired name, this 200-
year-old village inn is an all-season retreat. Rooms in the main inn and
the saltbox next door, five with whirlpool baths, are done in Laura Ash-
ley and Ralph Lauren prints. The suites, in the cottages, log cabin, and
dairy barn, have beam ceilings, fireplaces, and rustic Colonial furnishings.
Some standbys in the restaurant ($$–$$$) include chicken Dijon with

artichoke hearts and shiitake mushrooms, grilled swordfish with citrus salsa, and New York sirloin; soups and desserts vary nightly. ⊠ *Box CC, Rte. 16B, 03846,* ☎ *603/383–4313 or 800/443–5837,* FAX *603/ 383–6495. 34 rooms. Restaurant, pub, pool, sauna, hot tub, volleyball, cross-country skiing, recreation room. MAP. AE, MC, V.*

$$$–$$$$ ✕☷ **Inn at Thorn Hill.** Architect Stanford White designed this 1895 Vic-
★ torian house, which is a few steps from cross-country trails and Jackson Village. Romantic touches include rose-motif papers and antiques like a blue-velvet fainting couch. The restaurant (reservations essential; closed mid-week in April) serves new American dishes like the roasted pork tenderloin marinated with cider and chiles and the brook trout stuffed with herb-roasted tomatoes. Leave room for the Sacher torte or the cranberry sorbet. The inn is no-smoking. ⊠ *Box A, Thorn Hill Rd., 03846,* ☎ *603/383–4242 or 800/289–8990,* FAX *603/383–8062. 11 rooms, 8 suites. Restaurant, pub, pool, hot tub, cross-country skiing. MAP. AE, D, MC, V.*

$$$–$$$$ ✕☷ **Wentworth.** This resort built in 1869 retains a Victorian look with individually decorated rooms accented with antiques. All rooms have TVs and telephones; some have working fireplaces and two-person whirlpool tubs. The dining room ($$$) serves a five-course, candlelight dinner with a menu that changes seasonally. Try the pan-seared red snapper with Himalayan red rice. ⊠ *Rte. 16A, 03846,* ☎ *603/383–9700 or 800/637–0013,* FAX *603/383–4265. 60 rooms in summer, 52 in winter. Restaurant, bar, pool, tennis court, ice-skating, cross-country skiing, sleigh rides, billiards. MAP. AE, D, DC, MC, V.*

$$–$$$$ ✕☷ **Ellis River House.** Most of the period-decorated rooms in this ro-
★ mantic country inn on the Ellis River have fireplaces, and some have two-person whirlpool baths or private balconies. In winter, a snow bridge across the river connects you with the Ellis River Trail and Jackson's renowned cross-country trail system. The elegant dining room (reservations required; $$–$$$) serves nightly specials as well as standards like boneless breast of duck. The inn is no-smoking. ⊠ *Box 656, Rte. 16, 03846,* ☎ *603/383–9339 or 800/233–8309,* FAX *603/383–4142. 17 rooms, 3 suites, 1 cottage. Restaurant, pub, pool, hot tub, sauna. Full breakfast. AE, D, DC, MC, V.*

$$–$$$$ ☷ **Inn at Jackson.** The builders of this 1902 Victorian followed a design by Stanford White. The inn has spacious rooms—six with fireplaces—with oversize windows and an airy feel. Other than an imposing grand staircase in the front foyer, the house is unpretentious, with hardwood floors, braided rugs, a smattering of antiques, and mountain views. The hearty breakfast may fill you up for the entire day. ⊠ *Box 807, Thornhill Rd., 03846,* ☎ *603/383–4321 or 800/289–8600,* FAX *603/ 383–4085. 14 rooms. Hot tub, cross-country skiing. Full breakfast. AE, D, DC, MC, V.*

$$–$$$$ ☷ **Nordic Village Resort.** The light wood and white walls of these deluxe condos near several ski areas are as Scandinavian as the snowy views. The Club House has pools and a spa, and there is a nightly bonfire at Nordic Falls. Larger units have fireplaces, full kitchens, and whirlpool baths. ⊠ *Rte. 16, Jackson 03846,* ☎ *603/383–9101 or 800/472–5207,* FAX *603/383–9823. 140 condominiums. 1 indoor and 2 outdoor pools, hot tub, steam room, ice-skating, cross-country skiing, hiking, sleigh rides. D, MC, V.*

$$–$$$ ☷ **Eagle Mountain House.** This country estate, which dates from 1879, is close to downhill ski slopes and even closer to cross-country trails, which begin on the property. The public rooms of this showplace have a tycoon-roughing-it feel, and the bedrooms are large and furnished with period pieces. On a warm day, you can nurse a drink in a rocking chair on the wraparound deck. ⊠ *Carter Notch Rd., 03846,* ☎ *603/383–9111 or 800/966–5779,* FAX *603/383–0854. 93 rooms. Restau-*

rant, pool, hot tub, sauna, 9-hole golf course, 2 tennis courts, health club, playground. AE, D, DC, MC, V.

$$–$$$ 🏨 **Wildcat Inn & Tavern.** After a day of skiing, you can collapse on a comfy sofa by the fire in this small 19th-century tavern in the center of Jackson Village. The fragrance of home-baking permeates into suite-style guest rooms, which are full of interesting furniture and knickknacks. The tavern, where bands often perform, attracts many skiers. In summer, dining is available in the landscaped garden. ✉ *Rte. 16A, 03846,* ☎ *603/383–4245 or 800/228–4245,* 📠 *603/383–6456. 6 rooms, 4 with bath; 7 suites; 1 cottage. Restaurant, bar. Full breakfast; MAP available. AE, MC, V.*

Outdoor Activities and Sports

Nestlenook Farm (✉ Dinsmore Rd., ☎ 603/383–0845) maintains an outdoor ice-skating rink with rentals, music, and a bonfire. Going snow-shoeing or taking a sleigh ride are other winter options; in summer you can fly-fish or ride in a horse-drawn carriage.

Skiing and Snow Sports

BLACK MOUNTAIN

The atmosphere at Black Mountain is fun, friendly, and informal—perfect for families and singles who want a low-key skiing holiday. The Family Passport, which allows two adults and two juniors to ski at discounted rates, is a good value. Midweek rates here are usually the lowest in Mt. Washington Valley. ✉ *Box B, Rte. 16B, 03846,* ☎ *603/383–4490 or 800/698–4490.*

Downhill. The 38 trails and two glades on the 1,100-vertical-ft mountain are evenly divided among beginner, intermediate, and expert. There are a triple and a double chairlift and two surface tows. Most of the skiing is user-friendly, particularly for beginners—although recent expansion has added trails geared toward experts—and the southern exposure keeps skiers warm. In addition to trails, snowboarders can use two terrain parks and the halfpipe.

Child care. The nursery takes children from age 6 months to 5 years. Children from 3 to 12 can take classes at the ski school.

JACKSON SKI TOURING FOUNDATION

Rated as one of the top four cross-country skiing areas in the country and by far the largest in New Hampshire, Jackson offers 158 km (98 mi) of trails. Ninety-six kilometers (60 mi) are track groomed, 85 km (53 mi) are skate groomed, and there are 63 km (38½ mi) of marked backcountry trails. ✉ *Main St., 03846,* ☎ *800/927–6697.*

Mt. Washington

★ ㉙   *15 mi north of Jackson, 91 mi north of Concord.*

In summer, you can drive to the top of Mt. Washington, the highest mountain (6,288 ft) in the northeastern United States and the spot where weather observers have recorded 231-mph winds, the strongest in the world. But you'll have to endure the **Mt. Washington Auto Road** to get here. This toll road opened in 1861 and is said to be the nation's first manufactured tourist attraction. Closed in inclement weather, the road begins at **Glen House,** a gift shop and rest stop 15 mi north of Glen on Route 16. Allow two hours round-trip and check your brakes first. Cars with automatic transmissions that can't shift down into first gear aren't allowed on the road. A better option is to hop into one of the vans at Glen House for a 1½-hour guided tour (two hours if you purchase your ticket before 9:30 AM). In winter, the tours go to just above tree line and you have the option of cross-country skiing or snowshoeing down. (You can also take the Mt. Washington Cog Railway to the summit; ☞ Bretton Woods, *below*.) Up top, visit the **Sherman Adams Summit Building**, which contains a museum of memorabilia from each of the three hotels that have stood on this spot and a display of native plant life and alpine flowers. Stand in the glassed-in viewing area to hear the roar of that record-breaking wind. ☎ *603/466–3988.* ☒ *$15 per car and driver plus $6 for each adult passenger; van fare $20.* ☉ *Daily (weather permitting).*

Although not a town per se, scenic **Pinkham Notch** covers the eastern side of Mt. Washington and includes several ravines, including Tuckerman's Ravine, famous for spring skiing. It is one of the most eastern notches in the White Mountains. The **Appalachian Mountain Club** (☞ Hiking *in* The White Mountains A to Z, *below*) maintains a visitor center here on Route 16 that provides information to hikers and travelers and has guided walks.

Great Glen Trails Outdoor Center (☞ Skiing and Snow Sports, *below*) has an extensive trail network for hiking and mountain biking, as well as programs in mountain biking, canoeing, kayaking, and fly-fishing.

Skiing and Snow Sports

WILDCAT

Glade skiers head to Wildcat, which has official glade trails with 28 acres of tree skiing. Wildcat's runs include some stunning double-black-diamond trails. Skiers who can hold a wedge should check out the 4-km-long (3-mi-long) Polecat. Experts can zip down the Lynx. On a clear day, the views of Mt. Washington and Tuckerman's Ravine are superb. The trails are classic New England—narrow and winding. ☒ *Rte. 16, Pinkham Notch, Jackson 03846,* ☎ *603/466–3326; 800/643–4521 for snow conditions; 800/255–6439 for lodging.*

Downhill. Wildcat's expert runs deserve their designations and then some. Intermediates have mid-mountain-to-base trails, and beginners will find gentle terrain and a broad teaching slope. Snowboarders have several terrain parks and the run of the mountain. The 44 runs, with a 2,100-ft vertical drop, are served by a two-passenger gondola, one detachable quad, one double and three triple chairlifts.

Child care. The child-care center takes children ages 6 months and up. All-day SKIwee instruction is offered to children from age 5 to 12. Ski instruction for children takes place on a separate slope.

GREAT GLEN TRAILS OUTDOOR CENTER

There are 40 km (24 mi) of cross-country trails here and access to more than 1,100 acres of backcountry. You can even ski the lower half of the Mt. Washington Auto Road. Trees shelter most of the trails, so Mt. Washington's famous weather shouldn't be a concern. Evenings of cross-country skiing and snowshoeing by moonlight are scheduled throughout the winter. ☒ *Box 300, Rte. 16, Pinkham Notch (Mailing: Box 300, Gorham 03581),* ☎ *603/466–2333.*

Dixville Notch

🕥 *60 mi north of Mt. Washington, 166 mi north of Concord.*

Not everyone likes to venture this far north, but if you want to really get away from it all, Dixville Notch is the place to go. Just 12 mi from the Canadian border, this tiny community is known for two things. It's the home of the Balsams Grand Resort Hotel, one of the oldest and most celebrated resorts in New Hampshire. And Dixville Notch and Harts Location are the first election districts in the nation to vote in the presidential elections. Long before the sun rises on election day, the 30 or so Dixville Notch voters gather in the little meeting room beside the hotel bar to cast their ballots and make national news.

One of the favorite pastimes for visitors in this area is watching for moose, those large, ungainly, yet elusive members of the deer family. Although you may catch sight of one or more yourself, **Northern Forest Moose Tours** (☎ 603/752–6060) offers bus tours of the region that have a 97% success rate for spotting moose.

Dining and Lodging

$$$$ ✕⌘ **The Balsams Grand Resort Hotel.** At this resort founded in 1866,
★   you will find many nice touches: valet parking, dancing and entertainment, cooking demonstrations, wine tastings, and organized activities (many included in the cost). Families particularly enjoy late-night games of broomball. The Tower Suite, with its 20-ft conical ceiling, is in a Victorian-style turret and offers 360-degree views. Rooms vary in size but are generally spacious and comfortably furnished; all have views of the 15,000-acre estate and the mountains beyond. In the dining room ($$–$$$; jacket and tie), the summer buffet lunch is heaped upon a 100-ft-long table. Given the awesome amount of food, it's amazing that anyone has room left for the stunning dinners. A starter might be chilled strawberry soup spiked with Grand Marnier, followed by poached salmon with golden caviar sauce and chocolate hazelnut cake. ⌧ *Rte. 26, 03576,* ☎ *603/255–3400 or 800/255–0600; 800/255–0800 in NH;* ℻ *603/255–4221. 202 rooms. Restaurant, pool, 18-hole and 9-hole golf courses, driving range, 6 tennis courts, hiking, boating, fishing, mountain bikes, ice-skating, cross-country skiing, downhill skiing, children's programs. MAP in winter, AP in summer. AE, D, MC, V. Closed late Mar.–mid-May and mid-Oct.–mid-Dec.*

$$$ ⌘ **The Glen.** This rustic lodge with stick furniture, fieldstone, and cedar is on First Connecticut Lake, surrounded by log cabins, seven of which are right on the water. The cabins come equipped with efficiency kitchens and minirefrigerators—not that you'll need either, because rates include meals in the lodge restaurant. ⌧ *77 Glen Rd., 1 mi off U.S. 3, Pittsburg 03592,* ☎ *603/538–6500 or 800/445–4536. 8 rooms, 10 cabins. Restaurant, dock. AP. No credit cards. Closed mid-Oct.–mid-May.*

Outdoor Activities and Sports

Dixville Notch State Park (⌧ Rte. 26, ☎ 603/823–9959), the northernmost notch in the White Mountains, has picnic areas, a waterfall, and many hiking trails.

Skiing and Snow Sports

THE BALSAMS WILDERNESS

Skiing was originally provided as an amenity for hotel guests at the Balsams, but the area has become popular with day-trippers as well. ⌧ *Rte. 26, 03576,* ☎ *603/255–3400 or 800/255–0600; 800/255–0800 in NH; 603/255–3951 for snow conditions;* ℻ *603/255–4221.*

Downhill. Slopes with names like Sanguinary, Umbagog, and Magalloway may sound tough, but they're only moderately difficult, leaning toward intermediate. There are 12 trails and four glades from the top of the 1,000-ft vertical for every skill level. One double chairlift and two T-bars carry skiers up the mountain. There is a halfpipe for snowboarders.

Cross-country. Balsams has 86 km (53 mi) of cross-country skiing, tracked and groomed for skating (a cross-country technique). Natural-history markers annotate some trails; you can also try telemark and backcountry skiing, and 30 km (19 mi) of snowshoeing trails.

Child care. The nursery takes children up to age 6 at no charge to hotel guests. Lessons are for children 3 and up.

OFF THE
BEATEN PATH

PITTSBURG – Just north of the White Mountains, Pittsburg contains the four Connecticut Lakes and the springs that form the Connecticut River. The entire northern tip of the state—a chunk of about 250 square mi—lies within the town's borders, the result of a dispute between the United States and Canada. The two countries could not decide on a border, so the inhabitants of this region declared themselves independent of both countries in 1832 and wrote a constitution providing for an assembly, a council, courts, and a militia. They named their nation the Indian Stream Republic, after the river that passes through the territory—the capital of which was Pittsburg. In 1835 the feisty, 40-man Indian Stream militia invaded Canada—with only limited success. The Indian Stream war ended more by common consent than surrender; in 1842 the Webster-Ashburton Treaty fixed the international boundary. Indian Stream was incorporated as Pittsburg, making it the largest township in New Hampshire. Canoeing, fishing, and taking photos are favorite pastimes up here; the pristine wilderness teems with moose. Contact the **North Country Chamber of Commerce** (☞ Visitor Information *in* The White Mountains A to Z, *below*) for information about the region.

Bartlett

③ *7 mi southwest of Glen, 85 mi north of Concord.*

Bear Mountain to the south, Mt. Parker to the north, Mt. Cardigan to the west, and the Saco River to the east combine to create an unforgettable setting for the village of Bartlett, incorporated in 1790. Lovely Bear Notch Road in Bartlett has the only midpoint access to the Kancamagus Highway (closed winter).

Attitash Bear Peak (⊠ U.S. 302, ☎ 603/374–2368; ☞ Skiing and Snow Sports, *below*) has a dry alpine slide, a water slide, a children's area, and a driving range. A chairlift whisks passengers to the White Mountain Observation Tower, which delivers 270-degree views of the Whites.

Dining and Lodging

$$$–$$$$ ✕▥ **Grand Summit Hotel & Conference Center.** The gables and curves of this resort hotel at the base of Attitash Bear Peak (☞ *above*) mimic the mountain's peaks and slopes. The luxurious contemporary-style rooms have kitchenettes, VCRs, and stereo systems. Entrées in the Alpine Garden restaurant include pan-roasted chicken with garlic potato cakes and lobster spring rolls. ⊠ *Box 429, U.S. 302, 03812,* ☎ *603/374–1900 or 800/554–1900,* ℻ *603/374–3040. 143 rooms. Restaurant, bar, café, heated pool, hot tubs, sauna, steam room, exercise room, gift shop. AE, D, MC, V.*

$$$–$$$$ ▥ **Attitash Mountain Village.** The style at this condo-motel complex—across the street from the mountain via a tunnel—is alpine contemporary, and the staff is young and enthusiastic. The many amenities include indoor and outdoor pools and whirlpools. Units, some with fireplaces and kitchens, accommodate from 2 to 14 people. The restaurant has unobstructed views of the mountain. ⊠ *Rte. 302, 03812-0358,* ☎ *603/374–6501 or 800/862–1600,* ℻ *603/374–6509. 300 rooms. Restaurant, pub, indoor pool, sauna, recreation room. AE, D, MC, V.*

Skiing and Snow Sports

ATTITASH BEAR PEAK

This high-profile resort, which hosts many special events and ski races, continues to expand. Lodging at the base of the mountain is in condominiums and motel-style units, away from the hustle of North Conway. Attitash has a computerized lift-ticket system that in essence allows skiers to pay by the run. Skiers can share the ticket, which is good for two years. ⊠ *U.S. 302, 03812,* ☎ *603/374–2368; 603/374–0946; 800/223–7669 for snow conditions; 800/223–7669 for lodging.*

Downhill. Enhanced with massive snowmaking (97%), the trails now number 60 on two peaks, both with full-service base lodges. The bulk of the skiing and boarding is geared to intermediates and experts, with some steep pitches, glades, and good use of terrain. Beginners have a share of good terrain on the lower mountain and some runs from the top. Serving the 30 km (18 mi) of trails and the 1,750-ft vertical drop are two high-speed quads, one fixed-grip quad, three triples, four double chairlifts, and two surface tows.

Cross-country. Bear Notch Ski Touring Center (☎ 603/374–2277) has more than 70 km (43 mi) of cross-country trails, with more than 60 km (37 mi) skate groomed and tracked. Backcountry skiing is unlimited. Guests staying at the Grand Summit Hotel (☞ Dining and Lodging, *above*) can connect to the trail system from the hotel door.

Child care. Attitots Clubhouse takes children from age 6 months to 5 years. Other programs accommodate children up to 16 years of age.

En Route   Scenic U.S. 302 winds through the steep, wooded mountains on either side of spectacular Crawford Notch, north of Bartlett, and passes through **Crawford Notch State Park** (⊠ U.S. 302, Harts Location, ☎ 603/374–2272), where you can stop for a picnic and a short hike to Arethusa Falls or the Silver and Flume cascades.

Bretton Woods

③② *20 mi northwest of Bartlett, 95 mi north of Concord.*

Early in this century, as many as 50 private trains a day brought the rich and famous from New York and Philadelphia to the Mount Washington Hotel, the jewel of Bretton Woods. The hotel was the site of a famous World Monetary Fund conference in 1944 that greatly affected the post–World War II economy. The area is also known for its cog railway and for skiing.

In 1858, when Sylvester Marsh asked the state legislature for permission to build a steam railway up Mt. Washington, one legislator responded that he'd have better luck building a railroad to the moon.
★ Despite such doubters, the **Mt. Washington Cog Railway** opened in 1869 and has since provided a thrilling alternative to driving or climbing to the top. Allow three hours round-trip. ⊠ *U.S. 302, 6 mi northeast of Bretton Woods,* ☎ *603/846–5404; 800/922–8825 outside NH.* 🖾 *$39 round-trip.* ☉ *Mid-June–mid-Oct., daily 8–5, weather permitting; May–mid-June and mid-Oct.–early Nov., limited schedule.*

Dining and Lodging

$$$$ ✕🖾 **Mount Washington Hotel.** The 1902 construction of this leviathan
★   was one of the most ambitious projects of its day. It quickly became one of the nation's favorite grand resorts, most notable for its 900-ft-long veranda, which affords a full view of the Presidential Range. With its stately public rooms and large, Victorian-style bedrooms and suites, the hotel retains a turn-of-the-century formality; jacket and tie are required in the dining room. The regional cuisine highlights seasonal dishes such as lemon lobster ravioli with shrimp and scallops and roast pork with onions, mushrooms, and berry marmalade. This 2,600-acre property has an extensive recreation center. The hotel remains open in the 1999–2000 winter season for the first time in its long history,

making it a winter playground as well as a summer one. ⊠ *U.S. 302, 03575,* ☎ *603/278–1000 or 800/258–0330,* ℻ *603/278–8838. 200 rooms. 2 restaurants, indoor-outdoor pool, outdoor pool, sauna, 2 18-hole golf courses, driving range, 12 tennis courts, hiking, horseback riding, bicycles, cross-country skiing, sleigh rides, children's programs. MAP. AE, MC, V.*

$$–$$$ ✕🗔 **Bretton Arms Country Inn.** Built in 1896, this restored inn predates the Mount Washington Hotel (☞ *above*) across the way. Reservations are required in the dining room ($$$) and should be made on arrival. Guests are invited to use the facilities of the Mount Washington Hotel. ⊠ *U.S. 302, 03575,* ☎ *603/278–1000 or 800/258–0330,* ℻ *603/ 278–8838. 31 rooms, 3 suites. Restaurant, lounge. AE, D, MC, V.*

$–$$$ 🗔 **Bretton Woods Motor Inn.** Rooms here have contemporary furnishings, a balcony or patio, and mountain views. The Continental cuisine at Darby's Restaurant is served around a circular fireplace. The bar is a hangout for skiers. The motor inn, across from the Mount Washington Hotel, shares the hotel's facilities. ⊠ *U.S. 302, 03575,* ☎ *603/ 278–1000 or 800/258–0330,* ℻ *603/278–8838. 50 rooms. Restaurant, bar, indoor pool, sauna, recreation room. AE, D, MC, V.*

$ 🛆 **Dry River Campground.** This rustic campground in Crawford Notch State Park has 30 tent sites and is a popular base for hiking the White Mountain National Forest. ⊠ *U.S. 302, Harts Location; mailing address: Box 177, Twin Mountain 03595,* ☎ *603/374–2272. Closed mid-Dec.–mid-May.*

Skiing and Snow Sports

BRETTON WOODS

This area has a three-level, open-space base lodge, a convenient drop-off area, easy parking, and an uncrowded setting. On-mountain town houses are available as part of reasonably priced packages. The views of Mt. Washington alone are worth the visit; the scenery is especially beautiful from the Top o' Quad restaurant. ⊠ *U.S. 302, 03575,* ☎ *603/ 278–3300, 800/232–2972 for information, 800/258–0330 for lodging.*

Downhill. The skiing on the 33 trails is novice and intermediate, with steeper pitches near the top of the 1,500-ft vertical and glade skiing to satisfy expert skiers. Skiers and snowboarders can try a terrain park with jumps and halfpipes. The Accelerator halfpipe is for snowboarders only. One detachable quad, one triple, and two double chairlifts service the trails. The area has night skiing and snowboarding on Friday, Saturday, and holidays. A limited lift-ticket policy helps keep lines short.

Cross-country. The large, full-service cross-country ski center at Bretton Woods has 95 km (59 mi) of groomed and double-track trails and also rents snowshoes. Half the trails are in the White Mountain National Forest.

Child care. The nursery takes children from age 2 months to 5 years. The ski school has an all-day program for children ages 4 to 12, using progressive instructional techniques. There's also a snowboarding program for children 8 to 12. Rates include lifts, lessons, equipment, lunch, and supervised play.

Bethlehem

㉝ *25 mi west of Bretton Woods, 84 mi north of Concord.*

In the days before antihistamines, hay-fever sufferers came by the busload to the town of Bethlehem, elevation 1,462 ft, whose crisp air has a blissfully low pollen count.

Lodging

$$$–$$$$
★
🏨 **Adair.** In 1927 attorney Frank Hogan built this three-story Georgian Revival home as a wedding present for his daughter, Dorothy Adair. Walking paths on this luxurious country inn's 200 acres wind through gardens and offer magnificent mountain views. The rooms, which have garden or mountain views, are decorated with period antiques and antique reproductions. One suite has a large two-person hot tub, a fireplace, a balcony, and a king-size sleigh bed. The inn is no-smoking and has a two-night minimum on weekends, three on holiday weekends. ⊠ *80 Guider La., 03574,* ☎ *603/444–2600 or 888/444– 2600,* 𝔽𝔸𝕏 *603/444–4823. 7 rooms, 2 suites, 1 cottage. Tennis court, billiards. Full breakfast. AE, MC, V.*

Outdoor Activities and Sports

The Society for the Protection of New Hampshire Forests owns two properties in Bethlehem open to visitors. **Bretzfelder Park** (⊠ Prospect St., ☎ 603/444–6228), a 77-acre nature and wildlife park, has a picnic shelter, hiking, and cross-country ski trails. The **Rocks Estate** (⊠ 113 Glessner Rd., ☎ 603/444–6228) is a working Christmas-tree farm with walking trails, historic buildings, and educational programs.

Franconia

㉞ *8 mi south of Bethlehem, 74 mi north of Concord.*

Travelers first came to Franconia because the notch of the same name provided a north–south route through the mountains. The town, which is north of the notch, and the scenic notch itself are well worth a look. Famous literary visitors to the area have included Washington Irving, Henry Wadsworth Longfellow, and Nathaniel Hawthorne, who wrote a short story about the Old Man of the Mountain. I–93 is called the Franconia Notch Parkway as it passes through the notch.

The **Frost Place,** Robert Frost's home from 1915 to 1920, is where the poet wrote one of his most-remembered poems, "Stopping by Woods on a Snowy Evening." Two rooms contain memorabilia and signed editions of his books. Outside, you can follow short trails marked with lines from Frost's poetry. Occasional poetry readings take place here. ⊠ *Ridge Rd. (off Rte. 116; follow signs),* ☎ *603/823–5510.* 🎫 *$3.* ⊙ *Memorial Day–June, weekends 1–5; July–Columbus Day, Wed.–Mon. 1–5.*

Franconia Notch State Park, south of Franconia, contains a few of New Hampshire's best-loved attractions. A multiuse recreational path runs parallel to the Franconia Notch Parkway. **Cannon Mountain Aerial Tramway** will lift you 2,022 ft for one more sweeping mountain vista. It's a five-minute ride to the top, where marked hiking trails lead to the observation platform. ⊠ *Cannon Mountain ski area, Exit 3 off Franconia Notch Pkwy.,* ☎ *603/823–8800.* 🎫 *Tramway $9.* ⊙ *Tramway Memorial Day–3rd weekend in Oct., daily 9–4:30.*

The **New England Ski Museum,** north of Cannon Mountain at the foot of the tramway, has photographs and old trophies, skis and bindings, boots, and ski apparel dating from the late 1800s. A gift shop stocks ski-related books, posters, videos, and gift items. ⊠ *Franconia Notch Pkwy., Exit 2,* ☎ *603/823–7177.* 🎫 *Free.* ⊙ *Dec.–Mar., Thurs.–Tues. noon–5; Memorial Day–Columbus Day, daily noon–5.*

It would be a shame to come to the White Mountains and leave without seeing the granite profile of the **Old Man of the Mountain,** the icon of New Hampshire. Nathaniel Hawthorne wrote about it, New Hampshire resident Daniel Webster bragged about it, and P. T. Barnum wanted to buy it. The two best places to view the giant stone face are the highway parking area on the Franconia Notch Parkway or along the shores of Profile Lake.

The **Flume** is an 800-ft-long natural chasm with narrow walls that give the gorge's running water an eerie echo. The route through the flume has been built up with a series of boardwalks and stairways. The visitor center has exhibits on the region's history. ⊠ *Franconia Notch Pkwy., Exit 2,* ☎ *603/745–8391.* 🖭 *$7.* ☉ *May–Oct., daily 9–5.*

Dining and Lodging

$$ ✕🏨 **Franconia Inn.** This resort has recreations for all seasons. You can golf next door at Sunset Hill's nine-hole course, play tennis, ride horseback, swim in the pool or sit in the hot tub, order your lunch to go for a day of hiking—even try soaring from the inn's airstrip. The inn has a cross-country ski center, too (☞ Skiing and Snow Sports, *below*). Rooms have designer chintzes, canopy beds, and country furnishings; some have whirlpool baths or fireplaces. At meals ($$–$$$), children choose from a separate menu. Among the fare for adults are the medallions of veal with apple-mustard sauce and the filet mignon with green-chili butter and Madeira sauce. ⊠ *1300 Easton Rd., 03580,* ☎ *603/823–5542 or 800/473–5299,* 🖷 *603/823–8078. 34 rooms. Restaurant, pool, hot tub, 4 tennis courts, croquet, horseback riding, bicycles, ice-skating, cross-country skiing, sleigh rides. Full breakfast; MAP available. AE, MC, V. Closed Apr.–mid-May.*

$$ 🏨 **Horse and Hound Inn.** Off the beaten path yet convenient to the Cannon Mountain tram, this inn is on 8 acres surrounded by the White Mountain National Forest. Antiques and assorted collectibles provide a cheery atmosphere, and on the grounds are 65 km (39 mi) of cross-country ski trails. Pets are welcome ($8.50 per stay). ⊠ *205 Wells Rd., 03580,* ☎ *603/823–5501 or 800/450–5501. 10 rooms, 8 with bath. Restaurant, bar, cross-country skiing. Full breakfast. AE, D, DC, MC, V. Closed Apr. and Nov.*

$ ⛺ **Lafayette Campground.** This campground has hiking and biking trails, 97 tent sites, showers, a camp store, a bike trail, and easy access to the Appalachian Trail. ⊠ *Franconia Notch State Park, 03580,* ☎ *603/823–9513 for information; 603/271–3628 for reservations. No pets. MC, V.*

Nightlife and the Arts

Hillwinds (⊠ Main St., ☎ 603/823–5551) has live entertainment on weekends.

Shopping

The **Franconia Marketplace** (⊠ Main St., ☎ 603/823–5368) sells only products made in Franconia. Stores in the complex include the Grateful Bread Quality Bakery and Tiffany Workshop, which stocks clothing and crystal jewelry.

Skiing and Snow Sports

CANNON MOUNTAIN

Nowhere is the granite of the Granite State more pronounced than here. One of the first ski areas in the United States, Cannon, which is owned and run by the state, gives strong attention to skier services, family programs, snowmaking, and grooming. The New England Ski Museum (☞ *above*) is adjacent to the base of the tramway. ⊠ *Franconia Notch State Park, Franconia Notch Pkwy., Exit 3, 03580,* ☎ *603/823–8800; 603/823–7771 for snow conditions; 800/237–9007 for lodging.*

Downhill. The quality of this mountain's skiing is reflected in the narrow, steep pitches off the peak of the 2,146 ft of vertical rise. Some trails marked intermediate may seem more difficult because of the side-hill slant of the slopes (rather than the steepness). Under a new fall of snow, Cannon's 42 trails have challenges not often found at modern ski areas. For additional fun, try the two glade-skiing trails, Turnpike and Banshee. There is a 70-passenger tramway to the top, one quad, one triple, and two double chairlifts, and one surface lift.

Cross-country. Nordic skiing is available on a 13-km (8-mi) multiuse recreational path through Franconia Notch State Park.

Child care. Cannon's Peabody Base Lodge takes children ages 1 year and older. All-day and half-day SKIwee programs are available for children from age 4 to 12, and season-long instruction can be arranged.

FRANCONIA VILLAGE CROSS-COUNTRY SKI CENTER
This ski center at the Franconia Inn (☞ Dining and Lodging, *above*) has 65 km (39 mi) of groomed trails and 40 km (24 mi) of backcountry trails. One popular trail leads to Bridal Veil Falls, a great spot for a picnic lunch. There are horse-drawn sleigh rides and ice-skating on a lighted rink as well. ⊠ *1300 Easton Rd., 03580,* ☏ *603/823–5542 or 800/473–5299,* ℻ *603/823–8078.*

Sugar Hill

③⑤ *4 mi west of Franconia, 11 mi south of Bethlehem, 77 mi north of Concord.*

Sugar Hill, a town of 500 people, is deservedly famous for the spectacular sunsets and views of the Franconia Mountains, best seen from Sunset Hill, where a row of grand hotels and summer "cottages" once stood. Quiet country charm and good-quality bed-and-breakfasts and small inns make Sugar Hill an ideal spot for a romantic getaway.

The surprisingly well done **Sugar Hill Historical Museum** has permanent and changing exhibits that focus on the history of the area from settlement through the resort era. ⊠ *Rte. 117,* ☏ *603/823–5336.* 🎟 *$2.* ◔ *July–mid-Oct., Thurs. and weekends 1–4.*

Dining and Lodging

$ ✕ **Polly's Pancake Parlor** This local institution, originally a carriage shed built in 1830, was converted to a tea room during the depression, when the Dexters began serving "all you can eat" pancakes, waffles, and French toast for 50¢. The prices have gone up some, but the descendants of the Dexters continue to serve pancakes and waffles made from grains ground on the property, their own country sausage, and local maple syrup. ⊠ *Rte. 117,* ☏ *603/823–5575. MC, V. No dinner.*

$$–$$$$ ✕🏠 **Sugar Hill Inn.** The old carriage on the lawn and wicker chairs on the wraparound porch set a nostalgic mood before you even enter this converted 1789 farmhouse. Many rooms have hand-stenciled walls, views of the Franconia Mountains, and rippled antique windowpanes; all contain antiques. The late film star Bette Davis visited friends in this house before she bought her own farm nearby—the room with the best view is named after her. The restaurant ($$$; reservations required) serves meat, fish, and poultry dishes and delicious desserts. There are 10 rooms in the inn and 6 (some with fireplaces) in three country cottages. The inn is no-smoking. ⊠ *Rte. 117, 03585,* ☏ *603/823–5621 or 800/548–4748,* ℻ *603/823–5639. 16 rooms. Restaurant, pub, cross-country skiing. Full breakfast; MAP available (required during foliage season). AE, MC, V.*

$$–$$$ 🏠 **Hilltop.** Staying with innkeepers Mike and Meri Hern is just like dropping by Grandma's—they even welcome pets. The rooms in their 1895 country farmhouse are done in a quirky mix of antiques with handmade quilts, Victorian ceiling fans, piles of pillows, and big, fluffy towels. The TV room has hundreds of movies on tape. Rockers on the porch

are perfect for watching the sun set behind the mountains. The large country breakfast includes homemade jams, pancakes made with homegrown berries, soufflés, and smoked ham, bacon, or salmon. The no-smoking inn has a two-night minimum during foliage season, summer weekends, and on holidays. ⊠ *Rte. 117, 03585,* ☎ *603/823–5695 or 800/770–5695,* 𝔽𝔸𝕏 *603/823–5518. 3 rooms, 3 suites, 1 2-bedroom cottage. Restaurant, bar, library. Full breakfast. D, MC, V.*

$$–$$$ ⊞ **Foxglove.** Extensive gardens with hammocks for relaxing are just one of the sybaritic delights at this rambling turn-of-the-century home next to Lover's Lane. The delicious breakfast is different each day, as is the china on which it is served. Common areas are decorated in country-French style with antiques. Guest rooms are thoughtfully furnished, each in a different motif. The Serengeti Room has animal- print linens, a chandelier with carnival glass shades, and black and brass fixtures in the bath. The inn is no-smoking. ⊠ *Rte. 117, 03585,* ☎ *603/823–8840,* 𝔽𝔸𝕏 *603/823–5755. 6 rooms. Full breakfast.*

The White Mountains A to Z

Arriving and Departing

BY BUS

Concord Trailways (☎ 800/639–3317) stops in Chocorua, Conway, Franconia, Glen, and Jackson.

BY CAR

Access to the White Mountains is from I–93 via the Kancamagus Highway or U.S. 302. From the seacoast, Route 16 is the popular choice.

BY PLANE

Manchester Airport (☞ Arriving and Departing *in* New Hampshire A to Z, *below*) is about an hour's drive from the White Mountains region.

Getting Around

BY BUS

See Arriving and Departing, *above.*

BY CAR

I–93 and U.S. 3 bisect the White Mountain National Forest, running north from Massachusetts to Québec. The Kancamagus Highway (Route 112), the east–west thoroughfare through the White Mountain National Forest, is a scenic drive. U.S. 302, a longer, more leisurely east–west path, connects I–93 to North Conway.

BY PLANE

Charters and private planes land at **Franconia Airport & Soaring Center** (⊠ Easton Rd., Franconia, ☎ 603/823–8881) and **Mt. Washington Regional Airport** (⊠ Airport Rd., Whitefield, ☎ 603/837–9532).

Contacts and Resources

CAMPING

White Mountain National Forest (⊠ U.S. Forest Service, 719 N. Main St., Laconia 03246, ☎ 603/528–8721; 877/444–6777 for campground reservations) has 20 campgrounds with more than 900 campsites spread across the region; only some take reservations. All sites are subject to a 14-day limit.

CANOEING, KAYAKING, AND RAFTING

River outfitter **Saco Bound Canoe & Kayak** (⊠ Box 119, Center Conway 03813, ☎ 603/447–2177) leads gentle canoeing expeditions, guided kayak trips, and white-water rafting on seven rivers and provides lessons, equipment, and transportation.

Memorial Hospital (✉ 3073 White Mountain Hwy., North Conway, ☎ 603/356–5461).

FISHING

For trout and salmon fishing, try the Connecticut Lakes, though any clear stream in the White Mountains will do. Many are stocked, and there are 650 mi of them in the national forest alone. Conway Lake is the largest of the area's 45 lakes and ponds; it's noted for smallmouth bass and—early and late in the season—good salmon fishing. The **New Hampshire Fish and Game Office** (☎ 603/788–3164) has up-to-date information on fishing conditions.

The **North Country Angler** (✉ 3643 White Mountain Hwy., Intervale, ☎ 603/356–6000) schedules intensive guided fly-fishing weekends.

HIKING

With 86 major mountains in the area, the hiking possibilities are endless. Innkeepers can usually point you toward the better nearby trails; some inns schedule guided day-trips for guests. The **White Mountain National Forest** (☞ Visitor Information, *below*) has hiking information and information about parking passes ($5) required in the national forest. These are available at visitor centers; if you can't buy one in advance, you can park and you'll probably find an envelope with information on your windshield.

The **Appalachian Mountain Club** (✉ Box 298, Gorham 03581, ☎ 603/466–2721; 603/466–2725 for trail information; 603/466–2727 for reservations or a free guide to huts and lodges) headquarters at Pinkham Notch offers lectures, workshops, slide shows, and outdoor skills instruction from June to October. Accommodations include a 100-bunk main lodge, a 24-bed hostel in Crawford Notch, and two rustic cabins. The club's eight trailside huts provide meals and dorm-style lodging, June through October, on several trails in the Whites.

New England Hiking Holidays (✉ Box 1648, North Conway 03860, ☎ 603/356–9696 or 800/869–0949) conducts scheduled guided hiking tours with lodging in country inns for two to eight nights.

LODGING RESERVATION SERVICES

Country Inns in the White Mountains (☎ 603/356–9460). **Jackson Chamber of Commerce Reservation Service** (☎ 800/866–3334).

VISITOR INFORMATION

Jackson Chamber of Commerce (Box 304, Jackson 03846, ☎ 603/383–9356 or 800/866–3334). **Mt. Washington Valley Chamber of Commerce** (☎ 603/356–3171 or 800/367–3364). **Mt. Washington Valley Hot Line** (☎ 877/948–6867). **North Country Chamber of Commerce** (✉ Box 1, Colebrook 03576, ☎ 603/237–8939 or 800/698–8939). **White Mountain Attractions Association** (✉ Kancamagus Hwy., North Woodstock 03251, ☎ 603/745–8720 or 800/346–3687). **White Mountain National Forest** (✉ U.S. Forest Service, 719 N. Main St., Laconia 03246, ☎ 603/528–8721; 877/444–6777 for campground reservations).

WESTERN AND CENTRAL NEW HAMPSHIRE

Here is the unspoiled heart of New Hampshire. The beaches on the state's coast attract sun worshipers, and the resort towns to the north keep the skiers and hikers beating a well-worn path up I–93, but western and central New Hampshire have managed to keep the water slides and the outlet malls at bay. In the center of New Hampshire you'll see one pristine town green after another. Each village has its own historical society and tiny museum filled with odd bits of memorabilia.

Two other lures in this area are the shining waters of Lake Sunapee and the looming presence of Mt. Monadnock. When you're done climbing and swimming and visiting the past, look for the wares and small studios of area artists. The region has long been an informal artists' colony where people come to write, paint, and weave in solitude.

The towns in this region, beginning with Concord, are described in counterclockwise order. From Concord, take I–89 through the Lake Sunapee region to Hanover, follow the Connecticut River south to Keene, and then meander through the Monadnock region to Manchester.

Concord

36 *40 mi north of the Massachusetts border via I–93, 20 mi north of Manchester, 45 mi northwest of Portsmouth.*

New Hampshire's capital (population 38,000) is a quiet, conservative town that tends to the state's business but little else. The residents joke that the sidewalks roll up promptly at 6. The **Concord on Foot** walking trail winds through the historic district. Maps are available from the **Chamber of Commerce** (⌧ 244 N. Main St.) or stores along the trail. The **Pierce Manse** is the Greek Revival home in which Franklin Pierce lived before moving to Washington to become the 14th U.S. president. ⌧ *14 Penacook St.,* ☎ *603/224–9620 or 603/224–7668.* ⌔ *$3.* ☉ *Mid-June–Labor Day, weekdays 11–3.*

At the gilt-domed neoclassical **State House,** New Hampshire's legislature still meets in its original chambers. The building dates to 1819 and is the oldest in the United States in continuous use as a state capitol. ⌧ *107 N. Main St.,* ☎ *603/271–2154.* ☉ *Weekdays 8–4:30; guided tours by reservation.*

Among the artifacts at the **Museum of New Hampshire History** is an original Concord Coach. During the 19th century, when more than 3,000 coaches were built in Concord, this was about as technologically perfect a vehicle as you could find—many say it's the coach that won the West. Other exhibits provide an overview of New Hampshire's history, from the Abenaki to the settlers of Portsmouth up to current residents. ⌧ *6 Eagle Sq.,* ☎ *603/226–3189.* ⌔ *$5.* ☉ *Jan.–June and mid-Oct.– Nov., Tues.–Wed. and Sat. 9:30–5, Thurs.–Fri. 9:30–8:30, Sun. noon– 5; Dec. and July–mid-Oct., Mon.–Wed. and Sat. 9:30–5, Thurs.–Fri. 9:30–8:30, Sun. noon–5.*

☾ The high-tech **Christa McAuliffe Planetarium** presents shows on the solar system, constellations, and space exploration that incorporate computer graphics, sound, and special effects in the 40-ft dome theater. Children love seeing the tornado tubes, magnetic marbles, and other hands-on exhibits. Outside, explore the scale-model planet walk and the human sundial. The planetarium was named for the Concord teacher and first civilian in space, who was killed in the *Challenger* space-shuttle explosion in 1986. ⌧ *New Hampshire Technical Institute campus, 3 Institute Dr.,* ☎ *603/271–7827.* ⌔ *Exhibit area free, shows $6.* ☉ *Tues.–Thurs. 9–5, Fri. 9–7, weekends 10–5. Call for show times and reservations.*

Guided tours of the late-Victorian **Kimball-Jenkins Estate** focus on the craftsmanship of the mansion—including the woodwork, tilework, and frescoed ceilings—and stories of more than 200 years of life in Concord. The formal gardens are the perfect spot for a summer picnic. ⌧ *266 N. Main St.,* ☎ *603/225–3932.* ⌔ *$4.* ☉ *June–Oct. Call for hrs.*

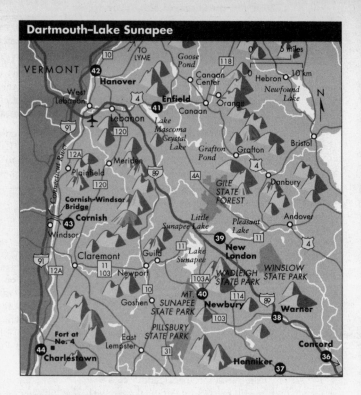

Dartmouth–Lake Sunapee

Dining and Lodging

$–$$$
★

✕ **Hermanos Cocina Mexicana.** The food at this popular two-level restaurant is standard Mexican but with fresher ingredients and more subtle sauces than might be expected. Everything on the menu is available à la carte, so you can mix and match to build a meal. ⊠ *11 Hills Ave.,* ☎ *603/224–5669. Reservations not accepted. D, MC, V.*

$$–$$$

✕▥ **Centennial Inn.** Built in 1896 for widows of Civil War veterans, this brick-and-stone building is set back from busy Pleasant Street. Much of the original woodwork has been preserved. Each room is decorated with antiques and reproduction pieces, and all have ceiling fans and VCRs. In the Franklin Pierce dining room, try the shredded-duck pizza and the roast medallions of venison. ⊠ *96 Pleasant St., 03301,* ☎ *603/ 225–7102 or 800/360–4839,* ℻ *603/225–5031. 27 rooms, 5 suites. Restaurant, bar, in-room data ports. AE, D, DC, MC, V.*

Nightlife and the Arts

The **Capitol Center for the Arts** (⊠ 46 S. Main St., ☎ 603/225–1111) has been restored to reflect its Roaring '20s origins. It hosts touring Broadway shows, dance companies, and musical acts. The lounge at **Hermanos Cocina Mexicana** (☞ Dining and Lodging, *above*) has live jazz on Sunday and Wednesday nights.

Outdoor Activities and Sports

Hannah's Paddles, Inc. (⊠ 15 Hannah Dustin Dr., ☎ 603/753–6695) rents canoes for use on the Merrimack River.

Shopping

CRAFTS

Capitol Craftsman and Romance Jewelers (⊠ 16 N. Main St., ☎ 603/ 224–6166 or 603/228–5683), which share adjoining shops, sell fine jewelry and handicrafts. The **Den of Antiquity** (⊠ 2 Capital Plaza, ☎ 603/225–4505) carries handcrafted country gifts and accessories. The

League of New Hampshire Craftsmen (⊠ 36 N. Main St., ☏ 603/228–8171) exhibits crafts in many media. **Mark Knipe Goldsmiths** (⊠ 2 Capitol Plaza, Main St., ☏ 603/224–2920) sets antique stones in rings, earrings, and pendants.

MALLS

Steeplegate Mall (⊠ 270 Loudon Rd., ☏ 603/224–1523) has more than 70 stores, including chain department stores and some smaller crafts shops.

Henniker

③⑦ *17 mi west of Concord.*

Governor Wentworth, the first Royal Governor of New Hampshire, named this town in honor of his friend John Henniker, a London merchant and member of the British Parliament (residents delight in their town's status as "the only Henniker in the world"). Once a mill town producing bicycle rims and other light-industrial items, Henniker reinvented itself after the factories were damaged, first by spring floods in 1936 and then by the hurricane and flood of 1938. New England College was established in the following decade. One of the area's covered bridges can be found on campus.

Dining and Lodging

$$–$$$$ ╳ ⊞ **Colby Hill Inn.** The cookie jar is always full in this Colonial farmhouse, where guests are greeted by Delilah, the inn dog. There is no shortage of relaxing activities: You can curl up with a book by the parlor fireplace, stroll through the gardens and 5 acres of meadow, or play badminton out back. Rooms in the main house contain antiques, Colonial reproductions, and frills like lace curtains. In the carriage-house rooms, plain country furnishings, stenciled walls, and exposed beams are the norm. The dining menu ($$$–$$$$) is excellent: Try the chicken Colby Hill (breast of chicken stuffed with lobster, leeks, and Boursin) or the crab crepes. ⊠ *Box 779, 3 The Oaks, 03242,* ☏ *603/428–3281,* ℻ *603/428–9218. 16 rooms. Restaurant, in-room data ports, pool, ice-skating, recreation room. Full breakfast. AE, D, DC, MC, V.*

$–$$ ╳ ⊞ **Meeting House Inn & Restaurant.** The owners of this 200-year-old farmhouse at the base of Pats Peak, who tout the complex as a lovers' getaway, start guests' days off with breakfast in bed. The old barn has become a restaurant ($$–$$$) that specializes in leisurely, romantic dining. Items like lobster pepito are served in a heart-shape puff pastry, and the chocolate-raspberry frozen mousse is also heart-shape. ⊠ *Rte. 114/Flanders Rd., 03242,* ☏ *603/428–3228,* ℻ *603/428–6334. 6 rooms. Restaurant, hot tub, sauna. Full breakfast. AE, D, MC, V.*

Shopping

The **Fiber Studio** (⊠ 9 Foster Hill Rd., ☏ 603/428–7830) sells beads, hand-spun natural-fiber yarns, spinning equipment, and looms.

Skiing and Snow Sports

PATS PEAK

Convenient for Bostonians who can make a quick trip up I–93, Pats Peak is geared to families. Base facilities are rustic, and friendly personal attention is the rule. ⊠ *Rte. 114, 03242,* ☏ *603/428–3245; 800/742–7287 for snow conditions.*

Downhill. Despite Pats Peak's size of only 710 vertical ft, the 20 trails and slopes have something for everyone. New skiers and snowboarders can take advantage of a wide slope and several short trails; intermediates have wider trails from the top; and advanced skiers have a couple of real thrillers. Night skiing and snowboarding take place in

January and February. One triple and two double chairlifts, one T-bar, and three surface lifts serve the runs. Pats Peak also has afternoon snow-tubing on weekends and holiday periods.

Child care. The nursery takes children from age 6 months to 5 years. Special nursery ski programs operate on weekends and during vacations for children from 4 to 12; all-day lessons for self-sufficient skiers in this age range are scheduled throughout the season.

Warner

③⑧ *18 mi north of Henniker, 22 mi northwest of Concord.*

Three New Hampshire governors were born in this quiet agricultural town just off I–89. Buildings dating from the late 1700s and early 1800s and a charming library give the town's main street a welcoming feel.

Mount Kearsarge Indian Museum, Education, and Cultural Center gives guided tours of the extensive collection of Native American artistry, including moose-hair embroidery, quillwork, and basketry. Signs on the self-guided Medicine Woods trail identify plants and explain how Native Americans used them as foods, medicines, and dyes. ⊠ *Kearsarge Mountain Rd., 03278,* ☎ *603/456–2600.* ➂ *$6.* ☉ *May–Oct., Mon.–Sat. 10–5, Sun. noon–5; Nov.–Dec., Sat. 10–5, Sun. noon–5.*

A scenic auto road at **Rollins State Park** (⊠ off Rte. 103) snakes nearly 3,000 ft up the southern slope of Mt. Kearsarge, where you can then tackle on foot the ½-mi trail to the summit.

New London

③⑨ *12 mi northwest of Warner, 10 mi west of Andover, 34 mi northwest of Concord.*

New London, the home of Colby-Sawyer College (1837), is a good base for exploring the Lake Sunapee region. A worthwhile stop is 10,000-year-old **Cricenti's Bog,** off Business Route 11 (Business Route 11 goes right through town; Route 11 goes around town). A short trail, maintained by the local conservation commission, shows off the shaggy mosses and fragile ecosystem of this ancient pond.

Dining and Lodging

$–$$ ✕ **Peter Christian's Tavern.** Exposed beams, wooden tables, a smattering of antiques, and half shutters on the windows make Peter Christian's a cool oasis in summer and a cozy haven in winter. Tavern fare like beef stew and shepherd's pie has been updated for this century. ⊠ *186 Main St., 03257,* ☎ *603/526–4042. AE, D, MC, V.*

$$–$$$ ✕▥ **Inn at Pleasant Lake.** This family-run property is aptly named for its location and ambience. The original farmhouse dates from 1790, and that early country look has been maintained by keeping frills to a minimum. Five acres of woods, fields, and gardens surround the inn. Candlelight and classical music accompany the restaurant's five-course prix-fixe dinner. ⊠ *Box 1030, 125 Pleasant St., 03257,* ☎ *603/526–6271 or 800/626–4907,* ℻ *603/525–4111. 12 rooms. Restaurant. Full breakfast. MC, V.*

$$–$$$ ✕▥ **New London Inn.** The two porches of this rambling 1792 country inn overlook Main Street. Rooms have a Victorian decor; those in the front of the house overlook the pretty campus of Colby-Sawyer College. The nouvelle-inspired menu in the restaurant starts with items like butternut squash with a sun-dried cranberry pesto and includes entrées such as grilled cilantro shrimp with a saffron risotto. The inn is no-smoking. ⊠ *Box 8, 140 Main St., 03257,* ☎ *603/526–2791 or 800/526–2791,* ℻ *603/526–2749. 28 rooms. Restaurant. Full breakfast. AE, MC, V.*

$$ 🛏 **Follansbee Inn.** Built in 1840, this quintessential country inn on the shore of Kezar Lake is a perfect fit in the 19th-century village of North Sutton, about 4 mi south of New London. The common rooms and bedrooms are loaded with collectibles and antiques. You can ice-fish on the lake and ski across it in winter and swim or boat from the inn's pier in summer. A 3-mi walking trail circles the lake. The inn is no-smoking. ⊠ *Rte. 114, North Sutton 03260,* ☎ *603/927–4221 or 800/ 626–4221. 23 rooms, 11 with bath; 1 cottage. Lake, hiking, boating, fishing, ice-skating, cross-country skiing. Full breakfast. MC, V.*

$ 🏕 **Otter Lake Camping Area.** The 28 sites on Otter Lake have plenty of shade, and there are numerous activities. Facilities include a beach, boating, fishing, a playground, and canoe and paddleboat rentals. ⊠ *55 Otterville Rd., 03257,* ☎ *603/763–5600.*

Nightlife and the Arts

The **New London Playhouse** (⊠ 209 Main St., ☎ 603/526–6710) presents Broadway-style and children's plays every summer in New Hampshire's oldest continuously operating theater.

Outdoor Activities and Sports

Pleasant Lake, off Route 11, has salmon, brook trout, and bass.

Shopping

Artisan's Workshop (⊠ Peter Christian's Tavern, 186 Main St., ☎ 603/ 526–4227) carries jewelry, hand-blown glass, and other local handicrafts.

Skiing and Snow Sports

NORSK CROSS COUNTRY SKI CENTER

The 75 km (46½ mi) of scenic cross-country ski trails here are also perfect for hiking in the warmer months. ⊠ *Rte. 11,* ☎ *603/526–4685 or 800/426–6775.*

Newbury

40 *10 mi south of New London, on the edge of Mt. Sunapee State Park; 38 mi northwest of Concord.*

Mt. Sunapee, which rises to an elevation of nearly 3,000 ft, and sparkling Lake Sunapee are the region's outdoor recreation centers. **Mt. Sunapee State Park** has 130 acres of hiking and picnic areas, a beach, and a bathhouse. You can rent canoes at the beach. In winter the mountain becomes a downhill ski area and host to national ski competitions. In summer the park holds the League of New Hampshire Craftsmen's Fair, a Fourth of July flea market, and the Gem and Mineral Festival. ⊠ *Rte. 103,* ☎ *603/763–2356.* 🎟 *$2.50.* ☉ *Daily dawn–dusk.*

The narrated cruises aboard **M/V Mt. Sunapee II** (⊠ Sunapee Harbor, ☎ 603/763–4030) provide a closer look at Lake Sunapee.

Lodging

$ 🏕 **Crow's Nest Campground.** This year-round campground on the Sugar River has 100 sites, some on the river. The facilities include a recreation hall, a swimming pool, a children's wading pool, miniature golf in summer, and a warm-up room with fireplace for winter use. River swimming and fishing are summer pastimes; you can skate or sled in the winter, and area snowmobile trails connect to the campground. ⊠ *Rte. 10, Newport 03773,* ☎ *603/863–6170.*

Outdoor Activities and Sports

Lake Sunapee has brook and lake trout, salmon, smallmouth bass, and pickerel.

Shopping

Dorr Mill Store (⊠ Rte. 11/103, Guild, ☏ 603/863–1197), the yarn and fabric center of the Sunapee area, has a huge selection of fiber.

Skiing and Snow Sports

MOUNT SUNAPEE

Although the resort is state-owned, the operation of Mount Sunapee is now leased to Vermont's Okemo Mountain resort, known for its family-friendly atmosphere. The lease agreement brought a necessary influx of capital to update aging lifts, snowmaking, and other facilities. ⊠ *Mt. Sunapee State Park, Rte. 103, 03772, ☏ 603/763–2356; 800/552–1234 for snow conditions; 800/258–3530 for lodging.*

Downhill. This mountain is 1,510 vertical ft, the highest in southern New Hampshire, and has 41 trails, mostly intermediate, with a couple of steep pitches. A nice beginner's section is beyond the base facilities, well away from other trails. Black-diamond slopes now number nine—including Goosebumps, a double-black diamond—so experts have some challenges. A new halfpipe expands the options for snowboarders. Two base lodges and a summit lodge supply the essentials. One high-speed detachable quad, one fixed-grip quad, one triple, and three double chairlifts and two surface lifts transport skiers.

Child Care. The Duckling Nursery takes children from ages 1 to 5. The Little Indians children's program gives ages 3 and 4 a taste of skiing, and SKIwee lessons are available for kids ages 5 to 12.

Enfield

④ *35 mi north of Newbury, 55 mi northwest of Concord.*

In 1782, two Shaker brothers from Mount Lebanon, New York, arrived at a community on the northeastern side of Mascoma Lake. Eventually, they formed Enfield, the ninth of 18 Shaker communities in this country, and moved it to the lake's southern shore, where they erected more than 200 buildings.

The **Enfield Shaker Museum** preserves the legacy of the Enfield Shakers. A self-guided walking tour takes you through 13 of the buildings that remain. The museum preserves and explains Shaker artifacts, and skilled craftspeople demonstrate Shaker techniques. Numerous special events take place each year. ⊠ *2 Lower Shaker Village Rd., ☏ 603/632–4346. ▣ $5. ⊙ Memorial Day–mid-Oct., Mon.–Sat. 10–5, Sun. noon–5; mid-Oct.–Memorial Day, Sat. 10–4, Sun. noon–4.*

Dining and Lodging

$$–$$$ ✕▥ **The Shaker Inn.** Built between 1837 and 1841, the Great Stone Dwelling is the largest main dwelling ever built by a Shaker community. Adjacent to the Enfield Shaker Museum (☞ *above*), it is now an inn, and the guest rooms in the original Shaker sleeping chambers have reproduction Shaker furniture and are decorated with the simplicity and style for which the religious community was known. The dining room serves Shaker-inspired cuisine such as pumpkin ravioli and maple-glazed baked ham. ⊠ *447 Rte. 4A, 03748, ☏ 603/632–7810 or 888/707–4257. 24 rooms. Restaurant. AE, D, MC, V.*

Outdoor Activities and Sports

Anglers can try for rainbow trout, pickerel, and horned pout in **Lake Mascoma.**

Hanover

42 *12 mi west of Enfield via Rte. 120 from Lebanon, 60 mi northwest of Concord.*

Eleazer Wheelock founded Hanover's Dartmouth College in 1769 to educate the Abenaki "and other youth." When he arrived, the town consisted of about 20 families. The college and the town grew symbiotically, with Dartmouth becoming the northernmost Ivy League school. Today Hanover is still synonymous with Dartmouth, but the town is also a respected medical center and the cultural center for the upper Connecticut River valley.

Robert Frost spent part of a brooding freshman semester at Ivy League **Dartmouth College** before giving up college altogether. The buildings that cluster around the green include the **Baker Memorial Library,** which houses literary treasures including 17th-century editions of Shakespeare's works. If the towering arcade at the entrance to the **Hopkins Center** (☎ 603/646–2422) appears familiar, it's probably because it resembles the project that architect Wallace K. Harrison completed just after designing it: New York City's Metropolitan Opera House at Lincoln Center. The complex includes a 900-seat theater for film and music, a 400-seat theater for plays, and a black-box theater for new plays. The Dartmouth Symphony Orchestra performs here, as does the Big Apple Circus (in summer). In addition to African, Peruvian, Oceanic, Asian, European, and American art, the **Hood Museum of Art** owns the Picasso painting *Guitar on a Table,* silver by Paul Revere, and a set of Assyrian reliefs from the 9th century BC. Rivaling the collection is the museum's architecture: a series of austere redbrick buildings with copper roofs arranged around a courtyard. Free guided tours are given on some weekend afternoons. ✉ *Museum: Wheelock St.,* ☎ *603/646–2808.* ▣ *Free.* ☉ *Tues. and Thurs.–Sat. 10–5, Wed. 10–9, Sun. noon–5.*

Dining and Lodging

$$$$ ✕▣ **Hanover Inn.** Owned and operated by Dartmouth College, this
★ Georgian brick house rises four white-trimmed stories. The building was converted to a tavern in 1780 and has been open ever since. Rooms have Colonial reproductions, Audubon prints, and large sitting areas. The formal Daniel Webster Room ($$$–$$$$) serves regional American dishes like stuffed rabbit with prunes, cognac, and kale. The contemporary Zins wine bar ($–$$$) prepares lighter meals. ✉ *Box 151, The Green, 03755,* ☎ *603/643–4300 or 800/443–7024,* FAX *603/ 646–3744. 92 rooms. 2 restaurants. AE, D, DC, MC, V.*

$$–$$$$ ▣ **Trumbull House.** This white Colonial-style house sits on 16 acres on the outskirts of Hanover. The sunny guest rooms are furnished with king- or queen-size beds, window seats, writing desks, and other comfortable touches. Breakfast is served in the formal dining room or in front of the fireplace in the living room. The inn is no-smoking. ✉ *40 Etna Rd., 03755,* ☎ *603/643–2370 or 800/651–5141. 5 rooms. Pond. Full breakfast. AE, D, DC, MC, V.*

Outdoor Activities and Sports

The Connecticut River is generally considered safe after June 15, but canoeists should always exercise caution. This river is not for beginners. **Ledyard Canoe Club of Dartmouth** (☎ 603/643–6709) provides canoe and kayak rentals and classes.

Shopping

Goldsmith Paul Gross of **Designer Gold** (✉ 3 Lebanon St., ☎ 603/643–3864) designs settings for gemstones—all one-of-a-kind or limited-edition. He also carries some silver jewelry by other artisans.

West Lebanon, south of Hanover on the Vermont border, has a busy commercial section. The owners of the **Mouse Menagerie of Fine Crafts** (⊠ Rte. 12A, West Lebanon, ☎ 603/298–7090) have created a collector's series of toy mice and also sell furniture, wind chimes, and other gifts. The **Powerhouse Mall** (⊠ Rte. 12A, 1 mi north of Exit 20 off I–89, West Lebanon, ☎ 603/298–5236), a former power station, comprises three buildings of specialty stores, boutiques, and restaurants.

Cornish

㊸ *18 mi south of Hanover on Rte. 12A, 70 mi northwest of Concord.*

Today Cornish is best known for its four covered bridges, but at the turn of the century the village was known primarily as the home of the country's then most popular novelist, Winston Churchill (no relation to the British prime minister). His novel *Richard Carvell* sold more than a million copies. Churchill was such a celebrity that he hosted Teddy Roosevelt during the president's 1902 visit. At that time Cornish was an enclave of artistic talent. Painter Maxfield Parrish lived and worked here, and sculptor Augustus Saint-Gaudens set up his studio and created the heroic bronzes for which he is known.

The 460-ft **Cornish-Windsor Bridge,** built in 1866, is the longest covered bridge in the United States. It spans the Connecticut River, connecting New Hampshire with Vermont.

★ The **Saint-Gaudens National Historic Site,** 1½ mi north of the Cornish-Windsor covered bridge, contains sculptor Augustus Saint-Gaudens's (1848–1907) house, studio, gallery, and 150 acres of grounds and gardens. Scattered throughout are full-size casts of his works. The property has two hiking trails, the longer of which is the 2½-mi Blow-Me-Down Trail. ⊠ *Off Rte. 12A,* ☎ *603/675–2175.* ☞ *$4.* ☉ *Buildings Memorial Day weekend–Oct., daily 9–4:30; grounds daily dawn–dusk.*

Dining and Lodging

$$$–$$$$ ✕🏨 **Home Hill Inn.** This restored 1800 mansion set back from the river on 25 acres of meadow and woods is a tranquil place best suited to adults. The owners have given the inn a French influence with 19th-century antiques and collectibles. Rooms in the main house have canopy or four-poster beds, and four have fireplaces; a suite in the guest house can be a romantic hideaway. Golf is on a nine-hole, par-3 executive course. The dining room serves classic and Mediterranean French cuisine like braised pheasant with apple and bacon sauerkraut or fresh, oven-poached turbot with sea urchin roe. ⊠ *River Rd., Plainfield 03781,* ☎ *603/675–6165. 6 rooms, 2 suites, 1 seasonal cottage. Pool, 9-hole golf course, tennis court, cross-country skiing. Continental breakfast. AE, D, MC, V.*

$$ 🏨 **Chase House Bed & Breakfast Inn.** Innkeepers Barbara Lewis and
★   Ted Doyle love sharing the history of this 1775 Federal house. It was the birthplace of Salmon P. Chase, who was Abraham Lincoln's secretary of the treasury, chief justice of the Supreme Court, and a founder of the Republican Party. Careful restoration with Colonial furnishings and Waverly fabrics has recaptured 19th-century elegance. Ask for a room with a canopy bed or one with a view of the Connecticut River valley and Mt. Ascutney. The inn is no-smoking. ⊠ *R.R. 2, Box 909, Rte. 12A (1½ mi south of Cornish-Windsor covered bridge), 03745,* ☎ *603/675–5391 or 800/401–9455,* 📠 *603/675–5010. 5 rooms, 3 suites. Exercise room, boating, snowshoeing. Full breakfast. MC, V. Closed Nov.*

Nightlife and the Arts

The beautifully restored 19th-century **Claremont Opera House** (⊠ Tremont Sq., Claremont, ☎ 603/542–4433) hosts plays and musicals from September to May.

Outdoor Activities and Sports

Northstar Canoe Livery (⊠ Rte. 12A, Balloch's Crossing, ☎ 603/542–5802) rents canoes for half- or full-day trips on the Connecticut River.

Charlestown

44 *20 mi south of Cornish, 32 mi north of Keene.*

Charlestown has the state's largest historic district: 63 homes of Federal, Greek Revival, and Gothic Revival architecture are clustered about the center of town; 10 of them were built before 1800. Several merchants on Main Street distribute brochures that contain an interesting walking tour of the district.

The **Fort at No. 4,** 1½ mi north of Charlestown, was in 1747 an outpost on the lonely periphery of Colonial civilization. That year fewer than 50 militia men at the fort withstood an attack by 400 French soldiers that changed the course of New England history by ensuring that northern New England remained under British rule. Costumed interpreters at the only living-history museum from the era of the French and Indian War cook dinner over an open hearth and demonstrate weaving, gardening, and candlemaking. Each year the museum holds full reenactments of militia musters and battles of the French and Indian War. ⊠ *Rte. 11/Springfield Rd.,* ☎ *603/826–5700.* ☞ *$6.* ☻ *Late May–mid-Oct., Wed.–Mon. 10–4 (weekends only 1st 2 wks of Sept.).*

On a bright, breezy day you might want to detour to the **Morningside Flight Park** (⊠ Rte. 12/11, ☎ 603/542–4416), not necessarily to take hang-gliding lessons, although you could. You can watch the bright colors of the gliders as they swoop over the school's 450-ft peak.

Walpole

45 *12 mi south of Charlestown, 20 mi north of Keene.*

Walpole possesses one of the state's perfect town greens. This one is surrounded by homes built about 1790, when the townsfolk constructed a canal around the Great Falls of the Connecticut River and brought commerce and wealth to the area. The town now has 3,200 inhabitants, more than a dozen of whom are millionaires.

OFF THE BEATEN PATH

SUGARHOUSES – Maple-sugar season—a harbinger of spring—occurs about the first week in March when days become warmer but nights are still frigid. A drive along maple-lined back roads reveals thousands of taps and buckets catching the fresh but labored flow of unrefined sap. Plumes of smoke rise from nearby sugarhouses where sugaring off, the process of boiling down this precious liquid, takes place. Many sugarhouses are open to the public; after a tour and demonstration, you can sample the syrup with traditional unsweetened doughnuts and maybe a pickle—or taste hot syrup over fresh snow, a favorite confection. Open to the public in this area of the state are **Bacon's Sugar House** (⊠ 243 Dublin Rd., Jaffrey, ☎ 603/532–8836); **Bascom Maple Farm** (⊠ Mt. Kingsbury, off Rte. 123A, Alstead, ☎ 603/835–6361), which serves maple pecan pie and maple milk shakes; and **Stuart & John's Sugar House & Pancake Restaurant** (⊠ Rtes. 12 and 63, Westmoreland, ☎ 603/399–4486), which offers a tour and pancake breakfast.

Keene

46   *20 mi southeast of Walpole, 53 mi west of Manchester.*

Keene is the largest city in the southwest corner of the state and the proud locus of the widest main street in America. Each year, on the Saturday before Halloween, locals use that street to hold a Pumpkin Festival, where they seek to retain their place in the record books for the most carved, lighted jack-o-lanterns—13,500 in 1997. **Keene State College,** hub of the local arts community, is on the tree-lined main street. The college's **Redfern Arts Center on Brickyard Pond** (☎ 603/358–2171) has three theaters and eight art studios. The **Thorne-Sagendorph Art Gallery** (☎ 603/358–2720) houses George Ridci's *Landscape* and presents traveling exhibitions. The **Putnam Art Lecture Hall** (☎ 603/358–2160) shows art films and international films.

Dining and Lodging

$–$$$ ✕ **Mangos Cafe on Main.** Paintings of fruits and vegetables on the wall and fruit-motif tablecloths adorn this restaurant, which serves vegetarian dishes—such as the grilled eggplant sandwich or the mixed grilled vegetables with a side of spicy pepper jelly—along with non-veggie fare like New Zealand rack of lamb and grilled Atlantic salmon. ⊠ *81 Main St.,* ☎ *603/358–5440. D, MC, V.*

$–$$ ✕ **One Seventy Six Main.** This restaurant in the heart of Keene has a relaxed atmosphere and a menu that runs the gamut from steak fajitas to blackened catfish. The bar stocks an equally wide selection of domestic and imported beers, with 16 on tap. ⊠ *176 Main St.,* ☎ *603/357–3100. AE, D, MC, V.*

$$$–$$$$ ✕🏠 **Chesterfield Inn.** Surrounded by gardens, the Chesterfield sits above
★   Route 9, the main Brattleboro–Keene road. The spacious rooms, decorated with armoires, fine antiques, and period-style fabrics, have telephones in the bathroom and refrigerators. The views from the dining room are of the gardens and the Vermont hills. Crab cakes with *rémoulade* (a seasoned sauce made with mayonnaise) and salmon with a mustard-mango glaze are among the menu highlights. ⊠ *Box 155, Rte. 9, Chesterfield 03443,* ☎ *603/256–3211 or 800/365–5515,* ℻ *603/256–6131. 13 rooms, 2 suites. Restaurant. Full breakfast. AE, D, DC, MC, V.*

$$ 🏠 **Carriage Barn.** Antiques and wide pine floors lend this inn across from Keene State College a cozy charm. An expansive buffet is served each morning in the breakfast room, but many guests savor a second cup of coffee in the summerhouse under the lilacs. ⊠ *358 Main St., 03431,* ☎ *603/357–3812. 4 rooms. Continental breakfast. MC, V.*

$ 🏕 **Swanzey Lake Camping Area.** This 82-site campground for tents and RVs has a sandy beach, a dock, a ball field, a recreation area, and boat rentals. ⊠ *88 E. Shore Rd.; mailing address: Box 115, W. Swanzey 03469,* ☎ *603/352–9880. Closed Nov.–Apr.*

Nightlife and the Arts

The **Apple Hill Chamber Players** (⊠ E. Sullivan, ☎ 603/847–3371) produce summer concert series. The **Colonial Theatre** (⊠ 95 Main St., ☎ 603/352–2033) opened in 1924 as a vaudeville stage. Recently refurbished, it now hosts folk and jazz concerts and has the largest movie screen in town. The **Redfern Arts Center at Brickyard Pond** (⊠ 229 Main St., ☎ 603/358–2171) has year-round music, theater, and dance performances.

Outdoor Activities and Sports

The Monadnock region has more than 200 lakes and ponds, most of which offer good fishing. Rainbow trout, smallmouth and largemouth bass, and some northern pike swim in **Spofford Lake** in Chesterfield. **Goose Pond** in West Canaan, just north of Keene, holds smallmouth bass and white perch.

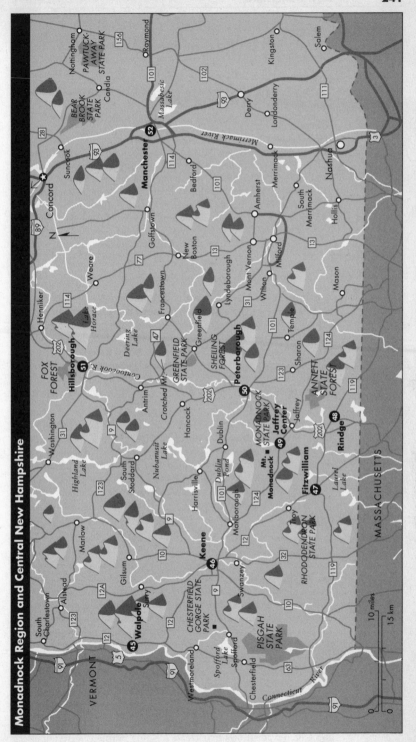

Shopping

ANTIQUES

The more than 240 dealers at **Antiques at Colony Mill** (⊠ 222 West St., ☎ 603/358–6343) sell everything from furniture to dolls.

BOOKS

The extraordinary collection of used books at the **Homestead Bookshop** (⊠ Rtes. 101 and 124, Marlborough, ☎ 603/876–4213) includes biographies, cookbooks, and town histories.

MARKETPLACE

Colony Mill Marketplace (⊠ 222 West St., ☎ 603/357–1240), an old mill building, holds 30-plus stores and boutiques such as Country Artisans (☎ 603/352–6980), which showcases the stoneware, textiles, prints, and glassware of regional artists; the Toadstool Bookshop (☎ 603/352–8815), which carries many children's and regional travel and history books; and Ye Goodie Shoppe (☎ 603/352–0326), whose specialty is handmade chocolates and confections.

Fitzwilliam

47 *12 mi southeast of Keene, 50 mi southwest of Manchester.*

A well-preserved historic district of Colonial and Federal houses has made the town of Fitzwilliam, on Route 119, the subject of thousands of postcards—particularly views of its landscape in winter, when a fine white snow settles on the oval common. Town business is still conducted in the 1817 meeting house. The **Amos J. Blake House,** maintained by the Fitzwilliam Historical Society, contains a museum with period antiques and artifacts and the law office of its namesake. ⊠ *Village Green,* ☎ *603/585–7742.* 🎟 *Free.* ☉ *Late May–mid-Oct., weekends 1–4 or by appointment.*

More than 16 acres of wild rhododendrons burst into bloom in mid-July at **Rhododendron State Park.** This is the largest concentration of *Rhododendron maximum* north of the Allegheny Mountains. Bring a picnic lunch and sit in a nearby pine grove, or follow the marked footpaths through the flowers. ⊠ *Off Rte. 12, 2½ mi northwest of the town common,* ☎ *603/532–8862.* 🎟 *$2.50 weekends and holidays; free at other times.* ☉ *Daily 8–sunset.*

Lodging

$$$–$$$$ 🏨 **Inn at East Hill Farm.** At this 1830 farmhouse resort at the base of Mt. Monadnock, children are not only allowed but expected. In fact, if you don't have kids, you might be happier elsewhere. Children collect the eggs for the next day's breakfast, milk the cows, feed the animals, and participate in arts and crafts, storytelling, hiking, and games. Three meals, all served family-style, are included in the room rate. The innkeepers schedule weekly sleigh rides or hay rides and can whip up a picnic lunch for families who want to spend the day away from the resort. ⊠ *Monadnock St., Troy 03465,* ☎ *603/242–6495 or 800/ 242–6495,* 📠 *603/242–7709. 65 rooms. Restaurant, 1 indoor and 2 outdoor pools, indoor and outdoor whirlpools, wading pool, sauna, tennis court, horseback riding, boating, water-skiing, fishing, cross-country skiing, baby-sitting. AP. D, MC, V.*

$$ 🏨 **Amos Parker House.** The garden of this old Colonial B&B is the
★ town's most stunning, complete with lily ponds, Asian stone benches, and Dutch waterstones that create a gently burbling waterfall effect. Two rooms have garden views; three have wood-burning fireplaces. In winter, breakfast is served in an elegant setting in front of a roaring fire. ⊠ *Box 202, Rte. 119, 03447,* ☎ *603/585–6540. 4 rooms. Full breakfast. No credit cards.*

$-$$ ⊞ **Hannah Davis House.** This 1820 Federal house just off the village
★   green has retained its elegance. The original beehive oven still sits in
the kitchen, and one suite has two Count Rumford fireplaces. Your
host has the scoop on area antiquing. ⊠ *186 Rte. 119W, 03447,* ☎
603/585–3344. 6 rooms. Full breakfast. D, MC, V.

Outdoor Activities and Sports

You can find rainbow and golden trout, pickerel, and horned pout in
Laurel Lake. Rainbow and brown trout line the **Ashuelot River.**

Rindge

48   *8 mi east of Fitzwilliam on Rte. 119, 42 mi southeast of Manchester.*

The small town of Rindge sits on a hill overlooking the Monadnock
region. Most diversions center on outdoor activities in this scenic setting. **Cathedral of the Pines** is an outdoor memorial to American men
and women, both civilian and military, who have sacrificed their lives
in service to their country. There's an inspiring view of Mt. Monadnock and Mt. Kearsarge from the **Altar of the Nation,** which is com-
posed of rock from every U.S. state and territory. All faiths are welcome
to hold services here; organ meditations take place at midday from Tuesday to Thursday in July and August. The **Memorial Bell Tower,** with
a carillon of bells from around the world, is built of native stone; Norman Rockwell designed the bronze tablets over the four arches. Flower
gardens, an indoor chapel, and a museum of military memorabilia share
the hilltop. ⊠ *75 Cathedral Entrance Rd., off Rte. 119,* ☎ *603/899–
3300.* ⊡ *Free.* ⊙ *May–Oct., daily 9–5.*

Lodging

$$–$$$ ⊞ **Woodbound Inn.** This rustic inn was built as a farmhouse in 1819
and became an inn in 1892. A favorite with families and people who
fish, it occupies 200 acres on the shores of Contoocook Lake. Accommodations are basic and range from traditional rooms in the main
inn to modern hotel-style rooms in the Edgewood building to cabins
by the water. ⊠ *62 Woodbound Rd., 03461,* ☎ *603/532–8341 or 800/
688–7770,* ℻ *603/532–8341 ext. 213. 35 rooms, 31 with bath, 4 rooms
share bath, 11 cottages. Restaurant, bar, lake, 9-hole golf course, tennis court, croquet, hiking, horseshoes, shuffleboard, volleyball, fishing, ice-skating, cross-country skiing, tobogganing, recreation room.
Full breakfast; MAP available. AE, MC, V.*

$ ⊞ **Cathedral House Bed and Breakfast.** This 1850s farmhouse on the
edge of the Cathedral of the Pines was the home of the memorial's
founders. Innkeepers Don and Shirley Mahoney are well versed in area
history. Rooms have high ceilings, flowered wallpapers, quilts, and well-
stocked cookie jars, all of which help create the feeling that you've just
arrived at Grandmother's house. ⊠ *63 Cathedral Entrance Rd., 03461,*
☎ *603/899–6790. 5 rooms, 1 with bath. Full breakfast. MC, V.*

Jaffrey Center

49   *7 mi north of Rindge, 46 mi west of Manchester.*

Novelist Willa Cather came to the historic village of Jaffrey Center in
1919 and stayed in the Shattuck Inn, which now stands empty on Old
Meeting House Road. She pitched a tent not far from here in which she
wrote several chapters of *My Ántonia.* She returned nearly every summer thereafter until her death and was buried in the Old Burying Ground.
Amos Fortune Forum, near the Old Burying Ground, brings nationally
known speakers to the 1773 meeting house on summer evenings.

The chief draw at **Monadnock State Park** is Mt. Monadnock. The oft-quoted statistic about the mountain is that it's the most-climbed mountain in America—second in the world to Japan's Mt. Fuji. Whether this is true or not, locals agree that it's never lonely at the top. Some days more than 400 people crowd its bald peak. Monadnock rises to 3,165 ft, and on a clear day the hazy Boston skyline is visible from its summit. The park maintains picnic grounds and some tent campsites and sells a trail map for $2. Five trailheads branch into more than two dozen trails of varying difficulty that wend their way to the top. Some are considerably shorter than others, but you should allow between three and four hours for any round-trip hike. A visitor center has exhibits documenting the mountain's history. ⊠ *2½ mi north of Jaffrey Center off Rte. 124, 03452,* ☎ *603/532–8862.* ⊡ *$2.50.*

Lodging

$–$$$ 🛏 **Benjamin Prescott Inn.** The working dairy farm surrounding this 1853 Colonial farmhouse makes guests feel as though they are miles out in the country rather than just minutes from Jaffrey Center. Stenciling, quilts handmade by innkeeper Jan Miller, and wide pine floors add to the country feel. A full breakfast of Welsh miner's cakes, baked French toast with fruit, and Jaffrey maple syrup prepares you for a day of antiquing or climbing Mt. Monadnock. ⊠ *Rte. 124, 03452,* ☎ *603/532–6637. 10 rooms, 3 suites. Full breakfast. AE, MC, V.*

Outdoor Activities and Sports

Gilmore Pond in Jaffrey has several types of trout.

Shopping

Sharon Arts Center (⊠ Rte. 123, Sharon, ☎ 603/924–7256) has a gallery that exhibits locally made pottery, fabric, and woodwork and also houses a school with classes in everything from photography to paper marbling.

Peterborough

🔟 *8 mi north of Jaffrey Center, 40 mi west of Manchester.*

The nation's first free public library opened in Peterborough in 1833. The town, which was the first in the region to be incorporated (1760), is still a commercial and cultural hub. The **MacDowell Colony** (⊠ 100 High St., ☎ 603/924–3886) was founded by the composer Edward MacDowell in 1907 as an artists' retreat. Willa Cather wrote part of *Death Comes for the Archbishop* here. Thornton Wilder was in residence when he wrote *Our Town*; Peterborough's resemblance to the play's Grover's Corners is no coincidence. Only a small portion of the colony is open to visitors.

In **Miller State Park** (⊠ Rte. 101, ☎ 603/924–3672), 3 mi east of town, an auto road takes you almost 2,300 ft up Mt. Pack Monadnock.

Dining and Lodging

$$–$$$ ✕ **Latacarta.** The innovative menu at Latacarta, where the dining room overlooks a waterfall, relies heavily on fresh, organic products. Start with *gyoza,* pan-grilled Japanese dumplings filled with vegetables and tofu, and then try the fresh Atlantic salmon or the hormone-free teppanyaki beef served with a sauce made from saki and apples. Dessert might be a mocha custard or wonderful hot pear crunch. ⊠ *Noone Falls, U.S. 202,* ☎ *603/924–6878. AE, D, MC, V. Closed Mon. No lunch weekends.*

$$–$$$$ ✕🛏 **Hancock Inn.** Dating from 1789, this Federal inn is the pride of the well-preserved town for which it's named. Common areas possess the warmth of a tavern, with fireplaces, big wing chairs, couches, dark wood paneling, and Rufus Porter murals. Rooms, done in traditional

Colonial style, have antique four-poster beds. One suite has the original domed ceiling from the inn's 1800s ballroom. Updated Yankee fare is served by candlelight in the dining room; the specialty is Shaker cranberry pot roast. ⊠ *Box 96, 33 Main St., Hancock 03449,* ☎ *603/525–3318,* FAX *603/525–9301. 11 rooms, 4 suites. Restaurant, bar. Full breakfast. AE, D, DC, MC, V.*

$$ ✕⊞ **Inn at Crotched Mountain.** This 1822 Colonial inn has nine fireplaces, four of which are in private rooms. The other five spread cheer in several common areas. The inn, whose rooms are furnished with early Colonial reproductions, is a particularly romantic place to stay when snow is falling on Crotched Mountain. The restaurant's multicultural menu includes Eastern specialties such as Indonesian charbroiled swordfish with a sauce of ginger, green pepper, onion, and lemon; cranberry-port pot roast is one of the regional entrées. ⊠ *Mountain Rd., Francestown 03043,* ☎ *603/588–6840. 13 rooms. Restaurant, bar, pool, tennis court, cross-country skiing. Full breakfast; MAP required weekends. No credit cards.*

$ ✕⊞ **Birchwood Inn.** Thoreau slept here, probably on his way to climb Monadnock or to visit Jaffrey or Peterborough. Country furniture and handmade quilts outfit the bedrooms of this no-smoking inn, as they did in 1775 when the house was new and no one dreamed it would someday be listed on the National Register of Historic Places. Allow time to linger in the dining room ($$; reservations essential; BYOB; no lunch; closed Sunday and Monday), where Rufus Porter murals cover the walls and she-crab soup, roast duckling, and fresh-fruit cobblers are among the specialties. ⊠ *Box 197, Rte. 45, Temple 03084,* ☎ *603/ 878–3285,* FAX *603/878–2159. 7 rooms, 5 with bath. Restaurant. Full breakfast. No credit cards.*

$ ⊞ **Apple Gate Bed and Breakfast.** With 90 acres of apple orchards across the street, this B&B is appropriately named. The four rooms and even the yellow labrador, Macintosh, are named for types of apples. Some rooms are small, but Laura Ashley prints and stenciling make them cheery and cozy. The house dates from 1832, and the original beams and fireplace still grace the dining room. A music and reading room has a piano and a television with VCR tucked in the corner. From June to October, there's a two-night minimum on weekends. ⊠ *199 Upland Farm Rd., 03458,* ☎ *603/924–6543. 4 rooms. Full breakfast. MC, V.*

Nightlife and the Arts

Monadnock Music (☎ 603/924–7610 or 800/868–9613) produces a summer series of concerts from mid-July to late August, with solo recitals, chamber music, and orchestra and opera performances by renowned musicians. The concerts, at locations throughout the region, usually take place in the evening at 8 and on Sunday at 4; many are free. The **Peterborough Players** (⊠ Stearns Farm, off Middle Hancock Rd., ☎ 603/924–7585) have performed for more than 60 seasons. Plays are staged in a converted barn. The **Temple Town Band** (☎ 603/924–3478) was founded in 1799. Members range from teenagers to septuagenarians. The band plays a selection of patriotic songs, traditional marches, and show tunes at the Jaffrey Bandstand, the Sharon Arts Center, and local festivals and events.

Outdoor Activities and Sports

Several types of trout swim in **Dublin Pond,** near Dublin.

Shopping

Artek Creations (⊠ 375 Jaffrey Rd., ☎ 603/924–0003) sells museum reproductions of jewelry, bookends, boxes, and other ornamental objects. The corporate headquarters and retail outlet of **Eastern Mountain Sports** (⊠ 1 Vose Farm Rd., ☎ 603/924–7231) sells everything from tents to skis to hiking boots, gives hiking and camping classes, and conducts kayaking and canoeing demonstrations. **Harrisville Designs** (⊠ Mill Alley, Harrisville, ☎ 603/827–3333) sells hand-spun and hand-dyed yarn sheared from local sheep, as well as looms for the serious weaver. The shop also hosts classes in knitting and weaving. **North Gallery at Tewksbury's** (⊠ Rte. 101, ☎ 603/924–3224) stocks thrown pots, sconces, candlestick holders, and woodworkings.

Hillsborough

❺❶   *20 mi north of Peterborough, 25 mi west of Manchester.*

The four villages that make up Hillsborough include the historic district, Hillsborough Center, where 18th-century houses surround the town green. Many houses are still occupied by descendants of the original settlers who founded the town in 1769.

President Franklin Pierce was born in Hillsborough and lived here until he married. The **Pierce Homestead,** operated by the Hillsborough Historical Society, welcomes visitors for guided tours. The house is decorated much as it was during Pierce's life. ⊠ Rte. 31, ☎ 603/478–3165. ▣ $2.50. ⊙ June and Sept.–Columbus Day, Sat. 10–4, Sun. 1–4; July–Aug., Mon.–Sat. 10–4, Sun. 1–4.

Lodging

$–$$ 🛏 **Inn at Maplewood Farm.** The white-clapboard 1794 farmhouse on the side of Peaked Hill beside a quiet country road may make you feel as if you've been transported back in time. The rooms, three with fireplaces, have antiques and quilts but contain modern bathrooms. The luxurious Garden suite has a queen-size canopy bed, a fireplace, a skylight over the bathtub, and a sitting area. All rooms have vintage radios so that you can listen to the old-time radio shows broadcast nightly on the inn's transmitter. The inn is no-smoking. ⊠ Box 1478, 447 Center Rd., 03244, ☎ 603/464–4242, FAX 603/464–5401. 2 rooms, 2 suites. Guest kitchen with refrigerator and coffeemaker. Continental breakfast. AE, D, DC, MC, V. Closed Nov.–May.

Outdoor Activities and Sports

Fox State Forest (⊠ Center Rd., ☎ 603/464–3453) has 20 mi of hiking trails and an observation tower.

Shopping

At **Gibson Pewter** (⊠ 18 East Washington Rd., ☎ 603/464–3410), the father-and-son team of Raymond and Jonathan Gibson create and sell museum-quality, lead-free pewter in contemporary and traditional designs. You are welcome to watch them work. **William Thomas, Master Cabinetmaker** (⊠ 217 Saw Mill Rd., ☎ 603/478–3488), a founding member of the New Hampshire Furniture Masters Association, creates well-crafted wood furniture.

Manchester

❺❷   *25 mi east of Hillsborough, 23 mi north of the Massachusetts border.*

Manchester, with just over 100,000 residents, is New Hampshire's largest city. The town grew around the power of the Amoskeag Falls on the Merrimack River, which fueled small textile mills through the 1700s. Today Manchester is mainly a banking and business center. The state's major airport is here, though, so you may want to spend a day visiting its museums or walking through the former mill yards.

By 1828, a group of investors from Boston had bought the rights to the Merrimack's water power and built on its eastern bank the

Amoskeag Textile Mills, which became a testament to New England's manufacturing power. In 1906, the mills employed 17,000 people and churned out more than 4 million yards of cloth per week. The enterprise formed the entire economic base of Manchester; when it closed in 1936, the town was devastated. As part of an economic recovery plan, the mill buildings have been converted into warehouses, classrooms, restaurants, and office space. You can wander among these huge blood-red buildings; contact the **Manchester Historic Association** (⊠ 129 Amherst St., ☎ 603/622–7531) for a map.

The **Currier Gallery of Art,** in a 1929 Beaux Arts Italianate building, has a permanent collection of European and American paintings, sculpture, and decorative arts from the 13th to the 20th century, including works by Monet, Picasso, Edward Hopper, and Georgia O'Keeffe. Also part of the museum is the Frank Lloyd Wright–designed **Zimmerman House,** built in 1950. Wright called this sparse, utterly functional living space "Usonian." The house is New England's only Wright-designed residence open to the public. ⊠ *201 Myrtle Way,* ☎ *603/669–6144, 603/626–4158 for Zimmerman House tours.* ☒ *$5; free Sat. 10–1; Zimmerman House $7 (reservations required).* ☉ *Sun.–Mon. and Wed.–Thurs. 11–5, Fri. 11–9, Sat. 10–5; call for tour times.*

Ⓒ Salmon, shad, and river herring "climb" the **Amoskeag Fishways** fish ladder near the Amoskeag Dam during the migration period, from May to June. The visitor center has an underwater viewing window, year-round interactive exhibits and programs, and a hydroelectric-station viewing area. ⊠ *Fletcher St.,* ☎ *603/626–3474.* ☉ *Call for hrs.*

Dining and Lodging

$$$–$$$$ ✕▣ **Bedford Village Inn.** This luxurious Federal-style inn, just minutes from Manchester, was once a working farm and still shows horse-nuzzle marks on its old beams. Gone, however, are the hayloft and the old milking room, which have been converted into lavish suites containing king-size beds, whirlpool baths, and three telephones. The tavern has seven intimate dining rooms, each with original wide pine floors and huge fireplaces. The menu, which often includes New England favorites like lobster and Atlantic salmon with a chardonnay beurre blanc, changes every two weeks. ⊠ *2 Village Inn La., Bedford 03110,* ☎ *603/472–2001 or 800/852–1166,* ℻ *603/472–2379. 12 suites, 2 apartments. Restaurant, meeting rooms. AE, DC, MC, V.*

Nightlife and the Arts

American Stage Festival (⊠ 14 Court St., Nashua, ☎ 603/886–7000) is the state's largest professional theater. The season, with shows presented at two locations, runs from March through October and includes five Broadway plays, one new work, and a children's-theater series.

Shopping

Bell Hill Antiques (⊠ Rte. 101 at Bell Hill Rd., Bedford, ☎ 603/472–5580) sells country furniture, glass, and china. The enormous **Mall of New Hampshire** (⊠ 1500 S. Willow St., ☎ 603/669–0433) has every conceivable store and is anchored by Sears and Filene's.

Western and Central New Hampshire A to Z

Arriving and Departing

BY BUS

Concord Trailways (☎ 800/639–3317) runs from Concord to Boston. **Vermont Transit** (☎ 603/351–1331 or 800/552–8737) links the cities of western New Hampshire with major cities in the eastern United States.

BY CAR

Most people who travel up from Massachusetts do so on I–93, which passes through Manchester and Concord before cutting a path through the White Mountains. I–89 connects Concord, in the Merrimack Valley, with Vermont. Route 12 runs north–south along the Connecticut River. Farther south, Route 101 connects Keene and Manchester, then continues to the seacoast.

BY PLANE

Manchester Airport (☞ Arriving and Departing *in* New Hampshire A to Z, *below*) is the main airport in western and central New Hampshire. Colgan Air offers flights to Rutland, Vermont, and Newark, New Jersey, from **Keene Airport** (⊠ Rte. 32 off Rte. 12, North Swanzey, ☎ 603/357–9835). **Lebanon Municipal Airport** (5 Airpark Rd., West Lebanon, ☎ 603/298–8878), near Dartmouth College, is served by US Airways. *See* Air Travel *in* Smart Travel Tips A to Z for airline phone numbers.

Getting Around

BY BUS

Advance Transit (☎ 802/295–1824) stops in Enfield and Hanover. **Keene City Express** (☎ 603/352–8494) buses run from 9 AM to 4 PM. **Manchester Transit Authority** (☎ 603/623–8801) has hourly local bus service around town and to Bedford from 6 AM to 6 PM.

BY CAR

On the western border of the state, Routes 12 and 12A are picturesque but slow-moving. U.S. 4 crosses the region, winding between Lebanon and the seacoast. Other pretty drives include Routes 101, 202, and 11.

Contacts and Resources

BIKING

Eastern Mountain Sports (☞ Shopping *in* Peterborough, *above*) and the **Greater Keene Chamber of Commerce** (⊠ 8 Central Sq., Keene 03431, ☎ 603/352–1303) have information about local bike routes.

EMERGENCIES

Cheshire Medical Center (⊠ 580 Court St., Keene, ☎ 603/352–4111). **Concord Hospital** (⊠ 250 Pleasant St., Concord, ☎ 603/225–2711). **Dartmouth Hitchcock Medical Center** (⊠ 1 Medical Center Dr., Lebanon, ☎ 603/650–5000). **Elliot Hospital** (⊠ 1 Elliot Way, Manchester, ☎ 603/669–5300 or 800/235–5468). **Monadnock Community Hospital** (⊠ 452 Old Street Rd., Peterborough, ☎ 603/924–7191). **Southern New Hampshire Medical Center** (⊠ 8 Prospect St., Nashua, ☎ 603577–2000).

Monadnock Mutual Aid (☎ 603/352–1100) responds to any emergency, from a medical problem to a car fire.

FISHING

For word on what's biting where, contact the **Department of Fish and Game** (☎ 603/352–9669) in Keene.

LODGING RESERVATION SERVICE

The **Sunapee Area Lodging and Information Service** (☎ 603/763–2495 or 800/258–3530) can help with reservations.

24-HOUR PHARMACY

Brooks Pharmacy (⊠ 53 Daniel Webster Hwy., Manchester, ☎ 603/623–1135). **CVS Pharmacy** (⊠ 271 Mammouth Rd., Manchester, ☎ 603/623–3995).

VISITOR INFORMATION

Concord Chamber of Commerce (⊠ 244 N. Main St., Concord 03301, ☎ 603/224–2508). **Hanover Chamber of Commerce** (⊠ Box A-105, Hanover 03755, ☎ 603/643–3115). **Keene Chamber of Commerce** (⊠

48 Central Sq., Keene 03431, ☎ 603/352–1303). **Lake Sunapee Business Association** (✉ Box 400, Sunapee 03782, ☎ 603/763–2495; 800/258–3530 in New England). **Manchester Chamber of Commerce** (✉ 889 Elm St., Manchester 03101, ☎ 603/666–6600). **Monadnock Travel Council** (✉ 8 Central Sq., Keene 03431, ☎ 603/355–8155). **Peterborough Chamber of Commerce** (✉ Box 401, Peterborough 03458, ☎ 603/924–7234). **Southern New Hampshire Visitor & Convention Bureau** (✉ 1 Airport Rd., Suite 198, Manchester 03103, ☎ 603/645–9889).

NEW HAMPSHIRE A TO Z

Arriving and Departing

By Bus

C&J (☎ 603/431–2424) serves the seacoast area of New Hampshire. **Concord Trailways** (☎ 603/228–3300) links the capital with other parts of the state. **Vermont Transit** (☎ 603/228–3300 or 800/451–3292) links the cities of western New Hampshire with major cities in the eastern United States.

By Car

Interstate 93 is the principal north–south route through Manchester, Concord, and central New Hampshire. To the west, I–91 traces the Vermont–New Hampshire border. To the east, I–95, which is a toll road, passes through the coastal area of southern New Hampshire on its way from Massachusetts to Maine. Interstate 89 travels from Concord to Montpelier and Burlington, Vermont.

By Plane

Manchester Airport (✉ 1 Airport Rd., Manchester 03103, ☎ 603/624–6539), the state's largest airport, has scheduled flights by Continental, Delta, United, and US Airways. **Lebanon Municipal Airport** (✉ 5 Airpark Rd., West Lebanon, ☎ 603/298–8878) has commuter flights by US Air Express, Delta Business Express, and Northwest. *See* Air Travel *in* Smart Travel Tips A to Z for airline phone numbers.

Getting Around

By Bus

See Arriving and Departing, *above,* and the A to Z sections of the New Hampshire regions covered in this chapter.

By Car

The official state map, available free from the New Hampshire Office of Travel and Tourism Development (☞ Visitor Information, *below*), has directories for each of the tourist areas.

Speed limits on interstate highways are generally 65 mph, except in heavily settled areas, where 55 mph is the norm. On state routes, speed limits vary considerably. On any given stretch, the limit may be anywhere from 25 mph to 55 mph, so watch the signs carefully. Right turns are permitted on red lights unless otherwise indicated.

By Plane

Small local airports that handle charters and private planes are **Berlin Airport** (✉ Rte. 16, Milan, ☎ 603/449–7383), **Concord Airport** (✉ 71 Airport Rd., Concord, ☎ 603/229–1760), **Laconia Airport** (✉ Rte. 11, Laconia, ☎ 603/524–5003), **Nashua Municipal Airport** (✉ Borie Field, Nashua, ☎ 603/882–0661), and, in Rochester, **Skyhaven Airport** (✉ 238 Rochester Hill Rd., ☎ 603/332–0005).

Contacts and Resources

Biking

Bike & Hike New Hampshire's Lakes (☎ 603/968–3775), **Bike the Whites** (☎ 800/933–3902), **Great Outdoors Hiking & Biking Tours** (☎ 603/356–3271 or 800/525–9100), **Monadnock Bicycle Touring** (☎ 603/827–3925), **New England Hiking Holidays** (☎ 603/356–9696 or 800/869–0949), and **Sunapee Inns Hike & Bike Tours** (☎ 800/662–6005) organize bike tours.

Bird-Watching

Audubon Society of New Hampshire (✉ 3 Silk Farm Rd., Concord 03301, ☎ 603/224–9909) schedules monthly field trips throughout the state and a fall bird-watching tour to Star Isle and other parts of the Isles of Shoals.

Camping

New Hampshire Campground Owners Association (✉ Box 320, Twin Mountain 03595, ☎ 603/846–5511 or 800/822–6764, FAX 603/846–2151) publishes a guide to private, state, and national-forest campgrounds.

Emergencies

Ambulance, fire, police (☎ 911).

Fishing

For information about fishing and licenses, call the **New Hampshire Fish and Game Office** (☎ 603/271–3421).

Foliage and Snow Hot Lines

A fall **foliage hot line** (☎ 800/258–3608) is updated twice weekly from mid-September through October. Two **snow hot lines** (☎ 800/258–3608 for information on New Hampshire alpine ski conditions; ☎ 800/262–6660 for cross-country ski conditions) provide updates on snow conditions at ski centers.

Visitor Information

New Hampshire Office of Travel and Tourism Development (✉ Box 1856, Concord 03302, ☎ 603/271–2343; 800/386–4664 for a free vacation packet). **Events** (☎ 800/258–3608 or 800/262–6660). **New Hampshire Parks Department** (☎ 603/271–3556). **New Hampshire State Council on the Arts** (✉ 40 N. Main St., Concord 03301, ☎ 603/271–2789).

INDEX

NOTES

NOTES

NOTES

NOTES

NOTES

L@@king
⊙ FOR A
great place to go?

We know just the place. In fact, it attracts more than 125,000 visitors a day, making it one of the world's most popular travel destinations. It's previewtravel.com, the Web's comprehensive resource for travelers. It gives you access to over 500 airlines, 25,000 hotels, rental cars, cruises, vacation packages and support from travel experts 24 hours a day. Plus great information from Fodor's travel guides and travelers just like you. All of which makes previewtravel.com quite a find.

Preview Travel has everything you need to plan & book your next trip.

air, car & hotel reservations

vacation packages & cruises

destination planning & travel tips

24-hour customer service

previewtravel.com

preview
travel℠

aol keyword: previewtravel
www.previewtravel.com